The 1986 Sandoz Lectures in Gerontology

Dimensions in Aging

The 1986 Sandoz Lectures in Gerontology

Dimensions in Aging

edited by

M. Bergener
M. Ermini
H. B. Stähelin

1986

ACADEMIC PRESS
HARCOURT BRACE JOVANOVICH, PUBLISHERS
LONDON   ORLANDO   SAN DIEGO
NEW YORK   AUSTIN   BOSTON
SYDNEY   TOKYO   TORONTO

ACADEMIC PRESS INC. (LONDON) LTD.
24/28 Oval Road,
London NW1 7DX

United States Edition published by
ACADEMIC PRESS INC.
Orlando, Florida 32887

Copyright © 1986 by
ACADEMIC PRESS INC. (LONDON) LTD.

All rights reserved. No part of this book may be reproduced or transmitted in any form or by any means, electronic or mechanical, including photocopy, recording, or any information storage and retrieval system without permission in writing from the publisher

British Library Cataloguing in Publication Data

Dimensions in aging. —(The 1986 Sandoz lectures in gerontology)
1. Aging
I. Bergener, M.   II. Ermini, M.
III. Stähelin, H. B.   IV. Series
612'.67   QP86
ISBN 0-12-090162-5

Phototypeset by Dobbie Typesetting Service, Plymouth, Devon
Printed by St Edmundsbury Press,
Bury St Edmunds, England

Contributors

L. Abisch *Sandoz Ltd, CH-4002 Basle, Switzerland.*

R. Adolfson *Umea Dementia Research Group, Department of Geriatric Medicine, University of Umea, S-901 87 Umea, Sweden.*

I. Alafuzoff *Umea Dementia Research Group, Department of Geriatric Medicine, University of Umea, S-901 87 Umea, Sweden.*

B. H. Anderton *Department of Immunology St George's Hospital Medical School, Cranmer Terrace, London SW17 0RE, UK.*

S. Azhar *Department of Medicine, Stanford University School of Medicine and the Palo Alto Veterans Administration, Medical Center, Palo Alto, CA 94304, USA.*

V. L. Bengtson *Director, Gerontology Research Center, Andrus Gerontology Center, University of Southern California, Los Angeles, CA 90089-0191, USA.*

E. Beregi *Hungary Gerontology Center, Semmelweis Medical University, Somogyi Bela u 33, H-1085 Budapest, Hungary.*

M. Bergener *Rheinische Landesklinik, Wilhelm Griesinger-Strasse 23, D-5000 Cologne, FRG.*

J.-P. Brion *Laboratoire d'Anatomie Pathologique et de Microscopie Electronique, Université Libre de Bruxelles, Route de Lennik, Bruxelles, Belgium.*

P. Ebbesen *Head, Institute of Cancer Research, Danish Cancer Society, Radiumstationen, DK-8000 Aarhus C, Denmark.*

K. Esser *Lehrstuhl für Allgemeine Botanik der Ruhr-Universität Bochum, Postfach 102148, D-4630 Bochum, FRG.*

C. Fowler *Umea Dementia Research Group, Department of Geriatric Medicine, University of Umea, S-901 87 Umea, Sweden.*

J. Flament-Durand *Laboratoire d'Anatomie Pathologique et de Microscopie Electronique, Université Libre de Bruxelles, Route de Lennik, Bruxelles, Belgium.*

W. J. Freed *Neuropsychiatry Branch, National Institute of Mental Health, Division of Special Mental Health Research, St Elizabeth's Hospital, Washington DC 20032, USA.*

C. G. Gottfries *Department of Psychiatry and Neurochemistry, St Jörgens Hospital, Gothenberg University, S-442 03 Hisings Backa, Sweden.*

S. Guttmann *Head of Pharmaceutical Research Department, Sandoz Ltd, CH-4013 Basel, Switzerland.*

J. Hardy *Umea Dementia Research Group, Department of Geriatric Medicine, University of Umea, S-901 87 Umea, Sweden.*

H. Haugh *Department of Immunology, St George's Hospital Medical School, Cranmer Terrace, London SW17 0RE, UK.*

L. Hayflick *Director, Center for Gerontological Studies, University of Florida, Gainesville, FL 32611, USA.*

B. B. Hoffman *Department of Medicine, Stanford University School of Medicine and the Palo Alto Veterans Administration, Medical Center, Palo Alto, CA 94304, USA.*

R. Holliday *Head, Division of Genetics, NIMR, The Ridgeway, Mill Hill, London NW7 1AA, UK.*

J. Husser *Rheinische Landesklinik, Wilhelm Griesinger-Strasse 23, D-5000 Cologne, FRG.*

J. Kahn *Department of Neuropathology, Institute of Psychiatry, University of London, Denmark Hill, London SE5 8AZ, UK.*

E. U. Kranzhoff *Rheinische Landesklinik, Wilhelm Griesinger-Strasse 23, D-5000 Cologne, FRG.*

E. G. Lakatta *Laboratory of Cardiovascular Science, Gerontology Research Center, National Institute of Aging, NIH, Baltimore, MD 21223, USA.*

L. de Medinaceli *Neuropsychiatry Branch, National Institute of Mental Health, Division of Special Mental Health Research, St Elizabeth's Hospital, Washington DC 20032, USA.*

J. Meites *Department of Physiology, Neuroendocrine Research Laboratory, Michigan State University, East Lansing, MI 48834-1101, USA.*

C. C. J. Miller *Department of Immunology, St George's Hospital Medical School, Cranmer Terrace, London SW17 0RE, UK.*

A. Probst *Department of Pathology, Neuropathology Division, University of Basel, CH-4065 Basel, Switzerland.*

G. S. Roth *National Institute of Health, National Institutes on Aging, Gerontology Research Center, Baltimore City Hospital, Baltimore, MD 21224, USA.*

M. Roth *Professor of Psychiatry, School of Clinical Medicine, University of Cambridge, Hills Road, Cambridge CB2 2QQ, UK.*

E. Steinhagen-Thiessen *Medizinische Kern- und Poliklinik, Universitäts-Krankenhaus Eppendorf, Martinistrasse 52, D-2000 Hamburg 20, FRG.*

R. B. Stewart *Department of Pharmacy Practice, College of Pharmacy, University of Florida, Gainesville, FL 32610 USA.*

A. Tsujimoto *Department of Pediatrics, Yamanashi Medical College, Tamaho, Nakakoma-gun, Yamanashi, 409-38 Japan.*

G. Tsujimoto *Department of Pharmacology, Yamanashi Medical College, Tamaho, Nakakoma-gun Yamanashi, 409-38 Japan.*

J. Ulrich *Department of Pathology, Neuropathology Division, University of Basel, CH-4065 Basel, Switzerland.*

W. Wallace *Umea Dementia Research Group, Department of Geriatric Medicine, University of Umea, S-901 87 Umea, Sweden.*

T. F. Williams *Director, National Institute on Aging, Department of Health & Human Services, Building 31, Room 2002, Bethesda, MD 20205, USA.*

B. Winblad *Umea Dementia Research Group, Department of Geriatric Medicine, University of Umea, S-901 87 Umea Sweden.*

R. J. Wyatt *Chief, Adult Psychiatry Branch, National Institute of Mental Health, Division of Special Mental Health Research, St Elizabeth's Hospital, Washington DC 20032, USA.*

Preface

This volume is a collection of papers, presented by eminent scientists at the 1986 Sandoz Lectures in Gerontology, on a wide range of topics of gerontological research.

The Sandoz Lectures aim to give scientists who have competed for the Sandoz Prize for Gerontological Research an opportunity to describe their own research work to a wider audience and at the same time discuss future research plans. The main objective is to further international and interdisciplinary collaboration and to investigate the possibilities of translating scientific knowledge into gerontological practice.

It was thus for the second time that the Sandoz Lectures in Gerontology were organized to follow-up the Sandoz Prize for Gerontological Research, awarded in 1985 equally to Professor Karl Esser (FRG) and Professor Sir Martin Roth (UK) for their respective outstanding research into genetic mechanisms of the aging process, and human brain diseases associated with aging.

As in 1984, when the rules were set for the first Sandoz Lectures in Gerontology, the scientific organizing committee was faced with the difficult task of selecting the speakers from the long list of contestants for the Sandoz Prize of the preceding year. Since it is the aim of the Lectures to bring together gerontologists from as diverse research areas as possible in order to stimulate the interdisciplinary exchange of thoughts in this complex field, representatives had preferably to be chosen from various domains of gerontological research. Fortunately, the high quality of the many applications once again made it possible to put together an excellent program with speakers from biological, medical and sociological research areas.

As in the published volume of the 1984 Sandoz Lectures in Gerontology, "Thresholds in Aging", one chapter of the present volume is devoted to the pre-program trigger meeting, which helped the invitees to become acquainted through an informal round table discussion, this time chaired by Professor Karl Esser and Dr L. Abisch and centering on the question "Is There a Functional Difference between Normal and Pathological Aging?" In an exceedingly animated discussion, the countless open questions of gerontology were discussed frankly without glossing over methodological shortcomings or controversial research findings, and once again the familiar problems of interdisciplinary communication were made evident.

Another goal of the Lectures is to inform not only the experts but also the interested lay public on the current state-of-the-art of gerontological research.

Because of the often highly specialized and technical nature of the presentations, it was felt by the organizers that the audience should be provided with a more general overview of the discussed topics. For that reason, at the end of each of the three sessions "Cellular Systems in Aging", "Aging at the Organ Level" and "Human Competences in Aging" Professor G. S. Roth, F. Williams and Sir Martin Roth were invited to make an *ad hoc* statement on the implications and outlook for future research in the respective areas. These "interpreters" have done a truly remarkable job and their words are deservedly included in this volume along with the fruitful discussions after each presentation.

We would like to express our thanks to all contributors for their efforts not only during the Lectures but also for their willing collaboration in the preparation of this book.

We are much obliged to all responsible at Sandoz Ltd of Basle who, encouraged by the great success and good response throughout the world, agreed to a continuation of the Sandoz Lectures providing generous financial and practical support.

Special thanks go to all members of the Honorary Committee: W. Arber (Basle), E. Beregi (Budapest), P. Binswanger (Zurich), S. Bravo Williams (Mexico City), E. W. Busse (Durham), G. Crepaldi (Padova), N. Exton-Smith (London), F. Forette (Paris), R. Hauri (Zurich), F. Huber (Basle), A. Svanborg (Gothenburg), T. F. Williams (Bethesda). Also the staff of the organizing committee of the 1986 Sandoz Lectures in Gerontology: L. Abisch (Basle), V. Ceresoli (Basle), Ch. Hesse (Cologne), and G. Nussbaumer (Basle) deserve our recognition. In addition, V. Biro (Arlesheim) is to be acknowledged for editing the discussions.

They all deserve our particular gratitude, as without their energy, imagination and involvement the realization of such a first-rate meeting and its subsequent publication would not have been possible.

M. Bergener, Cologne (FRG)
M. Ermini, Basle (CH)
H. B. Stähelin, Basle (CH)

Welcome Address

S. Guttmann

*Head of Pharmaceutical Research,
Sandoz Ltd, Basle, Switzerland*

It is a pleasure and a great honour for me to welcome you on behalf of the management of the Pharmaceutical Division to the 1986 Sandoz Lectures in Gerontology. This year's Lectures—the second in the series—bear witness that Sandoz as a company has accepted the challenge, and even the obligation, to contribute to the solution of the increasing problems arising with the elderly in our society. The lectures are associated with the Sandoz Prize for Gerontological Research.

The formal communications for the Lectures will be delivered by the candidates for the 1986 Prize. It is therefore a great pleasure for all of us to have with us today Professor Karl Esser of the University of Bochum and Professor Sir Martin Roth of the University of Cambridge, both of whom were recipients of the last Sandoz Prize for Gerontological Research in 1984.

For obvious reasons, the interest and major efforts of the medical and biological sciences were focussed in the past on those acute disorders and diseases, mainly infections, which threatened the so-called normal population in the best years of their lives. The tremendous progress made in these sciences in the last twenty to thirty years resulted in a dramatic reduction or even elimination of the causes of premature death and thus in a progressive increase of the number of elderly persons in the general population.

The problems emerging from this process are much more complex than the previous ones. Instead of "normal diseases" with more or less clear-cut acute pathophysiology, we are faced on the one hand with a constantly increasing elderly population presenting a very complex mixture of health and ill-health—of physical and of psychological problems—and on the other hand with the associated social and economic problems.

Whereas in the acute and in the "normal" diseases, therapies attacking the underlying cause are possible or at least aimed at, such an approach is at present rarely or not at all possible in the diseases of the elderly, since the cause is aging itself. The best we can currently do is discover adequate substitution therapy for the various deficiencies. An additional complication is the fact that the aging of different cellular structures, of cell populations, and of tissues, progresses in rather different ways and at different rates.

Since the causes of these diseases are so manifold, their therapy sometimes requires the contributions of a very large number of disciplines. In order to obtain an optimal effect, these contributions should proceed in a simultaneous and concerted manner. Due, however, to the different timings of awareness of the problems and different speed of progress in the various disciplines, we are far from the ideal conditions required for attaining optimal results.

Until the relatively recent past, and as can also be seen from the program of the present meeting, the main emphasis in geriatric research has been placed on the neural and the neuroendocrine system, although the process of aging affects the whole organism. It is evident that no academic or industrial research group alone can address in the necessarily comprehensive way the entire problem of aging. Only an intimate collaboration between all partners, academia and industry together, can contribute in an efficient way to the necessary enlargement of geriatric research. Our own research, which in the past has focussed its activity on the dysfunction of the central nervous system in the elderly, has now started to extend its interest to the peripheral disorders such as hypertension, atherosclerosis, and osteoporosis. It is our intention to reinforce basic and applied research in these fields, which finally should result in drugs and therapies which alleviate the illnesses of old age.

But in addition to our own research projects, we want to stimulate and encourage discussions and research activities in the field of geriatric medicine, whether they are similar to or different from our own activities.

For this reason, by creating the Sandoz Prize for Gerontological Research and the Sandoz Lectures in Gerontology, we are trying to establish a forum where in a multidisciplinary approach the problems of the elderly are met in as comprehensive a way as the current state of the art makes possible.

During the coming two days, a limited number of distinguished scientists will present and discuss the most recent progress made by themselves and by hundreds of their colleagues all over the world in academia, in industrial research laboratories, and in clinics. The conclusions of these lectures will enhance the state of the art and improve our knowledge of the aging process. They will also serve as a basis for further research and efforts to improve our understanding of the Dimensions of Aging. They will hopefully improve our ability to help elderly people to overcome their specific health problems and to enjoy a healthy and normal life also in their later years.

Contents

Contributors v

Preface ix

Welcome Address
S. GUTTMANN xi

Is There a Functional Difference
between Normal and Pathological Aging?
K. ESSER, L. ABISCH xvii

Cellular Systems In Aging

Foundations of Cytogerontology
L. HAYFLICK 3

Testing Molecular Theories of Cellular Aging
R. HOLLIDAY 21

Relationship between Aging of the Immune System
and Aging of the Whole Organism
E. BEREGI 35

Neuroendocrinological Aspects of Aging of the
Reproductive System
J. MEITES 51

Changes in the Neuronal Cytoskeleton in Aging
and Disease
B. H. ANDERTON, J.-P. BRION, J. FLAMENT-DURAND,
M. HAUGH, J. KAHN, C. C. J. MILLER, A. PROBST,
J. ULRICH 69

Cellular Systems in Aging—Implications
and Outlook
G. S. ROTH 91

Aging at the Organ Level

Age, Immunity and Cancer
P. EBBESEN 97

An Integrated Approach Toward
Understanding Myocardial Aging
E. G. LAKATTA 105

Influence of Age and Training on Bone and
Muscle Tissue in Humans and Mice
E. STEINHAGEN-THIESSEN 133

Functional Repair of the Nervous System:
A Focus on Aging
R. J. WYATT, L. de MEDINACELI, W. J. FREED 143

Mechanism of Age-related Alterations in Response
to α- and β-Adrenergic Stimulation in Rat Hepatocytes
and its Reverse in Primary Culture
G. TSUJIMOTO, A. TSUJIMOTO, S. AZHAR,
B. B. HOFFMAN 161

Aging at the Organ Level—Implications and Outlook
T. F. WILLIAMS 179

Human Competences in Aging

Neurochemical, Genetic and Clinical Aspects of Alzheimer's
Disease
B. WINBLAD, W. WALLACE, J. HARDY, C. FOWLER, G. BUCHT,
I. ALAFUZOFF, R. ADOLFSSON 183

Nosological Aspects of Differential Typology of Dementia of
Alzheimer Type
C. G. GOTTFRIES 207

Applied Pharmacology in the Elderly: An Overview of the
Dunedin Program
R. B. STEWART 221

Sociological Perspectives on Aging, Families and the Future
V. L. BENGTSON 237

Contributions to a Multi-level Model of Intervention in Psychogeriatrics
M. BERGENER, E. U. KRANZHOFF, J. HUSSER 263

Implications and Outlook
M. ROTH 293

General Conclusions
A. CARLSSON 301

Conclusion to the 1986 Sandoz Lectures in Gerontology
M. BERGENER 305

Is There a Functional Difference between Normal and Pathological Aging?

Karl Esser and Leo Abisch

*Ruhr-Universität Bochum, Federal Republic of Germany
and Sandoz Ltd, Basle, Switzerland*

On February 26, 1986, the Faculty of the Sandoz Lectures met informally—not with the aim of solving the above mentioned question—but rather to compare the different viewpoints of the various specialists. The main question gave rise to several subquestions: Are we discussing a purely academic question or does it have practical implications? What is "normal" as compared to "pathological" aging? Just a deviation from the mean? What does "pathological" mean on the molecular or cellular level since this is by definition a clinical term?

The cell biologist, indeed, sees that various cells of animal origin have a time-limited capacity to function including mitosis both *in vitro* and *in vivo*. There is also an inverse relationship between donor age and the numbers of population doublings that occur in a variety of cell types. It is difficult to distinguish between normal aging and pathology on the cellular level. Studies in the fungus *Podospora* suggest that there are plasmids which trigger aging but that there are nuclear genes which preclude aging of this organism. Conclusions from *Podospora* to Alzheimer's patients may be far reaching speculations but based on these experiences it might be interesting to study fibroblasts in Alzheimer's disease—and perhaps the clue to understanding Alzheimer's disease could be found on a molecular level in phenomena analogous to those observed in *Podospora*.

What role does pathology play if we accept that aging is genetically controlled and certainly a species-specific phenomenon? Even if we assume that aging is genetically controlled, environmental factors including the personal lifestyle, e.g. nutrition, stress etc. play an important role in processes which can clearly be defined as pathological. For example, genetic factors make an important contribution in relation to diabetes, dementia and to many psychiatric conditions, e.g. depression and schizophrenia.

These diseases are certainly also much influenced by environmental factors. In general, extrinsic factors may influence intrinsic factors, and both are involved in the aging process. A very simple formula would be: genotype + environment = phenotype.

For a cardiologist it might be difficult to see any evidence for an aging process with regard to cardiovascular functions. He might rather speak about an interaction of genetics, diseases and lifestyle variables. Hence, he might have great difficulty in distinguishing between functional and pathological aging.

One of the important biological changes connected with aging in mammals is the involution of the reproductive system but with clear species- and sex-related differences. The reproductive function declines in female rodents after only one-third of their lifespan whereas menopause occurs in women after two-thirds of normal lifespan. On the other hand, the aging process of the male reproduction system is much less clear-cut both in laboratory animals and in man. How do terms such as pathological or normal aging apply to these changes?

The clinician often sees that the aging organism is attacked by diseases more frequently that the young organism. This might be due to both a decreased functional capacity and a decreased reserve capacity in the aged. Often it is difficult to differentiate normal aging from pathological age-related changes. Therefore, age-standardized normal values are needed in clinical work. If we discuss changes in later years of life we must distinguish between normal age-related, abnormal and pathological changes due to secondary illnesses. Physiological processes should not be considered as diseases, but the situation is often complicated because most people over 70 years of age suffer from one or more clinically defined diseases. In this context a serious limitation of our knowledge of the aging process in man is due to the fact that many gerontological studies have been performed in elderly individuals who are apparently clinically healthy.

We also lack well designed prospective studies in humans to shed light on the development of diseases in the elderly under various conditions. We would particularly need to include "early cases" in such studies and to follow them up, in an interdisciplinary approach, over a long time. If one accepts that there is a difference between normal and pathological aging, emphasis should be laid on the various diseases with high prevalence in older age. Therapy by drugs and other means should therefore aim to prevent these diseases or to minimize their impact. Positive changes of lifestyle might have a further beneficial effect.

Aging and dying are certainly connected up to a certain degree. Therefore, the question discussed here could be continued to ask: Is there a difference between normal dying and pathological dying?

For a social scientist the term "normal" has several meanings based on socio-logical findings: the first definition is average behaviour within one or two standard deviations. The second definition is expectable behaviour and the third is valued behaviour. Therefore, the term "competence" should perhaps be used when we are talking about "normal" aging, because to maintain one's competence is the goal of successful aging, of successful life. The social psychologist would define competence as adequate role-performance, as the ability to cope and as the feeling of mastery, i.e. the opposite of hopelessness. Put into unfavourable conditions, an aged individual can be said to be incompetent even when he or she is biologically and physiologically normal.

The question arises as to what will happen in the future if, and when, science and technology will be in a position to implement "corrective measures" to the drawbacks of many diseases and age-related changes. Spectacles, hearing aids, pacemakers etc. have already become routine, and replacing diseased organs like kidneys, hearts and lungs becomes more and more frequent. Brain grafting is already being done on an experimental level and, theoretically, with the help of genetic engineering certain diseases such as diabetes, heart diseases etc. could possibly be eliminated. Will there still be such a thing as natural aging? What will then be the role of the physician? While the "prosthetic man" seems a utopian idea today, the situation could be much more realistic in 50 years from now, or even earlier.

There is no doubt that an involutionary process takes place during the aging process of man but there are also compensatory mechanisms working. It might prove fruitful to look upon pathological aging as a stage where compensation is not possible any more, i.e. where there is loss of adaptability. We should therefore study and define these compensatory mechanisms and hopefully find some measures to keep them active as long as possible.

An illustrious example of the problem "normality" versus "pathology" often discussed is Alzheimer's disease. Is it a separate disease entity or does it represent an exaggerated aging process? If it was primarily age-related, the prevalence of Alzheimer's disease would steadily increase with age, but, in fact, this increase seems to slow down beyond the age of about 90. There are also distinctive qualitative differences between Alzheimer patients and persons of the same age who are not affected by the disease, e.g. regarding semantic memory but also in many pathological findings. A final answer to this question will be found once a cause for Alzheimer's disease is identified, perhaps by molecular-genetic methods and/or by prospective, epidemiological studies. Hopefully, some years from now we will be able to give a more concrete answer to this important question.

If we limit the discussion of "normal" versus "pathological" aging to the central nervous system it has the advantage that we do know a great deal about what happens in the brains of individuals who merely grow old and what happens in the brain of individuals who not only grow old but become demented. The brain is a very special kind of system which has a fixed cell population since the nerve cells do not divide. Therefore, many of the findings of cell biologists in other cell populations cannot be transferred to the central nervous system.

Organs with a fixed cell population have a special problem because their reserve capacity is liable to be eroded. Moreover, personality changes are much more pronounced in persons with dementia and, above all, their life expectation is only about a quarter of that of individuals of comparable age in the general population. In summary, there is a difference between normal and pathological aging but besides this discontinuity between the norm and pathological, there is also continuity.

Part I

Cellular Systems in Aging

Foundations of Cytogerontology

Leonard Hayflick

Center for Gerontological Studies
University of Florida, Gainesville, Florida, USA

Keywords
Cytogerontology; Cell memory; Cell aging.

PREFACE

This contribution was prepared in response to a call for papers to compete for the "Second Sandoz Prize for Gerontological Research". Instructions for the competition stipulated that the submitted papers contain a summary of the research conducted by the candidate. It is for that explicit reason that this paper reports, almost exclusively, on the work of the author and his co-workers. The reader should be aware that, as a consequence of these instructions, many significant studies done by colleagues working in this field consciously have been excluded.

INTRODUCTION

The term "Cytogerontology" was proposed by me in 1974 (Hayflick 1974) to describe the field of cellular aging which was then an emerging subdiscipline of biogerontology. Our early observations, on which the foundations of modern cytogerontology rest, will be described first in order to better appreciate subsequent advances made in the past quarter century.

Twenty-four years ago Moorhead and I described the finite replicative capacity of cultured normal human fibroblasts and interpreted the phenomenon to be aging at the cellular level (Hayflick and Moorhead 1961). We demonstrated that when normal human embryonic cells were grown under the most favourable conditions, death was inevitable after about 50 population doublings. We called this the

Phase III phenomenon. We also showed that the death of cultured normal cells was not due to some trivial cause involving medium components or culture conditions but was an inherent property of the cells themselves (Hayflick 1965, Hayflick and Moorhead 1961).

Although there were many previous reports on the failure of cultured cells to proliferate continuously, none characterized the cells as normal, ruled out culture artifacts as the cause, or suggested that the phenomenon might be associated with aging (Puck *et al.* 1957, Puck *et al.* 1958, Swim and Parker 1957). However, the observation that cultured cells frequently failed to replicate indefinitely was probably made hundreds of times from the genesis of cell culture techniques in about 1900 to our report more than a half century later. Those previous "failures" went unreported because the then current dogma was that the failure of cells to proliferate indefinitely *in vitro* was attributable to errors in the "art" required to keep cells dividing indefinitely. That dogma was so well entrenched that our original manuscript (Hayflick and Moorhead 1961), which was first submitted to *The Journal of Experimental Medicine*, was rejected with the statement: "The largest fact to have come out from tissue culture in the last fifty years is that cells inherently capable of multiplying will do so indefinitely if supplied with the right milieu *in vitro*." The letter was signed by Peyton Rous.

As for our data showing that normal human diploid cells were more sensitive to human viruses than any other cell and our suggestion that they had many other advantages over primary cells for human virus vaccine production, Rous said, "The observations on the effect of viruses on cultures of these (cells) seem extraneous." With respect to our suggestion that the Phase III phenomenon represents aging, he said, "The inference that death of the cells is due to 'senescence at the cellular level' seems notably rash."

Our manuscript was then sent unchanged to *Experimental Cell Research* where it was quickly accepted.

The prevailing dogma that all cultured cells are intrinsically immortal received further support because dozens of continuously propagable cell populations indeed were then known. However, as we pointed out, the essential distinction between continuously propagable cell populations and those having a finite lifetime is that the former are composed of abnormal cells, frequently having characteristics of cancer cells, and the latter are normal cells or are composed of cells having properties of the cells found in the tissue of their origin (Hayflick and Moorhead 1961). The failure to recognize this crucial distinction, even to this day, is the reason why so much of the effort in modern cancer biology is without merit. In my view, and that of others, much current work is wrongly based on the assumption that certain popular continuously propagable cell lines like NIH 3T3 and BHK 21 are normal cells and as such can be used in attempts to convert them to cancer cells. NIH 3T3 cells and other immortal cell populations are abnormal and in most cases, already behave like cancer cells (Boone 1975, Boone *et al.* 1976, Hayflick and Moorhead 1961, Littlefield 1982).

Our finding that cultured normal cells have a finite capacity to replicate has had a profound impact on gerontological thought. Prior to our observation, the cellular basis of aging was dealt an almost lethal blow by the finding of the noted cell culturist Alexis Carrel that cells from a chick heart allegedly could be cultured indefinitely (Parker 1961). If chick heart cells, presumably normal, were capable of continuous culture for the 34 years attributed to them and if 34 years is in excess of the life span of *Gallus domesticus*, then it would be difficult to attribute age changes to events occurring at the cellular level. The reasoning was that if cultured normal cells, once released from *in vivo* controls, could function and proliferate indefinitely then age changes must be attributable to events that occur at the supracellular level.

Carrel's purported finding provided powerful evidence that cultured, presumably normal cells, did not age and die. Yet the interpretation of his results soon fell to a preponderance of opposing evidence including the fact that no one since Carrel has been able to keep normal chick embryo cells in a state of continuous propagation for periods of time even in excess of 1 year (Harris 1957, Hay and Strehler 1967, Lima and Macieira-Coelho 1972). Thus Carrel's studies have never been confirmed. I have proposed one explanation for Carrel's finding in which the method of preparation of chick embryo extract, used as a source of nutrients for his cultures, allowed for the survival and introduction of new viable fibroblasts into the so-called "immortal" culture at each feeding (Hayflick 1972). Although I believe that Carrel was unaware of this artifact, Witkowski, in a lengthy study of Carrel's "immortal" cells, suggests otherwise (Witkowski 1979, 1980).

Thus three major developments in the 1960s helped launch interest in the new field of cytogerontology. The first was recognition that Carrel's experiment was flawed (Hayflick 1972); second, our evidence that cultured normal cells do have an intrinsic, finite capacity to replicate (Hayflick 1965, Hayflick and Moorhead 1961); and third, our recognition that immortal cell populations consist of abnormal cells (Hayflick 1965, Hayflick and Moorhead 1961).

An interesting aside to the history of cytogerontology is the recent discovery that the great German biologist August Weismann, in 1891, was the first to propose that the somatic cells of higher animals would be found to have a limited doubling potential (Kirkwood and Cremer 1982). Although he provided no experimental evidence for his surmise, Weismann stated, ". . . death takes place because a worn-out tissue cannot forever renew itself, and because a capacity for increase by means of cell division is not everlasting but finite" (Weismann 1891).

THE INVERSE RELATIONSHIP BETWEEN DONOR AGE AND POPULATION DOUBLING POTENTIAL

In the decade that followed our first report (Hayflick and Moorhead 1961), further evidence appeared from studies in cytogerontology that provided important new insights into cellular aging. In 1965 I reported that cultured fibroblasts derived from older human donors replicated fewer times than those derived from embryos (Hayflick 1965). Because the technique for determining population doublings was crude at that time we were unable to establish a direct relationship between donor age and population doubling potential. Subsequently, studies done by others not only confirmed the principle that we had observed but extended it significantly. Martin and his colleagues derived cultures from human donors ranging from fetal to 90 years of age (Martin *et al.* 1970). Although the data reveal considerable scatter they observed a regression coefficient, from the first to the ninth decade, of −0.2 population doublings per year of life with a standard deviation of 0.05 and a correlation coefficient of −0.50. The scatter found is not unlike that reported to occur with virtually any age-related change that is measured cross-sectionally and not longitudinally. Nevertheless, at least eight more studies have confirmed the finding that the number of population doublings of cultured human cells is inversely proportional to donor age. This inverse relationship has now been shown to occur in normal human cells derived from such diverse human tissue as lung (Hayflick 1965), skin (Goldstein *et al.* 1978, Martin *et al.* 1970, Schneider and Mitsui 1976, Vracko and McFarland 1980), liver (Le Guilly *et al.* 1973), arterial smooth muscle (Bierman 1977) and T lymphocytes (Walford 1982, Walford *et al.* 1981).

These findings, however, must be tempered with observations that the relationship may be clouded when different tissue sites are compared (Schneider *et al.* 1977) or where the physiological state of the donor is abnormal. For example, strains derived from diabetics have been found to undergo fewer doublings *in vitro* than their normal age matched counterparts (Goldstein *et al.* 1978).

DIRECT PROPORTIONALITY BETWEEN MAXIMUM SPECIES LIFESPAN AND POPULATION DOUBLING POTENTIAL

In 1973 I suggested that the population doubling potential of cultured fibroblasts from several animal species revealed a surprisingly good direct correlation with maximum species lifespan (Hayflick 1973). In the years that followed several other reports appeared that have substantiated this idea, especially that of Röhme (1981). The embryonic fibroblasts of ten species studied now show a direct correlation with maximum lifespan (Fig. 1).

If this relationship is extended and confirmed it suggests the presence of a chronometer or pacemaker within all normal cells that is characteristic for each species and that dictates maximum cell doubling or functional capacity with an apparent evolutionary basis. The postulated chronometer may or may not be the same one that we postulate controls the inverse relationship between donor age and population doubling potential.

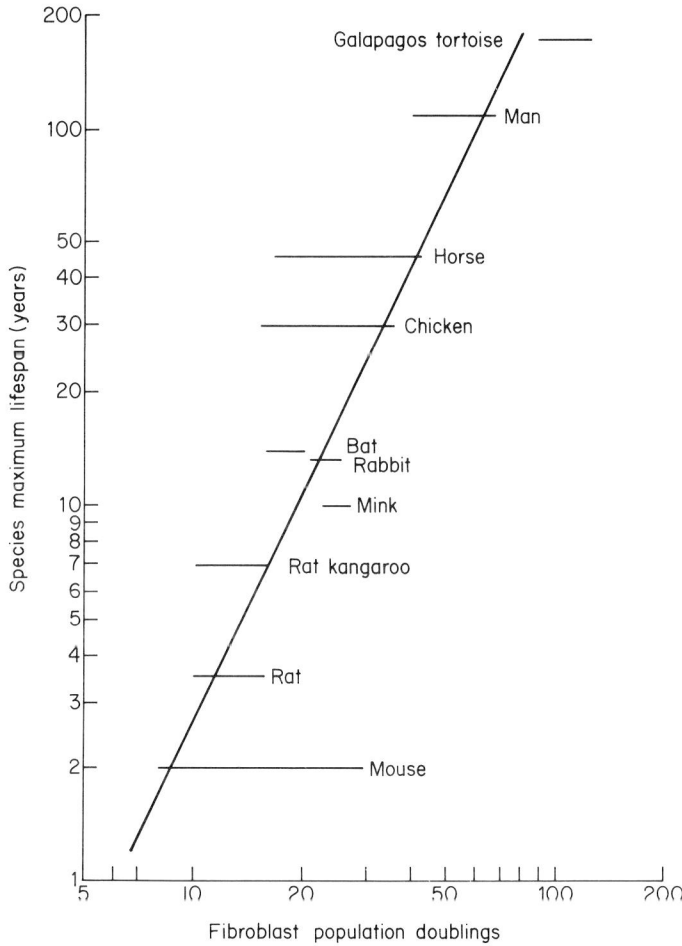

Fig. 1. Fibroblasts from the embryos of ten different species multiply in culture to a maximum number of population doublings that is roughly proportional to the lifespan for that species. Galapagos tortoise cells were derived from a juvenile animal.

THE MEMORY OF CULTURED NORMAL HUMAN CELLS

When I first established human diploid cell strains 25 years ago, it became apparent that their finite lifetime imposed a serious limit on the capacity to work with any single strain. I found that a strain derived from fetal tissue underwent 50 ± 10 population doublings over a period of about 1 year and was then lost. In order to circumvent this important limitation we succeeded in freezing viable normal human cells at subzero temperatures (Hayflick and Moorhead 1961). In this way it was possible to characterize fully a single human diploid cell strain and have it available for study for long periods of time. This observation had important practical applications in the field of human virus vaccine preparation as will be discussed subsequently.

In 1962 we developed, and placed in liquid nitrogen cryogenic storage, several hundred ampules of our normal human diploid cell strain WI-38 which became the most completely characterized normal human cell population in the world. It is today the archetypical normal human fibroblast and is used worldwide for countless applications in biological research, virus isolation and identification and the production of human virus vaccines.

WI-38 has been in cryogenic storage for 24 years. This represents the longest period of time that a viable normal human cell population has ever been stored at subzero temperatures. The ability to preserve normal cell strains has permitted experimentation directed toward answering a fundamental question in cytogerontology. If cells are frozen at various population doubling levels (PDLs) up to Phase III, how many population doublings will the cells undergo when they are thawed or reconstituted? Do they have a "clock" that is arrested in the cold at the population doubling level at which they were frozen so that the total cumulative number of doublings both before and after freezing is about 50 (in the case of a fetal strain) or is the "clock" recycled to zero or somehow randomly reset?

In the subsequent 24 years we have shown that WI-38 and other human cell strains have a remarkable memory. Even after 24 years they remember at which population doubling level they were frozen and, upon reconstitution, undergo a number of population doublings such that the total number before and after freezing equals about 50. More than 130 ampules have been reconstituted by us in the past 24 years and the memory of the cells is as accurate today as it was in 1962.

FUNCTIONAL FAILURES IN CULTURED NORMAL CELLS AS THEY APPROACH PHASE III

In 1971 we first reported the loss of functional properties in cultured normal human WI-38 cells after repeated population doublings or approach of Phase III (Houck et al. 1971). We found that the cells lost much of their ability to synthesize collagen and to induce collagenolytic activity after almost 40 population doublings. The loss of at least two fibroblastic functions prior to loss of cell division capacity suggested to us that other cell functions might also be altered as normal human cells approach Phase III.

In the subsequent decade a plethora of functional increments and decrements numbering in the hundreds have been discovered to occur in cultured normal human cells prior to their loss of replicative capacity. A full tabulation of these changes may be found in my recent review (Hayflick 1980a). The changes reported to occur cover virtually all aspects of cell biochemistry, morphology and behaviour. They include changes in lipids, carbohydrates, amino acids, proteins, RNA, DNA, enzymes, cell cycle dynamics, cell size and morphology, synthesis, incorporation and stimulation (Hayflick 1980a).

The importance of these findings is that many of the changes that have been reported to occur in cultured normal human cells as they age *in vitro* are identical to changes that are known to occur in cells *in vivo* as humans age (Hayflick 1980a). This observation adds additional weight to our suggestion that the Phase III phenomenon does indeed represent aging at the cellular level. Furthermore, it supports our original contention that it is unlikely that animals age because one or more important cell populations lose their proliferative capacity. Rather, we contend that although normal cells have a demonstrable finite capacity to replicate *in vitro*, that limit is never reached *in vivo*. This is because the age-related increments and decrements that herald the approaching loss of division capacity result in the aging and death of the animal well before the genetically determined replicative limit on cell division is reached.

It is also important to observe that age changes are equally likely to occur in cells other than fibroblasts. In fact, the changes that occur in time in non-dividing or slowly dividing cells may be even more important in aging than are those that occur in fibroblasts. However, it is crucial to understand that cell division in fibroblasts is as much a functional property as is any other function. Whatever the causes are that produce functional decrements in non- or slowly dividing cells, those factors are equally likely to cause that functional decrement recognized as cessation of proliferative ability in fibroblasts. There is no justification for distinguishing between non- or slowly dividing cells on the one hand, and dividing cells on the other hand, on the basis that the former are functioning cells and the latter are not. Cell division is, after all, a functional property whose likelihood for change with age is as probable as any other cell function. We do not believe that aging in animals is the result of the loss of cell proliferative capacity. What is more likely is that determinants that produce decrements in cell function with time also affect replicative capacity. We have suggested that the determinants are likely to repose in the cell genome (Hayflick 1976, 1980b).

HISTOCOMPATIBILITY ANTIGENS AND CELLULAR AGING

In 1972 our group launched a series of studies designed to determine whether the major histocompatibility antigens remain quantitatively and qualitatively stable throughout the entire limited lifetime of cultured normal human cells. These studies had two additional goals: (1) to determine the relationship, if any, between *in vitro* cell senescence and the expression of the major histocompatibility surface antigens, and (2) to determine whether the detection of HLA specificities could be useful in distinguishing between human diploid cell strains derived from different donors of the same sex. To these ends we employed a modification of the fluorochromatic cytotoxicity assay using 15 phenotypically different human fibroblast cell strains which were repeatedly typed for their HLA specificities from early population doubling levels until senescence.

We found that HLA specificities remained markedly stable throughout the *in vitro* lifetime of several human diploid cell strains derived from both fetal and adult sources (Brautbar *et al.* 1972). We concluded that any immunological theory of aging would not be tenable if it depended upon changes in fibroblast HLA specifications with age. We also found that the fluorochromatic cytotoxicity test could be used to distinguish between human diploid cell populations. This finding had important practical value as a test for identity of strains, such as WI-38, which were then being used worldwide as a substrate for human virus vaccine production (Hayflick 1969).

These qualitative studies were followed by quantitative measurements of the density of the histocompatibility determinants during cellular aging (Brautbar *et al.* 1973). We employed a quantitative microabsorption assay utilizing HLA alloantisera with a variety of human diploid cell strains. We found that the density of HLA determinants remained unchanged on normal human diploid cells throughout their *in vitro* lifetime (Brautbar *et al.* 1973).

In marked distinction with the behaviour of cultured normal human cells we found that several immortal SV40 transformed human fibroblast populations were found to acquire new antigenic sites (Pellegrino *et al.* 1976).

VARIATIONS IN THE LIFESPAN OF CLONES

An important consideration in the search for the mechanism that limits the proliferative capability of cultured normal human cells is the degree to which the cell population is homogeneous. Phase II or Phase III cells may represent a heterogeneous population composed of cells or cell lineages at different PDLs, such that the uncloned population behaves as the mean. In studying variables whose values depend upon the remaining doubling potential of cells in mass cultures, any heterogeneity of doubling potential among the cells within a culture is likely to increase the difficulty of detecting changes which occur during the finite *in vitro* lifetime of cultured normal cells.

Prior to the studies done by us on this question in 1974, I had previously found that for three clones isolated from a mass culture after the second population doubling, the doubling potential of each clone was about the same as that of the mass culture (Hayflick 1965). I interpreted this to mean that the doubling potential of each clonable cell was about the same. Studies subsequently done by Smith and Hayflick (1974) showed that clonal heterogeneity did occur at later PDLs and that this finding has a significant bearing on delineating the mechanism of the Phase III phenomenon.

We used for these studies our strains WI-26 and WI-38 from which we derived several hundred clones at various PDLs. Each clone was cultured and the cells composing them counted until all reached Phase III (Smith and Hayflick 1974).

In all cases we found a large variation in the population doubling potential, or lifespan, among the colonies isolated from a single mass culture. When clones were isolated from mass cultures which had undergone eight or nine population doublings, only about 50% of the clones were capable of more than eight population doublings. This percentage was further reduced when clones were isolated from mass cultures at higher PDLs. Mass cultures appear to be composed of two subpopulations: one with a low population doubling potential and the other with a high population doubling potential. Nevertheless, we found that the highest doubling potential observed in clones isolated from any single culture was about the same as the doubling potential of the mass culture from which the single cells were taken (Smith and Hayflick 1974).

The subpopulation of single cells having low doubling potential appears to increase with increasing PDLs of the mass culture at the time of cloning. About 50% of the clones isolated at PDLs eight or nine of the mass culture were capable of only eight population doublings, while 90% or more of the clones isolated at the thirtieth to fortieth PDL of the mass culture had a low doubling potential. It might be expected that all of the cells with low doubling potential would be eliminated from the mass culture within ten population doublings. However, this was found not to be the case. It appears that cells are recruited into the low doubling potential subpopulation as the mass culture approaches Phase III (Smith and Hayflick 1974).

THE FIDELITY OF PROTEIN BIOSYNTHESIS DURING CELLULAR AGING

One of the major hypotheses offered in recent years to explain age changes is based on the accumulation of errors over time in essential proteins. This theory, although intrinsically attractive, has been the recipient of more contrary data than supportive findings. In 1974 we published a series of experiments designed to test this hypothesis by detecting misspecified proteins in Phase III cells (Tomkins et al. 1974).

Our approach was to use DNA and RNA viruses as probes to detect and amplify putative cellular protein errors. We compared the behaviour of poliovirus type 1 and herpesvirus type 1 replicated in Phase II and Phase III WI-38 cells. We examined quantity of virus produced, pattern of cytopathology, plaque morphology and analysis of herpesvirus proteins by polyacrylamide gel electrophoresis. We found no difference in these variables in viruses that had replicated in old or young cells and concluded that these results did not support the notion that misspecification of proteins accounts for cell aging *in vitro* (Tomkins *et al.* 1974).

Following these studies we determined the susceptibility to proteolysis of the total proteins isolated from Phase II and Phase III cultures (Bradley *et al.* 1975). Here we found proteins with increased protolytic susceptibility only at the last population doubling in Phase III cultures of WI-38. This finding suggests that proteins from terminal Phase III cells are modified when compared to those from Phase II and early Phase III cultures. This modification could be due to errors in transcription, translation or to post-translational alterations that may be fundamental or incidental to the *in vitro* senescence phenomenon. Cells in the last population doubling should not be overlooked as a substrate for biochemical studies (Bradley *et al.* 1975).

In a final effort to assess the biosynthetic capabilities of young and old WI-38 cells, we compared, by radioautography, cells grown with labelled precursors of DNA, RNA, protein and lipids (Razin *et al.* 1977). We found that by incorporating radioactive thymidine, uridine, protein-hydrolysate, acetate, oleic acid and cholesterol, and measuring the number of grains per cell, that there was a decrease in the incorporation of all these substances with progressive age of the culture (Razin *et al.* 1977). However, the decrease in the incorporation of acetate, oleic acid and cholesterol was much smaller than that of the other precursors. This indicates that lipid synthesis is effected to a lesser degree than protein and nucleic acid synthesis in cellular aging. This result was found to be in accord with a higher lipid content and proliferation of intracellular membranes in cells of Phase III WI-38 cultures reported by others (Razin *et al.* 1977).

DNA SYNTHESIS IN WI-38 DURING CELLULAR AGING

The limited proliferative capacity of cultured normal human cells and our interpretation of it as aging at the cellular level has given rise to many studies directed toward understanding why normal cells ultimately lose their ability to replicate. In the years during which these studies have been conducted several important observations have been made on the population dynamics of these aging cell populations. Chief among these findings are that (1) cells plated at low density contain non-dividing cells, the proportion of which increases with the PDL of the culture (Absher *et al.* 1974, Martin *et al.* 1974, Merz and Ross 1969, Smith and Hayflick 1974), (2) cloned cells vary in their doubling potential (Martin *et al.* 1974, Smith and Hayflick 1974, Smith *et al.* 1977), (3) the percentage of labelled cells (labelling index) in an autoradiography study reached a plateau after a 24-30 h exposure to tritiated thymidine, and (4) the labelling index decreased as a function of PDL (Cristofalo and Sharf 1973).

Taken together, these observations reveal the variability of proliferation rate and metabolic activity of individual cells in a human diploid population as it ages *in vitro*. Because of the importance of this variability and the means of detecting it we sought to develop a method of autoradiographic analysis for the determination of that proportion of normal cells which does not enter S phase during exposure to tritiated thymidine (Matsumura *et al.* 1979a).

Our results supported the notion of the presence of subpopulations with an extremely slow rate of entrance into Phase III in a proliferating normal human cell population. The variable was shown to be a useful empirical estimate for the doubling potential of the cell population (Matsumura *et al.* 1979a).

In subsequent studies, we investigated the DNA synthetic abilities of WI-38 and WI-26 after the cessation of the last replicating cells in Phase III (Matsumura *et al.* 1979b). Phase III cultures, which we had earlier found could be maintained for months (Hayflick and Moorhead 1961), had not been studied systematically for clues that might provide an understanding of the process. We examined terminal Phase III cultures of WI-38 and WI-26 for cell morphology, survival and the ability to incorporate tritiated thymidine into their nuclei (Matsumura *et al.* 1979b). In these studies we found that terminal Phase III cultures reproducibly and quantitatively accumulated multinucleated cells. An analysis of DNA content revealed that multinucleation was not the result of simple fission of the nuclear region, but was accompanied by DNA synthesis and polyploidization. This observation suggests that the slow DNA synthesis found to occur during terminal Phase III is related to multinucleation and polyploidization.

Senescent WI-38 and WI-26 cells could be periodically transferred during this 6-month period of terminal Phase III with only a small loss of cells. A considerable percentage of cells continue to synthesize DNA during this period (Matsumura *et al.* 1979b).

THE GENETIC BASIS FOR PHASE III

The preceding studies on Phase III and our demonstration of its association with aging at the cell level led us to a series of investigations directed toward an understanding of the mechanism that places a limit on the replicative ability of cultured normal human cells. Our thesis was that this limitation is under genetic control. This was based on what we believe to be conclusive evidence produced by us that the Phase III phenomenon is caused by intracellular events (Hayflick 1965, Hayflick and Moorhead 1961), that there is an inverse relationship between donor age and population doubling potential (Bierman 1977, Goldstein *et al.* 1978, Hayflick 1965, Le Guilly *et al.* 1973, Martin *et al.* 1970, Vracko and McFarland 1980, Walford 1982, Walford *et al.* 1981) and that there is a direct relationship between species lifespan and population doubling potential (see

Fig. 1). In the last decade our studies have been directed toward an understanding of the genetic basis of Phase III and the demonstration of a putative molecular chronometer.

In 1972 Wright and I reported on a method for enucleating mass cultures of our normal human diploid cell strain WI-38 (Wright and Hayflick 1972). This method was based on previous observations that cytochalasin B (CB), a mould metabolite, interferes with cytokinesis in many eukaryotic cells and, in high concentrations, causes these cells to extrude their nuclei (Carter 1967). We found that CB-treated cells, exposed to high **g** forces, could be separated from their extruded nuclei, producing virtually pure cultures of enucleated cells called "cytoplasts" (Wright and Hayflick 1972). This technique was also independently described by others (Prescott *et al.* 1972). The technique permitted us to conduct an important series of experiments, the goal of which was to determine whether the mechanism limiting the proliferation of normal human cells was located in the nucleus or the cytoplasm. We enucleated cultures of young WI-38 cells and fused these cytoplasts to whole old WI-38 cells using Sendai fusion factor. By this procedure we intended to determine whether the introduction of "young" cytoplasm into "old" WI-38 cells, or the reciprocal, would affect doubling capacity. Our results showed that the presence of young cytoplasm had no effect on population doubling potential nor was there an effect when the reciprocal experiment was performed. We concluded that nuclear, rather than cytoplasmic factors, control the limitation on cell division (Wright and Hayflick 1975a,b).

These studies were followed by more direct experiments made by Muggleton-Harris and me (Muggleton-Harris and Hayflick 1976). We found that the nuclei released from whole WI-38 cells after CB treatment could be isolated and then fused to cytoplasts in the same way that cytoplasts were previously fused to whole cells. Our goal was to fuse isolated nuclei obtained from old WI-38 cells to cytoplasts obtained from young WI-38 cells (and the reciprocal) and to determine the number of population doublings remaining in these "cybrids". The results suggested again that the nucleus is governing. However, since the isolated nuclei are surrounded by a narrow cytoplasmic shell, these experiments are not unequivocally conclusive.

PRACTICAL USES FOR HUMAN DIPLOID CELLS

Although only indirectly associated with cytogerontology, our discovery of the human diploid cell strains resulted in several practical advances in biomedical research, many of which have tended to increase life expectation or have had a direct benefit for the elderly. In our original paper we described the exquisite sensitivity of human diploid cell strains to human viruses and showed that these cells had the widest human virus spectrum known (Hayflick and Moorhead 1961). The cells were so sensitive that in subsequent years we used them to identify a new common cold virus (rhinovirus) that was heretofore unknown (Tyrell et al. 1962). Others found many additional new human viruses using WI-38 and WI-26 cells. The use of WI-38 or its derivative strains is now a part of the standard procedures used in virus diagnostic laboratories throughout the world.

In addition to our recognition of the use of these cells to identify human viruses (Hayflick and Moorhead 1961) we also suggested their use as superior substrates for the production of human virus vaccines (Hayflick 1963, 1969, Hayflick and Moorhead 1961, Hayflick et al. 1962). We pointed out that the cells were normal and, unlike primary cells, could be thoroughly tested and found to be safe before use in vaccine production. In 1962 we reported the first successful production and human administration of a polio vaccine produced in a human diploid cell strain (Hayflick et al. 1962). In subsequent years recognition of the advantages of using WI-38 as a substrate for human virus vaccines was achieved and in 1972 the first polio vaccine produced in WI-38 was licensed in the United States. Many other human virus vaccines produced in human diploid cells have now been licensed for use in countries throughout the world. These vaccines have benefited tens of millions of people and include vaccines against poliomyelitis, adenoviruses, rubella, mumps, cytomegalovirus, rubeola, smallpox and, most recently, rabies.

CYTOGERONTOLOGY AND THE FUTURE OF AGING RESEARCH

Cytogerontology has, itself, now come of age. In the 25 years since its establishment, the discipline has become well recognized as a productive area for enquiry into the aging process. Belief that the Phase III phenomenon might be an artifact of *in vitro* culture conditions has vanished because the same phenomenon has been shown to occur even when normal cells are transplanted seriatim *in vivo* (Hayflick 1980a).

In recent years the research frontiers in cytogerontology have moved in directions designed to uncover the genetic and/or molecular mechanism that is thought to underlie the cause of the Phase III phenomenon. The successful, widespread use of cell enucleation procedures and fusion technology by a number of investigators suggests that a good understanding of the postulated intracellular chronometers will soon be forthcoming.

Of at least equal importance is the current recognition that the study of more differentiated cells *in vitro* might provide valuable new information in the field of cytogerontology.

It is becoming increasingly evident that all normal cells possess a means by which the passage of time and/or the passage of repetitive cellular events are measured or recorded. Future research in cytogerontology will undoubtedly yield information on the molecular nature of the pacemakers or chronometers that we propose are present in all normal cells. If this is ultimately proven and an understanding of the nature of biological clocks is achieved it will be a short step to intervention. How desirable is it for humans to possess the ability to tamper with their biological clocks? Society must determine the merits of that possibility now before it becomes a reality with the concomitant potential for undesirable consequences.

REFERENCES

Absher, P. M., Absher, R. G. and Barnes, W. D. (1974). Genealogies of clones of diploid fibroblasts. Cinemicrophotographic observations of cell division patterns in relation to population age. *Exp. Cell Res.* **88**, 95-104.

Bierman, E. L. (1977). The effect of donor age on the *in vitro* lifespan of cultured human arterial smooth-muscle cells. *In Vitro* **14**, 951-955.

Boone, C. W. (1975). Malignant hemangioendotheliomas produced by subcutaneous inoculation of Balb/3T3 cells attached to glass beads. *Science* **188**, 68-70.

Boone, C. W., Takeichi, N., Paranjpe, M. and Gilden, R. (1976). Vasoformative sarcomas arising from Balb/3T3 cells attached to solid substrates. *Cancer Res.* **36**, 1626-1633.

Bradley, M. A., Dice, J. F., Hayflick, L. and Schimke, R. T. (1975). Protein alterations in aging WI-38 cells as determined by proteolytic susceptibility. *Exp. Cell Res.* **96**, 103-112.

Brautbar, C., Payne, R. and Hayflick, L. (1972). Fate of HL-A antigens in human diploid cell strains. *Exp. Cell Res.* **75**, 31-38.

Brautbar, C., Pellegrino, M. A., Ferrone, S., Reisfeld, R. A., Payne, R. and Hayflick, L. (1973). Fate of HL-A antigens in aging cultured human diploid cell strains, II. Quantitative absorption studies. *Exp. Cell Res.* **78**, 367-375.

Carter, S. B. (1967). The effects of cytochalasins on mammalian cells. *Nature* **213**, 261-264.

Cristofalo, V. J. and Sharf, B. B. (1973). Cellular senescence and DNA synthesis. Thymidine incorporation as a measure of population age in human diploid cells. *Exp. Cell Res.* **76**, 419-427.

Goldstein, S., Moerman, E. J., Soeldner, J. S., Gleason, R. E. and Barnett, D. M. (1978). Chronologic and physiologic age effect replicative life-span of fibroblasts from diabetics, prediabetics, and normal donors. *Science* **199**, 781-782.

Harris, M. (1957). Quantitative growth studies with chick myoblasts in glass substrate cultures. *Growth* **21**, 149-166.

Hay, R. J. and Strehler, B. L. (1967). The limited growth span of cell strains isolated from the chick embryo. *Exp. Gerontol.* **2**, 123-135.

Hayflick, L. (1963). A comparison of primary monkey kidney, heteroploid cell lines and diploid cell strains for human virus vaccine preparation. *Am. Rev. Respir. Dis.* **88**, 387-393.

Hayflick, L. (1965). The limited *in vitro* lifetime of human diploid cell strains. *Exp. Cell Res.* **37**, 614-636.

Hayflick, L. (1969). A consideration of the cell substrates used in human virus vaccine preparation. *In* "Progress in immunobiological standardization" Vol. 3, pp. 86-93. Karger, Basel and New York.

Hayflick, L. (1972). Cell senescence and cell differentiation *in vitro*. *In* "Aging and development" (Academy of Science and Literature, Mainz, Germany), Vol. 4, pp. 1-15. F. K. Schattauer Verlag, Stuttgart.
Hayflick, L. (1973). The biology of human aging. *Am. J. Med. Sci.* **265**, 433-445.
Hayflick, L. (1974). Cytogerontology. *In* "Theoretical aspects of aging" (M. Rockstein, ed.) pp. 83-103. Academic Press, New York.
Hayflick, L. (1976). The cell biology of human aging. *N. Engl. J. Med.* **295**, 1302-1308.
Hayflick, L. (1980a). Cell aging. *In* "Annual review of gerontology and geriatrics", (C. Eisdorfer, ed.) Vol. 1, pp. 26-67. Springer Verlag, New York.
Hayflick, L. (1980b). The cell biology of human aging. *Scientific Am.* **242**, 58-66.
Hayflick, L. and Moorhead, P. S. (1961). The serial cultivation of human diploid cell strains. *Exp. Cell Res.* **25**, 585-621.
Hayflick, L., Plotkin, S. A., Norton, T. W. and Koprowski, H. (1962). Preparation of poliovirus vaccines in a human fetal diploid cell strain. *Am. J. Hygiene* **75**, 240-258.
Houck, J. C., Sharma, V. K. and Hayflick, L. (1971). Functional failures of cultured human diploid fibroblasts after continued population doublings. *Proc. Soc. Exp. Biol. Med.* **137**, 331-333.
Kirkwood, T. B. L. and Cremer, T. (1982). Cytogerontology since 1881: A reappraisal of August Weismann and a review of modern progress. *Hum. Genet.* **60**, 101-121.
Le Guilly, Y., Simon, M., Lenoir, P. and Bourel, M. (1973). Long-term culture of human adult liver cells: morphological changes related to *in vitro* senescence and effect of donor's age on growth potential. *Gerontologia* **19**, 303-313.
Lima, L. and Macieira-Coelho, A. (1972). Parameters of aging in chicken embryo fibroblasts cultivated *in vitro*. *Exp. Cell Res.* **70**, 279-284.
Littlefield, J. W. (1982). NIH 3T3 cell line. *Science* **218**, 214-215.
Martin, G. M., Sprague, C. A. and Epstein, C. J. (1970). Replicative lifespan of cultivated human cells. Effect of donor's age, tissue, and genotype. *Lab. Invest.* **23**, 86-92.
Martin, G. M., Sprague, C. A., Norwood, T. H. and Pendergrass, W. R. (1974). Clonal selection, attenuation and differentiation in an *in vitro* model of hyperplasia. *Am. J. Pathol.* **74**, 137-153.
Matsumura, T., Pfendt, E. A. and Hayflick, L. (1979a). DNA synthesis in the human diploid cell strain WI-38 during *in vitro* aging. An autoradiography study. *J. Gerontol.* **34**, 323-327.
Matsumura, T., Zerrudo, Z. and Hayflick, L. (1979b). Senescent human diploid cells in culture: Survival, DNA synthesis and morphology. *J. Gerontol.* **34**, 328-334.
Merz, G. S. and Ross, J. D. (1969). Viability of human diploid cells as a function of *in vitro* age. *J. Cell Physiol.* **74**, 219-221.
Muggleton-Harris, A. L. and Hayflick, L. (1976). Cellular aging studied by the reconstruction of replicating cells from nuclei and cytoplasms isolated from normal human diploid cells. *Exp. Cell Res.* **103**, 321-330.
Parker, R. C. (1961). *In* "Methods of tissue culture". Harper and Row, New York.
Pellegrino, M. A., Ferrone, S., Brautbar, C. and Hayflick, L. (1976). Changes in HL-A antigen profiles on S.V.$_{40}$ transformed human fibroblasts. *Exp. Cell Res.* **97**, 340-343.
Prescott, D., Myerson, O. and Wallace, J. (1972). Enucleation of mammalian cells with cytochalasin B. *Exp. Cell Res.* **71**, 480-485.

Puck, T. T., Cieciura, S. J. and Fisher, H. W. (1957). Clonal growth *in vitro* of human cells with fibroblastic morphology. *J. Exp. Med.* **106**, 145-158.

Puck, T. T., Cieciura, S. J. and Robinson, A. (1958). Genetics of somatic mammalian cells. III. Long-term cultivation of euploid cells from human and animal subjects. *J. Exp. Med.* **108**, 945-956.

Razin, S., Pfendt, E. A., Matsumura, T. and Hayflick, L. (1977). Comparison by autoradiography of macromolecular biosynthesis in "young" and "old" human diploid fibroblast cultures. *Mech. Age. Dev.* **6**, 379-384.

Röhme, D. (1981). Evidence for a relationship between longevity of mammalian species and life spans of normal fibroblasts *in vitro* and erythrocytes *in vivo*. *Proc. Natl Acad. Sci. USA.* **78**, 5009-5013.

Schneider, E. L. and Mitsui, Y. (1976). The relationship between *in vitro* cellular aging and *in vivo* human aging. *Proc. Natl Acad. Sci. USA* **73**, 3584-3588.

Schneider, E. L., Mitsui, Y., Aw, K. S. and Shorr, S. S. (1977). Tissue-specific differences in cultured human diploid fibroblasts. *Exp. Cell Res.* **108**, 1-6.

Smith, J. R. and Hayflick, L. (1974). Variation in the lifespan of clones derived from human diploid cell strains. *J. Cell Biol.* **62**, 48-53.

Smith, J. R., Pereira-Smith, O. and Good, P. I. (1977). Colony size distribution as a measure of age in cultured human cells. A brief note. *Mech. Age. Dev.* **6**, 283-286.

Swim, H. E. and Parker, R. F. (1957). Culture characteristics of human fibroblasts propagated serially. *Am. J. Hygiene* **66**, 235-243.

Tomkins, G. A., Stanbridge, E. J. and Hayflick, L. (1974). Viral probes of aging in the human diploid cell strain WI-38. *Proc. Soc. Exp. Biol. Med.* **146**, 385-390.

Tyrrell, D. A. J., Bynoe, M. L., Buckland, F. E. and Hayflick, L. (1962). The cultivation in human-embryo cells of a virus (D.C.) causing colds in man. *Lancet* August 18: 320-322.

Vracko, R. and McFarland, B. M. (1980). Lifespan of diabetic and non-diabetic fibroblasts *in vitro*. *Exp. Cell Res.* **129**, 345-350.

Walford, R. L. (1982). Studies in immunogerontology. *J. Am. Geriat. Soc.* **30**, 617-625.

Walford, R. L., Jawaid, S. Q. and Naeim, F. (1981). Evidence for *in vitro* senescence of T-lymphocytes cultured from normal human peripheral blood. *Age* **4**, 67-70.

Weismann, A. (1891). "Essays upon heredity and kindred biological problems" 2nd edn. Clarendon Press, Oxford.

Witkowski, J. A. (1979). Alexis Carrel and the mysticism of tissue culture. *Med. Hist.* **23**, 279-296.

Witkowski, J. A. (1980). Dr. Carrel's immortal cells. *Med. Hist.* **24**, 129-142.

Wright, W. E. and Hayflick, L. (1972). Formation of anucleate and multinucleate cells in normal and S.V.$_{40}$ transformed WI-38 by cytochalasin B. *Exp. Cell Res.* **74**, 181-194.

Wright, W. E. and Hayflick, L. (1975a). Contributions of cytoplasmic factors to *in vitro* cellular senescence. *Fed. Proc.* **34**, 76-79.

Wright, W. E. and Hayflick, L. (1975b). Nuclear control of cellular aging demonstrated by hybridization of anucleate and whole cultured normal human fibroblasts. *Exp. Cell Res.* **96**, 113-121.

Discussion

Verdonk: May I have your opinion on the experiments of McCay which proved that aging can be prolonged by about 50% over the normal lifespan by undernutrition. Furthermore, fewer tumours, fewer infections, less hypertension etc. can be seen in rats and mice. It is a disturbing and a rather pessimistic view that aging is only due to genetic factors.

Hayflick: The classic experiments by Clive McCay at Cornell University showed that undernutrition produces in rodents a substantial increase in life expectation. This was confirmed in a variety of other species in recent years. More recently it has been discovered that undernutrition even during early adulthood provides for additional increases in lifespan. The fundamental reason for this is not understood, but it seems that undernutrition alone does not simply slow down development; it must be a far more subtle mechanism.

Roth: We have to keep two things in mind when we consider these undernutrition experiments: firstly, this kind of experiment has never been done in any animal higher than a rodent and, secondly, we are not certain that the normal *ad libitum* diet which is offered to rats in captivity is not simply killing them by eating themselves to death.

Esser: Concerning the influence of nutrition on aging, I would mention that in the fungus *Podospora* the onset of senescence is strictly under control of nuclear genes. However, the longevity is modified by external conditions, such as nutrition. Undernutrition enhances lifespan as was shown experimentally.

Ulrich: You pointed out that there are probably molecular clocks in our cells which determine aging in various functions. Obviously these clocks are reset in each germ cell, probably at meiosis and cellular fusion. Do you know of research in this direction?

Hayflick: Aging probably did not evolve from a genetic process because aging in its extreme manifestations is a characteristic only of humans, domestic animals, pets and zoo animals. Wild animals do not age to the same degree that humans do. For example, humans, after sexual maturation, are capable of life expectations significantly greater than feral animals. The theory that aging may have developed from a selective process by evolution can not be defended, because there has never been a sufficient number of old feral animals to be selected for. Now to the clocks themselves: if they do exist, they have probably evolved due to genetic changes which deal with development and not with aging. The very interesting speculation about an apparent recycling of the clock during meiosis has been discussed. It was proposed that repair capacity is far more efficient and occurs far more regularly during meiosis than during any other part of the cell cycle.

Viidik: The other possibility to explain finite lifespan of cells and individuals is that clocks or active limiting mechanisms are passive phenomena, e.g. running out of genetic programs or accumulation of waste products. Could you comment on these two "opposite" mechanisms?

Hayflick: Any genetic process which might explain manifestations of age changes may be modified by environmental effects. Clearly, aging is a far too complex phenomena to be universal.

Testing Molecular Theories of Cellular Aging

Robin Holliday

Genetics Division, National Institute for Medical Research, Mill Hill, London

Keywords
Error theories; Cultured human fibroblasts; Epigenetic errors; DNA methylation.

INTRODUCTION

The experimental study of the processes of aging can be broadly divided into two alternative strategies. On the one hand, information is gained by a direct comparison of the cells, tissues or organs of young and old organisms, or at intervals throughout their lifespan. Such an approach may employ biochemical, physiological, histological or other procedures, and it is hoped that the information gained will provide insight into one or more of the underlying mechanisms of aging. On the other hand, the starting point may be theoretical: the formulation of a theory or hypothesis about a possible basis for the aging process, and then the execution of one or more experimental tests, which may either support the theory or discredit it.

Amongst theories of aging, it is very important to distinguish those which only try to account for those secondary changes in cells and tissues which produce the visible manifestations of senescence and are the final cause of death, from those which also address the primary causes and the more fundamental problem of a well defined finite lifespan. This second type of theory tries to explain the intrinsic changes which are occurring without any outward manifestation, but which will eventually give rise to the features of senescence. Theories of the first type may not attempt to explain these intrinsic changes, but only to account for their end result. For example, the free radical theory of aging may explain the steady deterioration of a variety of tissues in old animals, but it does not explain

Dimensions in Aging
ISBN 0 12 090162 5

Copyright © 1986 Academic Press, London
All rights of reproduction in any form reserved.

why the healthy adult is able to withstand free radical damage for a considerable part of its lifespan, whereas later on its defence against such damage succumbs.

Theories which attempt to explain the primary causes of aging fall into one or other of two major categories. Stochastic theories propose that the gradual accumulation of multiple errors or defects in macromolecules may initially have little or no effect on the organism, but will eventually lead to progressively severe changes in the phenotype. Programme theories propose that aging is determined by processes which may be related to those which occur during development, that is, aging is seen as a final development stage which inevitably follows the reproductive period of the adult. Such a programme would, of course, be genetically controlled because it must involve time dependent changes in gene activity. However, it is important to understand that aging from stochastic processes would also be under genetic control, because the frequency of defects in macromolecules, or the ability to remove defects, is known to be determined by the genotype of the organism (for reviews, see Kirkwood *et al.* 1986).

Aging must ultimately be understood at the level of the organism, but at present it is usually very hard to use organisms to devise tests of either stochastic or programme theories of aging. Although changes in a particular tissue or organ may be readily discernible, their molecular or cellular bases are much harder to identify. Moreover, a relatively slight change at the cellular level may have more profound consequences at higher levels of cellular organization. It is therefore a considerable advantage to be able to study cells directly. This can be done by growing diploid cells in culture until the end of their lifespan. The fact that many types of cell, including fibroblasts, glial cells, lymphocytes, endothelial and adrenal cells (Bierman 1978, Hayflick 1965, Hornsby 1978, Ponten and MacIntyre 1968, Walford *et al.* 1981 and A. A. Morley and M. McKarran, pers. comm.) all have a finite lifespan *in vitro* suggests that this is a property of all somatic cells, and provides a valid model for testing molecular theories of aging. However, this approach must eventually be complemented by studies of age related changes in non-dividing postmitotic cells.

STOCHASTIC THEORIES OF AGING

Somatic Mutations

Cells have a variety of mechanisms to protect the integrity of their DNA; nevertheless, damage can become fixed in the genome of a cell, either as a gene mutation or a chromosome aberration. What can be regarded as the earliest error theory of aging proposed that the accumulation of such damage would inevitably lead to the loss of cellular functions. Experiments with human fibroblasts do not provide support for this theory. Treatment of cells with the potent mutagens ethyl methane sulphonate and N-methyl-N'-nitrosoguanidine showed that there was no reduction in their subsequent lifespan (Gupta 1980), and similar experiments have been done with X-rays (Macieira-Coelho *et al.* 1977, 1978).

With regard to dividing cells, most mutations with dominant deleterious effects would be selected out, but recessive mutations would accumulate and have their effect when two homologous genes were altered. In this case, tetraploid cells with four gene copies should have a longer lifespan than diploid ones. Two different experimental approaches have shown that tetraploids have, in fact, the same lifespan as diploid cells (Hoehn *et al.* 1975, Thompson and Holliday 1978). Actual measurement of mutation frequencies showed only a two-fold increase during the first two-thirds of the *in vitro* lifespan of human cells (Gupta 1980). However, there is evidence that mutations may well increase more rapidly after that (Fulder and Holliday 1975) and it is well known that senescent human fibroblasts frequently have chromosome aberrations (Saksela and Moorhead 1963, Thompson and Holliday 1973). Studies on mutations *in vivo* also suggest that they do not accumulate linearly with time, but much more rapidly at the end of the lifespan (Morley *et al.* 1982). A possible explanation for the rapid increase in genetic defects during this period will be discussed later.

There are also strong theoretical grounds for believing that somatic mutations are unlikely to be one of the primary causes of aging (Maynard-Smith 1962). For human diploid fibroblasts the mutation frequencies would have to be unreasonably high (10^{-3}-10^{-4} per gene per cell generation), and one would expect far more early death during the serial subculture of diploid fibroblasts than is actually observed (Holliday and Kirkwood 1981).

Selfish DNA

A variant of the somatic mutation theory proposes that transposable elements may continually increase in somatic cells (V. Murray and T. B. L. Kirkwood in prep.). In principle, the replication of such elements and their insertion at random into the genome would lead to an exponential build-up and the inactivation of more and more genes. Molecular techniques are now available which should make it possible to identify such transposable elements and monitor their frequency during serial subculture of fibroblasts. It had been reported that repetitive DNA sequences accumulate as non-chromosomal closed circles during aging *in vitro* and *in vivo* (Schmookler Reis *et al.* 1983). However, this claim was later retracted (Schmookler Reis *et al.* 1985).

Mitochondrial DNA

The aging of growing vegetative cells of the fungus *Podospora anserina* has shown to be associated with the accumulation of truncated mitochondrial genomes and the loss of respiratory function (Cummings *et al.* 1979, Kuck *et al.* 1981, Stahl *et al.* 1980, Wright *et al.* 1982). Since cloned human mitochondrial DNA is available, it is possible to examine the integrity of the genomes of mitochondria from senescent human cells, using restriction enzyme patterns for detection of gross changes in DNA sequence. Two laboratories have reported that there is no significant change in mitochondrial DNA (Schmookler Reis and Goldstein 1983, R. F. Rosenberger in prep.) and there are no reports that respiratory function is severely impaired in senescent diploid fibroblasts. Although these results are negative, it is important to note that the elimination of a possible mechanism of aging is in itself an important advance.

Free Radical Damage

There is strong evidence that senescent cells or tissues contain abnormal lysosomes and accumulate the "age pigment" lipofuscin. This is thought to arise from lipid peroxidation which is one of the main effects of free radical attack. The exponential accumulation of lipofuscin in human fibroblasts has been shown by measuring their autofluorescence by flow cytometry (Rattan *et al.* 1982). The serial selection of a subfraction of the least fluorescent cells prevented this accumulation; nevertheless, the cells died out at the normal population doubling level (L. I. Huschtscha *et al.* unpublished observations). In studies of cultured human glial cells it was shown that secondary lysosomes accumulate in the centre of colonies, where the non-dividing cells are chronologically the eldest. However, the cells are the youngest in terms of cell divisions completed, and when they resume division, the lipofuscin and abnormal lysosomes disappear (Brunk *et al.* 1973, Ponten *et al.* 1973). Results with both fibroblasts and lymphocytes indicate that the accumulation of "age pigment" is a secondary consequence of other cellular changes and not a primary cause of aging.

An early report that treatment with the antioxidant vitamin E greatly extended the lifespan of human fibroblasts could not be confirmed (Packer and Smith 1974).

Protein Errors

The potential instability of the machinery for protein synthesis was first pointed out by Orgel (1963, 1970). He suggested that the feedback of protein errors into the pathways of information transfer from DNA to protein could lead to an exponential increase and ultimately to an "error catastrophe" in protein synthesis. Whether or not this occurred would depend on the extent of error feedback. In principle, the theory can explain why some cells, such as those which grow indefinitely, could avoid error accumulation, whereas others might eventually succumb (for reviews, see Holliday 1968a, Kirkwood *et al.* 1984). The theory predicts that senescent cells should contain a significantly increased frequency of errors in all proteins. However, to detect such errors is not at all easy, since abnormal molecules would be completely heterogeneous with regard to their amino acid substitutions. Thus a senescent cell may contain a major proportion of completely normal molecules and a subset of altered ones, but within this subset, any specific substitution would be present only in a minute amount. Very sensitive methods are therefore needed to detect such abnormal molecules, and these have not yet been developed. So far most tests of Orgel's theory have depended on indirect methods, such as the accumulation of a fraction of heat-labile enzyme. Some of these results provide support for the theory and others do not (Holliday 1984, 1986a, Kirkwood et al. 1984).

One promising approach involved measuring the fidelity of DNA polymerase, since this is one of the most important enzymes in information transfer. The argument is that alterations in its structure should lead to a decrease in its ability to copy faithfully defined templates *in vitro*. Two studies confirm that DNA polymerase α, and also γ, extracted from senescent human fibroblasts are less accurate than enzyme from young cells (Linn et al. 1976, Murray and Holliday 1981). In the most thorough series of experiments, a variety of controls were carried out to establish the validity of the measure of fidelity, and the results suggested that the polymerase became progressively altered during the final phase of the cell's lifespan (Murray and Holliday 1981). However, a later study suggested that the DNA polymerases from confluent non-dividing cells also had reduced fidelity (Krauss and Linn 1982). If errors in protein synthesis result in less accurate replication of DNA, then one would expect that mutations would accumulate during the senescent phase of growth, evidence for this has been obtained (Fulder and Holliday 1975).

The aminoglycoside antibiotics paramomycin and G418 have been shown to reduce the fidelity of protein synthesis in eukaryotes, both *in vitro* and *in vivo* (Buchanan et al. 1980, Burke and Mogg 1985, Palmer and Wilhelm 1978, Buchanan unpublished observations). Another test of the protein error theory, therefore, is to examine the effects of these agents on the *in vitro* lifespan of human fibroblasts. Low levels of antibiotic were used which had no initial effect on growth rate, but when the cells were grown continually in their presence, they became prematurely senescent on the basis of at least three criteria (Holliday and Rattan 1984). Treating an early passage culture once with a higher concentration of G418 also reduced its subsequent lifespan (R. Holliday unpublished observations).

In summary, indirect tests with the protein error theory have often provided support for it, but in other cases results have been negative. Direct tests of the theory have yet to be carried out.

Epigenetic Errors

Recently considerable evidence has accumulated that the postsynthetic methylation of cytosine (5mC) in DNA is related to the control of gene expression (for reviews, see Razin et al. 1984). In many cases it has been shown that hypomethylation is associated with transcription, and that silent non-transcribed genes are methylated in promoter or controlling sequences. Moreover, the pattern of methylation is inherited through the activity of a maintenance transmethylase which acts on hemimethylated DNA soon after replication, but does not act on non-methylated DNA. It has been shown that maintenance of 5mC in DNA is incomplete in mammalian diploid fibroblasts, and the rate of loss of methylation is inversely related to *in vitro* lifespan for the three species studied (human, hamster and mouse) (Wilson and Jones 1983). On the other hand, permanent lines retain a constant level of methylation. It has been known for a long time that the lifespan of human fibroblasts is related to elapsed cell divisions rather than to chronological time (Hayflick 1965), and it would be expected that loss of methylation would primarily occur in dividing cells. Taken together, these results suggest that the stochastic loss of 5mC might have progressively aberrant effects on gene expression, including expression of genes which are normally silent in fibroblasts. This does not mean that it would be easy to detect new proteins in senescent cells, because, as in the case of errors in proteins, the aberrant effects on gene expression would be expected to be heterogeneous. Thus, any particular new protein might be expressed only in a very small fraction of the total population.

Experiments have been carried out to test the possibility that the loss of methylation is a primary cause of aging. These made use of the analogues azacytidine or deoxyazacytidine, which are known to be potent inhibitors of DNA methylation (Creusot *et al.* 1982, Jones and Taylor 1981, Taylor and Jones 1982). A single treatment would be expected to reduce the total level of 5mC significantly, and subsequently there would be a more gradual decline from that level. Studies in two laboratories have now demonstrated that a single treatment does indeed have a heritable effect, since in all experiments the cells died out significantly sooner than the controls (Fairweather *et al.* 1986, Holliday 1985, 1986b). These results suggest that the stochastic loss of epigenetic controls of gene expression may be an important component in the aging process. There is also evidence that DNA methylation declines during aging *in vivo* (Holliday 1985).

Quantitative arguments also make the "epigenetic error" theory an attractive one. In human fibroblasts the frequency of loss of any individual 5mC is about 6×10^{-3} per cell division, which is far higher than the frequency of mutation (see above and Holliday and Kirkwood 1981). Also, the reactivation of silent genes would have dominant or co-dominant effects, and it would not be surprising if such epigenetic changes had more than additive interactions. An escalating impairment of normal cellular functions is necessary to explain the fact that cellular selection for continued growth does not prevent the demise of large populations of cells.

PROGRAMME THEORIES OF AGING

These theories are easily stated, but very difficult to formulate and test, because so little is known about the normal developmental programme of a complex organism. A mechanism for counting cell divisions based on the sequential methylation of short repeated DNA sequences has been suggested (Holliday and Pugh 1975), but at present this is purely speculative and cannot be tested experimentally. The concept of a strictly determined clock or programme for aging implies that lifespan would be fairly independent of environmental perturbations or insults. However, with regard to fibroblast aging, it has been shown that temperature (Thompson and Holliday 1973), 5-fluorouracil (Holliday and Tarrant 1972), aminoglycoside antibiotics (Holliday and Rattan 1984, R. Holliday unpublished observations) and azacytidine (Fairweather *et al.* 1986, Holliday 1985, 1986b) all have strong effects on lifespan.

A variant of the programme theory is that human fibroblasts cease growth because they become terminally differentiated (Bell *et al.* 1978, Martin *et al.* 1974). However, the morphology of late passage cells is extremely heterogeneous rather than uniform, and the term "senescent" appears to be a much more apt description. Moreover, the newly differentiated cells would be expected to synthesize new types of luxury protein which could be detected on two dimensional gels. In several studies, the appearance of new proteins has not been reported (Celis and Bravo 1984, Harley *et al.* 1980, Sakagami *et al.* 1979). It also seems very improbable that the several types of differentiated cell, previously mentioned, which all have a finite *in vitro* lifespan, should all undergo further terminal differentiation.

An attractive feature of programme theories is the possibility that the immortalization of diploid cells to form permanent lines is due to the bypass of the programme. Several laboratories are actively engaged in identifying the dominant genes which appear to confer finite lifespan on human cells (Bunn and Tarrant, 1980, Pereira-Smith and Smith 1983). This approach holds out one of the strongest hopes for the future understanding of the genetic control of cell aging, whether this aging is based on cumulative stochastic events, or a more direct control of division potential.

EVOLUTIONARY ASPECTS OF THE AGING PROCESS

So far, no satisfactory explanation for the evolution of a programme for aging has been proposed. The argument that aging evolved for the benefit of subsequent generations or the species has been exposed as largely fallacious (Medawar 1952, Williams 1957). On the other hand, evolutionary arguments not only provide support for error theories of aging, but also suggest further experimental tests (Kirkwood 1977, Kirkwood and Holliday 1979).

When an organism develops to a reproducing adult, it must be maintained for a given period of time. This maintenance demands the investment of metabolic resources, including (1) the repair of damage in DNA, (2) accuracy in the synthesis of macromolecules, which involves energy dependent proof reading steps,

(3) removal of defective molecules, for example, denatured or abnormal proteins, and (4) the replacement of malfunctioning or dead cells. If the ecological lifestyle is such that death from accident, predation, starvation or disease is a common event, as is the case for small mammals such as rodents, then it becomes counterproductive to invest resources to maintain the adult organism, or soma, for a long period. Such resources are more profitably channelled into rapid reproduction, since this will increase the Darwinian fitness of the organism, and consequently the lifespan of the animal is short. On the other hand, accidental death is much less common in large mammals. In this case, more resources are used to maintain the soma, reproduction is much slower and the lifespan is much longer. In all cases, however, it is proposed that to maximize the survival of the germ line, it is counterproductive to maintain the soma longer than is necessary for effective reproduction, and aging is the process which eventually disposes of the soma (Kirkwood 1977, Kirkwood and Holliday 1979).

This disposable soma theory makes two strong predictions. First, that cells from long lived organisms should invest more resources in maintenance than those from short lived species. This has been clearly shown for the repair of lesions in DNA. In five published studies, four show that the efficiency of repair of damage induced by ultra-violet light is correlated with the longevity of the donor species (Francis *et al.* 1981, Hall *et al.* 1984, Hart and Setlow 1974, Kato *et al.* 1980, Treton and Courtois 1982). These are striking observations. Apart from *in vitro* longevity itself, which correlates with *in vivo* lifespan (Rohme 1981), other aspects of cellular maintenance have not yet been examined. The second prediction of the disposable soma theory is that the potential immortality of germ line cells is due to their investment of the metabolic resources necessary for continued survival. Thus, their repair capacity, accuracy of synthesis of macromolecules and so on, should be greater than it is in somatic cells. This could be tested by experiment, but so far no such studies have been reported.

CONCLUSIONS

The majority of experimental studies of aging cells or animals employ empirical procedures which gather information about the phenotypic changes during senescence. For the most part, it is hard to interpret such changes and it is not often that they specifically support, or provide evidence against, any particular theory. Theories are most valuable if they suggest specific experimental tests, and this is particularly true of stochastic or error theories of aging. It is an important advance if specific possibilities can be ruled out, as has happened in some cases, but for the most part experimental evidence in favour of error theories is indirect and better tests are needed. A new possibility is that the process of aging is directly related to the breakdown of the normal controls of gene activity. The gradual loss of DNA methylation may alter the epigenetic control of gene expression in specialized cells, and this could lead to more than additive interactions between different epigenetic effects, a loss of cellular homeostasis, and an accelerating degeneration of normal tissue functions. Permanent cell lines and germ cells are able to escape these processes and they may achieve this by investing metabolic resources in the maintenance of cellular function. Alternatively, they may have bypassed a predetermined programme for aging. Although the concept of a programme has received wide support amongst gerontologists, so far it has not been formulated in any specific form which can be tested experimentally. Also, it is far from clear why programmes for aging, either at the cellular or the organism level, should have evolved in the first place.

One of the current challenges to cell and molecular biologists is the identification of genes which determine whether a cell will have finite or infinite growth. Immortalization, or the escape from senescence, is often an essential step in carcinogenesis and can in some cases be brought about in rodent cells by transfection with active oncogenic DNA (Land *et al.* 1983, Newbold and Overell 1983). However, other experiments with human cells strongly indicate that immortalization is due to the loss of gene function (Bunn and Tarrant 1980, Pereira-Smith and Smith 1983). If such "mortalization" genes exist, then it should be possible, in principle, to identify them using modern procedures, and find out whether they are activated during early development when somatic cells with finite lifespan are first formed. One function of such genes might be the turning off of those cellular maintenance mechanisms which are essential for the survival of germ line cells.

ACKNOWLEDGEMENTS

I would like to thank all my colleagues, past and present, for their many contributions to our experimental programme to test molecular theories of cellular aging. These include L. E. Orgel, G. M. Tarrant, K. V. A. Thompson, C. M. Lewis, S. J. Fulder, T. B. L. Kirkwood, L. I. Huschtscha, J. H. Buchanan, A. Stevens, V. A. Shakespeare, Zh. A. Medvedev, M. N. Medvedeva, C. L. Bunn, V. Murray, S. M. Linn, M. Kairis, A. A. Morley, S. Cox, S. I. S. Rattan and R. F. Rosenberger. Many of their relevant publications are cited in the References

REFERENCES

Bell, E., Marek, L. F., Levinstone, D. S., Merrill, C., Sher, S., Young, I. T. and Eden, M. (1978). Loss of division potential in vitro ageing or differentiation? *Science* **202**, 1158-1163.

Bierman, E. L. (1978). The effect of donor age on the *in vitro* life span of cultured human arterial smooth-muscle cells. *In Vitro* **14**, 951-955.

Brunk, U., Ericsson, J. L. E., Ponten, J. and Westermark, B. (1973). Residual bodies and "ageing" in cultured human glia cells. *Exp. Cell Res.* **79**, 1-14.
Buchanan, J. H. Bunn, C. L., Lappin, R. I. and Stevens, A. (1980). Accuracy of *in vitro* protein synthesis: translation of polyuridylic acid by cell free extracts of human fibroblasts. *Mech. Age. Dev.* **12**, 339-353.
Bunn, C. L. and Tarrant, G. M. (1980). Limited lifespan in somatic cell hybrids and cybrids. *Exp. Cell Res.* **127**, 385-396.
Burke, J. F. and Mogg, A. E. (1985). Suppression of a nonsense mutation in mammalian cells *in vivo* by the aminoglycoside antibiotics G418 and paromomycin. *Nucl. Acids Res.* **13**, 6265-6272.
Celis, J. E. and Bravo, R. (1984). Synthesis of the nuclear protein cyclin in growing, senescent and morphologically transformed human skin fibroblasts. *Febs Letters* **165**, 21-25.
Creusot, F., Acs, G. and Christman, J. K. (1982). Inhibition of DNA methyltransferase and induction of Friend erythroleukemia cell differentiation by 5 azacytidine and 5 aza-2'-deoxycytidine. *J. Biol. Chem.* **257**, 2041-2048.
Cummings, D. J., Belcour, L. and Grandchamp, C. (1979). Mitochondrial DNA from *Podospora anserina* II Properties of mutant DNA and multimeric circular DNA from senescent cultures. *Mol. Gen. Genet.* **171**, 239-250.
Fairweather, S., Fox, M. and Margison, G. P. (1986). The *in vitro* life span of MRC-5 cells is shortened by 5-azacytidine induced demethylation. *Exp. Cell Res.* (in press).
Francis, A. A., Lee, W. H. and Reagan, J. D. (1981). Relationship of DNA excision repair of ultraviolet-induced lesions to the maximum life span of mammals. *Mech. Age Dev.* **16**, 181-189.
Fulder, S. J. and Holliday, R. (1975). A rapid rise in cell variants during the senescence of populations of human fibroblasts. *Cell* **6**, 67-73.
Gupta, R. S. (1980). Senescence of cultured human diploid fibroblasts. Are mutations responsible? *J. Cell Physiol.* **103**, 209-216.
Hall, K. Y., Hart, R. W., Benirschke, A. K. and Walford, R. L. (1984). Correlation between ultraviolet-induced DNA repair in primate lymphocytes and fibroblasts and species maximum achievable life span. *Mech. Age. Dev.* **24**, 163-173.
Harley, C. B., Pollard, J. W., Stanners, C. P. and Goldstein, S. (1980). Protein synthetic errors do not increase during ageing of cultured human fibroblasts. *Proc. Natl Acad. Sci. USA* **77**, 1885-1889.
Hart, R. W. and Setlow, R. B. (1974). Correlation between deoxyribonucleic acid excision-repair and lifespan in a number of mammalian species. *Proc. Natl Acad. Sci. USA* **71**, 2169-2173.
Hayflick, L. (1965). The limited *in vitro* lifetime of human diploid cell strains. *Exp. Cell Res.* **37**, 614-636.
Hoehn, H., Bryant, E. M., Johnston, P., Norwood, T. H. and Martin, G. M. (1975). Non selective isolation, stability and longevity of hybrids between normal human somatic cells. *Nature (London)* **258**, 608-609.
Holliday, R. (1984). The unsolved problem of cellular ageing. *Monogr. Devl. Biol.* **17**, 60-77.
Holliday, R. (1985). The significance of DNA methylation in cellular ageing. *In* "Molecular biology of ageing" (A. D. Woodhead, A. D. Blackett and A. Hollaender, eds) pp. 269-283. Plenum Press, New York.
Holliday, R., ed. (1986a). *"Genes, proteins and cellular ageing."* Van Nostrand Reinhold, Pennsylvania.
Holliday, R. (1986b). Strong effects of 5-azacytidine on the *in vitro* lifespan of human diploid fibroblasts. *Exp. Cell Res.* (in press).

Holliday, R. and Kirkwood, T. B. L. (1981). Predictions of the somatic mutation and mortalisation theories of cellular ageing are contrary to experimental observations. *J. Theoret. Biol.* **93**, 627-642.

Holliday, R. and Pugh, J. E. (1975). DNA modification, mechanisms and gene activity during development. *Science* **187**, 226-232.

Holliday, R. and Rattan, S. I. S. (1984). Evidence that paramomycin induces premature ageing in human fibroblasts. *Mongr. Devl. Biol.* **17**, 221-233.

Holliday, R. and Tarrant, G. H. (1972). Altered enzymes in ageing human fibroblasts. *Nature (London)* **238**, 26-30.

Hornsby, P. J. (1978). Characterisation of adult bovine adrenocortical cells throughout their life span in tissue culture. *Endocrinology* **102**, 926-936.

Jones, A. P. and Taylor, S. M. (1981). Hemimethylated duplex DNAs prepared from 5 azacytidine-treated cells. *Nucl. Acids Res.* **9**, 2933-2947.

Kato, H., Harada, M., Tsuchiya, K. and Moriwaki, K. (1980). Absence of correlation between DNA repair in ultraviolet irradiated mammalian cells and lifespan of the donor species. *Japan J. Genet.* **55**, 99-108.

Kirkwood, T. B. L. (1977). Evolution of ageing. *Nature (London)* **270**, 301-304.

Kirkwood, T. B. L. and Holliday, R. (1979). The evolution of ageing and longevity. *Proc. Roy. Soc.* **205**(B), 531-546.

Kirkwood, T. B. L., Holliday, R. and Rosenberger, R. F. (1984). Stability of the cellular translation apparatus. *Int. Rev. Cytol.* **92**, 93-132.

Kirkwood, T. B. L., Rosenberger, R. F. and Galas, D. eds (1986). "Accuracy of molecular processes." Chapman and Hall, London.

Krauss, S. W. and Linn, S. (1982). Changes in DNA polymerases α, β, γ during the replicative life span of cultured human fibroblasts. *Biochemistry* **21**, 1002-1009.

Kuck, U., Stahl, U. and Esser, K. (1981). Plasmid-like DNA is part of mitochondrial DNA in *Podospora anserina*. *Curr. Genet.* **3**, 151-156.

Land, H., Paroda, L. F. and Weinberg, R. A. (1983). Tumorigenic conversion of primary embryo fibroblasts requires at least two co-operating oncogenes. *Nature (London)* **304**, 596-602.

Linn, S., Kairis, M. and Holliday, R. (1976). Decreased fidelity of DNA polymerase activity isolated from ageing human fibroblasts. *Proc. Natl Acad. Sci. USA* **73**, 2818-2822.

Maciera-Coelho, A., Diatloff, C., Billardon, C., Bourgeois, C. A. and Malaise, E. (1977). Effect of low dose rate ionising radiation on the division potential of cells *in vitro* III Human lung fibroblasts. *Exp. Cell Res.* **104**, 215-221.

Maciera-Coelho, A., Diatloff, C., Billard, M., Fertil, B., Malaise, E. and Fries, D. (1978). Effect of low dose rate irradiation on the division potential of cells *in vitro* IV Embryonic and adult human lung fibroblast like cells. *J. Cell. Physiol.* **95**, 235-238.

Martin, G. M., Sprague, C. A., Norwood, T. H. and Pendergrass, W. R. (1974). Clonal selection, attenuation and differentiation in an *in vitro* model of hyperplasia. *Am. J. Pathol.* **74**, 137-154.

Maynard-Smith, J. (1962). The causes of ageing. *Proc. Roy. Soc.* **157**(B), 115-127.

Medawar, P. B. (1952). "An unsolved problem in biology." Lewis, London; reprinted (1957). *In* "The uniqueness of the individual". Methuen, London.

Morley, A. A., Cox, S. and Holliday, R. (1982). Human lymphocytes resistant to 6-thioguanine increase with age. *Mech. Age. Dev.* **19**, 21-26.

Murray, V. and Holliday, R. (1981). Increased error frequency of DNA polymerases from senescent human fibroblasts. *J. Molec. Biol.* **146**, 55-76.

Newbold, R. E. and Overell, R. W. (1983). Fibroblast immortality is a prerequisite for transformation by E c-Ha-*ras* oncogene. *Nature (London)* **304**, 648-651.

Orgel, L. E. (1963). The maintenance of the accuracy of protein synthesis and its relevance to ageing. *Proc. Natl Acad. Sci. USA* **49**, 517-521.

Orgel, L. E. (1970). The maintenance of the accuracy of protein synthesis and its relevance to ageing: a correction. *Proc. Natl Acad. Sci. USA* **67**, 1476.

Packer, L. and Smith, J. R. (1974). Extension of the lifespan of cultured normal human diploid cells by vitamin E. *Proc. Natl. Acad. Sci. USA* **71**, 4763-4767.

Palmer, L. and Wilhelm, J. M. (1978). Mistranslation in a eucaryotic organism. *Cell* **13**, 329-334.

Pereira-Smith, O. M. and Smith, J. R. (1983). Evidence for the recessive nature of cellular immortality. *Science* **221**, 964-966.

Ponten, J. and MacIntyre, E. (1968). Long term culture of normal and neoplastic human glia. *Acta. Path. Microbiol. Scand.* **74**, 465-486.

Ponten, J., Westermark, B. and Brunk, U. (1973). In "Biology of fibroblast" (E. Kulchen and J. Pikkarainen, eds) pp. 183-188. Academic Press, New York.

Rattan, S. I. S., Keeler, K. D., Buchanan, J. H. and Holliday, R. (1982). Autofluorescence as an index of ageing in human fibroblasts in culture. *Biosci. Rep.* **2**, 561-567.

Razin, A., Cedar, H. and Riggs, A. D., eds (1984). "DNA methylation". Springer Verlag, New York.

Rohme, D. (1981). Evidence for a relationship between longevity of mammalian species and life spans of normal fibroblasts *in vitro* and erythrocytes *in vivo*. *Proc. Natl Acad. Sci. USA* **78**, 5009-5013.

Sakagami, H., Mitsui, Y., Murota, S. and Yamada, M. (1979). Two dimensional electrophoretic analysis of nuclear acidic proteins in senescent human diploid cells. *Cell Struct. Funct.* **4**, 215-225.

Saksela, E. and Moorhead, P. S. (1963). Aneuploidy in the degenerative phase of serial cultivation of human cell strains. *Proc. Natl. Acad. Sci. USA* **50**, 390-395.

Schmookler Reis, R. J. and Goldstein, S. (1978). Mitochondrial DNA in mortal and immortal human cells. Genome number, integrity and methylation. *J. Biol. Chem.* **258**, 9078-9085.

Schmookler Reis, R. J., Lumpkin, C. K., McGill, J. R., Riabowol, K. T. and Goldstein, S. (1983). Extrachromosal circular copies of an *"inter Alu"* unstable sequence in human DNA are amplified during *in vitro* and *in vivo* ageing. *Nature (London)* **301**, 394-398.

Schmookler Reis, R. J., Lumpkin, C. K., McGill, J. R., Riabowol, K. T. and Goldstein, S. (1985). Amplification of *inter-Alu* extrachromosomal DNA during cellular ageing; retraction and explanation. *Nature (London)* **316**, 167.

Stahl, U., Kuck, U., Tudzinski, P. and Esser, K. (1980). Characterisation and cloning of plasmid-like DNA of the Ascomycete *Podospora anserina*. *Mol. Gen. Genet.* **178**, 639-646.

Taylor, S. M. and Jones, P. A. (1982). Mechanism of action of eukaryotic methyl transferase. Use of 5-azacytosine containing DNA. *J. Molec. Biol.* **162**, 679-692.

Thompson, K. V. A. and Holliday, R. (1973). Effect of temperature on the longevity of human fibroblasts in culture. *Exp. Cell Res.* **80**, 354-360.

Thompson, K. V. A. and Holliday, R. (1978). The longevity of diploid and polyploid human fibroblasts: evidence against the somatic mutation theory of cellular ageing. *Exp. Cell Res.* **112**, 281-287.

Treton, J. A. and Courtois, Y. (1982). Correlation between DNA excision repair and mammalian lifespan in lens epithelial cells. *Cell Biol. Int. Rep.* **6**, 253-260.

Walford, R. L., Jawaid, S. Q. and Maeim, F. (1981). Evidence for *in vitro* senescence of T lymphocytes cultured from normal human peripheral blood. *Age* **4**, 67-70.

Williams, G. (1957). Pleiotropy, natural selection and the evolution of senescence. *Evolution* **11**, 398-411.

Wilson, V. L. and Jones, P. A. (1983). DNA methylation decreases in ageing but not in immortal cells. *Science* **220**, 1055-1057.

Wright, R., Horrum, M. A. and Cummings, D. J. (1982). Are mitochondrial structural genes selectivity amplified during senescence in *Podospora anserina*? *Cell* **29**, 505-515.

Discussion

Ermini: Usually, cultured cells are used for testing error theories. However, *in vivo*, it is especially the postmitotic cells, e.g. neurons, that are investigated for their primary role in the aging process. How about indications for error effects in such postmitotic cells of old animals e.g. changed proteins? You would think that such cells are the best candidates for cells likely to accumulate "faulty" proteins owing to mistranslation or mistranscription? For instance, in skeletal muscle fibres one would expect myosine molecules with different amino acid composition or even changed enzymatic properties. This, however, seems not to be the case.

Holliday: They certainly would be good candidates and you would expect long living cells to accumulate defects possibly even faster than dividing cells because there is no opportunity for cell selection, but to do the experiment under strictly controlled conditions is difficult. Are you talking about tissues from old animals *vs* young animals?

Ermini: Yes.

Holliday: I think a detailed experiment on protein synthesis has not yet been performed owing to technical difficulties.

Esser: I think I have to correct what you stated about *Podospora*. As we and others have published, the senescence is not primarily caused by decay of mitochondrial DNA. There is a plasmid and this plasmid is an intron of cytochrome-oxidase-1 gene, subunit 1. This intron contains an origin of replication, at its ends are inverted repeats. Our theory says that this intron when liberated makes a plasmid and this plasmid causes senescence. We have mutants which do not have the intron and these strains never become senescent. Thus mitochondrial DNA decay is not the primary cause. You might have seen, on the other hand, in a recent paper in *Nature*, that this intron, the DNA sequence of the *Podospora* plasmid, has an open reading frame which comes very close to the open reading frame of the retroviruses. Therefore, we must consider for fibroblasts also the possibility of infective DNA being present. Goldstein has a paper in preparation also showing that there are plasmid-like double-stranded DNA rings in fibroblasts. Therefore, it is not correct to say mitochrondrial DNA causes decay or mitochondrial DNA causes senescence.

Holliday: I had no intention of misinterpreting your results. What I understand is that if you look at the mitochondrial genome using modern methods you see changes in the mitochondrial genome during senescence in *Podospora* cultures. If you apply the same methods to human cells you do not see similar changes.

Esser: No, I am sorry, it is different. You cannot say that mitochondrial genome changes cause senescence, that's not true. There is also experimental evidence forthcoming which shows that the plasmid invades the nucleus and it acts like a transposon.

Holliday: The same methods you use to detect those changes have been applied to human cells without seeing similar changes.

Ulrich: There are rat strains which age very fast and others which get comparatively old. Have any studies concerning methylation or similar studies been done in these kinds of strains?

Holliday: There are no studies on methylation because people do not like to use rodent cells for *in vitro* aging experiments because they become transformed, which is always a complication that makes them difficult to study, but, in principle, one can do the experiments you have mentioned.

Relationship between Aging of the Immune System and Aging of the Whole Organism

Edit Beregi

*Gerontology Center,
Semmelweis Medical University, Budapest, Hungary*

Keywords

Aging; Lymphocyte; Autoimmunity; Immune dysfunction; Smoking; Mitochondrial degeneration.

INTRODUCTION

Several data indicate that aging is associated with immune dysfunction both in humans and experimental animals. The age-related changes in the human immune system are sometimes controversial, because it is difficult to separate physiological age-related changes from changes that are secondary and appear as consequences of disease. In addition, it is difficult to consider aged people as a homogeneous group, because there are marked differences in health, physical and mental activity, social background etc., which can influence organ function. Aging is characterized by a decrease in organ function and an increased variability of performance. These are also valid for the immune function. Data of longitudinal investigations are of the utmost importance in this respect. It is of interest to clarify whether age-related dysfunction of the immune system is only a consequence of the age alteration of the whole organism or, inversely, the age-related changes of the immune system result in changes of other organs.

AGE-RELATED CHANGES IN HUMORAL IMMUNITY AND THEIR CORRELATION WITH DISEASES AND MORTALITY

The total immunoglobulin concentration in the serum does not change with age but there is a change in the distribution of immunoglobulin classes. IgA and IgG concentrations increase with age (Weksler and Siskind 1984, Rajczy et al. 1986). Longitudinal investigations in healthy subjects showed increased IgG and IgA levels in two-thirds of the examined subjects over a period of 40 years (Buckley and Dorsey 1974). These authors hypothesized a relationship between increased serum IgG and IgA levels and longevity, while Hallgren et al. (1973) suggested a selective mortality of aged subjects with lower immunoglobulin levels.

The concentration of isoagglutinin to sheep erythrocytes declines in aged subjects, the antibody response to tick-borne meningoencephalitis virus (Biró and Regius 1985), to Japanese B encephalitis virus, pneumococcal polysaccharides, *Salmonella flagellin* and tetanus toxoid is depressed in the aged (Weksler and Siskind 1984), and after influenza vaccination the number of IgG-bearing cells proved to be higher in young than in old subjects (Biró and Beregi 1980). Most authors agree that primary antibody response declines with age, while the secondary response remains unchanged (Makinodan and Adler 1975, Beregi et al. 1975). However, there are some exceptions: no decline was observed in the primary antibody response to bacterial and viral vaccines in some cases; this can be explained as follows (Kay and Makinodan 1982):

(1) The examined individuals had been previously exposed to the antigen and thus the secondary response was observed;

(2) The examined reaction is a T cell independent antibody response.

Decreased antibody response results in susceptibility to infections i.e. the frequent occurrence of pneumonia and pyelonephritis.

While antibody production generally decreases with age, the number of subjects with autoantibodies increases. However, frequency of autoimmune diseases is not increased in the aged. Some authors found antinuclear antibodies in 45% of healthy 70–79 year-old subjects (Rowley et al. 1968). The typical age-associated antibodies are of low titre but persistent (Hijmans et al. 1983).

In our examinations we stated that the presence of antinuclear antibodies significantly increased with age. The increase was more frequent in smokers than in non-smokers (Regius et al. in prep.) (Fig. 1). Increased levels of autoantibodies were described in subjects over 80 years of age who had a low lymphocyte response to phytohaemagglutinin (PHA) (Hallgren et al. 1973). In addition, increased levels of autoantibodies correlated with increased mortality, independent of chronological age (Fong et al. 1985).

There are data indicating a correlation between the incidence of thyreogastric autoantibody and diabetes, between obesity and the presence of autoantibodies (Mathews et al. 1976). Mathews (1975) also reported that the high rate of ischaemic heart disease in Australia showed a correlation with the frequency of the HLA

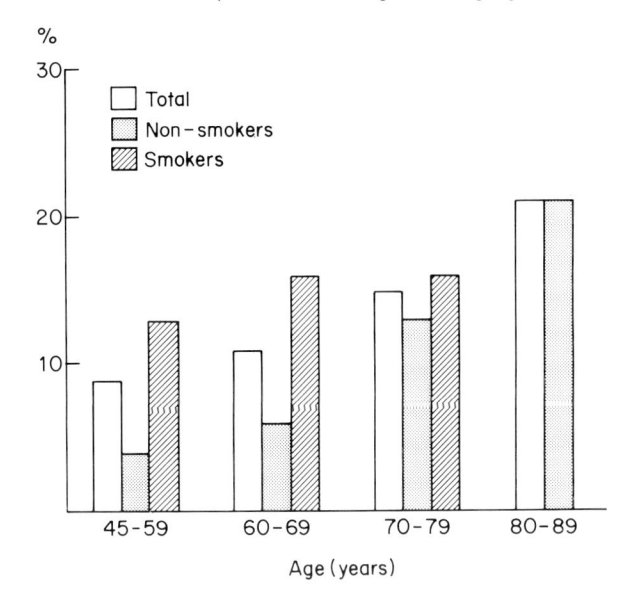

Fig. 1. Occurrence of antinuclear antibody in 518 subjects. Distribution in smokers and non-smokers.

haplotype 1-8; HLA-B8 shows a correlation with autoimmune diseases. In old age the high incidence of the rheumatoid factor was also described as well. A correlation could be stated between hypertension and the presence of the rheumatoid factor (Mathews *et al.* 1976). At present we have only a few data showing a correlation between the most frequent diseases of old age and the presence of autoantibodies.

AGE-RELATED CHANGES IN THE NUMBER, FUNCTION AND MORPHOLOGY OF T AND B LYMPHOCYTES, CORRELATION WITH DISEASES

Several authors have investigated the total number of T and B lymphocytes in the aged. The data are contradictory—some authors reported an increase in the proportion of circulating T lymphocytes (Hallgren *et al.* 1973), others described depressed (Girard *et al.* 1977, Ben-Zwi *et al.* 1977) and unchanged (Kishimoto *et al.* 1978) proportions. Some authors described that the number of peripheral human lymphocytes progressively decreases due to the decrease in the number of T lymphocytes (Kay and Makinodan 1982).

In our laboratory we have always found the lower limits of the normal T and B lymphocytes values in the aged. In addition, there are data showing that although the number of T and B lymphocytes does not change with age, the distribution of T and B cell subpopulations is altered (Weksler and Hüttenroth 1974, Walford 1982, Deviere et al. 1985, Schreibman et al. 1985). In males a significantly decreased percentage of SIg-positive, IgG-positive, IgM-positive and increased IgA-positive cells could be observed during aging (Bátory et al. 1985). Some of these changes may be due to *in vivo* activation of lymphocytes.

It is widely accepted that reactivity against allogeneic lymphocytes and response to special mitogens gives data about the functional parameters of the T lymphocytes. Weksler and Siskind (1984) found that healthy old persons have normal T lymphocyte values but the number of their mitogen-responsive T lymphocytes is greatly decreased. They stated that the capacity of these lymphocytes to divide sequentially in culture is also impaired (Hefton et al. 1980). A linear age-dependent decrease of reactivity against pooled allogeneic lymphocytes was found between 20 and 70 years of age (Ónody et al. 1980).

The maximal transformation values after PHA stimulation using different PHA doses showed a similar decrease to allogeneic reactivity. In PHA reactivity a dose-response type difference could be stated (Ónody et al. 1980).

The helper activity of T lymphocytes in response to pokeweed mitogen (PWM) has been shown to increase rather than decrease in aged humans (Kishimoto et al. 1973, Bátory et al. 1981) in accordance with the increased levels of serum IgG and, especially, IgA.

Disturbances in the suppressor cell function have been described in the aged (Callard 1981).

In mice natural killer activity declines with age (Herberman et al. 1975, Kiessling et al. 1975). In our laboratory we found that natural cell-mediated cytotoxicity (NCMC) and, especially, antibody-dependent cellular cytotoxicity (ADCC) activity increased with age in humans (Bátory et al. 1981).

Cutaneous delayed hypersensitivity (skin test) in humans decreased to five antigens when studied by Roberts-Thomson et al. (1974) and the mortality of very old people with hyporesponsive skin tests over a 2-year period was significantly higher than that of normally responsive old people (Fudenberg 1981); while others described no changes in the skin tests except in those elderly people who had some acute illness. It is presumed that the decreased delayed hypersensitivity is the consequence of the age-related changes in the skin (Kay and Makinodan 1982).

It is of interest that the so-called senescent cell antigen was recently observed on the surface of lymphocytes—described previously on the surface of erythrocytes, polymorphonuclear leukocytes, platelets etc. (Kay 1985). Macrophages are able to distinguish between mature and senescent red blood cells because of the presence of senescent cell membrane antigen (Kay 1985). There are no data to show whether macrophages are able to distinguish similarly mature lymphocytes from senescent lymphocytes.

In our laboratory electronmicroscopical investigations of the popliteal lymph nodes of CBA/Ca mice were carried out. We found emperipolesis in young and

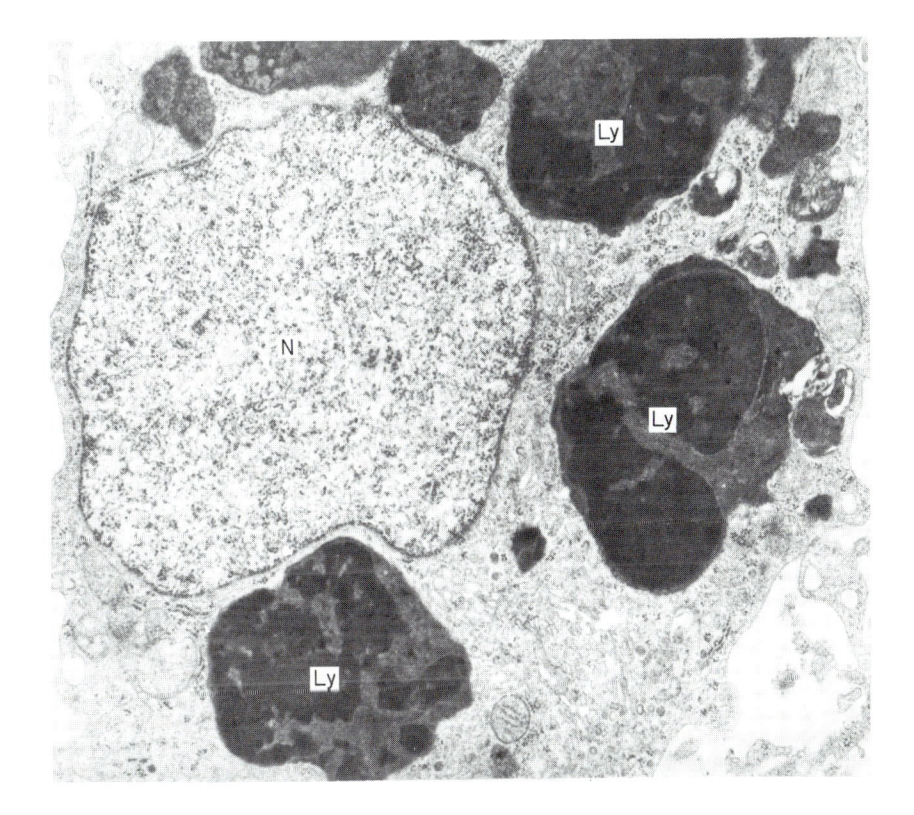

Fig. 2. Showing partly digested lymphocytes in the popliteal lymph node of CBA/Ca mice in the cytoplasm of the macrophage (×4980). Ly = lymphocyte; N = nucleus.

aged animals alike. Morphological investigation showed no age differences (Fig. 2).

Most authors agree that the functional capacity of lymphocytes, especially of T lymphocytes, decreases with age. It was interesting to investigate whether this functional change is based on morphological alterations. For the following reasons lymphocytes were chosen as a model of aging in our laboratory (Beregi et al. 1980):

(1) A number of data point to a decline of immune functions with a parallel increase in the frequency of autoimmunity and cancer in old age, both in men and animals;
(2) The lymphocyte stands at the centre of immune responses;
(3) Age-related immunological changes are connected with changes in the functions of T and B lymphocytes;
(4) It is easy to obtain lymphocytes from humans and experimental animals;

(5) Thus, lymphocytes can be used to examine the process of aging in both humans and experimental animals.

In our previous investigation we examined the primary and secondary immune responses of young and old Wistar rats and we found age-related morphological alterations in the lymphocytes of both immunized and untreated control aged rats. These findings and those of other authors about age-related functional changes in lymphocytes led us to examine the fine structure of lymphocytes in various species.

The same age-related damages were observed in the lymph node and spleen lymphocytes in old Wistar rats and CBA/Ca mice and in the peripheral lymphocytes of healthy humans. Electronmicroscopical investigations showed changes in the mitochondria and cytoplasm of the lymphocytes (Beregi *et al.* 1980). The mitochondria were sometimes swollen, the mitochondrial cristae had disappeared and were replaced by myelin-like lamellar structures (Fig. 3), by

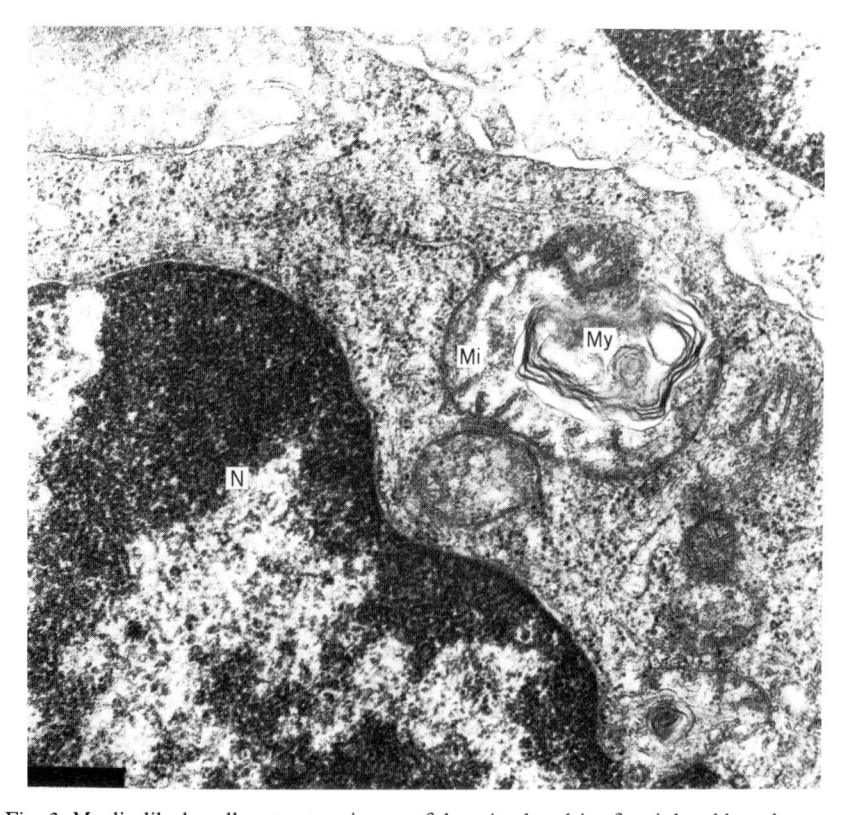

Fig. 3. Myelin-like lamellar structure in one of the mitochondria of peripheral lymphocytes in a 78-year-old subject (×9,000). Mi=mitochondria; My=myelin-like structure; N=nucleus.

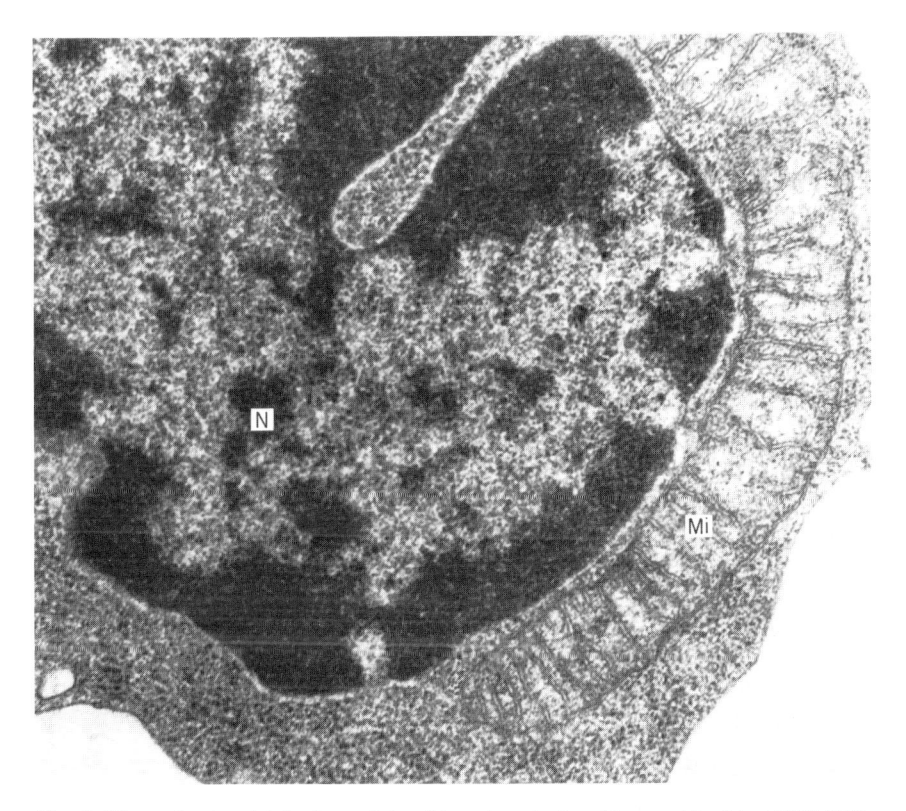

Fig. 4. Giant mitochondria in the peripheral lymphocytes in a 76-year-old-subject (×15,000). Mi = mitochondria; N = nucleus.

electron-dense and electron-translucent material. These changes were always found in the T lymphocytes. The structure of this material resembles lipofuscin or age pigment (Beregi and Regius 1983a). We found giant mitochondria too (Fig. 4). Lipofuscin was also observed in the cytoplasm of the lymphocytes. Over 60 years of age the most frequent alteration in the lymphocytes was the presence of myelin-like structures in the mitochondria (Fig. 5).

The lipofuscin can be identified by its yellowish green autofluorescence. In semithin sections of the cytoplasm of the lymphocytes we have demonstrated a dot-like fluorescence in unstained sections. The electron and fluorescence microscopic findings thus confirmed our supposition that the material in the mitochondria of the lymphocytes is lipofuscin (Beregi and Regius 1983a).

We examined the age distribution of the damaged mitochondria. We found that between 20 and 39 years of age only one out of 45 individuals had these alterations. Between 60 and 69 years of age 35% of 135 subjects had myelin-like lamellar structures in the mitochondria of lymphocytes and 12% had giant

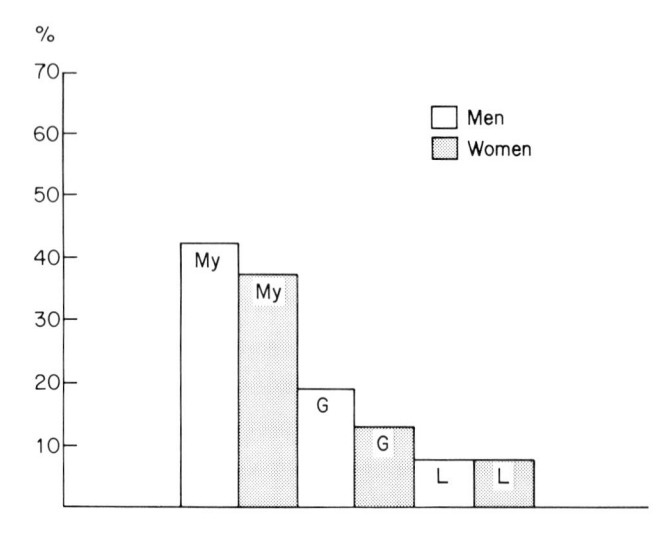

Fig. 5. Morphological changes in lymphocytes in 449 subjects over 60 years of age. My = myelin-like structure; G = giant mitochondria; L = lipofuscin.

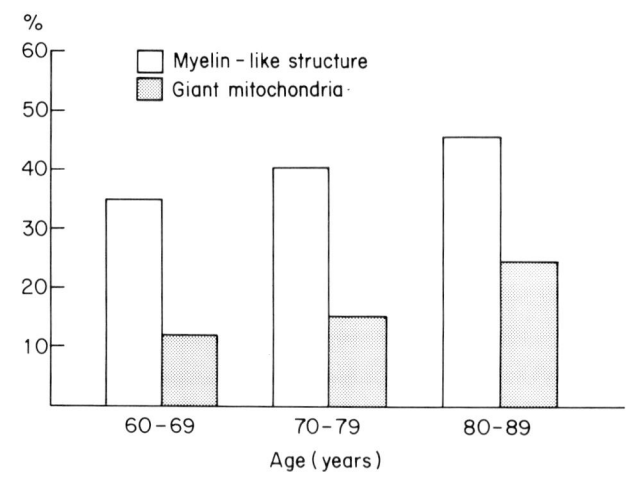

Fig. 6. Age distribution of myelin-like lamellar structures and giant mitochondria in the lymphocytes of 449 subjects.

mitochondria. Between 70 and 79 years of age 40% of 267 subjects had myelin-like structures in the mitochondria of lymphocytes and 15% had giant mitochondria. Between 80 and 89 years of age 45% of 97 persons had myelin-like structures and 24% giant mitochondria (Fig. 6).

Thus we can state that the occurrence of individuals with damaged mitochondria in the lymphocytes significantly increases ($P < 0.001$) with age. The changes in

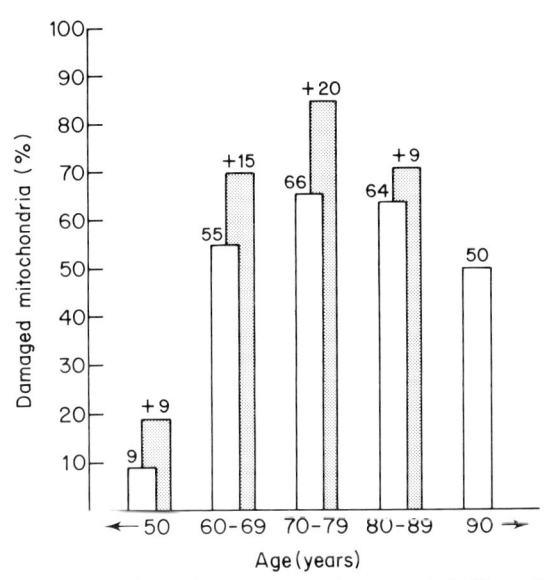

Fig. 7. Longitudinal study of lymphocytes over a 6-year period. (From Beregi and Regius 1984, with permission.)

the mitochondria, that is the presence of myelin-like structures and giant mitochondria, are in relation to age.

Most investigations in connection with aging lymphocytes have been short-term studies of cells removed from chronologically old individuals. It is always preferable to investigate age-related changes in the same individual longitudinally. In our work we have examined lymphocytes from the same subjects on three occasions during a 6-year period (Beregi and Regius 1984). The peripheral lymphocytes of 91 healthy individuals were examined every 2 years during this period. Twenty-one subjects were under 50 years of age. The age distribution over 60 years old was as follows: 22 subjects: 60-69 years of age; 23 subjects: 70-79 years of age; 21 subjects: 80-89 years of age, and over 90 years of age: four subjects.

In our examination we established that the number of subjects with damaged mitochondria significantly increased over 60 years of age ($P<0.05$). This finding correlated with our earlier results (Beregi and Regius 1983b). We controlled the morphology of the peripheral lymphocytes after 2, 4 and 6 years. In Fig. 7 we show the findings at the beginning of the study and after 6 years. The number of patients with damaged mitochondria increased significantly after 6 years in every age group (Beregi and Regius 1984). Recently, we analysed the data after eight years. The results of these analyses are identical with those after 6 years.

We decided to investigate whether there was a correlation between the mentioned age-related morphological changes of lymphocytes and the most frequent diseases suffered during aging? In addition, we studied the possibility

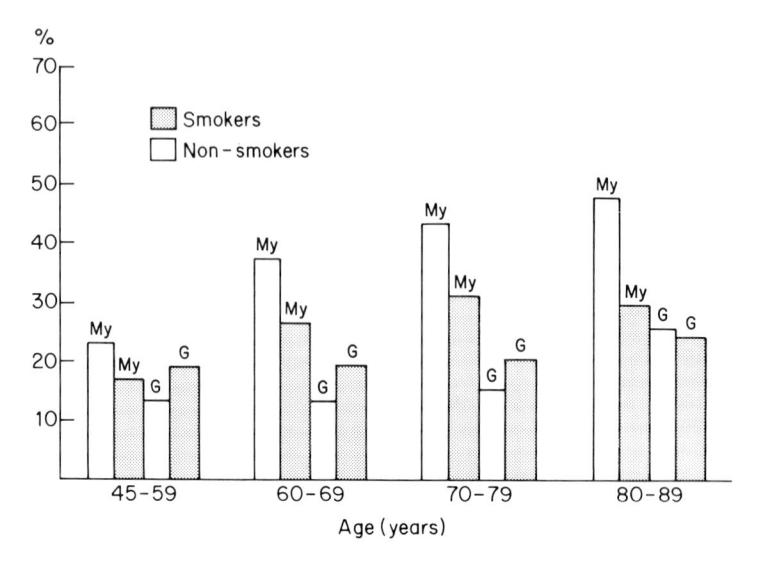

Fig. 8. Age-related morphological changes in the mitochondria of lymphocytes in smokers ($n=126$) and non-smokers ($n=392$). My = myelin-like structure; G = giant mitochondria.

of a relationship between these morphological alterations of the lymphocytes and smoking habits.

In the Gerontology Center in Budapest we examine aged people longitudinally without overt disease. In 518 subjects (214 men, 304 women) we analysed the relationship of morphological changes in the lymphocytes, smoking habits and the most frequent latent diseases using a computer (Regius *et al.* in prep.). We stated that the presence of myelin-like lamellar structures in the lymphocytes did not correlate with smoking. We also studied these alterations in chain smokers, but found no differences between chain smokers and non-smokers. At the same time we found a correlation between the presence of giant mitochondria in the lymphocytes and smoking. Giant mitochondria were found significantly more frequently in smokers than in non-smokers (Regius *et al.* in prep.) (Fig. 8).

Although aged subjects without overt disease are examined in the clinical department, we often find several latent diseases in the follow-up examinations. Therefore, it seemed to be of interest to analyse whether the morphological changes in the lymphocytes, myelin-like lamellar structures in the mitochondria and giant mitochondria are correlated with the most frequent diseases — hypertension, ischaemic heart disease, diabetes mellitus, emphysema and atherosclerosis (Regius *et al.* in prep.). It was verified unambiguously that the appearance of myelin-like lamellar structures in the mitochondria of lymphocytes is an age-dependent phenomenon and not a disease-dependent alteration. This could still be demonstrated over 80 years of age. Figure 9 shows that the above-mentioned lymphocyte alterations occur most frequently in healthy

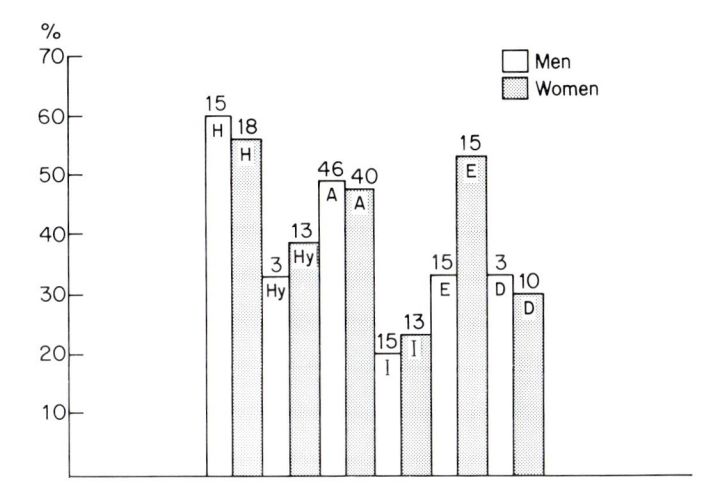

Fig. 9. Myelin-like lamellar structures in healthy and diseased subjects over 80 years of age. H = healthy; A = atherosclerosis; D = diabetes mellitus; E = emphysema; Hy = hypertension; I = ischaemic heart disease. (Number of subjects shown at top of columns.)

individuals. On the contrary, giant mitochondria occurred significantly more frequently in latent diseases, especially in ischaemic heart disease.

As we found the same age-related morphological changes in the lymphocytes of CBA/Ca mice as in humans, it was interesting to study whether a connection existed between these changes and the most frequent diseases in the animals. 661 CBA/Calati male inbred mice were used for these investigations.

The necropsy data of animals who died spontaneously were compared with those of killed animals. Some animals were killed randomly at different ages. Autopsy and histological examination of each animal were carried out. Organ weight of every animal was measured and organ indices were calculated (Beregi et al. 1986).

After the age of 601–750 days a significant decrease of spleen indices of animals without diseases could be demonstrated. It was also observed that diseases occurring in old age alter the indices (Fig. 10). Mitochondrial changes in the splenic lymphocytes developed after the age of 580 days.

During aging the number of animals with disease increased. The most frequent diseases in old animals were hepatocellular carcinoma and amyloidosis (Fig. 11). The first case with hepatocellular carcinoma occurred after 400 days of age and the highest number was found at the age of 601–750 days, thereafter the number of diseased mice decreased somewhat. In addition we observed amyloidosis in the youngest age group, but only associated with sarcoma. After the age of 500 days amyloidosis occurred independently of tumours. The highest incidence was in the age group of 751–900 days surpassing that of hepatocellular carcinoma. Pulmonary adenocarcinoma was found after the age of 451–600 days, with the

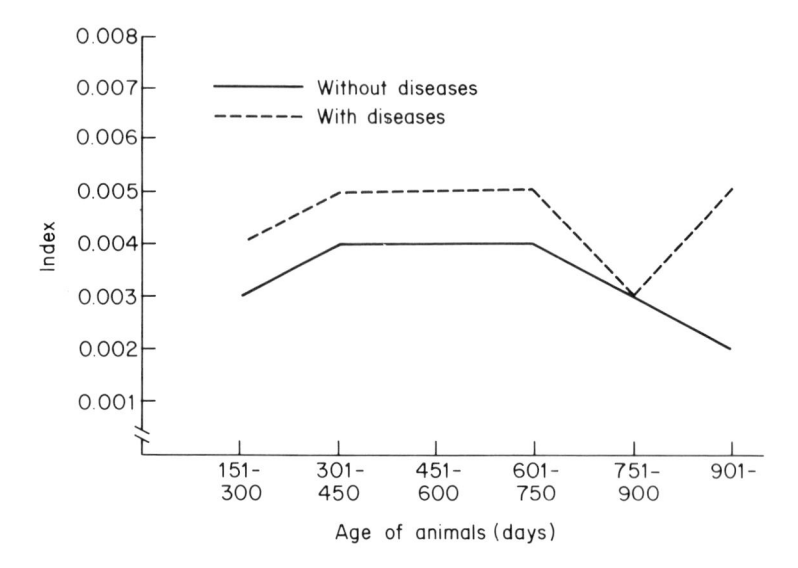

Fig. 10. Spleen indices.

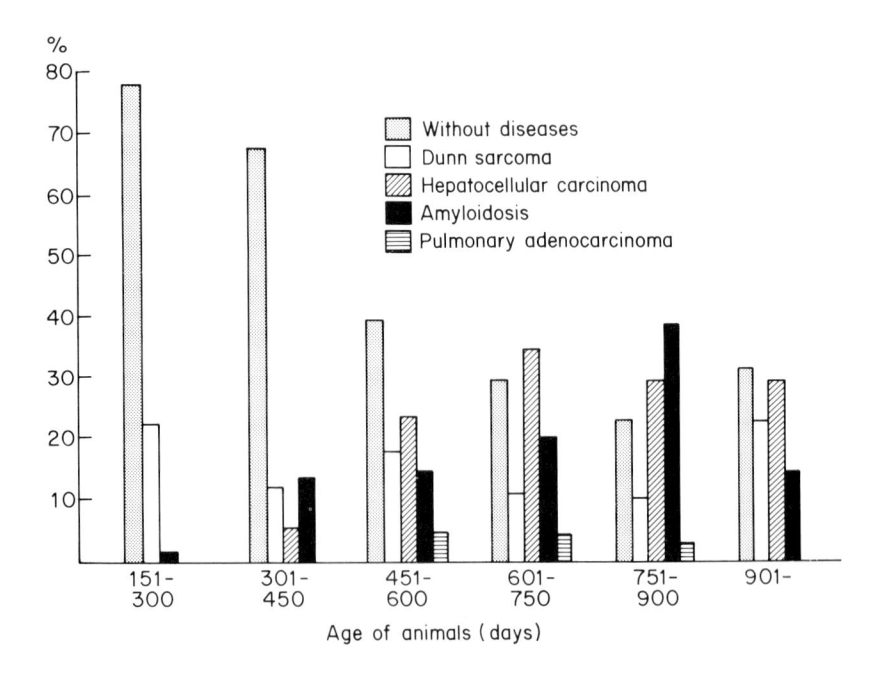

Fig. 11. Most frequent diseases in 661 CBA/Ca mice.

highest incidence after 900 days. This is an interesting finding, as the frequency of the other above-mentioned diseases decreased in the oldest animals. Dunns' sarcoma occurred most frequently in young mice and we did not observe it in the oldest age group.

The number of animals without diseases significantly decreased after the age of 451-600 days ($P<0.001$) and increased again in the oldest animals.

Electronmicroscopical investigation of lymphocytes was carried out using splenic samples from the animals. We could state that there was no connection between the most frequent diseases and the described morphological changes in the lymphocytes. The number of animals with morphological changes in the lymphocytes significantly increased with age in those without disease ($P<0.01$). Thus we could state that the frequency of morphological changes in the lymphocytes increased as a consequence of age and not of disease, similarly to humans. Giant mitochondria occurred infrequently, therefore, we could not analyse these changes separately.

The development and accumulation of lipofuscin or age pigment is one of the most characteristic phenomena in the aging cell. It is present in both dividing and non-dividing cells. Lipofuscin development has been connected with many organelles, thus the origin of lipfuscin is a much debated question. In our recent work we have strengthened the theory of the mitochondrial origin of lipofuscin.

The question is: what effects are produced by the accumulation of lipofuscin on the function of lymphocytes? Some researchers suggest that the pigment is a harmless by-product of cell metabolism (Körmendy and Bender 1971). Other authors are of the opinion that the presence of the pigment does not alter the activity of the cell and the inhibition of function develops only if the quantity of pigment is very high (Zeman 1971).

According to our opinion, when a large number of organelles are damaged and replaced by lipofuscin, the function of the organelles decreases. On the basis of our findings we hypothesized that the decreased immunological activity in old age is in connection with the mitochondrial alterations described.

It has long been the goal of researchers to establish an experimental system which is easy to obtain and which can be used to examine the process of aging and the factors influencing aging in both humans and experimental animals. As we found the same age related changes in lymphocytes of experimental animals and humans, we are using lymphocytes for testing the effect of different drugs in preventing age changes.

CONCLUSION

Aging is associated with immune dysfunction but there are only a few data indicating what kind of connections there are between the age-related immune dysfunctions and the most prevalent diseases in old age. Several data have shown that aging is associated with changes in the humoral and cellular immunity, in the function of lymphocytes. While antibody production generally decreases with age, the frequency of autoantibodies increases.

Authors have examined the morphological alteration of lymphocytes. Giant mitochondria and myelin-like lamellar structures and electron-dense material could be observed in the mitochondria of lymphocytes in old CBA/Ca mice, Wistar rats' lymph nodes and splenic lymphocytes, and in the peripheral lymphocytes in aged subjects without overt diseases. The occurrence of individuals with damaged mitochondria in lymphocytes increased significantly with age. Longitudinal investigations showed that the number of subjects with damaged mitochondria increased after 6 years in every age group. It could be stated that there was no correlation between smoking and degenerative mitochondrial damage in lymphocytes, but there was a correlation between the presence of giant mitochondria in the lymphocytes and smoking.

The correlation between the above-mentioned age-related morphological changes of lymphocytes and the most frequent diseases was studied in humans and CBA/Ca mice. It was verified that the appearance of myelin-like lamellar structures in the mitochondria of lymphocytes is an age- not disease-dependent alteration. On the contrary it was seen that giant mitochondria occurred more frequently in latent disease in aged subjects.

REFERENCES

Bátory, G., Benczur, M., Varga, M., Garam, T., Ónody, C. and Petrányi, G. Gy. (1981). Increased killer cell activity in aged humans. *Immunobiology* **158**, 393-402.

Bátory, G., Szondy, É., Falus, A., Füst, G., Beregi, E., Ónody, C. and Benczur, M. (1985). Autoimmunity and normal immune function in aged humans. *Arch. Gerontol. Geriatr.* **4**, 261-271.

Ben-Zwi, A., Galili, U., Russell, A. and Schlesinger, M. (1977). Age-associated changes in subpopulations of human lymphocytes. *Clin. Immunol. Immunopath.* **7**, 139-149.

Beregi, E. and Regius, O. (1983a). Lipofuscin in lymphocytes and plasma cells in aging. *Arch. Gerontol. Geriatr.* 2,229-235.

Beregi, E. and Regius, O. (1983b). Relationship of mitochondrial damage in human lymphocytes and age. *Akt. Gerontol.* **13**, 226-228.

Beregi, E. and Regius, O. (1984). Longitudinal study of lymphocytes. *Age Ageing* **13**, 201-204.

Beregi, E., Kelemen, J. and Szabó, D. (1975). Dei immunologischer Sekundärreaktion auftretende immunmorphologische Veränderungen in jungen und alten Ratten. *Akt. Gerontol.* **5**, 589-596.

Beregi, E., Biró, J. and Regius, O. (1980). Age-related morphological changes in lymphocytes as a model of aging. *Mech. Age. Dev.* **14**, 173-180.

Beregi, E., Regius, O., Pénzes, L. and Izsák, J. (1986). *Z. Altersforsch.* (in press).

Biró, J. and Beregi, E. (1980). The influence of influenza vaccinations on human peripheral blood lymphocytes relating to aging. *Akt. Gerontol.* **10**, 319-322.

Biró, J. and Regius, O. (1985). Aktives Immunisierung gegen Tick-Borne-Encephalitis im höheren Lebensalter. *Z. Gerontol.* **18**, 337-339.

Buckley, E. and Dorsey, F. C. (1974). Longitudinal changes in serum immunoglobulin levels in older humans. *Fedn. Proc.* **33**, 2036-2039.

Callard, R. E. (1981). Aging of the immune system. *In* "Handbook of immunology in aging" (M. M. B. Kay and T. Makinodan, eds) p. 103. CRC Press Inc., Florida.

Deviere, J., Kennes, B., Closset, J., De Maertelaer, V. and Neve, P. (1985). Immune senescence: effect of age, sex, and health on human blood mononuclear subpopulations. *Arch. Gerontol. Geriatr.* **4**, 285-293.

Fong, Sh., Chen, P. P., Vaughan, J. H. and Carson, D. A. (1985). Origin and age-associated changes in the expression of a physiologic autoantibody. *Gerontology* **31**, 236-250.

Fudenberg, H. H. (1981). Immunosuppression, autoimmunity and precocious aging: Observations and speculations. *In* "Handbook of immunology in aging" (M. M. B. Kay and T. Makinodan eds) p. 159. CRC Press Inc., Florida.

Girard, J. P., Paychere, M., Cuevas, M. and Fernandes, B. (1977). Cell mediated immunity in ageing population. *Clin. Exp. Immunol.* **27**, 85-91.

Hallgren, H. M., Buckley, C. E., Gilbertsen, V. A. and Yunis, E. J. (1973). Lymphocyte phytohemagglutinin responsiveness, immunoglobulins and autoantibodies in aging humans. *J. Immunol.* **111**, 1101-1107.

Hefton, J. M., Darlington, G., Casazza, B. A. and Weksler, M. E. (1980). Immunological studies of aging. V. Impaired proliferation of PHA responsive human lymphocytes in culture. *J. Immunol.* **125**, 1007-1010.

Herberman, R. B., Nunn, M. E. and Lavrin, D. H. (1975). Natural cytotoxic reactivity of mouse lymphoid cells against syngeneic and allogeneic tumors. I. Distribution of reactivity and specificity. *Int. J. Cancer* **16**, 216-229.

Hijmans, W., Radl, J., Bottazzo, G. F. and Doniach, D. (1983). Autoantibodies in highly aged humans. *Mech. Age. Dev.* **26**, 83-89.

Kay, M. M. B. (1985). Aging of cell membrane molecules leads to appearance of an aging antigen and removal of senescent cells. *Gerontology* **31**, 215-235.

Kay, M. M. B. and Makinodan, T. (1982). The ageing immune system. *In* "Lectures on gerontology" (A. Viidik, ed.) Part A, p. 143. Academic Press, London and New York.

Kiessling, R., Klein, E. and Wigzell, H. (1975). "Natural" killer cells in the mouse I. Cytotoxic cells with specificity for mouse Moloney leukemia cells. Specificity and distribution according to genotype. *Eur. J. Immunol.* **5**, 112-120.

Kishimoto, S., Shigemoto, S. and Yamamura, Y. (1973). Immune response in aged mice. Change of cell mediated immunity with ageing. *Transplantation* **15**, 455-462.

Kishimoto, S., Tomino, S., Inomata, K., Kotegava, S., Saito, T., Kuroki, M., Mitsuya, H. and Hisamitsu, S. (1978). Age-related changes in the subsets and functions of human T lymphocytes. *J. Immunol.* **121**, 1773-1780.

Körmendy, C. G. and Bender, A. D. (1971). Chemical interference with aging. *Gerontologia* **77**, 52-64.

Makinodan, T. and Adler, W. H. (1975). The effects of aging on the differentiation and proliferation potentials of cells of the immune system. *Fedn Proc.* **34**, 153-158.

Mathews, J. D. (1975). Ischaemic heart disease: Possible genetic markers. *Lancet* **2**, 681-682.

Mathews, J. D., Rodger, B. M. and Stenhouse, N. S. (1976). The significance of the association of tissue autoantibodies and rheumatoid factor with angina in the Busselton population. *J. Chronic Dis.* **29**, 345.

Ónody, C., Bátory, G. and Petrányi, G. Gy. (1980). Age dependent responsiveness of T lymphocytes to allogeneic and PHA stimulation. *Thymus* **1**, 205-213.

Rajczy, K., Vargha, P. and Beregi, E. (1986). *Z. Altersforsch.* (in press).

Roberts-Thomison, I. C., Wittingham, I., Youngchaiyud, U. and Mackay, I. R. (1974). Ageing, immune response and mortality. *Lancet* **ii**, 368-376.

Rowley, M. J., Buchanan, H. and Mackay, I. R. (1968). Reciprocal changes with age in antibody to extrinsic and intrinsic antigens. *Lancet* **ii**, 24-27.

Schreibman, M. P., Halpern-Sebold, L. and Margolis-Nunno, H. (1985). Age-related changes in lymphocyte subset proportions, surface differentiation, antigen density and plasma membrane fluidity: Application of the Eurage senior protocol admission criteria. *Mech. Age. Dev.* **33**, 39-66.

Walford, R. L. (1982). Studies in immunogerontology *J. Am. Geriat. Soc.* **30**, 617-625.

Weksler, M. E. and Hüttenroth, T. H. (1974). Impaired lymphocyte function in aged humans. *J. Clin. Invest.* **53**, 99-104.

Weksler, M. E. and Siskind, G. W. (1984). The cellular basis of immune senescence. *Monogr. Dev. Biol.* **17**, 110.

Zeman, W. (1971). The neuronal ceroid lipofuscinosis Batten-Vogt syndrome. A model for human aging? *In* "Advances in gerontological research" (B. L. Strehler, ed.) Vol. 3, p. 147. Academic Press, New York.

Discussion

Ermini: Do the lymphocytes of old donors show reduced or changed respiratory capacity when tested *in vitro*, as a possible consequence of the mitochondrial changes observed?

Beregi: I have no knowledge of such experiments.

Schoch: You mentioned several immunological dysfunctions in aged individuals, specifically affecting lymphocytes. Are there specific deficits of lymphocytes in Alzheimer patients?

Beregi: I don't know of any data referring to changes in the morphology in lymphocytes of Alzheimer patients.

Neuroendocrinological Aspects of Aging of the Reproductive System

Joseph Meites

Department of Physiology, Neuroendocrine Research Laboratory, Michigan State University, East Lansing, Michigan, USA

Keywords
Reproductive senescence; Neuroendocrinology; Reproductive decline; Hypothalamus; Reproductive aging; Reproductive decline; Animals and man.

INTRODUCTION

The major neuroendocrine mechanisms controlling reproduction in mammalian species are essentially similar. Control is exerted primarily by the hypothalamus, pituitary, gonads and reproductive tract, and is also influenced by hormones from the thyroid, adrenals and pancreas, and by external agents such as diet, temperature, light-dark cycles, stress, drugs etc. In female species, each component of the reproductive system must be activated in a definite time sequence to ensure reproduction of the species. The ovarian follicles must develop and the ova must mature at a definite time; the ova must be ovulated and released into the fallopian tubes and uterus; mating must occur during a limited time frame to ensure fertilization of the ova; the uterus must be properly prepared by the actions of the ovarian hormones to receive the zygote(s) so that the placenta can be formed; pregnancy must be maintained via the actions of hormones from the pituitary, gonads and placenta; mammary development and growth must be stimulated via the actions of gonadal hormones and prolactin to ensure that milk will be available for the newborn young; and the proper hormonal environment must be at hand at the end of gestation to induce parturition. Obviously these processes are highly integrated and interdependent, and if a fault develops in any single component of the reproductive system, cycles and pregnancies in females may be prevented, and in males testosterone and sperm production may be inhibited.

Rats and mice have been the most widely used animal models to study reproductive aging. The onset of oestrous cycles usually begins at about 35-40 days of age, and irregularities of the cycle first begin to appear at about 8-12 months of age. When male rats are placed in proximity to aging female rats, the occurrence of regular oestrous cycles was extended for several months, indicating a role for behavioural components in the reproductive decline (Nass *et al.* 1982). Initially the oestrous cycle becomes irregular and lengthened, followed by a prolonged state of persistent oestrus characterized by well developed ovarian follicles but no ovulation, then progress to long irregular pseudopregnancies with formation of numerous corpora lutea in the ovaries that actively secrete progesterone (owing to high prolactin secretion), and finally enter into a state of anoestrus in which the ovaries become atrophic and the follicles remain undeveloped and produce very few steroids (Aschheim 1976, Huang and Meites 1975, Meites 1982, Wise 1983). The ovaries of even the oldest rats and most mouse strains retain some follicles and ova and are capable of a considerable degree of function upon appropriate gonadotropic stimulation even to the end of life. When persistent oestrous old female rats are mated with vigorous young male rats, some become pseudopregnant, fewer become pregnant, and few fetuses survive to parturition.

In women approaching the menopause, menstrual cycles tend to become irregular and shortened rather than lengthened as in aging irregular cycling female rats. The ovaries show a reduction in ability to secrete ovarian hormones, resulting in a rise in follicle stimulating hormone (FSH) and luteinizing hormone (LH) secretion. In the postmenopausal period, the ovaries gradually become shrunken and fibrotic, lose their follicles and ova, and become essentially unresponsive to the high circulating levels of FSH and LH. In men, beginning at about 50 years of age, there is a gradual decline in testosterone secretion and spermatogenesis and a resultant rise in FSH and LH secretion that does not reach the high levels observed in postmenopausal women. Healthy aging men may retain the capacity to reproduce well into old age (Harman and Talbert 1985).

CAUSES OF THE REPRODUCTIVE DECLINE

Changes in Hypothalamic Secretion of Hypophysiotropic Hormones and Neurotransmitters

The principal cause(s) for the reproductive decline in rats and in most strains of mice have been shown to be due mainly to dysfunctions that develop in the hypothalamus, although there is also evidence for a decrease in hormonal responsiveness of the pituitary, gonads and reproductive tract (Aschheim, 1976,

Huang and Meites 1975, Meites 1982, Wise 1983). In some strains of mice (CBA and C57BL/6J), loss of follicles appears to be primarily responsible for cessation of oestrous cycles during aging (Finch *et al.* 1984), as in postmenopausal women. Evidence that the ovaries are not mainly responsible for reproductive senescence in old rats and most strains of mice is that transplantation of ovaries from old to young ovariectomized rats or mice has been shown to permit resumption of oestrous cycles in most of the young animals (Aschheim 1976, Peng 1983). Transplantation of the pituitary from old to young hypophysectomized rats also enabled some of the young rats to reinitiate cycles, indicating that the decrease in pituitary function is not primarily responsible for loss of oestrous cycles in the old rats (Peng 1983).

That hypothalamic dysfunction is mainly responsible for the reproductive decline in rats and most mouse strains is indicated by many observations. Thus, in old female rats there is loss of the positive feedback action by oestrogen on gonadotropin release and there is no surge in oestrogen, LH, FSH and prolactin release every 4–5 days as in young or mature cycling rats (Meites 1982). When old constant oestrous or pseudopregnant rats are ovariectomized, the rise in LH and FSH secretion is significantly below that of younger rats, and in the old anoestrous rats there is no rise in FSH and LH release after ovariectomy (Huang and Meites 1975). The high amplitude pulses of LH which appear after ovariectomy are markedly attenuated in old ovariectomized rats, providing evidence for reduced pulsatile release of luteinizing hormone-releasing hormone (LHRH) (Simpkins 1983). Old male rats similarly show a reduced ability to release FSH and LH after orchidectomy when compared to castrated young male rats (Huang and Meites, 1975, Meites 1982). The pituitary of old male and female rats retains its capacity to respond to LHRH administration (with the possible exception of the tumorous prolactin secreting pituitaries in the old anoestrous females), but the amounts of LH and FSH released are smaller than in young male rats (Bruni *et al.* 1977).

The first direct demonstration of hypothalamic involvement in the aging decline in reproductive functions was our report in 1969 (Clemens *et al.* 1969) that electrical stimulation of the medial preoptic area, an essential region for regulating LHRH and LH release in the rat, induced ovulation in old constant oestrous rats. This was confirmed by showing that electrical stimulation of the medial preoptic area induced elevations in circulating LH levels in old constant oestrous, but not in old pseudopregnant rats. The high prolactin secretion in the latter rats had to be reduced by use of ergot (dopaminergic) drugs to enable them to ovulate and cycle (Clemens and Bennett 1977). We reported that epinephrine and progesterone induced ovulation and/or cycling in old constant oestrous rats (Clemens *et al.* 1969), and subsequently observed that administration of the catecholaminergic precursor, L-dopa, or of iproniazid, a monamine oxidase inhibitor that prevents metabolism of catecholamines, induced resumption of oestrous cycles (Quadri *et al.* 1973). We suggested that this provided indirect evidence for a deficiency of catecholamine (CA) activity in the hypothalamus of old rats. Subsequently we showed that concentration and turnover (activity) of both norepinephrine and dopamine were significantly lower in the hypothalamus of old male and female rats than in young rats of both sexes (Simpkins *et al.* 1977), an observation confirmed by other investigators (Wise 1983, Simpkins 1984). Simpkins (1984) reported that dopamine (DA) and dihydroxyphenylacetic acid (DOPAC) concentrations were lower in the median eminence, medial basal hypothalamus, and preoptic area/anterior hypothalamus of 25- to 26-month-old constant oestrous than in 3- to 4-month-old cycling rats. Concentrations of norepinephrine (NE) were also reduced in the preoptic area/anterior hypothalamus and medial basal region, but not in the median eminence or striatum. Turnover rates of both CAs also were found to be decreased in old female and male rats. There is also some evidence for reduced CA concentrations in the brain, including the hypothalamus, of elderly human individuals, but a relation to reproduction has not been established.

The significance of the reduced concentration and turnover of CAs in the hypothalamus of old rats is that the CAs, particularly NE, have been shown to induce release of LHRH from the hypothalamus into the pituitary portal vessels, in turn inducing release of LH and FSH from the pituitary (Sarkar and Fink 1979). NE activity in the preoptic area/anterior hypothalamus has been shown to rise shortly before LH release on the afternoon of pro-oestrus in the cycling rat (Simpkins 1984). In addition to the CAs, other neurotransmitters may also modulate the release of gonadotropins. Hypothalamic serotonin (5-HT) concentration remains unchanged in aging rats, although turnover may be slightly increased (Simpkins 1984, Simpkins *et al.* 1977). However, the ratio of 5-HT to NE becomes greater, and this may contribute to the failure of cyclic release of LHRH and LH release in the old female rats. The rhythm of serotonin secretion appears to be controlled by the suprachiasmatic nucleus, a rhythm that apparently becomes disrupted during aging (Walker 1980). Serotonin may have a stimulatory role on LH release during the oestrous cycle, but there is also evidence that 5-HT can be inhibitory to LH release, and its precise role remains to be determined. It has been reported that restricting dietary intake of tryptophan, the precursor of 5-HT, or administering parachlorophenylalanine which inhibits 5-HT activity, extended the duration of oestrous cycles in aging rats. These treatments depressed food intake which alone can inhibit oestrous cycles. Less is known about the role of other hypothalamic neurotransmitters on LHRH and LH release during aging.

Measurement of LHRH concentrations in the hypothalamus of old rats and mice has revealed no consistent changes in old persistent oestrous or pseudopregnant rats, but a significant reduction was found in old anoestrous rats (Steger *et al.* 1979). Simpkins (1983) observed a decrease in LHRH in the median eminence, arcuate nucleus and organum vasculosum of the lamina terminalis in old male rats. Measurements of hypothalamic concentrations of LHRH are not necessarily indicative of the release rate into the portal vessels. The best evidence that LHRH release is reduced in old rats was the report by Wise and Ratner (1980) that hypothalamic LHRH concentration did not change after castration in old rats, in contrast to the rapid fall in hypothalamic LHRH concentration that normally occurs after castration in young rats. The fall in LHRH concentration in young rats after castration reflects its increased release and accounts for the rise in LH and FSH secretion by the pituitary.

Prolactin secretion is increased with aging in the rat, more so in females than in males, and this is associated with development of numerous mammary and pituitary tumours (prolactinomas) in the female rats (Meites 1982). Apparently no age-related increase in prolactin secretion occurs in mice unless they develop pituitary tumours (Finch *et al.* 1984). The stimulus for the progressive rise in prolactin secretion appears to come mainly from the decline in hypothalamic DA activity, since DA is the primary inhibitor of prolactin secretion. The increased ratio of 5-HT to DA during aging may also contribute to the rise in prolactin secretion, since 5-HT has been shown to elevate prolactin secretion in the rat. The incidence of mammary tumours may reach 80% in old female Sprague-Dawley rats, and is also high in some strains of old female mice. The incidence of pituitary tumours in old female rats and in some strains of mice may reach 50% or more (Russfield 1966). There is no evidence for any change in prolactin secretion in elderly women and men nor of any definite relationship between prolactin and development of breast cancer in women. However, the occurrence of microadenomas of the pituitary, mainly prolactinomas, was reported to be 8-25% in human subjects and to show some increase with aging (Post *et al.* 1980).

Other evidence that hypothalamic CAs have a central role in the decline of reproductive functions and the increase in mammary and pituitary tumours in aging rats is that administration of central acting drugs that increase hypothalamic CA activity can induce reversal of these aging events. Thus administration of L-dopa, the precursor of CAs, can delay the loss of oestrous cycles and induce resumption of oestrous cycles after they have ceased in old constant oestrous rats (Meites 1982, Quadri *et al.* 1973). L-Dopa and dopaminergic ergot drugs also can induce regression of mammary and pituitary tumours in old rats. Clonidine, a NE agonist, has also been shown to restore the amplitude of LH pulses in old ovariectomized rats to the same peak levels as in young ovariectomized rats (Simpkins 1984). Cooper and Linnoila (1980) reported that L-tyrosine, the amino acid precursor of L-dopa, extended the period of ovarian cycles in aging rats when added to the diet at 7.5 months of age.

Why Do CAs Decline during Aging?

The role of oestrogen and prolactin

There is evidence that prolonged oestrogen action or high circulating prolactin levels can damage hypothalamic neurons that normally regulate secretion of gonadotropins and prolactin. Aschheim (1976) reported more than 20 years ago that when rats were ovariectomized at 6 or 12 months of age, followed by grafting either young or old ovaries at 24–27 months of age, this resulted in resumption and extension of oestrous cycles whereas intact 24- to 27-month-old control rats had long ceased to cycle. He suggested that ovariectomy produced suspension of aging of the hypothalamic apparatus that controlled oestrous cycles in the rat. This report was confirmed and extended by Finch et al. (1984) who observed in C57BL/6J mice that ovariectomy followed many months later by ovarian grafting significantly extended the normal cycling period in these mice.

Clarification of some of the mechanism(s) by which chronic oestrogen exposure can damage hypothalamic neurons regulating reproduction in the rats and mouse was provided by Brawer et al. (1978). They reported that when ovariectomized mature rats were chronically exposed to oestrogen, this resulted in the development of gliosis, a characteristic of degenerating neurons, in the arcuate nucleus and medial basal hypothalamus (MBH). These degenerative changes consisted of swollen and distorted cell bodies, degenerating axons and axonal endings, excess accumulation of lipofuscin, and decreased vascularity. Similar changes in the arcuate nucleus and MBH have been observed in normal aging female rats and may be partly the consequence of chronic exposure to oestrogen during the many recurrent oestrous cycles of earlier life and during persistent oestrus in aging rats. Since the arcuate nucleus serves as an intermediate pathway between the medial preoptic area, essential for controlling LHRH release, and the median eminence, any impairment in transmission of signals from the medial preoptic area to the median eminence could adversely affect reproductive functions. A 30% neuronal loss has been reported in the arcuate nucleus and medial preoptic area of 2-year-old female rats (Peng 1983), but others have reported no loss of tyrosine hydroxylase containing neurons in rats in C57BL/6J mice (Finch et al. 1984).

Some reports have appeared in the literature that appear to contradict the view that long-term oestrogen treatment can damage neurons in the hypothalamus. Aschheim (1976) observed that when rats were treated with an oestrogen-progestogen mixture for 4 or 8 months beginning at 4–5 months of age, oestrous cycles resumed following cessation of treatment and were maintained for at least 4 months. When steroid treatment was begun at 10 months of age in cycling rats, there were no age-retarding effects on oestrous cycles. He explained this difference as due to a central "desensitization" to oestrogen during early treatment, counteracting the normal age-related increase in sensitivity to oestrogen. However, it is possible that the progestogen used inhibited the harmful effects of the oestrogen in this experiment. More difficult to explain is that ovarian resection or hemiovariectomy of young rats or mice actually advances the onset of acyclicity in these animals (Finch et al. 1984, Huang 1977). Finch et al. (1984) reported that when mice were ovariectomized when young and given ovarian grafts at 24–30 months of age, only few ovulations occurred. They had no explanation as to why prolonged ovariectomy in these rats failed to preserve hypothalamic reproductive function in these rats. However, recent work by Thompson *et al.* (1985) showed that after ovariectomy of middle-aged rats for 10-20 weeks, the rise in circulating LH was smaller than in young ovariectomized rats. This indicates that oestrogen is not alone responsible for the decreased ability to secrete LH during aging in rats. Finally, aging male rats exhibit decrements in hypothalamic and reproductive functions, as do aging female rats, despite the fact that they secrete very little oestrogen.

Effects of elevated oestrogen and prolactin levels on dopaminergic neurons

It is not clear from the work of Aschheim (1976), Finch *et al.* (1984) and Brawer *et al.* (1978) which kind of neurons are damaged by prolonged oestrogen treatment. Oestrogen has been shown to be present in both NE and DA neurons, as well as in neurons containing tyrosine hydroxylase, the rate limiting enzyme for CA synthesis (Sar 1984). Our laboratory has reported that either chronic exposure to oestrogen or to persistent high circulating prolactin can damage DA neurons in the arcuate nucleus (Sarkar *et al.* 1982, 1984). As in the report by Brawer *et al.* (1978), the neurons in the arcuate nucleus were shrunken, the nerve fibres were distorted and increased deposits of lipofuscin were observed in the neurons. When young, ovariectomized rats were implanted subcutaneously with a Silastic capsule containing β-oestradiol for 30 days, followed by removal of the capsule for 26 weeks, the median eminence showed decreased capacity to release DA *in vitro* in response to electrical stimulation or to hypertonic K (Gottschall and Meites 1986). It was concluded that long-term oestrogen treatment can permanently damage TIDA neurons. Similar observations were made in rats implanted with prolactin-secreting pituitary tissue for prolonged periods (Sarkar *et al.* 1984), and it was found that there was less DA in the hypophysial portal vessels. In apparent contradiction to these observations, Morgan *et al.* (1985) recently reported that either long-term oestrogen or chronic high prolactin exposure in intact male rats increased hypothalamic DA synthesis. They implanted a capsule of diethylstilboestrol subcutaneously, or three anterior pituitaries under the kidney capsule for 2 months, and killed the oestrogen-implanted rats 8 months after capsule removal and the pituitary-grafted rats 4-12 months after surgery. The oestrogen-implanted rats had hyperplastic pituitaries and both treatments produced hyperprolactinaemia. However, DA synthesis in the median eminence was found to be elevated in rats given either treatment, when measured by liquid chromatography with electrochemical detection. NE levels were not significantly altered in the median eminence. The reason(s) for these apparently contradictory results on the effects of chronic high oestrogen or prolactin on DA activity are not clear, but it is possible that less DA was released from the median eminence despite the increase in synthesis. Also, there may have been a recovery of the DA neurons after the oestrogen and prolactin were removed; and finally, there may be a difference in the hypothalamic response of intact male rats to chronically elevated oestrogen or prolactin exposure as compared to similarly treated ovariectomized female rats.

Other agents that may alter hypothalamic CA neurons during aging

Other agents may be partly responsible for the decline in hypothalamic DA and NE activity in aging rats. Mention has already been made of the reports that there is a decrease in tyrosine hydroxylase, the rate limiting enzyme for CA synthesis (Meites 1982). There is also some evidence for a decrease in dopamine-β-hydroxylase in 16- to 20-month-old mice (Finch *et al.* 1984). In addition, there are reports of loss of neurons during aging in the locus coeruleus, located in the mid-brain and the major source of NE in the hypothalamus (Meites 1982, Simpkins 1984). Also, monoamine oxidase, the major enzyme responsible for the metabolism of CAs, has been reported to be increased in the hypothalamus during aging (Meites 1982). Although there is no definite evidence reported that either testosterone or adrenal cortical steroids (the glucocorticoids) can damage CA neurons, it is well established that testosterone can be aromatized in the hypothalamus to oestrogen, and that glucocorticoids can damage neurons in the hippocampus of the rat. Other hormones from the pituitary and target glands may damage CA neurons as well, and their effects on these neurons over a long period of time need to be investigated. To what degree free radicals, cross-linkages, lipofuscin or other agents are responsible for damage to CA neurons in the hypothalamus remains to be determined.

Changes in Pituitary Function during Aging

Although believed to be of only secondary importance in the aging of the reproductive system in rats, there is convincing evidence that the pituitary becomes less responsive to LHRH stimulation. Thus, in old male rats the *in vivo* pituitary response to multiple injections of synthetic LHRH resulted in significantly lower release of LH than in young male rats (Bruni *et al.* 1977). Similarly, in old female rats a single injection of LHRH evoked smaller release of LH than in young rats (Watkins *et al.* 1975). Harman (1983) observed a progressive decrease with age in ability of LHRH to elicit LH and FSH release in human male subjects. The decreased capacity of LHRH to induce LH release in old male rats was reported by Sonntag *et al.* (1984) not to be due to a reduction in LHRH receptors in the pituitary of old male rats since the number of LHRH receptors was similar in both old and young rats. It was suggested that the loss in pituitary responsiveness to LHRH was probably due to faults that developed within the cells during aging e.g. reduced Ca ion entry, deficits in cAMP, deficits in interaction with genome etc.

It is of interest that when oestrogen was administered to aging ovariectomized rats, the afternoon rise in LH was lower than in young ovariectomized rats, but the rise in prolactin release was greater than in young rats (Wise 1983). There is other evidence that the lactotrophs of the pituitary show progressively increased sensitivity to oestrogen stimulation with aging (Ascheim 1976). Whether this action of oestrogen on prolactin release is exerted directly on the pituitary, via the hypothalamus, or both, remains to be determined.

Although the ability to release LH and FSH in response to different stimuli appears to be definitely decreased in old female and male rats, this is not necessarily reflected in measurements of basal circulating levels of these hormones. Thus, basal serum FSH levels were higher and basal serum LH levels were about the same in old constant oestrous rats as in young rats on the afternoon of pro-oestrus or morning of oestrus (Huang and Meites 1975). Serum FSH values were lower and serum LH levels were about the same in old pseudopregnant as in constant oestrous rats; serum gonadotropins were undetectable in old anoestrous rats (Huang and Meites 1975). The rise in circulating LH that normally occurs on the afternoon of pro-oestrus was found to be lower in middle-aged cycling rats than in young cycling rats (Wise 1983), probably reflecting both the reduction in hypothalamic release of LHRH as well as the reduced responsiveness of the pituitary to LHRH stimulation.

Changes in Gonadal Function during Aging

There is evidence that the gonads of old rats do not respond as well as the gonads of young rats to gonadotropin stimulation. After cessation of regular oestrous cycles in aging rodents, gonadotropic hormone stimulation may induce fewer eggs to ovulate and less steroids may be secreted. In old constant oestrous rats, cystic follicles are very common, perhaps owing to absence of the normal preovulatory surge of LH and also because of faults that develop within the follicles. It is not clear whether ovarian receptors to gonadotropin are reduced during aging. Huang et al. (1978) reported that old constant oestrous rats secreted more oestradiol than either old pseudopregnant or anoestrous rats but less than cycling rats on the day of pro-oestrus. Old pseudopregnant rats secreted more progesterone than old constant oestrous or anoestrous rats, but less than cycling rats on the day of pro-oestrus (Huang et al. 1978). The enzymes necessary to synthesize progesterone were reported to be reduced in the ovaries of old rats and mice, but most workers have not found any significant reduction in progesterone levels during pregnancy in aging rats and mice (Harman and Talbert 1985).

In women during the few years prior to the menopause, the ovarian response to gonadotropins is reduced due to the smaller number of follicles present and the decrease in oestrogen-secreting tissue (Harman and Talbert 1985). The atrophic, fibrotic ovaries of the postmenopausal state respond little or not at all to gonadotropic stimulation, due to disappearance of follicles and loss of oestrogen-secreting tissue. Most of the oestrogen produced in the postmenopausal state comes from peripheral conversion of androgens secreted by the adrenal glands.

In aging male animals and men, the testes become less responsive to stimulation by gonadotropins. Human chorionic gonadotropin (HCG) has been widely used to test the ability of the testes to secrete testosterone in both aging men and rats, and the results have generally shown a reduction in testicular response. In elderly men, the lower testicular response appears to be due to a decrease in Leydig cell number and/or decline in ability of individual Leydig cells to secrete testosterone (Harman and Talbert 1985). In the rat lower testosterone secretion appears to be due mainly to the reduction in secretion of pituitary gonadotropins (Simpkins et al. 1977).

Wide variations have been reported in blood levels of testosterone in aging men, probably owing to the physical state of the individuals at the time of blood collection. Factors such as illness, drug or alcohol intake, and environmental agents (diet, stress, temperature etc.) can influence secretion of testosterone. Also, the time of day of blood collection is important since there are diurnal variations in testosterone secretion, with higher values in the morning than in the afternoon. In healthy elderly men, little or no change in circulating testosterone levels has been reported, but most investigators observed a decline in testosterone secretion, particularly after the age of 50 years (Harman and Talbert 1985). Despite the reduction in testosterone secretion and spermatogenesis in aging male rats and men, the capacity to reproduce may be retained practically to the end of life in healthy individuals.

Relation of Aging Theories to the Reproductive Decline

Most gerontological investigators agree that no one theory can explain general body aging, although a particular theory may be favoured by an individual investigator, often because it is his/her own theory. It is generally agreed that heredity has a major role in determining aging of body tissues and organs, as shown by the different lifespans among various species and to some extent even within the same species. In addition, aging of tissues is influenced by external environmental factors such as diet, temperature, stress, health factors and light-dark cycles, as well as by internal environmental factors such as reproductive cycles, pregnancies, lactation, and immune functions. Through which mechanisms do genes and environmental agents exert their effects on aging processes?

One view is that genes and environmental agents act mainly at the cellular level to regulate developmental events throughout life, including aging and death of cells. Hayflick (1977) has demonstrated that cultures of human fibroblast cells *in vitro* show a maximum of about 50 cell divisions they can undergo before they die. From this work, it was deduced that not only fibroblasts but other cell types can undergo only a finite number of divisions. However, fibroblast cells rarely undergo division *in vivo* unless they are stimulated or injured, and other cells do not divide after they are formed. The latter includes the important brain cells (neurons), relatively few of which are lost during aging (perhaps about 5-7% in the human brain), and are believed by some, including myself, to be the major regulator of aging changes in the body. Other theories of aging stress that errors appear in transfer of information from DNA via mRNA, perhaps as a result of reduced ability to repair damage to DNA, leading to errors in protein synthesis; there is loss of important enzymes or reduction in their activities; an increase occurs in free radicals and cross-linkages, leading to damaged cell function; there is accumulation of cellular debris (lipofuscin), leading to decreased cellular function etc. There is some evidence in favour and some against each of these cellular theories, but it is doubtful whether any one of them or all together are adequate to explain general body aging or aging of specific body organs and tissues.

Different from the cellular theories is the view that genetic and environmental determinants of aging are mediated primarily via the two great integrating systems of the body, namely the brain and the endocrine glands (the neuroendocrine system). This view is based on the established evidence that the neuroendocrine system controls general body growth and development, reproduction, metabolism of protein, fat, carbohydrate, minerals and vitamins, immune functions, haemopoiesis, gastrointestinal activity, and greatly influences activities of the brain, kidneys, liver, heart etc. The neuroendocrine system is also involved in development and growth of many tumours, including those of the pituitary, thyroid, adrenals, ovaries, testes, breast, prostate and reproductive tract. It appears logical to hypothesize that, if the neuroendocrine system controls or greatly influences so many important body functions during early and mature life, it should have an equally important role in determining the onset and progression of decremental changes in these body functions during aging. In the three aging events we have studied in the rat, namely the decline of reproductive functions, development of numerous mammary and pituitary tumours, and decrease in pulsatile growth hormone (GH) secretion and the associated decline in protein synthesis (Meites 1984), it has become evident that dysfunctions that develop in the hypothalamic portion of the brain are mainly responsible for these aging events. It appears probable that many other aging changes in body organs and tissues also result primarily because of malfunctions that develop in the neuroendocrine system.

In such a complex mechanism as the neuroendocrine system, it is clear that if a fault develops in a single component of the system, this can "trigger" a chain of events that can lead to many decrements in body functions. The major fault that develops with aging in the rat that leads to the three aging events we have studied is the decrease in hypothalamic CA activity. The three aging events do not usually all occur at the same time. The decline in reproductive function usually appears first at about mid-life, followed some months later by a decrease in pulsatile GH secretion, and finally in the oldest rats by development of large numbers of mammary and pituitary tumours. These sequential aging events are believed to be the result of a progressive fall in hypothalamic CA activity, resulting first in a decrease in ability to secrete gonadotropins, followed next by a reduction in GH secretion, and last by an increase in prolactin secretion sufficient to induce development of pituitary and mammary tumours. There is considerable evidence for a progressive increase in prolactin secretion with age in the female rat (Aschheim 1976, Huang and Meites 1975).

The possible causes for the decline in hypothalamic CA activity with aging have been dealt with elsewhere. It was also shown that loss of oestrous cycles and development of mammary and pituitary tumours can be delayed in aging female rats and can be reversed after their occurrence by treatments that increase hypothalamic CA activity. Reduced pulsatile GH secretion in old male rats can also be returned to levels present in young male rats by L-dopa treatment. In addition, *some of these aging events can be induced in young rats* by treatments that depress hypothalamic CA activity. Thus oestrogen treatment in young intact rats can inhibit oestrous cycles, increase prolactin secretion and result in development of mammary and pituitary tumours. Chronic administration of neuroleptic drugs such as haloperidol or reserpine, or placement of a lesion in the median eminence, result in cessation of oestrous cycles, development of prolonged pseudopregnancies and development of mammary tumours (Welsch and Aylsworth 1983). Lesions placed in the anterior hypothalamus of young rats result in a constant oestrous state, whereas lesions placed in the preoptic nucleus result in prolonged pseudopregnancies (Clemens and Bennett 1977). Thus the decline in reproductive function and development of prolactin-related tumours in the rat are not dependent on age, but on a specific alteration(s) in hypothalamic function that can be induced even relatively early in life.

Recently, we have found that a 50% reduction in caloric intake for 10 weeks in 4-month-old and 12-month-old female rats, followed by *ad libitum* feeding, can delay loss of oestrous cycles in the young rats and induce resumption of oestrous cycles in the older rats (Quigley and Meites unpublished observations). Underfeeding is well known to reduce secretion of pituitary hormones, including the gonadotropins, prolactin and GH (Campbell *et al.* 1977). The endocrine state produced by severe underfeeding has sometimes been referred to as "pseudohypophysectomy" because it produces a syndrome similar to that of hypophysectomy. Everitt (1980) has demonstrated that hypophysectomy in rats retards collagen formation and aging of the heart, kidneys, skeletal muscle, bone and *ovaries*, and *inhibits tumour formation*. Part of the beneficial effects of reducing food intake on reproductive function in our study in rats may be the result of the temporary cessation of oestrous cycles in the young rats and the decrease in oestrogen secretion by the ovaries of the older rats, most of whom were in a state of constant oestrus at the time of initiation of underfeeding. Thus, the possible deleterious effects of oestrogen on the hypothalamic mechanisms regulating oestrous cycles may temporarily have been reduced or removed. In addition, the decrease in secretion of other hormones by the hypothalamus and pituitary may have helped to preserve functions of other organs and tissues in the body. It is of interest that the decrease in caloric intake induced temporary resumption of oestrous cycles in the older acyclic rats upon refeeding, suggesting the occurrence of a temporary *rejuvenation* of the reproductive system. We have previously noted that underfeeding followed by *ad libitum* feeding resulted in augmented gonadotropin secretion (Campbell *et al.* 1977). The one method that has definitely been shown to inhibit aging and significantly prolong life in the rat and mouse is reduced food intake (Masoro 1985, McCay *et al.* 1935), and there is increasing evidence that underfeeding may be beneficial even in older animals. It also is of interest that daily intake of L-dopa by mice has been reported to prolong the lifespan significantly (Cotzias *et al.* 1974).

Our studies in the rat indicate that at least three aging developments are not necessarily *progressive* or *irreversible*. Indeed, it is possible that oestrous cycles, normal GH secretion and prevention of mammary and pituitary tumours can be maintained to the end of life in the female rat, although this remains to be demonstrated. It is also possible that many other body functions can at least be improved by neuroendocrine intervention. To what extent aging of organs and tissue can be inhibited or reversed in elderly human individuals remains to be determined. Obviously the atrophic ovaries of the postmenopausal state cannot be rejuvenated, but small doses of oestrogen or oestrogen–progestin combinations are frequently used to produce a number of beneficial effects as well as some increased risks. It would be of great interest to determine the possible beneficial effects of reducing caloric intake in aging individuals.

It is clear from our studies in the rat that genetic and environmental factors act via the neuroendocrine system to initiate at least three major aging changes in the body. To what extent the various cellular-molecular theories may apply to these aging events is not clear at present. We have emphasized the role of declining hypothalamic activity, which may be due to the prolonged and perhaps permanent damage exerted by steroids and other hormones, to accumulated damage by chronic usage of hypothalamic mechanisms ("wear and tear") which apparently can be attenuated by underfeeding, to increased formation of free radicals or cross-linkages, to a genetically programmed decline in function of these cells, etc. A major defect of many cellular molecular theories is the tendency to ignore or give little note to the importance of environmental influences on aging processes. The ability of reduced food intake (external environment effect) to preserve body tissues and prolong life, or of chronic steroid exposure (internal environment effect) to shorten reproductive life, are good examples of the importance of extracellular influences. Both of these and indeed most environmental influences on body functions are exerted via the neuroendocrine system.

We have emphasized the decline in hypothalamic CAs in our studies. However, it is evident that enough capacity remains in the hypothalamus of old rats to secrete CAs, since administration of CA precursors can induce resumption of oestrous cycles, regression of mammary and pituitary tumours and increase GH secretion and protein synthesis. The experimental induction of similar aging changes in young animals by reducing hypothalamic CA activity, apparently without eliciting other aging phenomena, casts doubt on the view that aging is caused by some common cellular dysfunctions that occur only at a relatively late stage in life, as implied by the various cellular-molecular theories of aging. There is ample evidence that many aging events, including the decline in reproductive function and development of tumours, can appear earlier in life than many other decrements in body functions. Our studies indicate that the "command" cells of the body, namely the cells of the neuroendocrine system, have a special and specific role in determining when and where in the body aging changes will occur.

ACKNOWLEDGEMENTS

This work was aided in part by NIH grant AG00416. I would like to thank Victoria Kingsbury for her careful typing of this manuscript.

REFERENCES

Aschheim, P. (1976). Aging of the hypothalamic-hypophyseal ovarian axis in the rat. *In* "Hypothalamus, pituitary and aging" (A. V. Everitt and J. A. Burgess, eds), pp. 376-418. C. C. Thomas, Springfield, Illinois.

Brawer, G. R., Naftolin, F., Martin, J. and Sonnenschein, C. (1978). Effects of a single injection of estradiol valerate on the hypothalamic arcuate nucleus and on reproductive function in the female rat. *Endocrinology* **103**, 501-512.

Bruni, J. F., Huang, H. H., Marshall, S. and Meites, J. (1977). Effects of single and multiple injections of synthetic GnRH on serum LH, FSH and testosterone in young and old male rats. *Biol. Reprod.* **17**, 309-312.

Campbell, G. A., Kurcz, M., Marshall, S. and Meites, J. (1977). Effects of starvation in rats on serum levels of follicle stimulating hormone, luteinizing hormone, thyrotropin, growth hormone and prolactin; response to LH-releasing hormone and thyrotropin-releasing hormone. *Endocrinology* **100**, 580-587.

Clemens, J. A. and Bennett, D. R. (1977). Do aging changes in the preoptic area contribute to loss of cyclic endocrine function? *J. Gerontol.* **32**, 19-24.

Clemens, J. A., Amenomori, Y., Jenkins, T. and Meites, J. (1969). Effects of hypothalamic stimulation, hormones, and drugs on ovarian function in old female rats. *Proc. Soc. Exp. Biol. Med.* **132**, 561-563.

Cooper, R. L. and Linnoila, M. (1980). Effect of centrally and systemically administered L-tyrosine and L-leucine on ovarian function in the old rat. *Gerontology* **26**, 270-275.

Cotzias, G. C., Miller, S. T., Nicholson, A. R. Jr, Matson, W. H. and Tang, L. C. (1974). Levodopa, fertility, and longevity. *Proc. Natl Acad. Sci. USA* **71**, 2466-2469.

Everitt, A. V. (1980). The neuroendocrine system and aging. *Gerontology* **26**, 108-119.
Finch, C. E., Felicio, L. S., Mobbs, C. V. and Nelson, J. F. (1984). Ovarian and steroidal influences on neuroendocrine aging processes in female rodents. *Endocrine Rev.* **5**, 467-497.
Gottschall, P. E. and Meites, J. (1986). Persistence of low hypothalamic dopaminergic activity after removal of chronic estrogen treatment. *Proc. Soc. Exp. Biol. Med.* **181**, 78-86.
Harman, S. M. (1983). Relation of the neuroendocrine system to the reproductive decline in men. *In* "Neuroendocrinology of aging" (J. Meites, ed.) pp. 203-220. Plenum Press, New York.
Harman, S. M. and Talbert, G. B. (1985). Reproductive aging. *In* "Handbook of the biology of aging" 2nd edn (C. E. Finch and E. L. Schneider, eds) pp. 457-510. Van Nostrand Reinhold, New York.
Hayflick, L. (1977). The cellular basis for biological aging. *In* "Handbook of the biology of aging" (C. E. Finch and L. Hayflick, eds) pp. 159-188. Van Nostrand Reinhold, New York.
Huang, H. H. (1977). Relation of neuroendocrine system to loss of reproductive function in aging female rats. Ph.D. dissertation, Michigan State University, East Lansing, USA.
Huang, H. H. and Meites, J. (1975). Reproductive capacity of aging female rodents. *Neuroendocrinology* **17**, 289-295.
Huang, H. H., Steger, R. W., Bruni, J. F. and Meites, J. (1978). Patterns of sex steroid and gonadotropin secretion in aging female rats. *Endocrinology* **103**, 1855-1859.
Masoro, E. J. (1985). Metabolism. *In* "Handbook of biology of aging" 2nd edn (C. E. Finch and E. L. Schneider, eds) pp. 540-563. Van Nostrand Reinhold, New York.
McCay, C. M., Crowell, M. F. and Maynard, L. A. (1935). The effect of retarded growth upon the length of life span and upon the ultimate body size. *J. Nutrition* **10**, 63-79.
Meites, J. (1982). Changes in neuroendocrine control of anterior pituitary function during aging. *Neuroendocrinology* **34**, 151-156.
Meites, J. (1984). Role of the neuroendocrine system in aging processes. *In* "Comparative pathobiology of major age-related diseases: current status and research frontiers" (D. E. Scarpelli and G. Migaki, eds) pp. 89-108. Allan R. Liss, Inc., New York.
Morgan, W. M., Bartke, A. and Herbert, D. C. (1985). The effect of long-term diethylstilbestrol treatment or hyperprolactinemia on the response of the tubero-infundibular dopamine neurons to elevated prolactin. *Brain Res.* **335**, 330-333.
Nass, T. E., La Polt, P. S. and Lu, J. K. H. (1982). Alterations in ovarian steroid and gonadotrophin secretion preceding the cessation of regular oestrous cycles in aging female rats. *Biol. Reprod.* **27**, 609-615.
Peng, M. T. (1983). Changes in hormone uptake and receptors in the hypothalamus during aging. *In* "Neuroendocrinology of aging" (J. Meites, ed.) pp. 61-72. Plenum Press, New York.
Post, K. D., Jackson, J. M. D. and Reichlin, S. (1980). "The pituitary adenoma." Plenum Press, New York.
Quadri, S. K., Kledzik, G. S. and Meites, J. (1973). Reinitiation of estrous cycles in old constant estrous rats by central-acting drugs. *Neuroendocrinology* **11**, 248-255.
Russfield, A. B. (1966). "Tumors of endocrine glands and secondary sex organs." Public Health Service Pub. No. 1332, Washington, D. C.
Sar, M. (1984). Estradiol is concentrated in tyrosine hydroxylase-containing neurons of the hypothalamus. *Science* **223**, 938-940.
Sarkar, D. K. and Fink, G. (1979). Luteinizing hormone releasing factor in pituitary stalk plasma from long-term ovariectomized rats: effects of steroids. *J. Endocrinol.* **80**, 303-313.

Sarkar, D. K., Gottschall, P. E. and Meites, J. (1982). Damage to hypothalamic dopaminergic neurons is associated with development of prolactin-secreting pituitary tumors. *Science* **218**, 684-686.

Sarkar, D. K., Gottschall, P. E. and Meites, J. (1984). Decline of tuberoinfundibular dopaminergic function resulting from chronic hyperprolactinemia in rats. *Endocrinology* **115**, 1269-1274.

Simpkins, J. W. (1983). Changes in hypothalamic hypophysiotrophic hormones and neurotransmitters during aging. *In* "Neuroendocrinology of aging" (J. Meites, ed.) pp. 41-60. Plenum Press, New York.

Simpkins, J. W. (1984). Regional changes in monoamine metabolism in the aging constant estrous rats. *Neurobiol. Aging* **4**, 3309-3314.

Simpkins, J. W., Mueller, G. P., Huang, H. H. and Meites, J. (1977). Evidence for depressed catecholamines and enhanced serotonin metabolism in aging male rats: possible relation to gonadotropin secretion. *Endocrinology* **100**, 1672-1678.

Sonntag, W. E., Forman, L. J., Fiori, J. M. and Hylka, V. (1984). Decreased ability of old male rats to secrete LH is not due to alterations in pituitary LH-releasing hormone receptors. *Endocrinology* **114**, 1657-1664.

Steger, R. W., Huang, H. H. and Meites, J. (1979). Relation of aging to hypothalamic LHRH content and serum gonadal steroids in female rats. *Proc. Soc. Exp. Biol. Med.* **161**, 251-254.

Thompson, D. L., Pomerantz, D. K. and Weick, R. F. (1985). Characteristics of pulsatile luteinizing hormone secretion in middle-aged ovariectomized rats. *Biol. Reprod.* **33**, 827-834.

Walker, R. F. (1980). Serotonin neuroleptics change patterns of preovulatory secretion of luteinizing hormone in rats. *Life Sci.* **27**, 1063-1068.

Watkins, B. E., Meites, J. and Riegle, G. D. (1975). Age-related changes in pituitary responsiveness to LHRH in the female rat. *Endocrinology* **97**, 543-548.

Welsch, C. W. and Aylsworth, C. F. (1983). Relation of the neuroendocrine system to the development of mammary tumors in rats during aging. *In* "Neuroendocrinology of aging" (J. Meites, ed.) pp. 333-352. Plenum Press, New York.

Wise, P. M. (1983). Aging of the female reproductive system. *Rev. Biol. Res. Aging* **1**, 195-222.

Wise, P. M. and Ratner, A. (1980). Effect of ovariectomy on plasma LH, FSH, estradiol, and progesterone and medial basal hypothalamic LHRH concentrations in old and young rats. *Neuroendocrinology* **30**, 15-19.

Discussion

Berthel: Have you any data about increase or decrease of neurons in the hypothalamus during aging?

Meites: The number of neurons in various areas of the hypothalamus has been measured and an approximate 30% decrease in neurons in these regions was found with aging (Peng, 1983). If this can be confirmed by further studies, it would certainly be a very important observation.

Verdonk: Are there any practical implications with the use of contraconceptive pills, i.e. would an oestrogen abuse damage cerebral centres or accelerate aging?

Meites: Unfortunately, we know much more about the neuroendocrinology of aging in the rat than we do in humans. However, work in rats showed that the effects of chronic administration of oestrogen can be damaging to the brain. The evidence that oestrogen and perhaps testosterone can produce permanent changes in the brain, including the hypothalamus, has been noted in the rat but has not been studied in man.

Holliday: If rats were allowed to breed, would they remain fertile longer than if they were not allowed to breed?

Meites: A former student of mine at UCLA (Dr John Lu) has recently shown that when aging female rats are exposed to males in nearby cages, they will continue to cycle for a number of months beyond control rats. Therefore, it appears that exposing female rats to males has an influence on their ability to cycle. There is no convincing evidence that breeding has any effect on length of fertility.

Changes in the Neuronal Cytoskeleton in Aging and Disease

Brian H. Anderton,[1] Jean-Pierre Brion,[2]
Jacqueline Flament-Durand,[2] Margaret Haugh,[1]
Jacob Kahn,[3] Christopher C. J. Miller,[1]
Alphonse Probst[4] and Jurg Ülrich[4]

[1]*Department of Immunology, St George's Hospital Medical School, London, UK*
[2]*Laboratoire d'Anatomie Pathologique et de Microscopie Electronique, Universite Libre de Bruxelles, Bruxelles, Belgium*
[3]*Department of Neuropathology, Institute of Psychiatry, University of London, London, UK*
[4]*Department of Pathology, Neuropathology Division, University of Basel, Switzerland*

Keywords
Alzheimer's disease; Pick's disease; Parkinson's disease; Lewy bodies; Neurofibrillary tangles; Senile plaques.

INTRODUCTION

The Cytoskeleton

The cytoskeleton is the term used to describe the intracellular system of fibres present in eukaryotic cells. The cytoskeleton participates in many cellular functions which include cell migration, cell division, determination of cell shape, endocytosis, exocytosis, intracellular organization and transport of cytoplasmic constituents. In neurons the cytoskeleton presumably participates in the special neuronal adaptations of these functions and so insult or injury to the neuronal cytoskeleton through natural disease or by toxic agents can be expected to have serious consequences for the normal functioning of the nerve cell. A number of age-related degenerative diseases now seem to have a pathology which includes an abnormal neuronal cytoskeleton and here we describe several examples.

The most important of these age-related degenerative diseases is senile dementia of Alzheimer type (SDAT), which, when occurring before the age of 65 is called Alzheimer's disease (AD); together, these diseases are termed dementia of the Alzheimer type (DAT). DAT afflicts some 2-3% of all those older than 65 years (Katzman 1976, Ulrich *et al.* 1986). Deeper insights into the nature of the cytoskeletal changes associated with this disease might help to alleviate or even to prevent this very common, disabling and humiliating condition.

The cytoskeleton is composed of three fibrous organelles. These are microtubules which are 24 nm in diameter, 6-7 nm microfilaments and 9-11 nm intermediate filaments (Anderton 1981, 1982, Lazarides 1982). The intermediate filaments are subdivided into five tissue-related types and are represented by neurofilaments in neurons. The evidence at the time of writing implicates principally the neurofilaments in the neurofibrillary pathology of DAT, elderly Down's syndrome, Parkinson's disease, Pick's disease and progressive supranuclear palsy (Wisniewski *et al.* 1979). The involvement of neurofilaments in the pathology of axonal injury and in the effects of certain neurotoxic agents has been reviewed previously (Anderton 1982).

Neurofilaments are the Neuronal Intermediate Filaments

Neurofilaments of a width of 10 nm are the neuronal type of intermediate filaments (Lazarides 1982, Anderton 1981). In addition to neurofilaments, the other four types of intermediate filaments are glial filaments (astrocytes, Bergman glia), desmin filaments (muscle cells), vimentin filaments (mesenchymal cells) and keratin filaments (epithelial cells).

Neurofilaments and microtubules are the two principal components of the neuronal cytoskeleton although the proportions of the two varies in axons and dendrites. Neurofilaments are relatively more abundant in axons than in dendrites and the larger myelinated axons have the most. There is evidence to suggest that the calibre of some axons may be determined by the number of neurofilaments (Hoffman *et al.* 1985).

Further information on the ultrastructure and neuronal distribution of microtubules, microfilaments and neurofilaments can be found in the review of Wuerker and Kirkpatrick (1972).

INTRANEURONAL FIBROUS ACCUMULATIONS IN AGE-RELATED DISEASES

Alzheimer Neurofibrillary Tangles

Dementia of the Alzheimer type has a characteristic brain pathology which includes neurofibrillary tangles, senile neuritic plaques and granulovacuolar degeneration (Figs 1 and 2). The number of tangles and plaques have been reported to show a correlation with the severity of dementia (Perry *et al.* 1978, Wilcock *et al.* 1982). Neurofibrillary tangles are large fibrous accumulations which fill many neuronal perikarya, particularly the pyramidal cells of the hippocampus but also many cortical neurons in severe cases. Ultrastructurally, they are mostly

Fig. 1. Alzheimer neurofibrillary tangle in a pyramidal cell of the hippocampus. (Nomarski optic; Holmes-Luxol stain ×1440.)

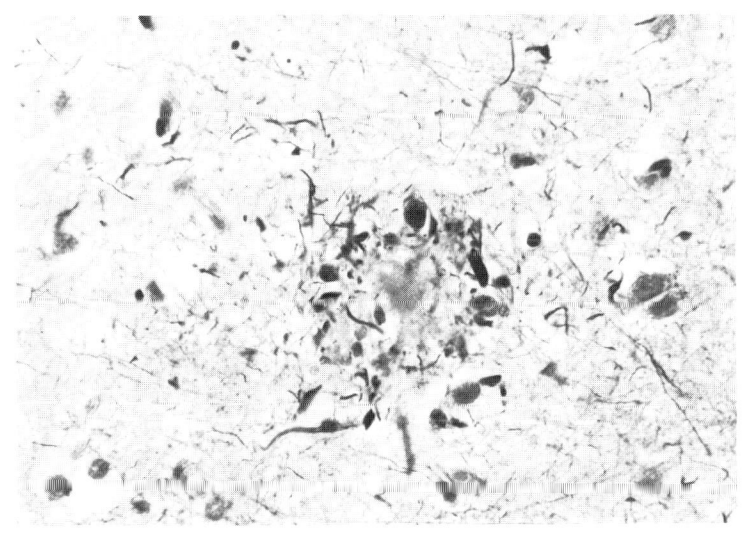

Fig. 2. Senile plaque. Dark abnormal neurites surround amyloid deposits (pale grey) in the centre. (Combined Holmes-Luxol stain ×448.)

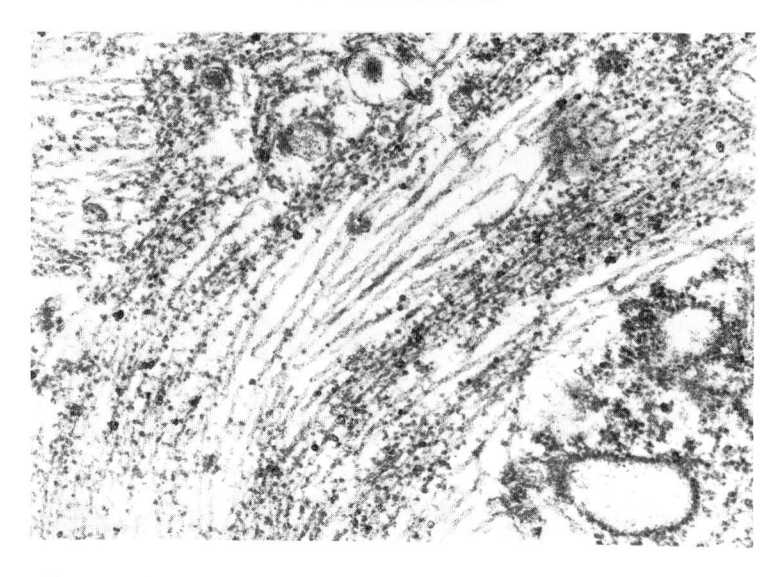

Fig. 3. Electron micrograph of PHF showing helically twisted pairs of filaments (×48,000).

composed of paired helical filaments (PHF) which appear to be either a twisted ribbon structure or helically twisted pairs of 10 nm filaments with a cross-over approximately every 80 nm (Fig. 3) (Kidd 1963, Wischik et al. 1985, Wisniewski et al. 1984, Wiesniewski and Wen 1985). Tangles may also contain straight 10–15 nm filaments alone as bundles or admixed with PHF (Metuzals et al. 1981, Yagishita et al. 1981). PHF are also found in the abnormal neurites located in the senile plaques (Kidd 1963, Gonatas et al. 1967).

The chemical composition of PHF is not yet established. Some PHF when isolated, are resistant to the usual protein-solubilizing and denaturing agents e.g. urea and sodium dodecyl sulphate (SDS) (Selkoe et al. 1982). However, depending upon the particular brain specimen it seems that a proportion can be solubilized giving rise to several polypeptides. The two major components possess molecular weights of 57,000 and 62,000, but they still have a strong tendency to aggregate even in SDS (Iqbal et al. 1984). Recently, Masters et al. (1985) have used pepsin digestion and formic acid to isolate from a PHF fraction a 4,000 mol. wt polypeptide. However, PHF are susceptible to pepsin (Yen and Kress 1983) and so this polypeptide may only represent a proteolytic fragment of the PHF subunit. Selkoe et al. (1986) have suggested that this polypeptide might originate from contaminating amyloid and so further efforts will have to be made before this result can be regarded as unequivocal.

Immunochemical studies have given rise to two findings. Firstly, tangles *in situ* have been stained by some but not all antibodies to neurofilaments and microtubule associated proteins (MAPs) (Grundke-Iqbal et al. 1979, Yen et al. 1981, Nukina and Ihara 1983, Kosik et al. 1984, Brion et al. 1985a,

Table 1

Monoclonal antibody	Antigen specificity	Epitope location in NFs	Labelling of Alzheimer tangles In situ	Labelling of Alzheimer tangles SDS-isolated	Labelling of Pick bodies	Labelling of Lewy bodies	Labelling of PSP tangles
8D8	NF-H, NF-M	NF side-arm	All or most +ve	90% +ve	+ve	+ve	ND
RT97	NF-H, NF-M	NF side-arm	All or most +ve	20-50% +ve	+ve	+ve	ND
1215	NF-H, NF-M	NF side-arm	All or most +ve	20-50% +ve	+ve	+ve	ND
EF10	NF-M	NF side-arm	All or more +ve	1% +ve	+ve	+ve	ND
147	NF-H, NF-M	NF side-arm	−ve	−ve	−ve	+ve	ND
F.S18	NF-H, NF-M	NF side-arm	−ve	−ve	ND	+ve	ND
155	NF-M	NF helical rod	−ve	−ve	ND	+ve	ND
Anti-IFA	All intermediate filaments	NF helical rod	−ve	−ve	ND	ND	ND

Polyclonal antisera

Anti-PHF	PHF	Not applicable	All or most +ve	90% +ve	ND	ND	+ve
Anti-NF-H	NF-H, NF-M	ND	−ve	−ve	−ve	+ve	ND
Anti-NF-M	NF-H, NF-M	ND	−ve	−ve	−ve	+ve	ND

ND = not determined; +ve = positive; −ve = negative.

Perry et al. 1985, Gambetti et al. 1980, Ihara et al. 1981, Anderton et al. 1982, 1985, Autilio-Gambetti et al. 1983, Elovaara et al. 1983, Probst et al. 1983b, Rasool et al. 1984, Rasool and Selkoe 1984, Kahn et al. 1980). Secondly, antibodies to preparations enriched in SDS-insoluble PHF stain tangles *in situ*, some of which recognize a variety of polypeptides in the 50,000-70,000 mol. wt range, but so far none of these proteins have been characterized further and unequivocally established as PHF precursors or constituents (Grundke-Iqbal et al. 1984, Ihara et al. 1983, Wang et al. 1984, Brion et al. 1985b, Yen et al. 1985). This latter group of anti-PHF antibodies label the isolated SDS-insoluble and morphologically identifiable neurofibrillary tangles in the light microscope but the cytoskeletal antibodies that stain tangles *in situ* often stain only a proportion, if any, of the SDS-insoluble tangles (Kosik et al. 1984, Rasool et al. 1984, Brion et al. 1985a). Ultrastructural studies of isolated PHF have also shown them to be different from neurofilaments and microtubules and the fragmentation pattern of PHF has been found to be inconsistent with a fibrous α-helical protein substructure which comprises the backbone of neurofilaments (Wischik et al. 1985).

We have studied a panel of eight monoclonal antibodies, one polyclonal anti-PHF serum and two polyclonal antineurofilament sera (Table 1). Monoclonal antibodies 8D8, RT97, 1215, BF10, 147, RS18 and 155 are all neurofilament-specific antibodies. Neurofilaments are a triplet of polypeptides, NF-H, NF-M and NF-L, corresponding to polypeptides with apparent molecular weights on SDS-PAGE of approximately 200,000, 160,000 and 70,000 (cf. Geisler et al. 1985). Antibodies 8D8, RT97, 1215, 147 and RS18 label most strongly on Western blots the NF—H, while antibodies BF10 and 155 recognize predominantly the NF-M polypeptide (Anderton et al. 1982). The monoclonal antibody, anti-IFA, recognizes a conserved epitope present in all intermediate filament polypeptides so far studied. This epitope is located towards the carboxy-terminus of the helical rod segment of intermediate filaments (Pruss et al. 1981, Geisler et al. 1985). The polyclonal neurofilament antisera were raised against either the NF-H or NF-M bands cut from SDS gels but both antisera react with both NF-H and NF-M because they contain antibodies to shared epitopes. The anti-PHF serum has been previously described (Brion et al. 1985b).

Alzheimer neurofibrillary tangles and their constituent PHF can be isolated as a crude preparation in SDS because of their relative insolubility. Western blots of SDS-insoluble PHF preparations with all the neurofilament antibodies did not produce any bands in the positions of the NF-H and NF-M polypeptides but a band corresponding to the top of the stacking gel was differentially labelled with antibodies 8D8, RT97, 1215 and the anti-PHF serum (Miller et al. 1986).

All the neurofilament antibodies stained cerebellum in a pattern characteristic of neurofilaments (cf. Anderton et al. 1982). In contrast, on Alzheimer brain sections, antibodies RT97, BF10, 1215 and 8D8 labelled virtually all of the neurofibrillary tangles (Figs 4 and 5) whereas antibodies 147, RS18, 155 and anti-IFA failed to stain the tangles as did the polyclonal anti-NF-H and anti-NF-M

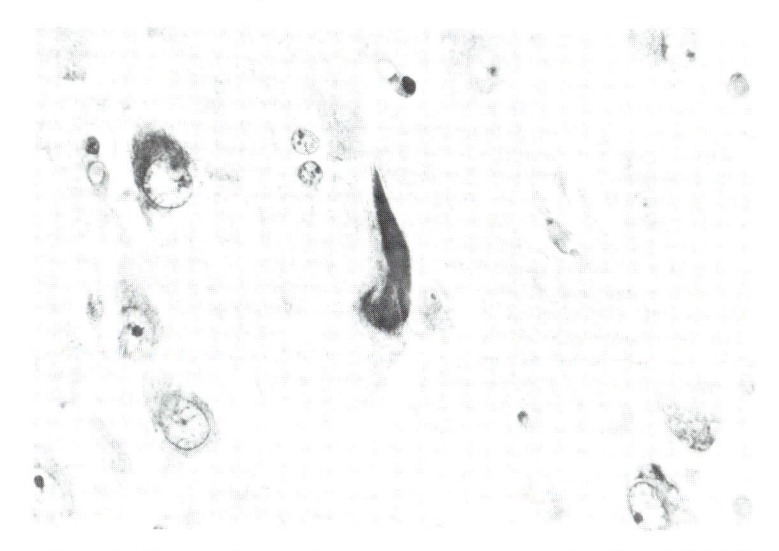

Fig. 4. Neurofibrillary tangle strongly reacting with monoclonal antibody RT97. (Paraffin section; PAP method ×448.)

Fig. 5. Small senile plaque. Abnormal neurites surrounding pale amyloid centre strongly react with monoclonal antibody RT97. (Paraffin section; PAP method ×448.)

sera (Table 1). The anti-PHF serum was raised against an enriched fraction of PHF and has previously been shown to label tangles and PHF *in situ* but not to stain axons containing neurofilaments (Brion *et al.* 1985b).

It was of interest, therefore, to begin mapping the relative positions of the epitopes for the monoclonal antibodies within the NF-H and NF-M polypeptides

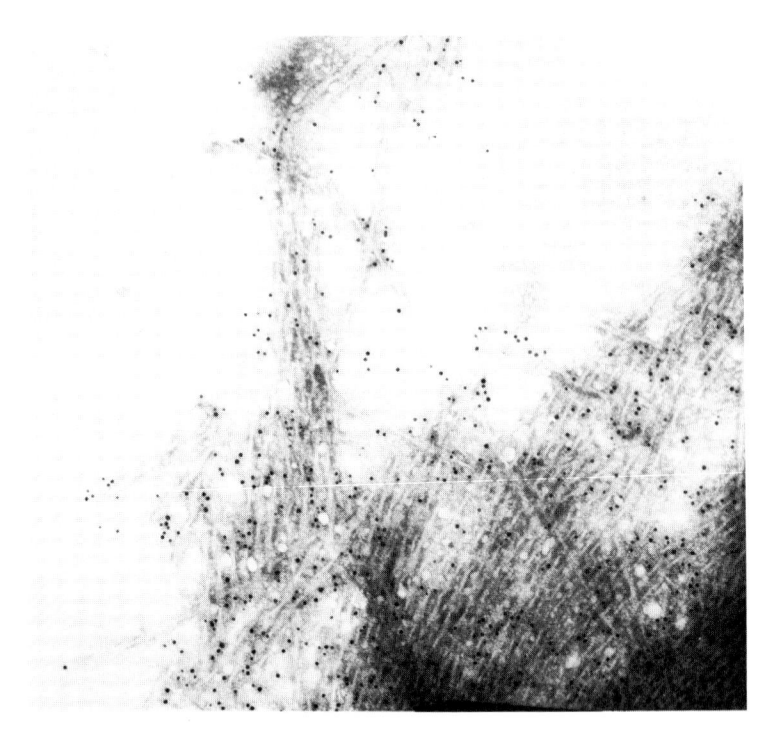

Fig. 6. Isolated PHF immunogold labelled with monoclonal antibody 8D8. (Negatively stained with PTA ×60,000.)

after chymotryptic digestion (Chin et al. 1983). Antibodies 8D8, RT97, 1215, BF10, 147 and RS18 were found to be in the side-arm fragments of NF-H and/or NF-M whereas antibodies 155 and anti-IFA were in the helical rod segment of the neurofilament polypeptides (Table 1) (Miller et al. 1986).

The very different antigenic specificities of the tangle-reactive neurofilament monoclonal antibodies and the anti-PHF serum made it important to establish that all the antibodies recognize the PHF *per se* and not either straight contaminating neurofilaments or other components. We have found that antibodies 8D8, RT97, BF10 and the anti-PHF serum do label the PHF by indirect immunogold staining of tangles *in situ* as assessed by electron microscopy (Brion et al. 1985b, Miller et al. 1986, Brion et al. in prep.). We have also studied the SDS-isolated enriched tangle fractions by immunolabelling in the light and electron microscopes (Miller et al. 1986).

Isolated tangle preparations were stained by double immunofluorescence with the monoclonal antibodies and the anti-PHF serum. Double immunostained preparations were analysed by counting the number of structures and small

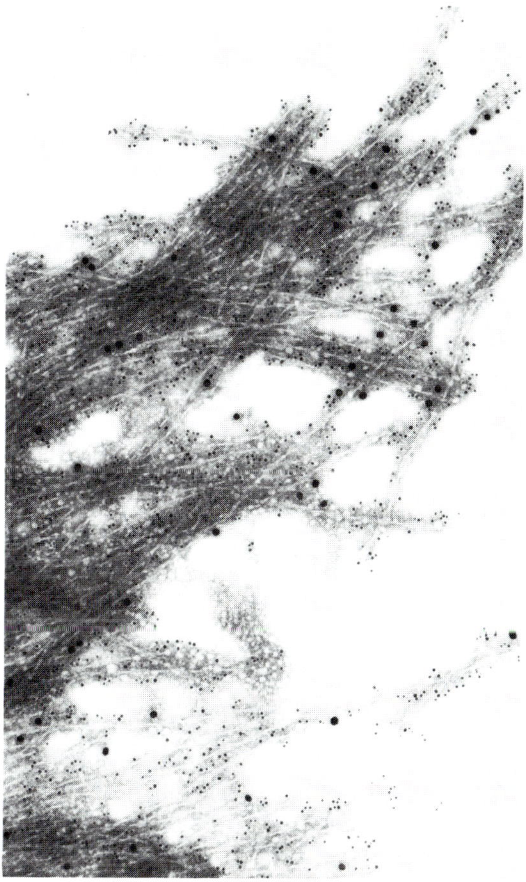

Fig. 7. Isolated PHF double immunogold labelled with monoclonal antibody 8D8 (5 nm gold particles) and rabbit anti-PHF (15 nm gold particles). (Negatively stained with PTA ×90,000.)

fragments stained by each antibody. On average, more than 90% of the anti-PHF positive structures were labelled with 8D8. Antibodies RT97 and 1215 labelled differing proportions of the SDS-insoluble anti-PHF labelled particles and BF10 labelled only very few. Table 1 summarizes the data on the proportion of tangles labelled by the various antibodies. Two different Alzheimer cases gave differing proportions labelled with antibodies RT97 and 1215 but 8D8 seemed to be independent of the specimen source.

The same 8D8 insoluble tangles were immunogold labelled with the monoclonal antibodies and the anti-PHF serum and analysed in the electron microscope. These SDS-insoluble tangles contained many PHF as well as some contaminating collagen and amyloid. More than 90% of the PHF were decorated by 8D8 (Fig. 6).

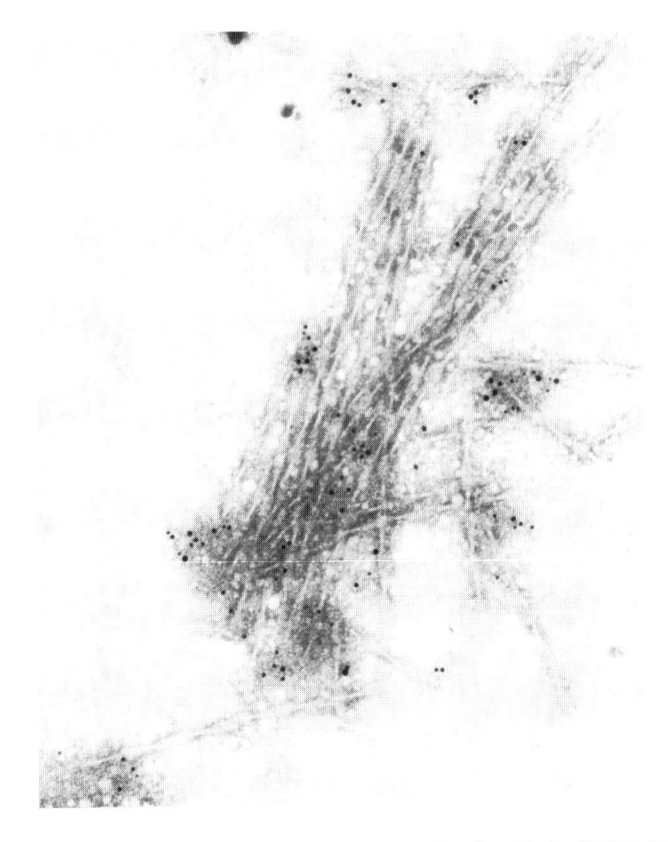

Fig. 8. Isolated PHF immunogold labelled with monoclonal antibody RT97. (Negatively stained with PTA ×90,000.)

Normal neurofilaments were not observed in any of these preparations. The PHF fractions were also double immunolabelled with 8D8 and anti-PHF using different sized gold particles conjugated to second antibodies. Still more than 90% of the PHF were labelled with both antibodies (Fig. 7) showing that the 8D8 and PHF epitopes are present on the same structures. Antibodies RT97 and 1215 labelled some but not all tangle fragments (Fig. 8). This labelling was often in a more patchy distribution than 8D8. When individual PHF were examined some were found to be labelled and others not at all. These results are consistent with the observations made by light microscopy. PHF were not seen to be labelled with antibody BF10 and this presumably reflects the low number of BF10-positive tangles seen by immunofluorescence and the much smaller sample observed in the electron microscope.

Thus, whilst neurofilament antibodies 8D8, RT97, 1215 and BF10 label all tangles *in situ* (Anderton *et al.* 1982, Miller *et al.* 1986), they label differing proportions of SDS-insoluble tangles in extracted material. 8D8 labels more than 90% whereas RT97 and 1215 label only 20–50% and BF10 just a small minority (Table 1) Rasool et al. 1984, Miller et al. 1986). Independent observations have demonstrated that tangles in situ are stained by only certain antibodies to the cytoskeleton (Anderton et al. 1982, Autilio-Gambetti et al. 1983, Gambetti et al. 1980, Kosik et al. 1984, Yen et al. 1981) which indicates that there are abnormal cytoskeletal elements in tangle bearing neurons. If labelling of tangles with these antibodies was due simply to admixing of normal neurofilaments and microtubules with PHF, then all antibodies labelling these organelles in human brain sections should also label tangles. This is borne out by the immunogold labelling of tangles in the electron microscope since antibodies 8D8, RT97, BF10 and the anti-PHF serum all labelled PHF and not simply admixed straight filaments. This result was found for both tangles in situ and isolated tangles. Perry et al. (1985) have also reported that one monoclonal and two polyclonal antibodies to neurofilaments label the majority of isolated PHF. In fact, we have found that in cases where Alzheimer tangles do contain many straight filaments, these are labelled by anti-PHF antibodies which show that such straight filaments are not simply normal neurofilaments (Brion unpublished results).

The labelling of subpopulations of isolated tangles by antibodies RT97 and 1215 is interesting and illustrates the variability of PHF composition which may be due to temporal changes since tangle formation and maturation probably extends over several years. Iqbal et al. (1984) have also reported variability in the solubility properties of PHF.

The tangle-reactive antibodies which we have examined all recognize epitopes on the side-arms of the NF-H and NF-M neurofilament polypeptides. Not all side-arm epitopes (e.g. 147, RS18) seem to be preserved in the PHF and those which are present in situ are not all equally stably associated with the insoluble PHF core, this suggests that proteolysis of neurofilaments may occur in any neurofilament/PHF transition. If proteolytic processing of neurofilaments is involved in PHF formation, then only the proteolytically more resistant fragments may contribute to PHF. Since the side-arms are known to be more resistant to proteolysis than the α-helical rod domains (Chin et al. 1983, Geisler et al. 1983), the substructure of PHF may not necessarily be fibrous which would be consistent with structural analyses (Wischik et al. 1985).

Masters et al. (1985) have recently reported that the majority of PHF can be solubilized in formic acid to give a 4000 mol. wt polypeptide. The amino-terminal sequence of this protein does not correspond to the known sequence of any neurofilament protein however, the sequences of the carboxy terminal side-arm extensions of NF-H and NF-M remain largely unknown (Geisler et al. 1985). It is not possible, therefore, to know whether this sequence bears any homology to the epitopes recognized by 8D8, RT97, 1215 and BF10. However, as described above, Selkoe et al. (1986) have questioned whether or not this 4 000 mol wt polypeptide is derived from PHF.

One hypothesis which could account for some aspects of the cytoskeletal contribution to neurofibrillary tangles assumes activation of an endogenous protease. A candidate is the calcium-dependent neutral protease which is known to be capable of degrading neurofilaments in injured neurons (Schlaepfer et al. 1985). A raised level of intracellular calcium as part of the degenerative process could destabilize microtubules and cause proteolysis of neurofilaments; aberrant protein phosphorylation might also be a result of a changed calcium metabolism (Sternberger et al. 1985). Overall, this might influence the accumulation of neurofilaments in the perikaryon. Proteolysis could cleave the neurofilament polypeptides resulting in destruction and loss of all or part of the α-helical domains and leave the side-arms as several fragments. The side-arm fragments would then adopt a new configuration, aggregate and be incorporated, perhaps along with non-cytoskeletal components, to form a stable structure i.e. PHF. The BF10, RT97 and 1215 epitopes must be on separate fragments from the 8D8 epitope and a proportion of them only loosely associated with the PHF since a fraction are relatively easily lost from PHF on isolation. The insoluble structure could be cross-linked as has been proposed but this may not be obligatory since some PHF can apparently be solubilized by extensive SDS extraction (Iqbal et al. 1984). A schematic representation of this hypothesis (without discriminating between NF-H and NF-M) is shown in Fig. 9. Since MAPs are probably involved in neurofilament–microtubule interaction, then proteolysed MAP fragments could be easily substituted in this scheme.

The above is a hypothesis aimed at accounting for the apparent contribution of neurofilaments to neurofibrillary tangles. It does not preclude additional events such as exogenous components or an infectious agent being incorporated into PHF nor the activation of a silent endogenous gene, the product of which may be a PHF component.

One important question is, obviously, how neurofibrillary tangles may contribute to the severe cerebral dysfunction, often leaving the patient unable to recognize time, place and even his own person. One way in which they do this is to kill the cell: a relationship has been demonstrated between the severity of tangle formation and nerve cell loss in the hippocampus (Ball 1977). Furthermore, some of the tangles originally located in nerve cells can still be demonstrated extracellularly once the neuron is dead (Probst et al. 1982).

The nerve cell processes within the senile plaque also contain PHF as described above (Kidd 1964, Krigman 1965, Gonatas et al. 1967). Dendrites within senile plaques are often grossly abnormal, as can be shown with the Golgi technique (Probst et al. 1983a). So far it has not been possible to demonstrate if the PHF-containing dendrites are identical with those whose shape is abnormal. If this is the case, the alteration of the dendrites i.e. the synapse-bearing cell process, would be closely related to the presence of PHF. Since the degree of dementia is paralleled by the number of plaques and tangles (Blessed et al. 1968), it is probable that these intracellular morphological alterations interfere severely with

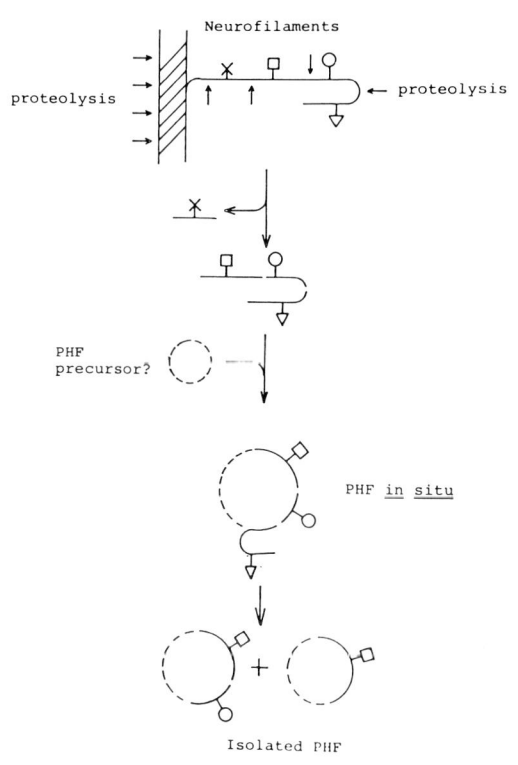

Fig. 9. Schematic representation of how neurofilaments may contribute to PHF. Neurofilaments may be cleaved proteolytically (↑—cleavage sites) some polypeptide segments and therefore epitopes being lost during this process (e.g. ✗ epitope for antibodies 147 and RS18) with others being incorporated into PHF. Of the latter some are easily lost on isolation of PHF (e.g. ↑ epitope for BF10) whereas others are differentially retained (e.g. ↑ epitopes for RT97 and 1215; ▯ epitopes for 8D8). Non-neurofilamentous molecules may also contribute to PHF (i.e. ○). This scheme makes no attempt to differentiate between NF-H and NF-M nor does it imply that the relative positions of particular epitopes on neurofilament side-arms are known.

neuronal function, even if they do not induce cell death. Because of the role played by the cytoskeleton in axonal transport and secretion, it is also conceivable that the deficiency of neurotransmitter synthesis observable in DAT (for review see Berger 1984) is related to the cytoskeletal alterations described here.

As mentioned in the introduction, the cytoskeleton participates in many cellular functions, which include cell migration, determination of cell shape, endocytosis, exocytosis, intracellular organization and transport of cytoplasmic constitutents. In neurons all these functions, especially the maintenance of the complicated shape and the transport of substances and organelles in axons and dendrites, are probably important for the maintenance of mental health. In regard to the function of the various parts of the neuronal cytoskeleton, an observation made by Ludwig and Nancy Sternberger (Sternberger and Sternberger 1983) may be very important. They noticed that in normal neurons, axonal neurofilaments contain phosphorylated epitopes, while those in the perikarya do not. Thus the presence or absence of phosphorylated neurofilaments indicates an important functional and morphological differentiation of the various parts of the neuron. More recently the same authors (Sternberger et al. 1985) demonstrated that in Alzheimer's disease phosphorylated neurofilament epitopes appear in tangles, i.e. in the perikaryon. This finding was confirmed by Haugh et al. (1986). Considering the relationship between the functional differentiation of the various parts of the normal neuron and phosphorylation of neurofilaments, the abnormally localized phosphorylated epitopes might be related to severe dysfunction of the affected neuron. With the advent of immunocytochemistry, these still poorly understood functional and morphological relationships become accessible to both biochemical and morphological studies. The probability that the appearance of phosphorylated epitopes of neurofilament protein represents a decisive event in the pathogenesis of the clinical symptoms is further increased by the observation of phosphorylated perikaryonal epitopes in Pick's disease — a disease which is clinically similar to Alzheimer's but morphologically different (Ulrich et al. 1986).

Pick Bodies

Pick bodies are spherical inclusions in the perikaryon of affected neurons. They contain a mixture of straight 10-15 nm filaments, membranous and amorphous material (Brion et al. 1973, Wisniewski et al. 1972, Takauchi et al. 1984). PHF are sometimes found mixed in with straight filaments in the Pick bodies (Schochet et al. 1968). So far, there have been no reports describing the isolation of Pick bodies but several laboratories have studied the immunochemical relationship of Pick bodies to Alzheimer tangles. We have shown that with our panel of neurofilament monoclonal antibodies, Pick bodies and Alzheimer tangles are stained by the same antibodies; those antibodies unreactive with Alzheimer tangles failed to stain Pick bodies (Fig. 10, Table 1) (Probst et al. 1983b). We have not tested our anti-PHF serum on Pick bodies, but Rasool and Selkoe (1985) reported that they were stained by their anti-PHF serum. Thus it may be that similar processing of neurofilaments occurs in diseased neurons in Pick's disease as in Alzheimer's disease. However, these immunochemical observations report on only a small fraction of the total neurofilament polypeptide mass and so there could well be differences in the neurofilamentous contributions to both types of inclusion. They do indicate, however, that if immunochemical cross-reactivity between these lesions and neurofilaments is not spurious but due to neurofilament polypeptides (whole or fragments) being integral constituents, then ultrastructural analyses in isolation are of limited value for establishing the likely origin of PHF and Pick body filaments. Clearly, it is now essential to obtain

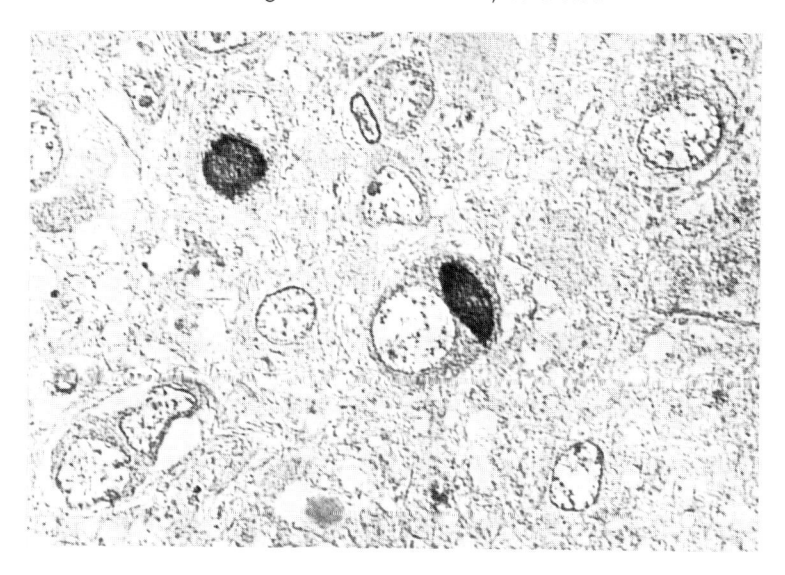

Fig. 10. Pick bodies in fascia dentata showing strong immunoreactivity with monoclonal antibody RT97. Semithin plastic section. (Nomarski optics. PAP method ×1,000.)

sequence data on all the constituent proteins including those bearing the epitopes labelled by the different types of tangle-reactive antibodies.

Lewy Bodies

We have now found that Lewy bodies which are a characteristic pathological feature of Parkinson's disease are also stained by neurofilament antibodies (Kahn et al. 1985). The classical Lewy body with a core and halo is only stained by these antibodies in the halo, the core remains unstained. Cytoplasmic inclusions which lack the core and halo organization are also found in other neurons in this disease and they were uniformly stained by all the neurofilament antibodies tested. These results are similar to those of Goldman et al. (1983) and demonstrate that the changes in neurofilament organization in Parkinson's disease are different to those in Alzheimer's and Pick's diseases.

Progressive Supranuclear Palsy

Neurofilamentous accumulations are found in neurons of mid-brain and pontine nuclei in progressive supranuclear palsy (PSP). These tangles are constituted by straight 10 15 nm filaments (Tellez Nagel and Wisniewski 1973; Bugiani et al. 1979), although "twisted" filaments with constrictions of up to 300 nm (Takauchi et al. 1983) have been described, mixed with the straight filaments or alone (Yagishita et al. 1979). We found that tangles in pontine nuclei in a case of PSP were labelled by our anti-PHF serum. Dickson et al. (1985) also observed a labelling of angles in PSP using monoclonal antibodies to PHF and to neurofilaments.

The aetiology of the degeneration and neuronal loss in these neurological diseases remains unknown. It is reasonable to assume that understanding the chemical composition and structure of the characteristic lesions discussed here will enable us to identify specific abnormalities in protein metabolism which results in a deranged cytoskeleton. This in turn may lead us to the key events which initiate the neurodegeneration and hopefully enable us to formulate new strategies for prevention or treatment of these diseases.

ACKNOWLEDGEMENTS

This work was supported by the Medical Research Council and The Wellcome Trust of the United Kingdom, Lekime-Ropsy Fund of Belgium and Sandoz Ltd.

REFERENCES

Anderton, B. H. (1981). Intermediate filaments: a family of homologous structures. *J. Muscle Res. Cell Motil.* **2**, 141-166.

Anderton, B. H. (1982). The neuronal cytoskeleton: proteins and pathology. In "Recent advances in neuropathology" (W. T. Smith and J. B. Cavanagh, eds) Vol 2, pp. 29-51. Churchill Livingstone, Edinburgh.

Anderton, B. H., Breinburg, D., Downes, M. J., Green, P. J., Tomlinson, B. E., Ulrich, J., Wood, J. N. and Kahn, J. (1982). Monoclonal antibodies show that neurofibrillary tangles and neurofilaments share antigenic determinants. *Nature* **298**, 84-86.

Anderton, B. H., Haugh, M. C., Kahn, J., Miller, C., Probst, A. and Ulrich, J. (1985). The nature of neurofibrillary tangles. In "Advances in applied neurological sciences, senile dementia of the Alzheimer type" (J. Traber and W. H. Gispen, eds) pp. 205-216. Springer-Verlag, Berlin and Heidelberg.

Autilio-Gambetti, L., Gambetti, P. and Crane, R. C. (1983). Paired helical filaments: relatedness to neurofilaments shown by silver staining and reactivity with monoclonal antibodies. "Banbury Reports 15: Biochemical aspects of Alzheimer's disease" (R. Katzman, ed.) pp. 117-124. Cold Spring Harbor Laboratory, Cold Spring Harbor, USA.

Ball, M. J. (1977). Neuronal loss, neurofibrillary tangles and granulovacuolar degeneration in the hippocampus with ageing and dementia. *Acta Neuropathol.* **37**, 111-118.

Berger, B. (1984). Anomalies des neurotransmetteurs dans la maladie de Alzheimer. *Rev. Neurol.* **140**, 539-552.

Blessed, G., Tomlinson, B. E. and Roth, M. (1968). The association between quantitative measurements of dementia and of senile changes in the cerebral gray matter of elderly subjects. *J. Psychiat.* **114**, 797-805.

Brion, S., Mikol, J. and Psimaras, A. (1973). Recent findings in Pick's disease. In "Progress in neuropathology" (H. M. Zimmerman, ed.) Vol. 2, pp. 421-452. Grune & Stratton, New York and London.

Brion, J. P., van den Bosch de Aguilar, P. and Flament-Durand, J. (1985a). Senile dementia of the Alzheimer type: morphological and immunocytochemical studies. In "Advances in applied neurological sciences, senile dementia of the Alzheimer type" (J. Traber and W. H. Gispen, eds) pp. 164-174. Springer-Verlag, Berlin and Heidelberg.

Brion, J. P., Couck, A. M., Passareiro, E. and Flament-Durand, J. (1985b). Neurofibrillary tangles of Alzheimer's disease: an immunocytochemical study. *J. Submicrosc. Cytol.* **17**, 89-96.

Bugiani, O., Mancardi, G. L., Brusa, A. and Ederli, A. (1979). The fine structure of subcortical neurofibrillary tangles in progressive supranuclear palsy. *Acta Neuropathol. (Berlin)* **15**, 147-152.

Chin, T. K., Eagles, P. A. M. and Maggs, A. (1983). The proteolytic digestion of ox neurofilaments with trypsin and α-chymotrypsin. *Biochem. J.* **215**, 239-252.

Dickson, D. W., Kress, Y., Crowe, A. and Yen, S.-H. (1985). Monoclonal antibodies to Alzheimer neurofibrillary tangles. 2. Demonstration of a common antigenic determinant between ANT and neurofibrillary degeneration in progressive supranuclear palsy. *Am. J. Pathol.* **120**, 292-303.

Elovaara, I., Paetau, A., Lehto, V.-P., Dahl, D., Virtanen, I. and Palo, J. (1983). Immunocytochemical studies of Alzheimer neuronal perikarya with intermediate filament antisera. *J. Neurol. Sci.* **62**, 315-326.

Gambetti, P., Valasco, M. E., Dahl, D., Bignami, A., Roessman, U. and Sindely, S. P. (1980). Alzheimer neurofibrillary tangles: an immunohistochemical study. In "Aging of the brain and dementia" (L. Amaducci, A. N. Davison and P. Antuono, eds) "Aging" Vol. 13. Raven Press, New York.

Geisler, N., Kaufman, E., Fischer, S., Plessman, U. and Weber, K. (1983). Neurofilament architecture combines structural principles of intermediate filaments with carboxy-terminal extensions increasing in size between triplet proteins. *EMBO J.* **2**, 1295-1302.

Geisler, N., Fischer, S., Vanderkerckhove, J., Van Damme, J., Plessmann, U. and Weber, K. (1985). Protein-chemical characterisation of NF-H, the largest mammalian neurofilament component; intermediate filament-type sequences followed by a unique carboxy-terminal extension. *EMBO J.* **4**, 57-63.

Goldman, J. E., Yen, S.-H., Chin, F. C. and Peress, N. S. (1983). Lewy bodies of Parkinson's disease contain neurofilament antigens. *Science* **221**, 1092-1084.

Gonatas, N. K., Anderson, W. and Evangelista, I. (1967). The contribution of altered synapses in the senile plaque: an electron microscope study in Alzheimer's dementia. *J. Neuropathol. Exp. Neurol.* **26**, 25-39.

Grundke-Iqbal, K., Johnson, A. B., Wisniewski, H. M., Terry, R. D. and Iqbal, K. (1979). Evidence that Alzheimer neurofibrillary tangles originate from neurotubules. *Lancet* **i**, 578-580.

Grundke-Iqbal, K., Iqbal, K., Tung, Y.-C. and Wisniewski, H. M. (1984). Alzheimer paired helical filaments: immunochemical identification of polypeptides. *Acta Neuropathol.* **62**, 259-267.

Haugh, M. C., Probst, A., Ulrich, J., Kahn, J. and Anderton, B. H. (1986). Alzheimer neurofibrillary tangles contain phosphorylated and hidden neurofilament epitopes. *J. Neurol. Neurosurg. Psychiatry* (in press).

Hoffman, P. N., Thompson, G. W., Griffin, J. W. and Price, D. L. (1985). Changes in neurofilament transport coincide with alterations in the caliber of axons in regenerating motor fibres. *J. Cell Biol.* **101**, 1332-1340.

Ihara, Y., Nukina, N., Sugita, H. and Toyokura, Y. (1981). Staining of Alzheimer's neurofibrillary tangles with antiserum against 200K components of neurofilament. *Proc. Jap. Acad.* **57**(Ser. B), 152-156.

Ihara, Y., Nukina, N., Sugita, H. and Toyokura, Y. (1981). Staining of Alzheimer's neurofibrillary tangles with antiserum against 200K components of neurofilament. *Proc. Jap. Acad.* **57**(Ser. B), 152-156.

Ihara, Y., Abraham, C. and Selkoe, D. J. (1983). Antibodies to paired helical filaments in Alzheimer's disease do not recognise normal brain proteins. *Nature* **304**, 727-730.

Iqbal, K., Zaidi, T., Thompson, C. H., Merz, P. A. and Wisniewski, H. M. (1984). Alzheimer paired helical filaments: bulk isolation, solubility, and protein composition. *Acta Neuropathol.* **62**, 167-177.

Kahn, J., Anderton, B. H., Gibb, W. R. G., Lees, A. J., Wells, F. R. and Marsden, C. D. (1985). Neuronal filaments in Alzheimer's, Pick's and Parkinson's diseases. *N. Engl. J. Med.* **313**, 520-521.

Kahn, J., Green, P. G., Thorpe, R. and Anderton, B. H. (1980). Immunohistochemistry of neurofilaments in Alzheimer's disease. *J. Clin. Exp. Gerontol.* **2**, 199-210.

Katzman, R. (1976). The prevalence and malignancy of Alzheimer disease. *Arch. Neurol.* **33**, 217-218.

Kidd, M. (1963). Paired helical filaments in electron microscopy of Alzheimer's disease. *Nature* **197**, 192-193.

Kidd, M. (1964). Alzheimer's disease—an electron microscopic study. *Brain* **87**, 307-321.

Kosik, K. S., Duffy, L. K., Dowling, M. M., Abraham, C., McCluskey, A. and Selkoe, D. J. (1984). Microtubule-associated protein 2: monoclonal antibodies demonstrate the selective incorporation of certain epitopes into Alzheimer neurofibrillary tangles. *Proc. Natl Acad. Sci. USA* **81**, 7941-7945.

Krigman, M. R., Feldman, R. G. and Bensch, K. (1965). Alzheimer's presenile dementia. A histochemical and electron microscopical study. *Lab. Invest.* **14**, 381-396.

Lazarides, E. (1982). Intermediate filaments: a chemically heterogeneous, developmentally regulated class of proteins. *Ann. Rev. Biochem.* **51**, 219-250.

Masters, C. L., Multhaup, G., Simms, G., Pottgiesser, J., Martins, R. N. and Beyreuther, K. (1985). Neuronal origin of a cerebral amyloid: neurofibrillary tangles of Alzheimer's disease contain the same protein as the amyloid plaque cores and blood vessels. *EMBO J.* **4**, 2757-2763.

Metuzals, J., Montpetit, V. and Clapin, D. F. (1981). Organization of the neurofilamentous network. *Cell. Tiss. Res.* **214**, 455-482.

Miller, C. C. J., Brion, J.-P., Calvert, R., Chin, T. K., Eagles, P. A. M., Downes, M. J., Flament-Durand, J., Haugh, M., Kahn, J., Probst, A., Ulrich, J. and Anderton, B. H. (1986). Alzheimer's paired helical filaments share epitopes with neurofilament side arms. *EMBO J.* **5**, 269-276.

Nukina, N. and Ihara, Y. (1983). Immunocytochemical study on senile plaques in Alzheimer's disease. *Proc. Jap. Acad.* **59**(Ser. B), 284-292.

Perry, E. K., Tomlinson, B. E., Blessed, G., Bergmann, K., Gibson, P. H. and Perry, R. H. (1978). Correlation of cholinergic abnormalities with senile plaques and mental test scores in senile dementia. *Br. Med. J.* **2**, 1457-1459.

Perry, G., Rizzuto, N., Autilio-Gambetti, L. and Gambetti, P. (1985). Paired helical filaments from Alzheimer disease patients contain cytoskeletal components. *Proc. Natl Acad. Sci. USA* **82**, 3916-3920.

Probst, A., Ulrich, J. and Heitz, Ph.D. (1982). Senile dementia of Alzheimer type: astroglial reaction to extracellular neurofibrillary tangles in the hippocampus. An immunocytochemical and electron microscopic study. *Acta Neuropathol.* **57**, 75-79.

Probst, A., Basler, V., Bron, B. and Ulrich, J. (1983a). Neuritic plaques in senile dementia of Alzheimer type. A Golgi analysis in the hippocampal region. *Brain Res.* **268**, 249-254.

Probst, A., Anderton, B. H., Ulrich, J., Kohler, R., Kahn, J. and Heitz, P. U. (1983b). Pick's disease: an immunocytochemical study of neuronal changes. Monoclonal antibodies show that Pick bodies share antigenic determinants with neurofibrillary tangles and neurofilaments. *Acta Neuropathol.* **60**, 175-182.

Pruss, R. M., Mirsky, R., Raff, M. C., Thorpe, R., Dowding, A. J. and Anderton, B. H. (1981). Intermediate filaments contain a common as well as class-specific proteins all of which share an antigenic domain. *Cell* **27**, 419-421.

Rasool, C. G. and Selkoe, D. J. (1984). Alzheimer's disease: exposure of neurofilament immunoreactivity in SDS-insoluble paired helical filaments. *Brain Res.* **322**, 194-198.

Rasool, C. G. and Selkoe, D. J. (1985). Sharing of specific antigens by degenerating neurons in Pick's disease and Alzheimer's disease. *N. Engl. J. Med.* **312**, 700-705.

Rasool, C. G., Abraham, C., Anderton, B. H., Haugh, M., Kahn, J. and Selkoe, D. J. (1984). Alzheimer's disease: immunoreactivity of neurofibrillary tangles with anti-neurofilament and anti-paired helical filament antibodies. *Brain Res.* **310**, 249-260.

Schlaepfer, W. W., Lee, C., Lee, V. M.-Y. and Zimmerman, U.-J. P. (1985). An immunoblot study of neurofilament degradation *in situ* and during calcium-activated proteolysis. *J. Neurochem.* **44**, 502-509.

Schochet, S. S., Lampert, P. W. and Lindenberg, R. (1968). Fine structure of the Pick and Hirano bodies in a case of Pick's disease. *Acta Neuropathol.* **11**, 330-337.

Selkoe, D. J., Ihara, Y. and Salazar, F. J. (1982). Alzheimer's disease: insolubility of partially purified paired helical filaments in sodium dodecyl sulphate and urea. *Science* **215**, 1243-1245.

Selkoe, D. J., Abraham, C. R., Podlisny, M. B. and Duffy, L. (1986). Isolation of low molecular weight proteins from amyloid plaque fibres in Alzheimer's disease. *J. Neurochem.* **45**, 1820-1834.

Sternberger, L. A. and Sternberger, N. H. (1983). Monoclonal antibodies distinguish phosphorylated and non phosphorylated forms of neurofilaments in situ. *Proc. Natl Acad. Sci. USA* **80**, 6126-6130.

Sternberger, N. H., Sternberger, L. A. and Ulrich, J. (1985). Aberrant neurofilament phosphorylation in Alzheimer's disease. *Proc. Natl Acad. Sci. USA* **82**, 4274-4276.

Takauchi, S., Mizuhara, T. and Miyoshi, K. (1983). Unusual paired helical filaments in progressive supranuclear palsy. *Acta Neuropathol. (Berlin)* **59**, 225-228.

Takauchi, S., Hosomi, M., Marassigan, S., Sato, M., Hayashi, S. and Miyoshi, K. (1984). An ultrastructural study of Pick bodies. *Acta Neuropathol.* **64**, 344-348.

Tellez-Nagel, I. and Wisniewski, H. M. (1973). Ultrastructure of neurofibrillary "tangles" in Steele-Richardson-Olszewski syndrome. *Arch. Neurol.* **29**, 324-327.

Ulrich, J., Probst, A. and Wuest, M. (1986). The brain diseases causing senile dementia. *J. Neurol.* (in press).

Wang, G. P., Grundke-Iqbal, I., Kascsak, R. J., Iqbal, K. and Wisniewski, H. M. (1984). Alzheimer neurofibrillary tangles: monoclonal antibodies to inherent antigen(s). *Acta Neuropathol.* **62**, 268-275.

Wilcock, G. K., Esiri, M. M., Bowen, D. M. and Smith, C. T. T. (1982). Alzheimer disease. Correlation of cortical choline acetyltransferase activity with severity of dementia and histological abnormalities. *J. Neurol. Sci.* **57**, 407-417.

Wischik, C. M., Crowther, R. A., Stewart, M. and Roth, M. (1985). Subunit structure of paired helical filaments in Alzheimer's disease. *J. Cell Biol.* **100**, 1905-1912.

Wisniewski, H. M. and Wen, G. Y. (1985). Substructure of paired helical filaments from Alzheimer's disease neurofibrillary tangles. *Acta Neuropathol. (Berlin)* **66**, 173-176.

Wisniewski, H. M., Coblentz, J. and Terry, R. D. (1972). Pick's disease. A clinical and ultrastructural study. *Arch. Neurol.* **26**, 97-108.

Wisniewski, K., Jervis, G. A., Moretz, R. C. and Wisniewski, H. M. (1979). Alzheimer neurofibrillary tangles in diseases other than senile and presenile dementia. *Ann. Neurol.* **5**, 288-294.

Wisniewski, H. M., Merz, P. A. and Iqbal, K. (1984). Ultrastructure of paired helical filaments of Alzheimer's neurofibrillary tangle. *J. Neuropath. Exp. Neurol.* **43**, 643-656.

Wuerker, R. B. and Kirkpatrick, J. B. (1972). Neuronal microtubules, neurofilaments and microfilaments. *Int. Rev. Cytol.* **33**, 45-75.

Yagishita, S., Itoh, Y., Amano, N., Nakano, T. and Saitoh, A. (1979). Ultrastructure of neurofibrillary tangles in progressive supranuclear palsy. *Acta Neuropathol. (Berlin)* **48**, 27-30.

Yagishita, S., Itoh, Y., Nan, W. and Amano, N. (1981). Reappraisal of the fine structure of Alzheimer's neurofibrillary tangles. *Acta Neuropathol.* **54**, 239-246.

Yen, S.-H. and Kress, Y. (1983). The effect of chemical reagents or proteases on the ultrastructure of paired helical filaments. *In* "Biological aspects of Alzheimer's disease", Banbury Reports No. 15 (R. Katzman, ed.) pp. 155-165. Cold Spring Harbor Laboratory, Cold Spring Harbor, USA.

Yen, S.-H., Gaskin, F. and Terry, R. D. (1981). Immunocytochemical studies of neurofibrillary tangles. *Am. J. Pathol.* **104**, 77-89.

Yen, S.-H., Crowe, A. and Dickson, D. W. (1985). Monoclonal antibodies to Alzheimer neurofibrillary tangles. *Am. J. Pathol.* **120**, 282-291.

Discussion

Reichenfeld: Is there a possibility of differentiating between different cases of DAT by means of labelling tangles?

Anderton: Yes, there may be a possibility. We do not have enough data to be able to say that there is variability which is quite predictable. However, we do have suggestions that there is heterogeneity from case to case. For example, the monoclonal antibodies which label a proportion of tangles; the proportion does seem to vary somewhat with the source of material in individual cases. But, so far, we have not done enough studies, nor have we actually looked at the case histories of those individuals to see whether any of these change, but there is certainly variation from individual to individual and that now needs to be looked into.

Sir Martin Roth: You appear to have concluded that the neurofibrillary tangle is made up of normal cytoskeletal protofilaments such as neurofilaments. One would expect such protofilaments to show fraying when filaments unwind and, under certain conditions, extensive breakages occur. Yet, in the Cambridge studies you have quoted (Wischik *et al.* 1985) the typical break is a clear-cut transverse break without any hint of fraying. This was one line of evidence favouring a double helical stack of transversely disposed subunits for the paired helical filament—a structure possibly made up of a *de novo* assembly of an aberrant protein.

Anderton: Depending on the time of proteolysis, cleavage of the neurofilament protein fragments will occur to differing degrees. Under certain conditions, the fragments bearing the determinants for the antibodies against neurofilaments and labelling Alzheimer tangles are cleaved off. The filament core will carry side-arm fragments but structurally modified, which could form the subunit structure identified by Wischik and Crowther as the building block of the PHF. Individual neurofilaments and associated proteins of microtubules are released from the main structural units, somehow forming a conformation on their own. This would be consistent with the studies of Wischik and Crowther.

Sir Martin Roth: They have worked with a very pure preparation of PHF. Does your explanation suppose that the side-arms are essential, indispensable components of the PHF structure?

Anderton: No. It is not possible to say from our and others' data on antibody labelling how many of the side-arms are involved in forming the subunit of the PHF or whether they are just a component. It is impossible to say what the proportion of that subunit derived from neurofilaments is.

Brion: Regarding Pick's bodies, is there a special pattern of monoclonal marking in Pick's bodies or is it the same as in neurofibrillary tangles? Were they also tested with antisera?

Anderton: We have used the same antibodies for staining Pick's bodies as in the Alzheimer tangles. Although we did not use an anti-PHF serum, others have done so.

Brion: Is there an accumulation of neurofilaments resembling Pick's bodies in axon reaction of neurons of various origin, especially in the small pyramidal neurons?

Anderton: The question of axon reaction is complicated by the fact that neurofilaments are highly phosphorylated in axons and that the majority of antibodies from different laboratories are in fact detecting phosphorylated determinants on neurofilaments but react weakly if at all, with non-phosphorylated neurofilaments. Antibodies specifically against non-phosphorylated neurofilaments tend to stain all cell bodies of many more neurons otherwise unstained with the other antibodies. It was shown by others that after sciatic nerve lesions in mice the axon reaction in the spinal cord corresponded quite closely with antibody staining. However, whether this is due to abnormal neurofilament accumulation or whether neurofilaments normally present in the cell body become abnormally phosphorylated remains to be clarified.

Cellular Systems in Aging—Implications and Outlook

George S. Roth

*National Institute of Health,
Baltimore City Hospitals, Baltimore, Maryland, USA*

I think that it is clear that despite the rather concise nature of the title of this session, "Cellular Systems in Aging", the data presented has been extremely diverse. To tie everything together I think it is necessary to divide the discussion into two parts; first, to consider the phenomena that have been described and then, secondly, to look a little more at the mechanisms.

Basically there have been two kinds of presentations: those on the aging of cellular systems and those on the aging of neuroendocrine and neurohumoral systems. From the paper by Dr Hayflick and Dr Holliday, which dealt with *in vitro* cellular aging or, if you will, *in vitro* programmed cessation of cell division, it seems reasonably clear that at least some cell types must age intrinsically. Probably this intrinsic cellular aging is related to the *in vivo* dysfunctions that occur at the cellular level as well. The best evidence for this comes from one experiment that Dr Hayflick discussed, which was first done by George Martin. Fibroblasts taken from donors of different ages showed differences in *in vitro* division potential, which are inversely proportional to the amount of the *in vivo* lifespan completed. Secondly, there were the differences in the *in vitro* lifespans of fibroblasts taken from different species which have different maximal longevities. Finally, a great number of biochemical changes are seen in fibroblasts aging *in vitro*.

Many of these mimic in some way the kinds of changes that we see *in vivo*. Now, certainly, we do not die from a loss of fibroblasts and I think Dr Hayflick made that point. However, it is conceivable that there may be two applications for the information obtained from these kinds of studies. First of all, changes in division potential may result in some functional changes. In the case of fibroblasts, one can imagine a phenomenon such as impaired wound healing which is a well characterized manifestation of aging. Secondly, as Dr Hayflick pointed out, cessation of fibroblast division *in vitro* does provide an interesting model with which to explore the mechanisms involved in cellular aging.

We can make a logical transition from the division problem of the fibroblast to the immune system as Dr Beregi discussed. A number of the changes (the immune dysfunctions that occur during aging) may be the result of an impaired ability of lymphocytes to respond to challenges, e.g. to respond to antigenic stimuli. This model can be used *in vitro* as well. In order to stimulate DNA synthesis and cell division, lymphocyte cultures can be treated with plant lectins. In response to these agents, certain types of lymphocytes show a very marked impaired ability to divide and to incorporate thymidine into DNA. Thus, this phenomenon might be somewhat analogous to the altered ability of fibroblasts to respond to a serum signal which enables the cells to propagate themselves *in vitro*. If serum is not included in the cultures, there is no division.

One question with regard to Dr Beregi's paper that needs to be answered is whether or not structural changes in mitochondria and lipofuscin accumulation are causes or effects of immune dysfunction. What do they really mean in terms of the cells' impaired ability to respond to antigens or to perform their cellular functions?

Next, beyond the intrinsic aspects of immunological (lymphocyte) aging, we must recognize that the neurohumoral or neuroendocrine systems also impacts on the ability of the immune system to function. It has been known for some time that if lymphocytes are transplanted from old donors into young or vice-versa, some of the age change seems to be intrinsic to the cells. However, there are some host factors which can account for perhaps 20–25% of the dysfunctions. Thus, we know that some sort of a neurohumoral factor exists within the host to modulate the ability of lymphocytes to respond, and it is also known that thymic hormones, such as thymosin and other thymic-derived hormones can in some cases reconstitute some of the age-related changes in immune functional capacity.

These observations bring us next to Dr Meites and his discussion of neuroendocrine changes. We know and have known for some time, that many investigators consider the hypothalamus to be a biological clock, to be a pacemaker of aging. There have been a number of reports of changes in hypothalamic threshold during aging. The fact that the aged hypothalamus seems to require higher levels of stimulation in order to exert its proper control in older individuals supports this hypothesis. One question that emerges from Dr Meites's paper with regard to the hypothalamic decline in neuroendocrine aging is how alterations in norepinephrine metabolism result in reduced luteinizing hormone-releasing hormone (LHRH) secretion. Exactly what is the signal transduction mechanism that occurs at that point? The hypothalamic changes that he described could, of course, be due, as was suggested, to neuronal loss or even more likely to neuronal degeneration.

Dr Anderton, showed some of the structural changes that occur in the brain and central nervous system with age. Knowing that some of the symptoms of dementia (plaques and tangles) do apparently occur as a consequence of normal aging, although to a lesser degree, one wonders whether these are truly qualitative differences. Alternatively, are there simply quantitative differences between normal aging and some of these neurological diseases?

Having reviewed the data, let me now briefly consider the mechanisms that I envision to be common to the aging of all of these systems. Dr Holliday suggested that many of these changes may be due to something occurring at the genomic level: mutations, errors, damage or even some epigenetic modification of gene expression. Dr Hayflick discussed nuclear transplantation experiments in which it was found that nuclei from late passage fibroblasts can confer senescence on early passage cells. I believe that one can do the same thing to tumour cells if senescent nuclei are transplanted. These observations suggest that something at the genomic level exerts control of division potential.

Furthermore, essentially all of the systems discussed in this session—fibroblasts, lymphocytes, endocrine cells, and neurons—may have the following common signal sequence for regulating their particular functions and the changes that occur with age. First, there must be a stimulus. In the case of fibroblasts this is a serum factor. In the case of neurons, this may be a neurotransmitter. In the case of lymphocytes this may be some foreign antigen. The stimuli must then interact with receptors which are generally proteins located on the surface of cells. In the case of some agents, however, (e.g. steroid hormones) receptors are intracellular. After this initial interaction there is a sequence of signal transduction events which can vary depending on the stimulus and the cell type in question. Some examples of this are the production of cyclic nucleotides from the adenylate and guanylate cyclase enzymes which are connected to some types of hormone receptors. In other cases we may have changes in ion fluxes. Calcium is an ion which acts very much like a second messenger. It can be mobilized in response to changes in phospholipid metabolism as well as by other mechanisms. It may come from outside the cell in some cases, or it may come from intracellular sources such as mitochondria or the endoplasmic reticulum. Finally, after all of these various single transduction events have occurred, the cell makes a response. In the case of nerve cells it may be the conduction of a nerve impulse. In the case of the lynphocytes it may be antibody production or cell division. In the case of fibroblasts it is of course cell division. In the case of endocrine cells it is the production of particular hormones.

From our own work at the National Institute on Aging we are seeing certain patterns emerge with respect to the kinds of changes in signal transduction mechanisms that occur with age. We work primarily with three systems. One of these is striatal dopaminergic control of motor function. This is a system in which we are fairly certain now that some of the motor dysfunctions that occur with age may be due to the loss of receptors for dopamine. We are not exactly sure as to the specific mechanism yet, but we have pretty good, at least correlative data, that support a loss of receptors as a cause of loss in function. The second system that we work with is the α-adrenergic system of the parotid gland. In this particular case, we find that deficits in cellular secretory capacity are not due to loss of receptors. α-Adrenergic receptors seem to be fairly stable with aging, but in this particular case we have a problem at the level of calcium mobilization. Finally, we are examining steroid action; in particular oestrogen action in the uterus and the pituitary gland. In these cases we find both types of changes. Alterations occur at the level of the receptor, but we also see changes in the signal transduction events. With increasing age, we observe an impaired ability of oestrogen receptors to interact with the chromatin in the nucleus and to regulate gene expression at that level.

If one examines the literature and considers the systems that we have discussed in this session, one can see several patterns consistently emerging. There may be a change in receptor function. For example some of the studies of *in vitro* fibroblast aging from Dr Cristofalo's laboratory in Philadelphia have suggested that fibroblast growth factor receptor function is altered with passage. The ability of the receptor to autophosphorylate and thereby become activated to enable the cells to respond to the serum signal, diminished with increasing passage. There are a number of other systems in which there occur postreceptor impairments such as altered ability to mobilize calcium. Finally, changes occur at both the receptor and postreceptor levels. This may be apparent in lymphocytes in terms of being able to respond to the antigen. Dr Beregi discussed a change in interleukin production as well as receptors with age.

All these types of changes are probably symptomatic rather than a first cause of the dysfunction. We must return then to the intrinsic and extrinsic alterations that might be occurring. Are these dysfunctions the results of something at the level of the DNA which is no longer specifying proper receptor proteins or no longer properly generating the enzyme systems necessary to mobilize calcium or to produce cyclic nucleotides? Ultimately, we must demonstrate that any particular cause which we have identified may be reversible. The experiment that Dr Holliday presented, in which it was possible to change the methylation patterns of fibroblast DNA and thereby shorten their lifespan is an example. If we really feel that changes at this level are involved in the *in vitro* cessation of cell division then we need to find a selective agent that has the opposite effect of 5-azacytidine and see if we can extend *in vitro* fibroblast lifespan. It is always easy to shorten lifespan; it is more difficult, however, to take the phenomenon which you feel is responsible for lifespan determination and alter it in a positive direction so that function and/or lifespan is improved.

In any case, we can conclude two things from these papers. They offer us excellent opportunities to first understand and attempt to deal with the functional impairments that occur during senescence, and secondly, to obtain fundamental information with regard to the basic mechanisms of aging.

Part II

Aging at the Organ Level

Age, Immunity and Cancer

Peter Ebbesen

The Institute of Cancer Research, Danish Cancer Society, Radiumstationen, Aarhus, Denmark

Keywords
Skin grafting; Autoreactivity; Dying; Carcinogens.

The AIDS (acquired immune deficiency syndrome) epidemic has added greatly to our understanding of the influence of cellular immune reactivity on tumour development. During the 1970s much experimental work was done to test the old immune surveillance hypothesis (Ehrlich 1909), but no clear proof was forthcoming. In particular, attempts to demonstrate immune rejection of syngeneic, primary tumour usually failed (Middle and Embleton 1981).

AIDS victims have an extremely high incidence of cancer emerging from months to a few years after primary infection (Volberding 1985). There is, at present, nothing to suggest that these cancers are directly caused by LAV/HTLV-III.

Today few doubt the role of systemic immune and hormone responsiveness for at least some types of tumour, and the role of age-related decline in immune capacity for the tumour crop in the old.

With this in mind a few experiments that testify to the importance of other factors for tumour development in old tissue will be described in this paper.

In animal experiments, the conditions are better defined than in humans with regard to carcinogens and the doses involved. However, the dosage needed to induce tumours in a manageable number of animals usually exceeds the exposures humans encounter. The high doses of carcinogen used in animal experiments may conceal possible differences in susceptibility when carcinogen doses do not exceed detoxification and/or repair capacities (Pegg et al. 1976). Available experimental evidence thus concerns high-dose carcinogenesis.

When senescent (>2-year-old) BALB/c mouse skin is exposed to small doses of carcinogens there is a greater susceptibility than in younger adult skin. This is

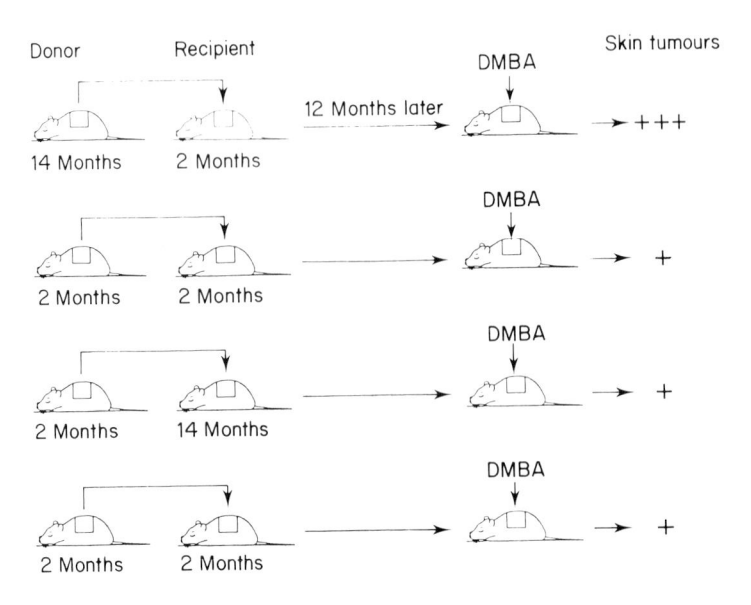

Fig. 1. DMBA carcinogenesis in age chimeras produced by skin grafting in inbred BALB/c mice.

the case when tumours are induced with a small dose of 7-12-dimethylbenz(alfa)anthracene (Ebbesen 1974), β-irradiation (Ebbesen 1980), UV light (Ebbesen and Kripke 1982), and TPA (Ebbesen 1985) (Fig. 1). Skin grafted from middle-aged to young recipients developed the same increased susceptibility as non-grafted skin to carcinogens with further aging. The high susceptibility to carcinogens of senescent skin must therefore derive from local, autonomously developing alterations in the skin itself, independent of age-dependent systemic changes in immune or hormone status.

In studies with carcinogen doses inducing high incidence of colon carcinomas in C57B1 mice, Defries et al. (1981) reported the same incidence in 6- and 22-month-old mice treated with 1,2-dimethylhydrazine. However, chemically induced colon cancer in mice, once established, advances more rapidly in old than in young animals (Clapp et al. 1981). Injecting 4-fluoronebiphenylacetamide resulted in more kidney tumours in the older test animals (Reuber 1975). Polycyclic aromatic hydrocarbons, when administered to rats mainly caused mammary tumours in young animals (Huggins et al. 1961). As the same relation to age was found with N-nitroso-N-methylurea, which does not require metabolic activation, important age-related changes probably occur within the mammary glands themselves (Grubbs Clinton et al. 1983).

The general impression from the literature on animal experiments is that the initial effect of a carcinogen may be either increased or decreased by aging — depending on the type of carcinogen and the biological properties of the target tissue. Age-related changes in the micro- and macro-environment of a transformed cell are often factors facilitating the stages of promotion and progression in carcinogenesis (Anisimov 1985).

Human fetuses after completion of organogenesis, children and adolescents are more susceptible to cancer induction by some agents than are adults. Examples are adenocarcinomas of the vagina in offspring of mothers treated with stilbestrol during pregnancy (Herbst *et al.* 1975), leukaemia after X-ray irradiation of children (Schwartz and Upton 1958) and breast cancer also after irradiation, where the adolescent girl is most at risk (McGregor *et al.* 1977). Rapid cell proliferation in these age groups is likely to be a major reason for the high susceptibility to carcinogens at that age.

Most studies indicate that the risk of cancer development in the adult increases as an exponential function of the person's age at first exposure to carcinogen, the risk being directly proportional to age raised to an exponent bladder cancer in dyestuff workers (Case *et al.* 1954), skin warts after tar exposure (Fisher 1958, Doll 1964), lung cancer in asbestos workers (Knox *et al.* 1968), and sinus cancer in nickel workers (Doll *et al.* 1970). Direct measurements of chromosome aberrations also show that more abnormalities are produced by *in vitro* carcinogen treatment of leukocytes from old than from young human donors (Bochov and Kulestrov 1972). The same relation to age for cancer development is reported for adult humans exposed to irradiation. The excess cancer cases caused by irradiation increase with age at first treatment. The ratio of observed cancer incidence to expected incidence, however, does not necessarily change with age, as the spontaneous incidence of many tumours also increases with age. Examples are cancer following treatment of ankylosing spondylitis (Court and Doll 1965, Smith and Doll 1982) and uterine cancer after irradiation treatment of metropathia haemorrhagica (Smith and Doll 1976). Studies by Jablon and Kato (1972) and Beebe *et al.* (1977) on atomic bomb survivors clearly demonstrated an increase in risk with increase in age at time of detonation. Not all data are in line with this trend. The incidence of lung cancer in nickel workers which increases with age at first exposure up to 25 years of age and then, for unknown reasons, falls off again (Doll *et al.* 1970).

After this survey of experimental and epidemiologic data a short report on work in progress will be given. The goal is to test how chronic stress influences tumour induction in various carcinogen tissue combinations at different ages. Model development is not completed—but the work has yielded some unexpected results from very old animals.

The basic observation is that when male mice are kept crowded for life with other males in conventional mouse boxes they develop a series of symptoms and a 25% shortening of the mean survival time. Beginning 3–5 months after the formation of a group there is a progressive loss of fur lustre, loss of weight, loss of vigour, development of spleen, amyloid, and in some cases a mild anaemia (Ebbesen and Rask-Nielsen 1967) (Fig. 2).

Fig. 2. Three 1-year old DBA/2 males. The two smaller ones have been subject to chronic psychosocial (crowding) stress.

Later experiments showed that keeping males together causes the above symptoms, whereas sex segregated, crowded females and males kept one to a cage were unaffected. Mixing males with females had no influence on the health of either sex. Tranquilizer in the drinking water and castration both retarded the stress disease. Pheromone may play a role, but not a decisive one, as males kept one to a cage in the same room as boxes with crowding-stressed males did not develop any symptoms (Table 1).

A major point is that the severe physical alterations observed are already known to be induced by means other than fighting wounds, as the consequences of grouping males with males is the same irrespective of whether the strain studied shows fighting or not. Results also indicate that infection is not instrumental in the development of degenerative lesions in these chronically stressed animals (Ebbesen 1968, 1972). A psychologic response is the highly likely explanation for the stress observed. This interpretation is in harmony with that of investigations on wild animals (Christian 1956).

So far, the stress model described has only been used once (Amkraut and Solomon 1972). They tested the susceptibility of middle-aged, crowding-stressed and non-stressed mice to murine sarcoma virus. Stressed animals were the most susceptible. More extensive experiments are in preparation.

Table 1
Influence of grouping and various treatments on mean survival time of three strains of mice.
The animals were segregated at weaning

	Mean survival time in months						
	Sex segregated 10 per box	One of one sex 9 of opposite sex	Half and half (5/5)	Only one per box	Sex segregated 10 per box reserpine tranquilizer	One male 9 castrated males	Castrates
Males							
DBA	12	19	9	21	17	18	20
BALB/c	13	21		22			21
CBA	14	19					
Females							
DBA	19	17	16				
BALB/c	21	21	20	20			18
CBA	17	16					

Table 2
Cellullar cytotoxicity of spleen lymphocytes towards syngeneic fibroblast and YAC cells*

			Target cells			
			Fibroblasts		YAC cells	
Strain	No. of groups (3 young, 3 old healthy, 3 dying old)	Subgroup	No. of subgroup with highest count in each group	% Increase (mean)	No. of subgroups with highest count in each group	% Increase (mean)
CBA	18	young	1	Baseline	1	Baseline
		old healthy	5	9	2	19
		dying old	12 $P<0.01$	13	15 $P<0.01$	32
DBA	18	young	1	Baseline	1	Baseline
		old healthy	3	5	3	5
		dying old	14 $P<0.01$	10	14 $P<0.01$	41

*Test for difference between dying and healthy old animals was done with χ^2 test.

Another general factor influencing susceptibility to carcinogens may be the nutritional state. In our model selenium supplementation of non-stressed animals decreases the susceptibility to skin tumour induction with ultraviolet light (Overvad et al. 1985). Experiments in progress will show the effect of caloric underfeeding on development of stress response symptoms.

A surprising observation during the first studies on the immune status of stressed mice was evidence of immunological alterations shortly before spontaneous death.

Untreated, old CBA and DBA/2 male and female mice were picked from the mouse colony when clinically deemed likely to die within the next 48 h. (In a separate study such a prediction was found correct in more than 90% of the cases.) In addition a similar number of like-aged healthy old mice and healthy young mice were studied.

The percentage of lymphoid cells considered dead by *in vitro* test with trypan blue staining was higher in the dying than the old, non-dying animals. Furthermore, unfractionated single-cell suspensions of spleen cells showed an enhanced (natural) killer cell activity towards syngeneic fibroblasts when harvested from dying animals (Table 2).

It is noteworthy that these two characteristics of dying mice occurred independently of any histologic lesions the animals had at time of death (Ebbesen *et al.* 1982).

One possible explanation is a terminal autoaggressive process that might be part of normal dying.

Summary

Epidemiologic and experimental studies show that senescence is accompanied by an increase in susceptibility to tumour induction in many carcinogen tissue combinations. In the case of mouse skin reciprocal syngrafting among animals of different age indicates that the related changes are autonomous local processes. A murine model for chronic stress is now being developed. Future work will reveal if mouse skin susceptibility to tumour induction is also independent of the general stress response. Finally, the process of spontaneous dying in old mice seems to include autoreactivity by lymphoid cells.

References

Amkraut, A. and Solomon, G. F. (1972). Stress and murine sarcoma virus (Moloney)-induced tumors. *Cancer Res.* **32**, 1428-1433.

Anisimov, V. N. (1985). Relevance of age to some aspects of carcinogenesis. In "Age-related factors in carcinogenesis" (A. Likhachev, V. Anisimov, and R. Montesano, eds) pp. 115-126. WHO IARC Scientific Publications No. 58, Lyon.

Beebe, G. W., Kato, A. and Land, C. E. (1977). Studies of the mortality of A-bomb survivors. 8. Mortality experience of A-bomb survivors 1950-1974. RERF Technical Report, pp. 1-77. Radiation Effects Research Foundation, Hiroshima.

Bochov, M. P. and Kulestrov, N. P. (1972). Age sensitivity of human chromosomes to alkylating agents. *Mutat. Res.* **14**, 345-353.

Case, R. A. M., Hoster, M. E., McDonald, D. B. and Pearson, J. T. (1954). Tumours of the urinary bladder in workmen engaged in the manufacture and use of certain dyestuff intermediates in the British chemical industry. *Br. J. Ind. Med.* **11**, 75-104.

Christian, J. J. (1956). Adrenal and reproductive responses to population size in mice from freely growing populations. *Ecology* **37**, 258-273.

Clapp, N. K., Perkins, E. H., Klima, W. C. and Cacheiro, L. H. (1981). Temporal advancement of diethylnitrosamine carcinogenesis in aging mice. *J. Gerontol.* **36**, 158-163.

Court, B. W. M. and Doll, R. (1965). Mortality from cancer and other causes after radiotherapy for ankylosing spondylitis. *Br. Med. J.* **ii**, 1327-1332.

Defries, E. A., Rowlatt, C., and Sheriff, M. V. (1981). The effects of age on tumor induction in C575BL mice using 1,2-dimethylhydrazine. *Toxicol. Letters* **8**, 87-88.

Doll, R. (1964). Epidemiological observations on susceptibility to cancer in man with special reference to age. *Acta Unio Int. Contra Cancrum* **20**, 747-752.

Doll, R., Morgan, L. and Speitzer, F. E. (1970). Cancers of the lung and nasal sinuses of nickel workers. *Br. J. Cancer* **24**, 623-632.

Ebbesen, P. (1968). Spontaneous amyloidosis in differently grouped and treated DBA/2, BALB/c and CBA mice and thymus fibrosis in estrogen-treated BALB/c males. *J. Exp. Med.* **127**, 387-396.

Ebbesen, P. (1972). Long survival time of isolated BALB/c and DBA/2 male mice. *Acta Path. Microbiol. Scand.* **80**(Section B), 149-150.

Ebbesen, P. (1974). Aging increases susceptibility of mouse skin to DMBA carcinogenesis independent of general immune status. *Science* **183**, 217-218.

Ebbesen, P. (1980). Increased susceptibility to beta-irradiation of senescent mouse skin irrespective of grafting to young recipients. *Int. J. Radiat. Biol.* **37**, 563-567.

Ebbesen, P. (1985). Papilloma development on young and senescent mouse skin treated with 12-0-tetradecanoyl-13-phorbol acetate. *In* "Age-Related Factors in Carcinogenesis" (A. Likhachev, V. Anisimov and R. Montesano, eds) pp. 167-170. WHO IARC Scientific Publications No. 58, Lyon.

Ebbesen, P. and Kripke, M. L. (1982). The influence of age and anatomical site on ultraviolet carcinogenesis in BALB/c mice. *J. Natl Cancer Inst.* **68**, 691-694.

Ebbesen, P. and Rask-Nielsen, R. (1967). Influence of sex-segregated grouping and of inoculation with subcellular leukemic material on development of non-leukemic lesions in DBA/2, BALB/c and CBA mice. *J. Natl Cancer Inst.* **39**, 917-932.

Ebbesen, P., Faber, T. and Fuursted, K. (1982). Dying old mice: occurrence of non-viable lymphocytes and autoaggressive cells. *Exp. Geront.* **17**, 425-428.

Ehrlich, P. (1909). Uber den jetzigen Stand der Karzinomforschung. *Ned. Tijdschr. Geneeskd. Eerste Helft* No. 5, 273-290.

Fisher, R. E. W. (1958). The effect of age upon the incidence of tar warts. *In* "Twelfth International Congress on Occupational Health", p. 402. Valtancuvoston Kirjapaino, Helsinki.

Grubbs Clinton, J., Peckham, J. and Cato, K. D. (1983). Mammary carcinogenesis in rats in relation to age at time of N-nitroso-N-methylurea administration. *J. Natl. Cancer Inst.* **70**, 209-212.

Herbst, A. L., Poskanzer, D. C. Robboy, S. J., Friedlander, L. and Scully, R. E. (1975). Prenatal exposure to silbestrol. A prospective comparison of exposed female offspring with unexposed controls. *New Engl. J. Med.* **292**, 334-339.

Huggins, C., Grand, L. C. and Brillantes, F. P. (1961). Mammary cancer induced by a single feeding of polynuclear hydrocarbons, and its suppression. *Nature* **189**, 204-207.

Jablon, S. and Kato, H. (1972). Studies of the mortality of A-bomb survivors. *Radiat. Res.* **50**, 649-698.

Knox, J. F., Holmes, S., Doll, R. and Hill, I. D. (1968). Mortality from lung cancer and other causes among workers in an asbestos textile factory. *Br. J. Ind. Med.* **25**, 293-303.

McGregor, D. H., Land, C. E., Chor, K., Tokvuku, S., Liv, P. I., Watabayashi, T. and Beebe, G. W. (1977). Breast cancer incidence among atomic bomb survivors, Hiroshima and Nagasaki, 1950-1969. *J. Natl Cancer Inst.* **59**, 799-811.

Middle, J. G. and Embleton, M. J. (1981). Naturally arising tumors of the inbred WAB/Not rat strain. II. Immunogenicity of transplanted tumors. *J. Natl Cancer Inst.* **67**, 637-643.

Overvad, K., Thorling, E. B., Bjerring, P. and Ebbesen, P. (1985). Selenium inhibits UV-light-induced skin carcinogenesis in hairless mice. *Cancer Lett.* **27**, 163-170.

Pegg, A. E., Nicoll, J. W., Magee, P. N. and Swann, P. F. (1976). Importance of DNA repair in an organ. Specificity of tumour induction by N-nitroso carcinogens. *Proc. Eur. Soc. Toxicol.* **17**, 39-54.

Reuber, M. D. (1975). Hyperplastic and neoplastic lesions of the kidney in buffalo rats of varying ages ingesting N-4(4-fluorobiphenyl)-acetamide. *J. Natl Cancer Inst.* **54**, 427-429.

Schwartz, E. E. and Upton, A. C. (1958). Factors influencing the incidence of leukemia: Special consideration of the role of ionizing radiation. *Blood* **13**, 845-864.

Smith, P. G. and Doll, R. (1976). Late effects of X irradiation in patients treated for metropathia hemorragica. *Br. J. Radiol.* **49**, 224-232.

Smith, P. G. and Doll, R. (1982). Age- and time-dependent changes in the rates of radiation-induced cancers in patients with ankylosing spondylitis following a single course of X-ray treatment. *IAEA-SM* **224**, 205-218.

Volberding, P. (1985). Kaposi's sarcoma. *In* "AIDS: a basic guide for clinicians" (P. Ebbesen, R. J. Biggar and M. Melbye, eds) pp. 99-110. Munksgaard, Copenhagen.

Discussion

Stähelin: Is there an inborn "dying mechanism" that could explain why there is an exponential increase in the death rate at a certain age irrespectively of the causes of death?

Ebbesen: If you compare the records of mice that died spontaneously with those with different diseases, a common mechanism becomes likely.

Holliday: In relation to the last part of your paper, do you have any comments about the fact that inbred mice, in an apparently uniform environment, have a very different lifespan with a large standard deviation about the mean? Does it not suggest that stochastic and probabilistic events are important in aging?

Ebbesen: I can only comment that possibly the social order may be important.

An Integrated Approach Toward Understanding Myocardial Aging

Edward G. Lakatta

Laboratory of Cardiovascular Science, Gerontology Research Center, National Institute on Aging, National Institutes of Health, Baltimore, Maryland, USA

Keywords

Aging myocardium; Excitation-Contraction coupling; Myoplasmic calcium; Sarcoplasmic reticulum; β-Adrenergic modulation.

Cardiovascular function is determined by a complex interaction of many variables (Fig. 1), the effectiveness of each is determined by basic cellular and extracellular biophysical mechanisms which are subject to autonomic modulation.

Our research over the last decade has focussed on how aging affects (a) overall cardiovascular function as depicted in Fig. 1, (b) the basic mechanisms that determine the intrinsic myocardial cell performance, sometimes also referred to as the contractile or inotropic state or the effectiveness of excitation-contraction coupling, and (c) β-adrenergic modulation of the factors in Fig. 1. The results of research are highlighted below.

EXCITATION-CONTRACTION COUPLING MECHANISMS

The myocardium of normotensive rodents of advanced age exhibits a constellation of changes in excitation-contraction coupling mechanisms. The interplay of these mechanisms in mammalian cardiac muscle is illustrated in a general scheme of excitation-contraction coupling (Fig. 2). An active potential produces a transient increase in the myoplasmic $[Ca^{2+}]$ resulting in a transient increase in force. This transient increase in myoplasmic free Ca^{2+} results primarily from

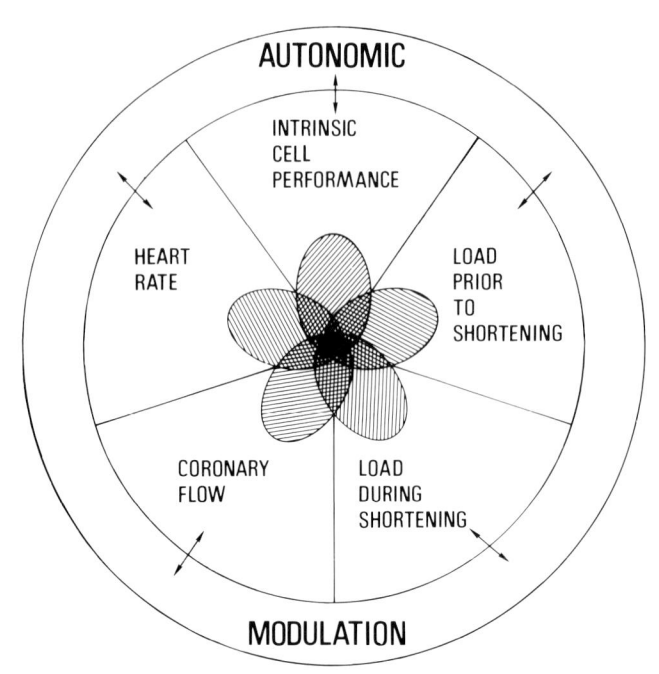

Fig. 1. Multiple factors that govern cardiac output. The overlap depicted in the centre of the figure indicates the interdependence of these factors. The bidirectional arrows indicate that each function not only is modulated by autonomic tone but also demonstrates a negative feedback on this modulation. Reprinted from Lakatta (1983) with permission from Pergamon Press.

sarcoplasmic reticulum (SR) Ca^{2+} release and is the net result of the amount of Ca^{2+} released and the extent of Ca^{2+} binding to cell proteins, which include the SR itself, other membraneous organelles, e.g. the myofilaments, sarcolemmal phospholipids, and calmodulin.

The sensitivity of the force generating sites within myofilaments for Ca^{2+} can be inferred from the shape of the force-pCa relation measured in preparations in which the membraneous organelles have been destroyed. This permits buffering of the $[Ca^{2+}]$ surrounding the myofilaments at constant levels over ranges that are encountered in the intact cell during contraction. Neither the maximum force nor the shape of the force-pCa relationship is altered with aging (Fig. 3). When isolated muscles with intact membrane function are studied at low stimulation rates neither twitch force nor the magnitude of the myoplasmic $[Ca^{2+}]$ transient which can be monitored by measuring the luminescence of the Ca^{2+} sensitive protein, aequorin, differs with age (Fig. 4). In response to an increase in the bathing $[Ca^{2+}]$ parallel increases in the peak Ca^{2+} transient and force occur in both adult and senescent muscles (Lakatta and Yin 1986, Orchard and Lakatta 1985). Similarly, peak twitch force in cardiac muscle isolated from senescent

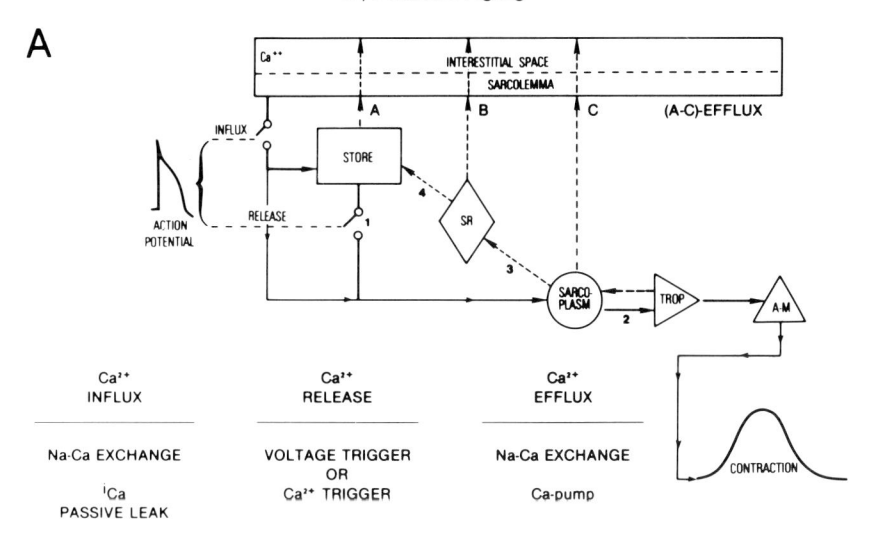

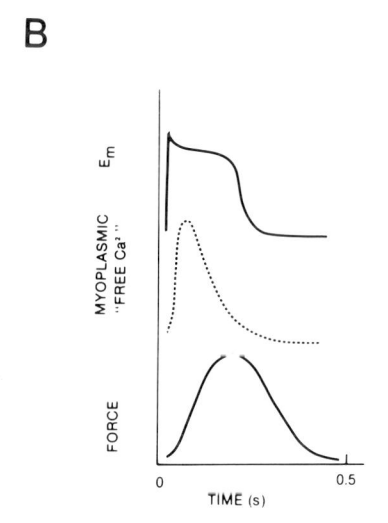

Fig. 2. A. A simplified scheme of excitation-contraction coupling mechanisms in cardiac muscle. See text for explanation. B. The relative time course of the transmembrane action potential, myoplasmic free Ca^{2+} transient, and contractile force following stimulation in isometric cardiac muscle. From Lakatta (1986).

animals is maintained at those in response to varying degrees of stretch applied to the muscle (Lakatta and Yin 1982).

The duration of the cardiac contraction becomes prolonged with aging (Lakatta and Yin 1982, Orchard and Lakatta 1985, Bhatnagar et al. 1984, Froehlich et al. 1978, Lakatta 1978). Contraction duration is highly dependent on the time course of the

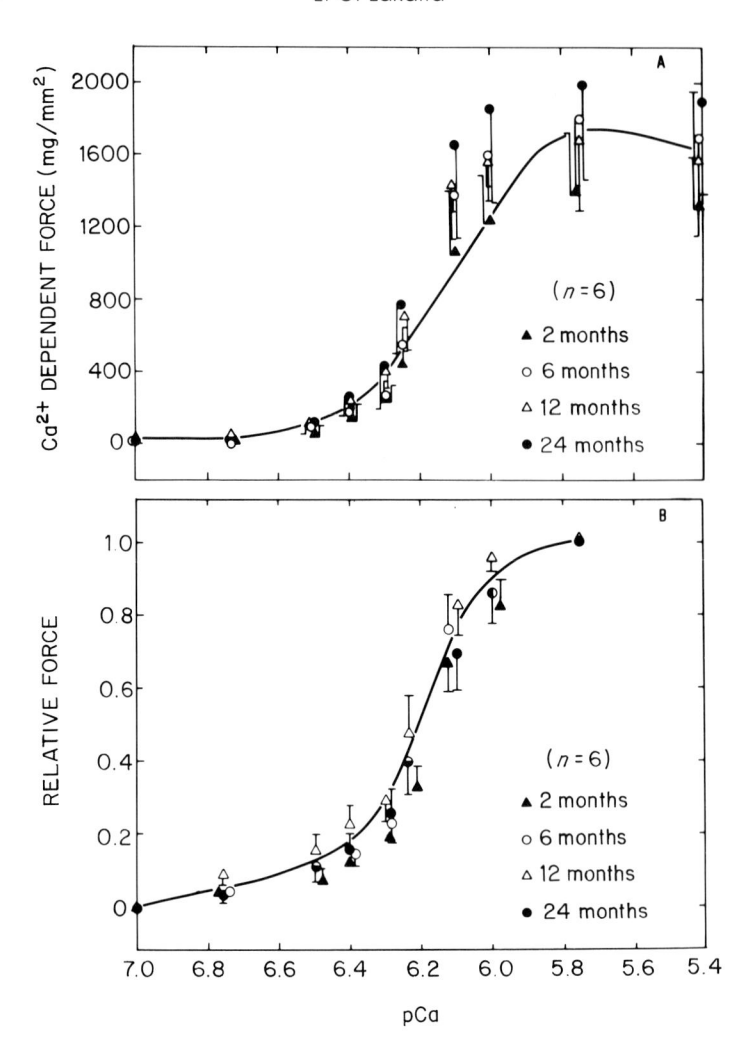

Fig. 3. A. Ca^{2+}-dependent force as a function of pCa in thin papillary muscle from Wistar rats of a broad age range that have been "chemically skinned" with a non-ionic detergent (Triton X). B. Force is normalized to the maximum level in each muscle. From Bhatnagar et al. (1984).

Ca^{2+}-myofilament interaction. This is determined by (a) the time course of the myoplasmic $[Ca^{2+}]$ transient, which is determined, in part, by the rates of SR Ca^{2+} release and pumping and the duration of sarcolemmal depolarization and (b) the extent and rate of myofilament shortening in response to the transient increase in $[Ca^{2+}]$. This is determined, in part, by the amount of Ca^{2+} bound to the myofilaments prior to the onset of contraction, and in part, by the rates of

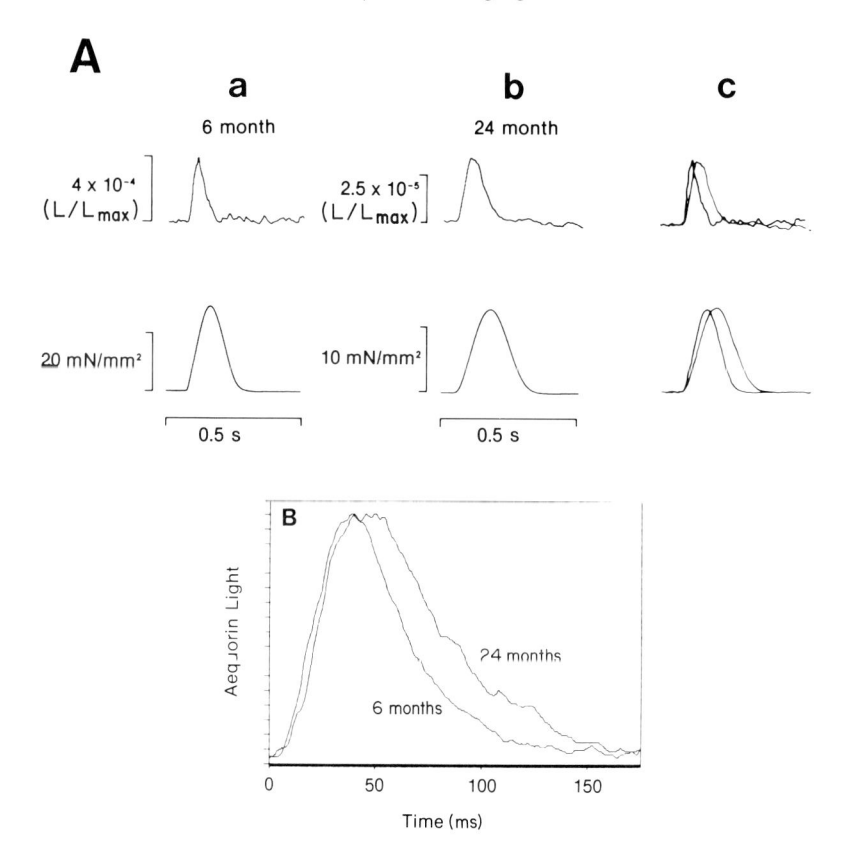

Fig. 4A. Aequorin luminescence and contraction in cardiac muscle. Aequorin was injected into 30–100 cells of a right ventricular papillary muscle from a 6 (a) and 24 (b) month old Wistar rat bathed in 2 mol Ca^{2+}. The luminescence transient, (top tracing) is the average of 100 consecutive steady state contractions at 0.33 Hz at 30°C at L_{max}. Concomitant isometric force records are shown in lower tracings and in (c) the force and light tracings from each muscle are superimposed. Note that both light and force are prolonged in the 24 month muscle.

Fig. 4B. The time course of aequorin luminescence in representative muscles from a 6- and 24-month old rat on an expanded time scale. The average time for aequorin luminescence to decay 50% in 11 young and 7 senescent muscles was 21.3±1.5 and 32.9±4.3 ms, respectively. Time to peak force was 88.8±33.1 and 110.4±6.8 ms and half relaxation time was 54.9±2.3 and 73.4±4.4 ms in young and senescent muscles, respectively. The average peak aequorin luminescence did not differ with age. From Orchard and Lakatta (1985).

myofilament ATP hydrolysis and cross-bridge cycling. The duration of the myoplasmic Ca^{2+} transient, is prolonged in isometric muscle isolated from aged versus younger adult rats (Fig. 4).

The rate at which SR pumps Ca^{2+} out of the myoplasm is a major factor that determines the decay rate of the myoplasmic $[Ca^{2+}]$ transient. This velocity

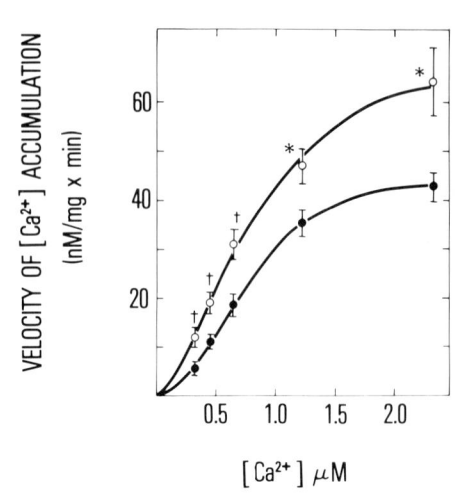

Fig. 5. The velocity of Ca^{2+} accumulation in sarcoplasmic reticulum isolated from 6- to 8-month (○) and 24- to 25-month (●) Wistar rat hearts. From Froehlich et al. (1978).

of SR Ca^{2+} pumping by SR from hearts of senescent animals is diminished compared with that of younger animals (Fig. 5).

The transmembrane action potential (TAP) in ventricular muscle of senescent rats is markedly prolonged compared with that in young controls (Fig. 6). Note that the overshoot and level of depolarization at all relative repolarization times are greater in the older than in the younger Wistar rat muscles. The mechanism for the prolonged TAP (enhanced inward versus reduced outwardly directed current(s)) remains to be established. Rat cardiac muscle does indeed have a slow inward current and when the [Ca^{2+}] bathing it is reduced below 2 mM, a beat-to-beat reduction in contractile force occurs and varies directly with the beat-to-beat reduction in the TAP overshoot (Lakatta and Yin 1982). When bathing [Ca^{2+}] is changed over this range parallel changes in TAP and twitch force occur in senescent but not in younger muscles (Lakatta and Yin 1982). This suggests a link between inward flux via Ca^{2+} channels and the magnitude of contractile force. The magnitude of the slow inward current may determine its effectiveness of a trigger for SR Ca^{2+} release and likely also serves to load the cell and thus the SR with Ca^{2+}. Since the diminution in SR Ca^{2+} pumping rate in the senescent myocardium might result in less SR Ca^{2+} loading, under some conditions at least, the amplification of the TAP may be a requirement for maintaining sufficient SR Ca^{2+} release in the senescent myocardial cell. This particular hypothesis requires the assumption that in the senescent heart the magnitude of the slow inward current or some other Ca^{2+} source, e.g. the Na-Ca exchanger, is the mechanism for the greater extent and duration of sarcolemmal depolarization during the TAP. An alternative hypothesis is that the changes in the TAP could *result from* age-related differences in SR Ca^{2+} release (Lakatta 1984).

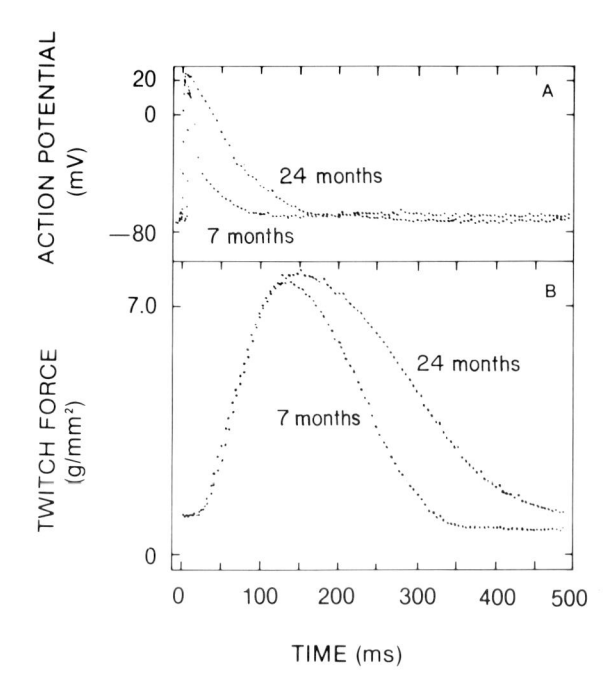

Fig. 6. Typical computer resynthesizations of simultaneously measured transmembrane potential (Panel A) and isometric contractions (Panel B) in adult and senescent right ventricular rat muscles stimulated at L_{max} 24 min_{-1} at 30°C in [Ca^{2+}] of 2.5. From Wei et al. (1984).

In a given contraction, the prolonged myoplasmic Ca^{2+} transient and TAP, and the diminished SR Ca^{2+} pumping rate can effect the restitution time for optimal excitation-contraction coupling in subsequent contractions. In response to electrical stimulation at short coupling intervals, cardiac muscle from senescent rat hearts, fail to generate a contraction at those same coupling intervals younger muscles do (Fig. 7). Similarly, when the interstimulus interval is reduced under the optimal Ca^{2+} loading conditions, the extent of Ca^{2+} release, as estimated from the peak of the aequorin light transient, is diminished in senescent but not in younger adult muscles (Orchard and Lakatta 1985).

A decline in the rate of ATP hydrolysis has been observed in various contractile myofilament protein preparations isolated from the myocardium of aged animals compared with those from younger ones (Lakatta and Yin, 1982). The extent of this decline varies with the particular myofilament preparation. Ca^{2+} activated myosin ATPase activity progressively declines with age from the maturation through senescence (Effron et al.). This activity is governed by the myosin isoenzyme profile (Effron et al.). The proportion of V_1 isozyme, i.e. that which has the most rapid ATP hydrolytic rate, declines progressively with age from

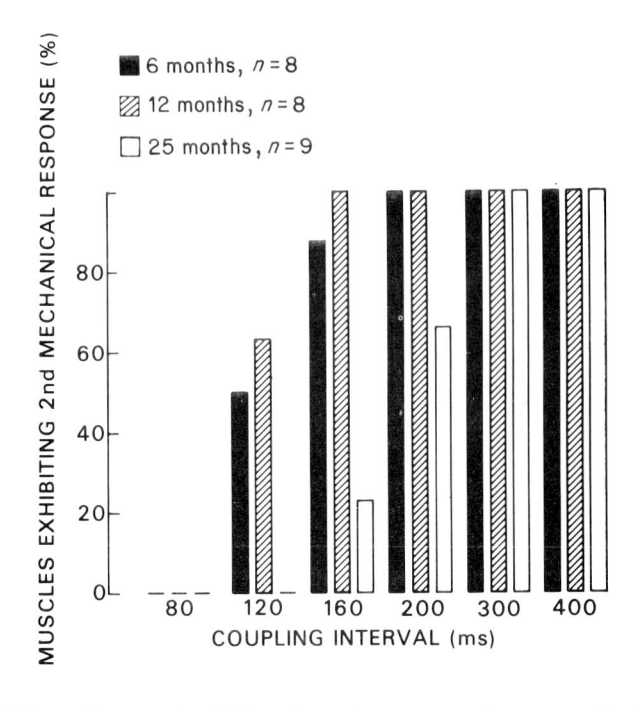

Fig. 7. Effect of age on the ability of muscles to respond to a second stimulus during paired pacing at varied coupling intervals. As the coupling interval shortens, fewer muscles in the aged group exhibit a second mechanical response ($P<0.01\,[\chi^2]$). From Lakatta et al. (1975a).

maturation through senescence, while the proportion of V_3, that isozyme with the slowest ATP hydrolytic rate, progressively increases with age (Fig. 8). Note that by 24 months of age V_3 comprises $>80\%$ of the total myosin isoenzyme content. In the isometric contraction, the time to peak tension and contraction duration are directly related to the % V_3 (or inversely related to the % V_1). An increase in the dynamic stiffness of cardiac muscle during myofilament activation occur with adult aging (Yin et al. 1980). This may attribute to age differences in cross-bridge dynamics that result from the age differences in isozyme composition (Effron et al.). The impact of the isozyme composition and myosin ATPase activity on functional parameters of muscle, however, can be overridden by some other factors that modulate muscle function, e.g. the time course of the myoplasmic free [Ca^{2+}] transient (Fig. 5).

The prolonged contraction time in senescent myocardium can be abolished by throxine injections (Fig. 9) or mild chronic exercise (Fig. 9) (Orchard and Lakatta 1985, Yin et al. 1982, Rodeheffer et al. 1984), and the altered myosin isozyme profile can be modulated by thyroid injections (Fig. 9) so that it resembles that from hearts of younger animals (Effron et al. 1986, Spurgeon et al. 1983).

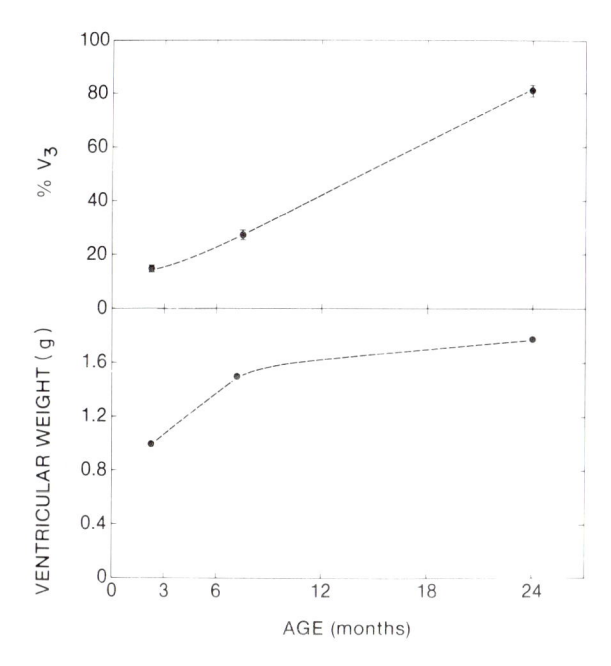

Fig. 8. Relative proportion of myosin V_3 (% of heterodimer not included) isozyme in Wistar heart preparations as a function of age (0, 0). From Effron *et al.*

The left ventricular myocardium hypertrophies to a moderate extent with advancing adult age (Fig. 8). This is due largely to an increase in myocyte mass (Yin *et al.* 1982). Many of the apparent age-related changes in excitation–contraction coupling mechanisms discussed above are also observed experimentally when the myocardium of younger rats is caused by hypertrophy in response to a chronic hypertension (Lakatta 1986). It might be argued, therefore, that the age-related changes discussed above, e.g. prolonged contraction or increased dynamic stiffness are the result of cardiac hypertrophy rather than aging *per se*. This is not the case, however, for two reasons: (a) the prolonged contraction and increased stiffness can be reversed by exercise (Fig. 10) or thyroid hormone (Fig. 9) in the absence of a reversal of the myocardial hypertrophy, (b) the prolonged duration of contraction, action potential, and myoplasmic $[Ca^{2+}]$ transient, and altered myosin isozyme composition are observed in right ventricular muscle; the right ventricle does not hypertrophy with adult aging in this rat model. An hypothesis to explain the similar alterations to myocardium of aged normotensive rats and those in hearts of younger animals with experimentally induced chronic hypertension is that these alterations are mediated by a common messenger, e.g. a change in cell Ca^{2+} secondary to altered cell loading. This then might stimulate an increase in myocyte mass and modulates other aspects of cell function as well.

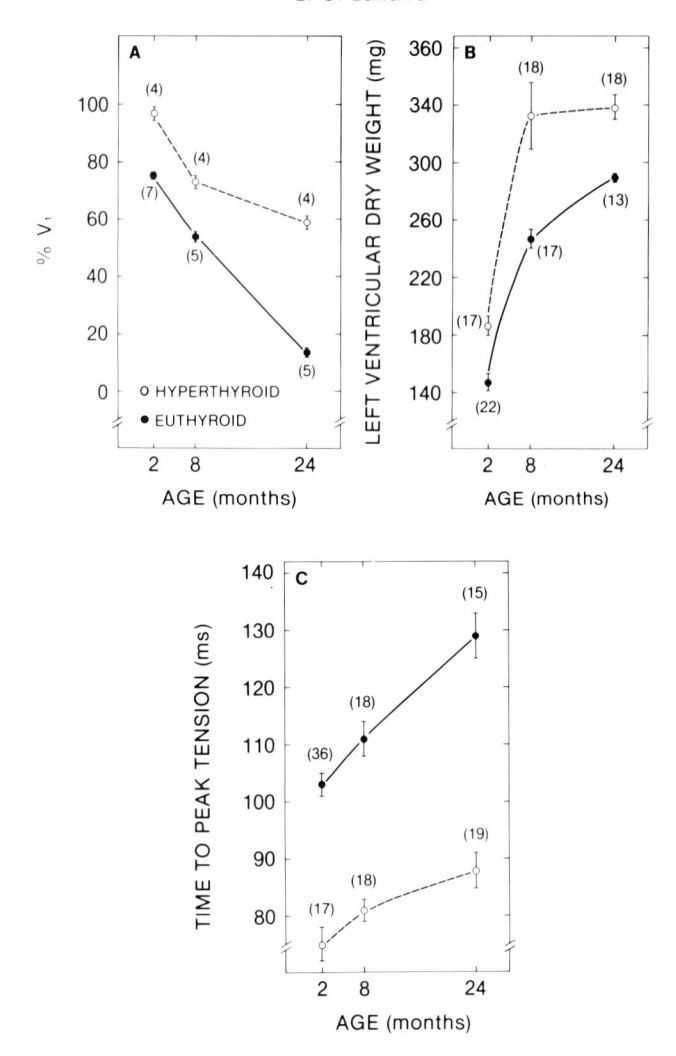

Fig. 9. The relative proportion of V_1 isomyosin (A) left ventricular weight (B) and time to peak tension (C) in cardiac muscle from euthyroid and hyperthyroid rats of varying age. Redrawn from Effron et al.

To summarize thus far, we have found that the myocardium of normotensive rodents of advanced age exhibits a constellation of changes in excitation–contraction coupling mechanisms which include (a) a two-fold increase in the TAP duration; (b) a 30% increase in the duration of the myoplasmic [Ca^{2+}] transient that occurs with excitation; (c) a 25% prolongation of twitch duration; (d) a 50% reduction in the net Ca^{2+} pumping rate by isolated SR; (e) prolonged restitution of the excitation–contraction coupling cycle,

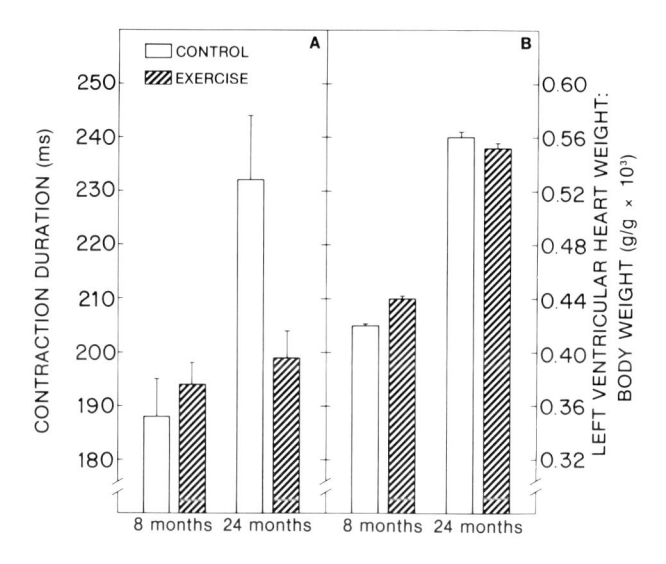

Fig. 10. The effect of chronic (4 months) daily wheel exercise on (A) contraction duration (time to peak force plus time from peak to 50% force decay in isometric muscles stimulated L_{max} at 29°C at 24 min^{-1} in [Ca^{2+}] of 2.5 mM) and (B) relative heart mass in right ventricular papillary muscles from adult (8 months) and senescent (24 months) rats. From Spurgeon et al. (1983).

manifested by an inability to respond to test stimuli at short coupling intervals; and (f) a marked reduction to 25% of that in the 2-month animal in the preparation of V_1 myosin isozme. The force response to Ca^{2+} in myofibrillar preparations and peak twitch force at optimal coupling intervals in intact preparations are unaltered in senescence but the velocity of isotonic shortening declines.

These age-related alterations in intrinsic excitation–contraction coupling mechanisms, and other yet to be defined age-related differences in mechanisms that regulate cardiac myocyte function may alter the response to pharmacologic perturbations that modulate excitation–contraction coupling. For example, we have demonstrated the inotropic response elicited by cardiac glycosides in cardiac muscle markedly declines with age (Gerstenblith et al. 1979, Guarnieri et al. 1979). Thus, these age-related changes in the myocardium have apparent implications in pharmacologic therapeutic strategies for treatment of cardiovascular disease in the elderly (Guarnieri et al. 1979). The age-related changes described above may also modify the response to the stress imposed on the senescent heart by disease states or exercise. The response to the stress of exercise which has been a major focus of our laboratory experiments (Lakatta 1980, Lakatta 1985a, Filburn and Lakatta 1984) is discussed below.

ALTERED β-ADRENERGIC MODULATION OF CARDIOVASCULAR PERFORMANCE WITH ADVANCING AGE

β-Adrenergic stimulation during exercise has two effects on myocardial contraction: it enhances its contractile strength and abbreviates the contraction duration. This latter effect is particularly necessary in the intact circulation since the heart rate can increase up to three-fold during exercise and the contraction must be more brief in order to permit myocardial relaxation and proper filling of the ventricle during a shorter diastole. In isolated cardiac muscle or perfused myocardium from rats of advanced age, the catecholamine enhancement of the contractile state is diminished compared with that in muscle or myocardium from younger adults rats (Lakatta *et al.* 1975b, Guarnieri *et al.* 1980). The effect of catecholamines to abbreviate the contraction duration is not age-related (Fig. 11). Studies designed to investigate mechanism(s) involved in this deficit must consider the diverse effects of hormonal modulation of cardiac cell performance. Figure 12 depicts our present level of understanding of these effects and how they are mediated at the cellular level. In brief, β-agonists bind to receptors which are coupled to the enzyme adenylate cyclase; this step is modulated by pyridine

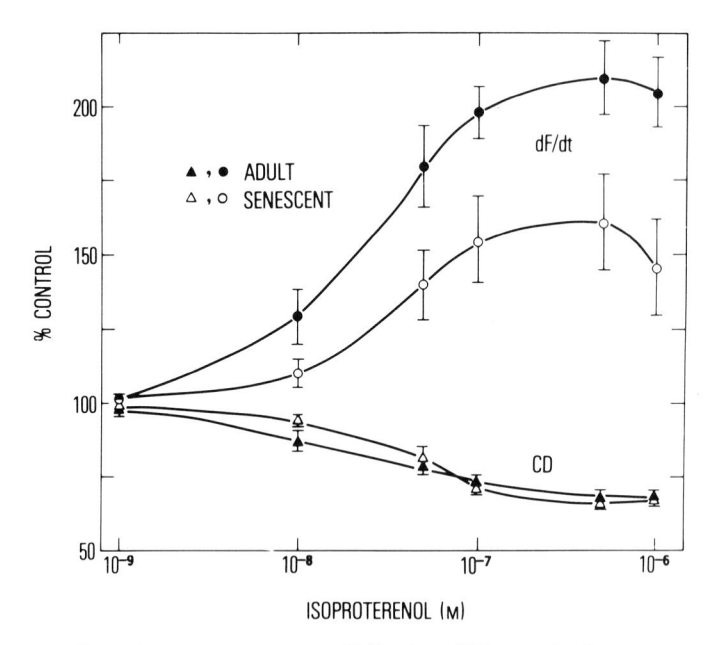

Fig. 11. A. Effect of age on response to dF/dt. Age difference in dose-response curves of dF/dt is significant at $P<0.005$ level (regression analysis of variance, $n=6$ in each age group at each isoproterenol concentration). From Guarnieri *et al.* (1980).

nucleotide binding; ATP is split to produce cAMP which converts a protein kinase from an inactive to an active form. The activated form of the enzyme catalyses the phosphorylation of cell proteins such as glyogen phosphorylase, troponin, myosin, phospholamban (SR) and likely sarcolemmal proteins as well. Sarcolemmal proteins that become phosphorylated are likely those that govern the function of the slow channel though which Ca^{2+} influx occurs with depolarization, those that are associated with ATP-dependent Ca^{2+} pumping from the cell, and possibly those involved with Na-K pumping. These phosphorylations result in a net increase in cell Ca^{2+}, greater loading of SR with Ca^{2+}, a more effective trigger to release Ca^{2+} from the SR and enhanced energy mobilization from glycogen. These effects permit a contraction of greater strength that is briefer in duration, due to enhancement of relaxation mechanisms. Enhanced relaxation is thought to be mediated by the combined effects of troponin phosphorylation, which causes weaker Ca^{2+} binding, SR phosphorylation, causing a greater rate of Ca^{2+} resequestration, and sarcolemmal Ca^{2+} pump phosphorylation, effecting more efficient Ca^{2+} efflux from the cell. The effect of phospholamban (SR) appears to be the dominant one in modulating relaxation (McIvor *et al.*). With the change in cell Ca^{2+} loading that occurs in response to β-stimulation, additional modulation of the Na–Ca exchanger, of sarcolemmal channels, and of SR Ca^{2+} pumping by Ca^{2+} itself occurs (Fig. 11B). The interaction of such modulation and that due to specific β-adrenergic induced phosphorylation complicates dissection of the mechanisms that account for the diminished inotropic response of the aged myocardium to catecholamines.

Age-related changes that are distal to the receptor-cyclase system appear to be required to explain the diminished myocardial contractile response to isoproterenol as depicted in Fig. 11. In that study (Guarnieri *et al.* 1980), neither the receptor number nor affinity for β-receptor antagonists or isoproterenol was altered with age, and neither basal levels of cAMP, nor the increased level achieved during the peak contractile response differed with age. When dibutyryl cAMP was employed as the agonist, the age deficit in enhancement of contractility observed with isoproterenol persisted (Fig. 13). The relationship between protein kinase activation and enhanced contractility in the perfused rat heart under the experimental conditions of Fig. 11 is depicted in Fig. 14. Neither the basal nor isoproterenol stimulated levels of protein kinase activity in the same myocardial preparations in which the contractile response was measured (Fig. 11) differed with age (Fig. 14). This result does not preclude the possibility that measurements of kinase activation prior to peak contractile response, i.e. within the first 15–30 seconds following infusion of the agonist may have differed with age, or that there is an age difference in compartmental kinase activation. However, since the effect of Ca^{2+} on force production is not altered with age (Figs 3 and 13), age differences in the extent of phosphorylation (Fig. 12A), or differences in the change in ion flux or binding that results from a given level of phosphorylation (Fig. 12A), are plausible explanations for the combined results in Figs 11, 13

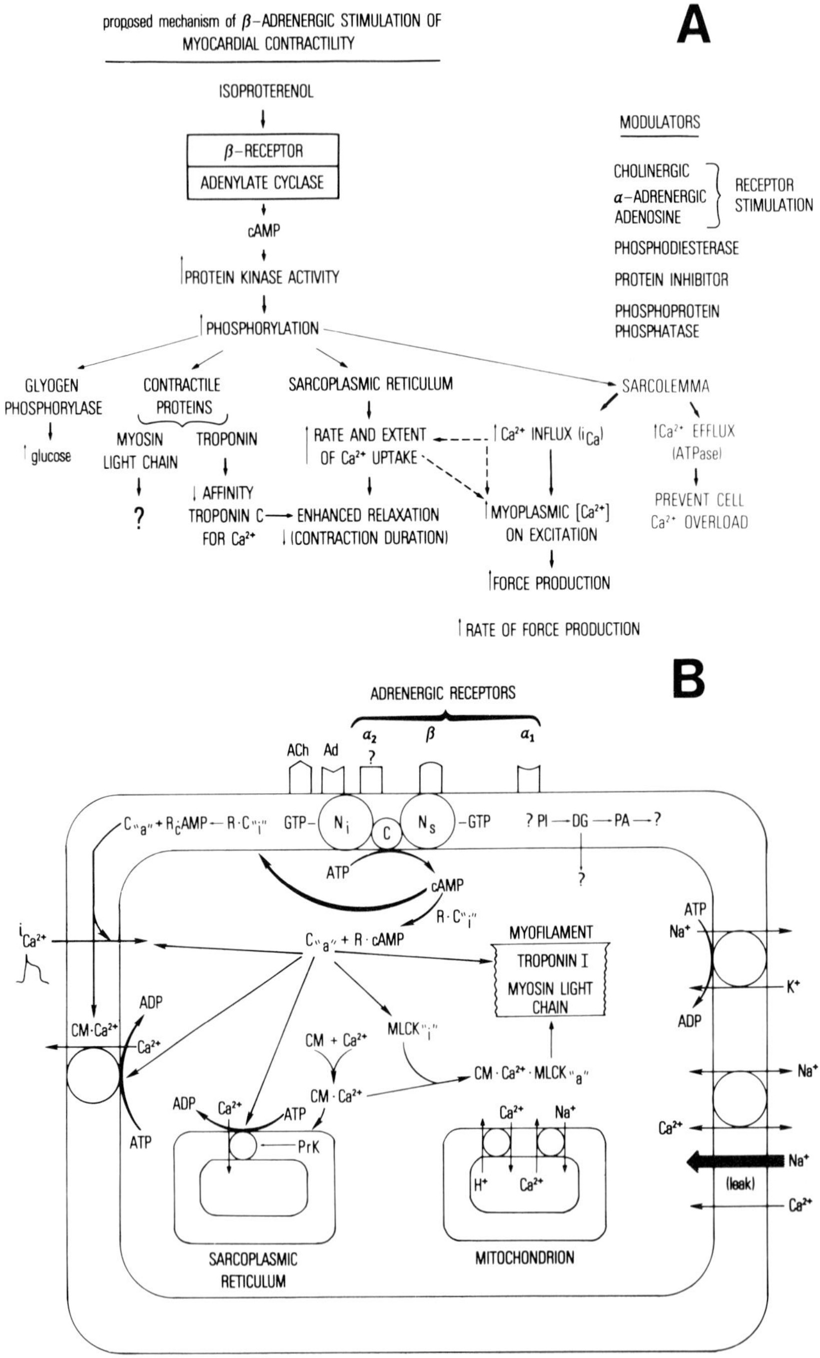
A
proposed mechanism of β–ADRENERGIC STIMULATION OF MYOCARDIAL CONTRACTILITY
ISOPROTERENOL
β–RECEPTOR
ADENYLATE CYCLASE
cAMP
↑PROTEIN KINASE ACTIVITY
↑PHOSPHORYLATION
MODULATORS
CHOLINERGIC
α–ADRENERGIC
ADENOSINE
RECEPTOR STIMULATION
PHOSPHODIESTERASE
PROTEIN INHIBITOR
PHOSPHOPROTEIN PHOSPHATASE
GLYCOGEN PHOSPHORYLASE
↑glucose
CONTRACTILE PROTEINS
MYOSIN LIGHT CHAIN
?
TROPONIN
↓AFFINITY TROPONIN C FOR Ca2+
SARCOPLASMIC RETICULUM
↑RATE AND EXTENT OF Ca2+ UPTAKE
ENHANCED RELAXATION
↓(CONTRACTION DURATION)
SARCOLEMMA
↑Ca2+ INFLUX (iCa)
↑MYOPLASMIC [Ca2+] ON EXCITATION
↑FORCE PRODUCTION
↑RATE OF FORCE PRODUCTION
↑Ca2+ EFFLUX (ATPase)
PREVENT CELL Ca2+ OVERLOAD
B
ADRENERGIC RECEPTORS
ACh
Ad
α2
?
β
α1
C"a" + RcAMP ← R·C"i"
GTP–
Ni
C
Ns
–GTP
? PI → DG → PA → ?
?
ATP
cAMP
R·C"i"
C"a" + R·cAMP
iCa2+
MYOFILAMENT
TROPONIN I
MYOSIN LIGHT CHAIN
ADP
CM·Ca2+
Ca2+
ATP
MLCK"i"
CM + Ca2+
CM·Ca2+
CM·Ca2+·MLCK"a"
ADP
Ca2+
ATP
PrK
Ca2+
Na+
H+
Ca2+
SARCOPLASMIC RETICULUM
MITOCHONDRION
ATP
Na+
K+
ADP
Na+
Ca2+
Na+
(leak)
Ca2+

and 14. A 20% increase in phosphoprotein phosphatase activity in the senescent hearts studied in Fig. 11 has in fact been measured (Guarnieri et al. 1980). Some other modulating influences of the cascade listed in Fig. 12B, should they differ with respect to age, might also have a role in the age difference in response to β-agonists. These have not yet been studied.

Figure 11 shows that the relaxant effect of β-adrenergic agonists is not altered with aging. Additional studies in isolated SR from adult and senescent rat hearts indicate that the cAMP + protein kinase stimulate the Ca^{2+} pump rate equally at other ages (Lakatta 1985a,b).

Our studies in man have investigated the β-adrenergic modulation of cardiovascular function (Rodeheffer et al. 1984, Lakatta 1985b, Fleg et al. 1985, Renlund et al. 1985). The precise impact of β-adrenergic modulation of cardiovascular function (Fig. 1) during exercise can be determined when the exercise is performed in the presence of β-adrenergic blockade (Fig. 15). Note that, in this representative subject, during exercise in the absence of β-blockade a fourfold increase in cardiac output is due to a marked increase in heart rate (Panel A), and a smaller increase in stroke volume (Panel B); it is important to note also that the cardiac size at end-diastole and, in particular, at end-systole does not increase. While the same cardiac output is achieved during exercise in the presence of β-blockade with propranolol, the haemodynamic profile differs: the heart rate is 40 beats/min less and the decrease in end-systolic volume is only

---

Fig. 12A. The relationship of β-adrenergically mediated changes in cellular biochemical reactions to enhancement of contractility in cardiac muscle. From Filburn and Lakatta (1984).

Fig. 12B. Scheme of the regulatory interactions involving cyclic AMP and Ca^{2+} in a cardiac myocyte. Agonists binding to specific receptors stimulate or attenuate cyclic AMP synthesis or stimulate breakdown of phosphatidylinositol. Cyclic AMP activates a protein kinase, present both in organelle membranes and cytosol, which then catalyses phosphorylation of various proteins involved in the metabolism or fluxes of intracellular Ca^{2+}. Intracellular Ca^{2+} interacts with calmodulin to form a complex which interacts with various enzymes involved in metabolism and action of both Ca^{2+} and cyclic AMP. The abbreviations used are: Ad: adenosine receptor, ACh, acetylcholine receptor; α_1 and α_2, α-1 and α-2 adrenergic receptors, β, β-adrenergic receptor, C, catalytic subunit of adenylate cyclase; N_s and N_i, stimulatory and inhibitory GTP binding proteins associated with catalytic subunit; GTP, guanosine triphosphate; ATP, adenosine triphosphate; ADP, adenosine disphosphate; cAMP, cyclic AMP; PDE_i and PDE_a, inactive and active forms of phosphodiesterase; CM, calmodulin; AMP, adenosine monophosphate; C_i and C_a, inactive and active protein kinase catalytic subunit; R, regulatory cyclic AMP-binding subunit of protein kinase; $MLCK_i$ and $MLCK_a$, inactive and active forms of myosin light chain kinases; PK_i and PK_a, inactive and active forms of protein kinase; iCa^{2+}, inward Ca^{2+} current; PI, phosphatidylinositol; DG, diacylglycerol; PA, phosphatidic acid. Recent evidence indicate that IP_3 (not shown in figure) a product of the hydrolysis of phosphatidylinositol in response to $\alpha^1\alpha_1$ agonists may be the second messenger in the $\alpha^1\alpha_1$ system. From Filburn and Lakatta (1984).

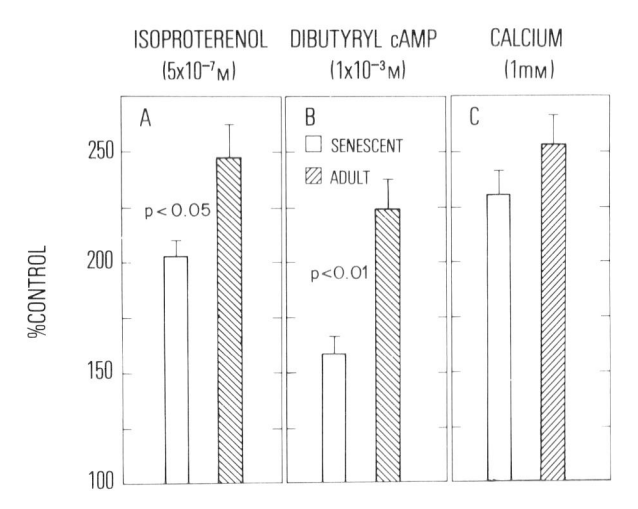

Fig. 13. The effect of isoproterenol (Panel A), dibutyryl cAMP (Panel B) and an increase in calcium concentration in the perfusate (Panel C) on the maximum rate of force production (dT/dt) in interventricular septa isolated from adult (6-9 months) and senescent (24-26 months) rat hearts. All muscles were contracting isometrically at the peak of their length-tension curve, stimulated 75/min at 29°, and perfused with Krebs-Ringer bicarbonate solution containing Ca^{2+} of 0.3 ml. Baseline dT/dt prior to the interventions in Panels A-C was not age-related. Redrawn from Guarnieri *et al.* (1980).

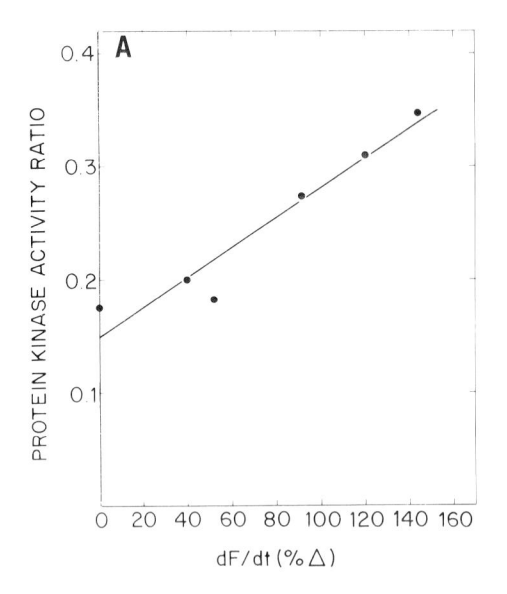

Fig. 14A.

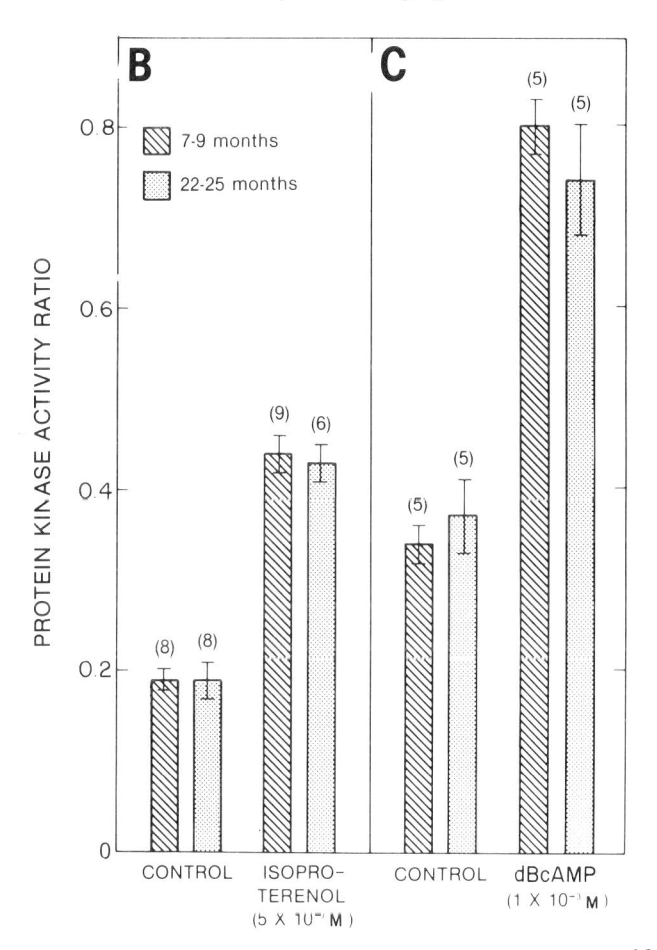

Fig. 14A *(opposite)*. The relationship of protein kinase activity ratio $\frac{-cAMP}{+cAMP}$ in the soluble fraction of the homogenate to the change in maximum rate of force production in the intact rat perfused interventricular septum. Data points are the mean of five different hearts studied in control (dF/dt of 0%) and at each of progressively incremented isoproterenol concentrations ranging from $1 \times 10^{-8} - 5 \times 10^{-7}$ M. From Filburn and Lakatta (1984).

Fig. 14B,C. The protein kinase activity ratio measured as in Panel A in septa that were perfused with control solution or with 5×10^{-7} M isoproterenol (B) or 1×10^{-3} M dibutyryl cAMP (dB cAMP) (C) and freeze-clamped at the peak of the contractile response. (The protein kinase assay in both control and after dibutyryl cAMP in Panel C was made in the presence of charcoal.) In control septa, maximum protein kinase activity measured in the soluble and particulate fraction of the heart homogenates were not differed with respect to age. Note that neither control nor stimulated levels by the agonists were age-related, but the contractile response evoked by these agents in the very same hearts was diminished in the senescent versus the younger adult (see Figs 11 and 13A for isoproterenol and Fig. 13B for dibutyryl cAMP). Redrawn from Guarnieri *et al.* (1980).

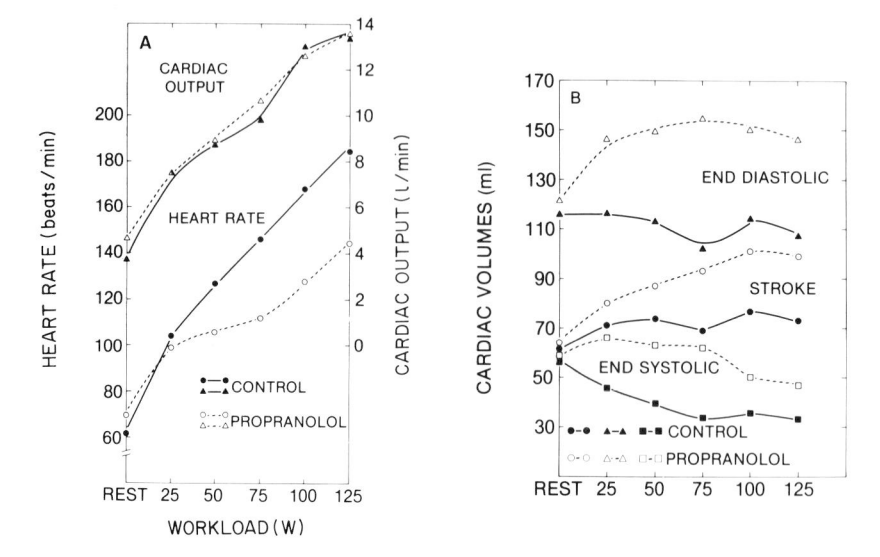

Fig. 15. The effect of β-adrenergic blockade (propranolol IV, 0.15 mg/kg) on (A) cardiac output and heart rate and (B) cardiac volumes (Panel B) during graded upright bicycle exercise. From Renlund et al. (1985).

half of that in the absence of β-blockade. However, the end-diastolic volume increases substantially and this permits a larger (about 30%) stroke volume than in the absence of β-blockade. Thus, the decrease in exercise cardiac output which would have occurred due to the 40 beat/min heart rate deficit was compensated for by an enhanced stroke volume. This was accomplished not by a greater reduction in heart size at the end of systole, but rather by an increase in the end-diastolic volume. Thus, the study in Fig. 13 shows how the interaction among parameters in Fig. 1 maintains cardiac output when a deficit in adrenergic modulation is present. In this case, cardiac dilatation, or the use of the Frank-Starling mechanism prevails.

A most striking finding in our studies of the haemodynamic response to stress in highly motivated, volunteer, community dwelling, subjects of a broad age range who had been rigorously screened during exercise for signs of clinical and occult disease (Rodeheffer et al. 1984) is that with advancing age, the haemodynamic profile during exercise takes on the appearance of that due to β-adrenergic blockade as in Fig. 15. Specifically, as age increased, a high cardiac output during exercise was maintained by a lower heart rate, a greater stroke volume, and increased end-diastolic and end-systolic volumes (Fig. 16). This finding and those of other studies which demonstrate a diminution with aging in cardiovascular reflexes mediated by the adrenergic system (Gerstenblith et al. 1979) suggest that a deficit in the effectiveness of adrenergic cardiovascular modulation occurs with advancing adult age.

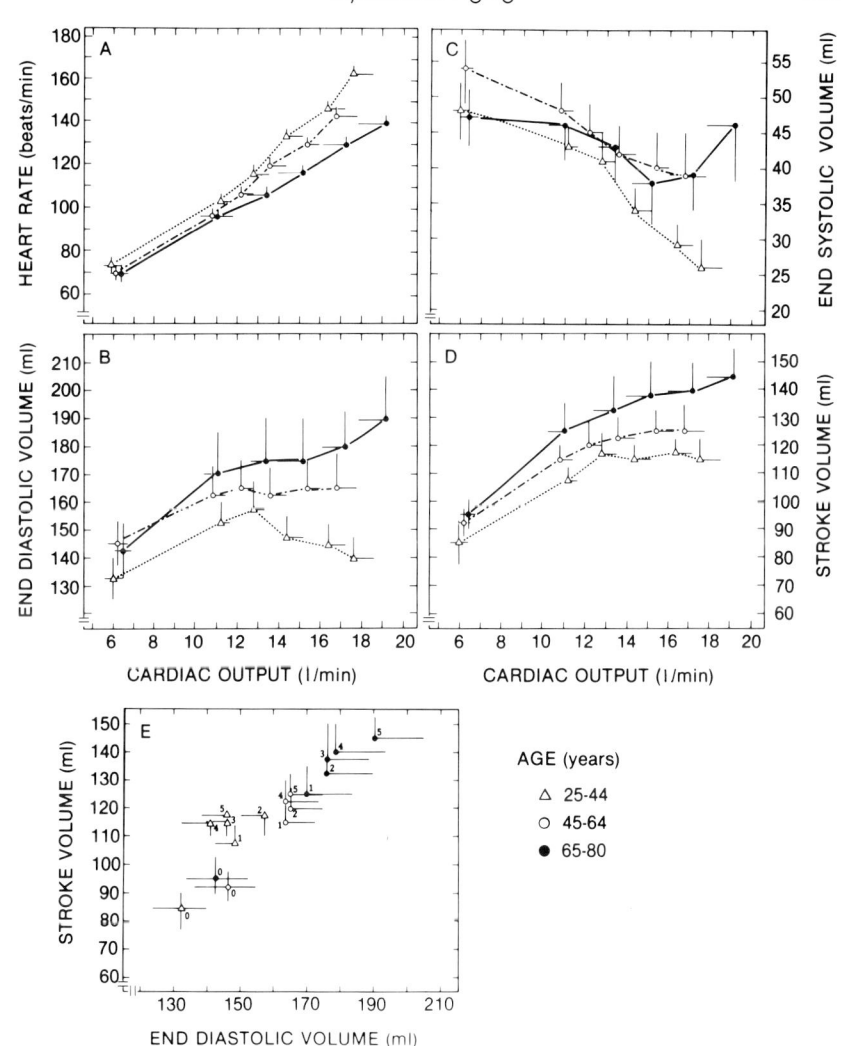

Fig. 16. The relationship of heart rate (A), end-diastolic volume (B), end-systolic volume (C), and stroke volume (D), to cardiac output at rest and during graded upright bicycle exercise in human subjects of the Baltimore Longitudinal Study of Aging who have rigorously been screened to exclude the presence of both clinical and occult cardiovascular disease (screening included ECG monitoring and thallium scanning during a prior maximum treadmill exercise). The major point of the figure is that a *unique* mechanism for augmentation of cardiac output during exercise does not exist in all subjects: to achieve the same high output as in younger subjects, elderly subjects increase heart rate to a lesser extent but increase stroke volume to a greater extent than younger subjects; this is not accomplished by a greater reduction in end-systolic volume but rather by an increase (as much as 30%) in end-diastolic volume, i.e. Starling's law of the heart. The relationship between stroke and end-diastolic volume is depicted in Panel E (0 = rest; 1-5 = progressive incremental work loads). Redrawn from Rodeheffer *et al.* (1984).

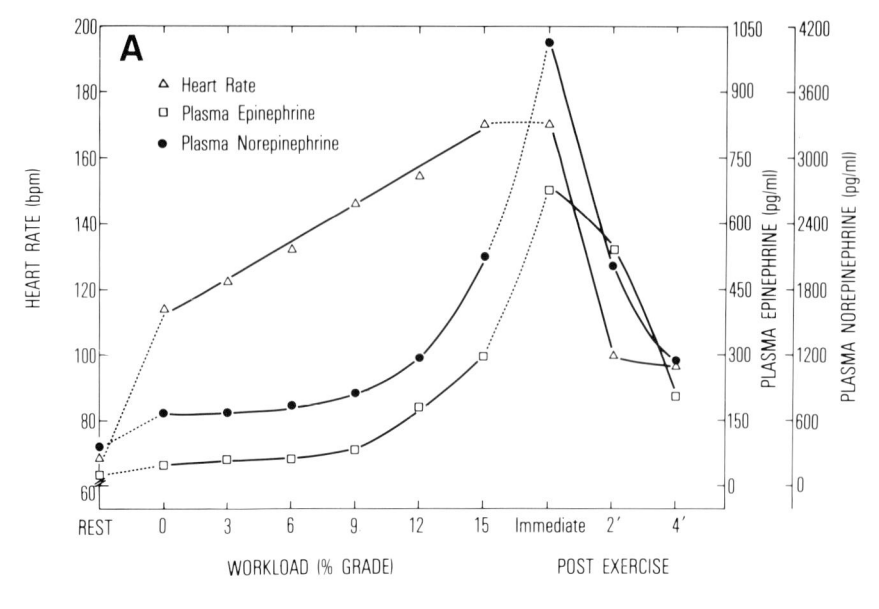

Fig. 17A.

One possible explanation for this apparent diminution in the effectiveness of β-adrenergic modulation of cardiovascular performance during exercise is that the secretion of norepinephrine during exercise stress declines with advancing age. Although this cannot be measured directly in intact animals, the plasma levels of these substances may provide some index of secretion. Figure 17A shows how plasma catecholamines change with incremental demands placed upon the cardiovascular system by incremental exercise work loads. Plasma levels of norepinephrine and epinephrine have been measured during exercise in a subset of older and young adult subjects of the same population studied in Fig. 15. It has been observed that these levels are *increased* rather than decreased in the older versus younger subjects (Figs 17B and C). This lack of evidence for a diminished secretion of catecholamines during exercise suggests that if a decline in tissue catecholamine content as occurs with adult aging in animal models (Lakatta *et al.* 1975a) also occurs in man, it is of little functional importance, at least for short-term stress.

The most obvious explanation for the apparent age-related differences in β-adrenergic modulation of cardiovascular function in man is that the neurotransmitters or hormones are not as effective at the level of the target organs, e.g. as shown in Fig. 11 for rat myocardium. Studies that address the issue of the effect of β-adrenergic modulation of heart rate have been performed. The effect on heart rate of an infusion of the β-adrenergic agonist, isoproterenol, in a subset of the subjects in Fig. 16 is depicted in Fig. 18. In normal men aged 62 to 80 versus those aged 18 to 34 isoproterenol resulted in less of an increment in

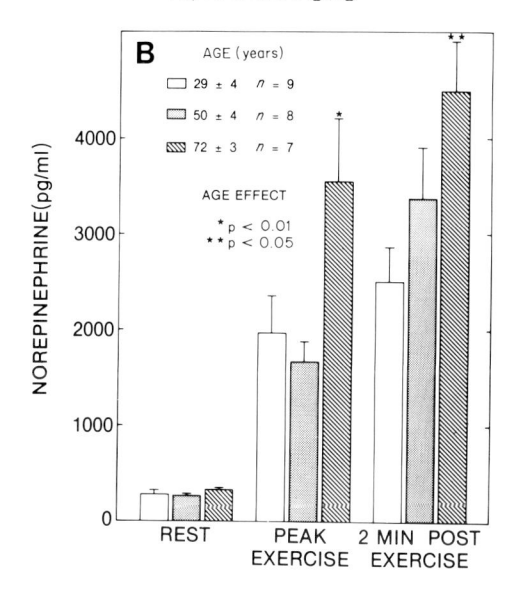

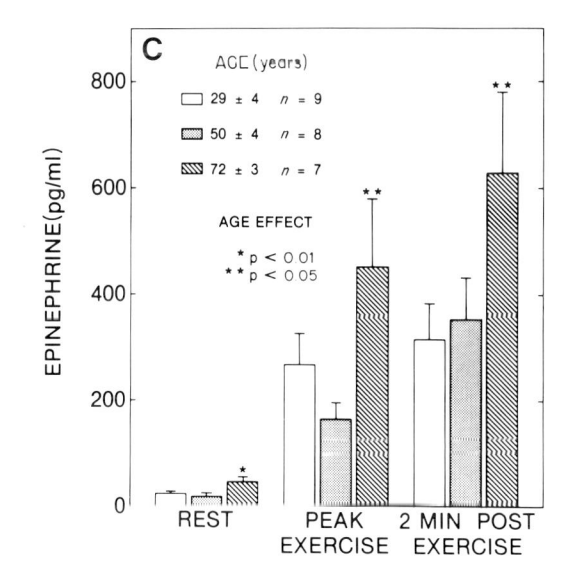

Fig. 17A *(opposite)*. The rise in heart rate (HR), oxygen consumption (VO$_2$), plasma epinephrine (EPI) and norepinephrine (NE) as a function of graded treadmill exercise. From Fleg *et al.* (1985).

Fig. 17B,C. The effect of advanced age on (B) plasma norepinephrine levels and (C) epinephrine at rest, during maximum treadmill exercise, and shortly following exercise. Subjects were participants of the Baltimore Longitudinal Study of Aging who were judged free from occult coronary artery disease by a thorough examination which include prior stress testing with ECG monitoring. From Fleg *et al.* (1985).

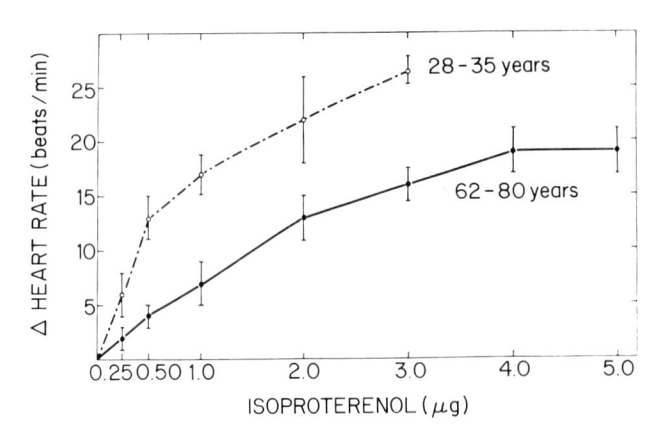

Fig. 18. The effect of age on the increase in heart rate in response to varying concentrations of isoproterenol in the Baltimore Longitudinal Study of Aging participants screened prior to study as in Fig. 16. Points indicate mean ± SEM. At all concentrations above 0.5 g, the effect of age is significant at $P < 0.005$. Adult age = 18-34 years, $n = 16$; senescent = 62-80 years, $n = 20$. From Lakatta (1978), redrawn from Yin et al. (1978).

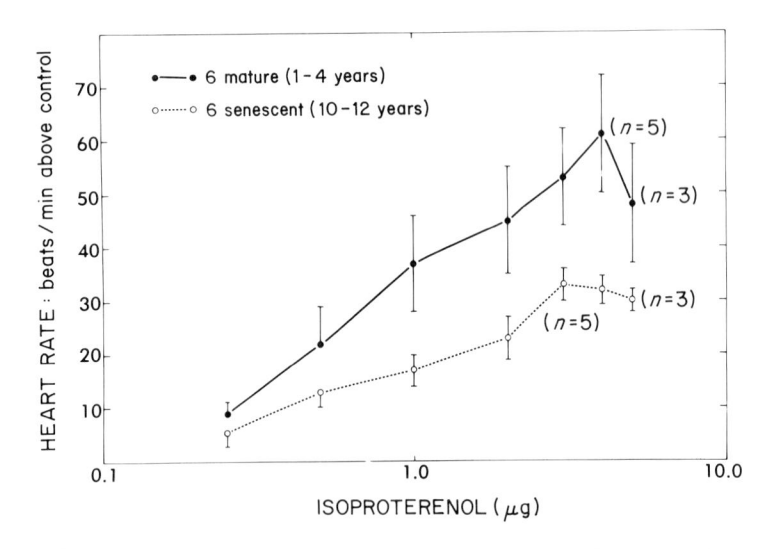

Fig. 19. The effect of age on the heart rate response to rapid bolus intravenous isoproterenol injection in anesthetized dogs. Six dogs in each age group were studied at each concentration, unless otherwise noted in the figure. Baseline heart rates were 157 ± 8 and 143 ± 11 respectively in the senescent and mature groups (NS). The maximum heart rate during isoproternol infusion was greater in the mature group than in the senescent (260 ± 11 vs 220 ± 8, $P < 0.02$. From Yin et al. (1975).

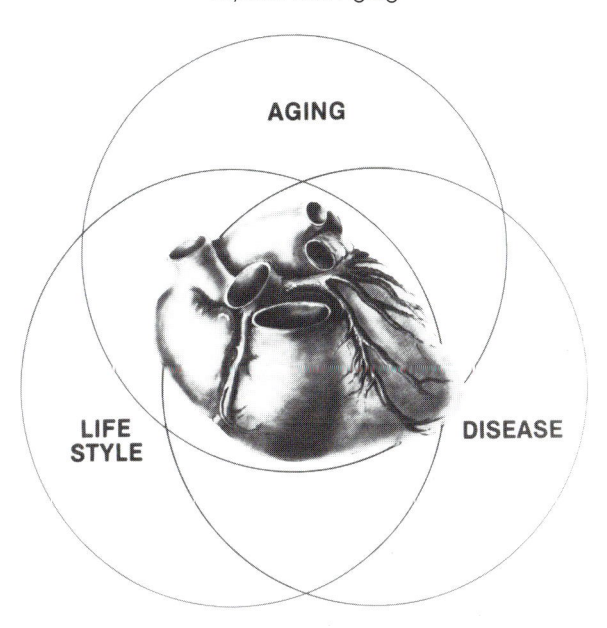

Fig. 20. Changes in lifestyle and diseases occur with advancing age and interactions among these and aging that occur make it difficult to identify or characterize the presence of an "aging process" in the cardiovascular system. From Lakatta (1985c).

heart rate in the elderly group (Lakatta 1978, Yin *et al.* 1976). Although these results are clear-cut in demonstrating that the heart rate response to isoproterenol declines with advancing age, the interpretation of the results is not unique, and they could be explained either by a diminished response to the adrenergic stimulation or by an enhanced vagal modulation of resting heart rate and myocardial function with advancing age, or by both factors. Studies of this sort in the presence of vagal blockade would clarify the interpretation somewhat. In these additional studies in the canine model we have demonstrated that the maximum heart rate response to isoproterenol infusion is diminished in senescent dogs when compared to the adult and the diminished response persisted in the presence of full vagal blockade with atropine. This suggests that age differences in cholinergic tone were not a factor contributing to the aging difference in response to the infused catecholamine (Fig. 19). It is noteworthy that while an age difference in the heart rate response to isoproterenol was observed, no difference in the response of the heart to external pacing at rates more than doubled those elicited by isoproterenol.

In summary, the results in Figs 11 and 13–19, when considered *in toto*, suggest that a diminished responsiveness to β-adrenergic modulation may be among the most significant changes in the cardiovascular system that occurs with advancing age. The differing manifestations of this diminution on cardiovascular performance are appreciated when perspectives from studies that range from measurement of the stress response in intact man to measurements of excitation-contraction coupling and of subcellular protein reactions in animal tissues are integrated. Further investigation of these mechanisms appears to be a fruitful opportunity for future study. Should these mechanisms prove to be similar among organ systems, a global hypothesis of an aging "process", might be legitimately defined and tested. For example, one such hypothesis might be, that "aging is determined in part by a deficiency in cell-cell communication and functional integration among organ systems." However, it must not be forgotten that studies intended to examine an effect of aging on organ function, such as those discussed here for adrenergic modulation of the cardiovascular system, compare younger and older subjects or tissues. Measured differences in function between different age groups in these studies, however, cannot uniquely be interpreted as a manifestation as the "aging process". Even a casual review of the literature that describes such functional declines in various organ systems reveals striking variation in the rate of decline among individual subjects. Conversely, within a given individual there is a wide scatter in the functional decline among different organ system (Rodehoffer *et al.* 1984). This implies that some other factor(s), e.g. lifestyle or the occurrence of disease are potent modulators of a "biological clock" or genetic mechanisms that determine how we age. With advancing age the prevalence of disease increases sharply and that major changes in lifestyle occur, i.e. aging, disease, and lifestyle, are intertwined (Fig. 20). This renders elucidation of the presence and nature of a distinct "aging process" that is independent of the interaction depicted in Fig. 20 a formidable task indeed.

REFERENCES

Bhatnagar, G. M., Walford, G. D., Beard, E. S., Humphreys, S. H. and Lakatta, E. G. (1984). ATPase activity and force production in myofibrils and twitch characteristics in intact muscle from neonatal, adult, and senescent rat myocardium. *J. Mol. Cell. Cardiol.* **16**, 203-218.

Effron, M. B., Bhatnagar, G. M., Spurgeon, H. A., Ruano-Arroyo, G. and Lakatta. Changes in myosin isoenzymes, ATPase activity, and contractile duration in rat cardiac muscle with aging can be modulated by thyroxine. (Submitted for publication.)

Filburn, C. R. and Lakatta, E. G. (1984). Aging alterations in β-adrenergic modulation of cardiac cell function. *In* "Aging and cell function" (J. E. Johnson, Jr., ed.) pp. 211-246. Plenum Press, New York.

Fleg, J. L., Tzankoff, S. P. and Lakatta, E. G. (1985). Age-related augmentation of plasma catecholamines during dynamic exercise in healthy males. *J. Appl. Physiol.* **59**, 1033-1039.

Froehlich, J. P., Lakatta, E. G., Beard, E., Spurgeon, H. A., Weisfeldt, M. L. and Gerstenblith, G. (1978). Studies of sarcoplasmic reticulum function and contraction duration in young adult and aged rat myocardium. *J. Mol. Cell. Cardiol.* **10**, 427-438.

Gerstenblith, G., Spurgeon, H. A., Froehlich, J. P., Weisfeldt, M. L. and Lakatta, E. G. (1979). Diminished inotropic responsiveness to ouabain in aged rat myocardium. *Circ. Res.* **44**, 517-523.

Guarnieri, T., Spurgeon, H., Froehlich, J. P., Weisfeldt, M. L. and Lakatta, E. G. (1979). Diminished inotropic response but unaltered toxicity to acetylstrophanthidin in the senescent beagle. *Circulation* **60**, 1548-1554.

Guarnieri, T., Filburn, C. R., Zitnik, G., Roth, G. S. and Lakatta, E. G. (1980). Contractile and biochemical correlates of beta-adrenergic stimulation of the aged heart. *Am. J. Physiol.* **239** (*Heart Circ. Physiol.* **8**), H501-508.

Lakatta, E. G. (1978). Alterations in the cardiovascular system that occur in advanced age. *Fedn Proc.* **38**, 163-167.

Lakatta, E. G. (1980). Age-related alterations in the cardiovascular response to adrenergic mediated stress, *Fedn Proc.* **39**, 3173-3177.

Lakatta, E. G. (1983). Determinants of cardiovascular performance: modification due to aging. *J. Chronic. Dis.* **36**, 15-30.

Lakatta, E. G. (1984). Excitation-contraction in cardiac muscle of the adult senescent rat. In "Functional aspects of the normal, hypertrophied and failing heart" (F. L. Abel and W. H. Newman, eds) pp. 351 368. Martinus Nijhoff, Boston.

Lakatta, E. G. (1985a). Altered autonomic modulation of cardiovascular function with adult aging: perspectives from studies ranging from man to cell. In "Pathobiology of cardiovascular injury" (H. L. Stone and W. B. Weglicki, eds) pp. 441-460. Boston, Martinus Nijhoff, Boston.

Lakatta, E. G. (1985b). Age-related changes in the heart. In "Handbook of the biology of aging" (C. E. Finch and E. L. Schneider, eds) pp. 377-413. Van Nostrand Reinhold, New York.

Lakatta, E. G. (1985c). Health, disease, and cardiovascular aging. In "Health in an older society" (Institute of Medicine and National Research Council, Committee on an Aging Society, eds) pp. 73-104. National Academy Press, Washington, DC.

Lakatta, E. G. (1986). Do hypertension and aging similarly affect the myocardium? *Circulation* (in press).

Lakatta, E. G. and Yin, F. C. P. (1982). Myocardial aging: functional alterations and related cellular mechanisms. *Am. J. Physiol.* **242** (*Heart Circ. Physiol.* **11**), H927-H941.

Lakatta, E. G., Gerstenblith, G. Angell, C. S., Shock, N. W. and Weisfeldt, M. L. (1975a). Prolonged contraction duration in aged myocardium. *J. Clin. Invest.* **55**, 61-68.

Lakatta, E. G., Gerstenblith, G., Angell, C. S., Shock, N. W. and Wiesfeldt, M. L. (1975b). Diminished inotropic response of aged myocardium to catecholamines. *Circ. Res.* **36**, 262-269.

McIvor, M. E., Orchard, C. H. and Lakatta, E. G. Autonomic modulation of cardiac twitch relaxation is independent of myofibrillar sensitivity to Ca^{2+}. Submitted for publication.

Orchard, C. H. and Lakatta, E. G. (1985). Intracellular calcium transients and developed tensions in rat heart muscle. A mechanism for the negative interval-strength relationship. *J. Gen. Physiol.* **86**, 637-651.

Renlund, D., Gerstenblith, G., Rodeheffer, R. J., Fleg, J. L. and Lakatta, E. G. (1985). Potency of the Frank Starling reserve in normal man. *J. Am. Coll. Cardiol.* **5**, 514.

Rodeheffer, R. J., Gerstenblith, G., Becker, L. C., Fleg, J. L., Weisfeldt, M. L. and Lakatta, E. G. (1984). Exercise cardiac output is maintained with advancing age in healthy human subjects: cardiac dilatation and increased stroke volume compensate for a diminished heart rate. *Circulation* **69**, 203-213.

Spurgeon, H. A., Steinbach, M. F. and Lakatta, E. G. (1983). Chronic exercise prevents characteristic age-related changes in rat cardiac contraction. *Am. J. Physiol.* **244** (*Heart Circ. Physiol.* **13**), H513-H518.

Wei, J. Y., Spurgeon, H. A. and Lakatta, E. G. (1984). Excitation-contraction in rat myocardium: alterations with adult aging. *Am. J. Physiol.* **246** (*Heart Circ. Physiol.* **15**), H784-H791.

Yin, F. C. P., Spurgeon, H. A., Raizes, G. S., Greene, H. L., Weisfeldt, M. L. and Shock, N. W. (1976). Age associated decrease in chronotropic response to isoproterenol. *Circulation* **54**, II-167.

Yin, F. C. P., Spurgeon, H. A., Greene, H. L., Lakatta, E. G. and Weisfeldt, M. L. (1979). Age-associated decrease in heart rate response to isoproterenol in dogs. *Mech. Age Dev.* **10**, 17-25.

Yin, F. C. P., Spurgeon, H. A., Weisfeldt, M. L. and Lakatta, E. G. (1980). Mechanical properties of myocardium from hypertrophied rat hearts: A comparison between hypertrophy induced by senescence and by aortic banding. *Circ. Res.* **46**, 292-300.

Yin, F. C. P., Spurgeon, H. A., Rakusan, K., Weisfeldt, M. L. and Lakatta, E. G. (1982). Use of tibial length to quantify cardiac hypertrophy: application in the aging rat. *Am. J. Physiol.* **243** (*Heart Circ. Physiol.* **12**), H941-H947.

Discussion

Goedhard: When talking about cardiac output in relation to aging, should not also the afterload of the heart be observed? Would you comment on possible changes in afterload with age?

Lakatta: One of the major determinants of the afterload is the systolic blood pressure and this is determined by aortic compliance and stroke volume. The aortic stiffness with age is partly compensated by aortic dilatation. At rest, stroke volume is not compromised and the heart is not bigger. Another adaptive mechanism permits normal function at rest, e.g. ventricular thickening compensates for increased afterload, higher blood pressure. During exercise, however, blood pressure increases from 120 or 130 to 200 systolic. The diastolic pressure increases also slightly. While there is an age difference at rest, there is no difference at peak exercise. From blood pressure measurements we have no evidence that there is a greater impedence in the old heart during exercise. Recent studies have shown that, while blood pressure increases during exercise, the impedance does not. The reason for this is aortic dilatation.

Hesser: Could you comment on the aging of vessels?

Lakatta: All factors mentioned work together. The question is, how stroke volume is limited by stiffer vessels. The data showed that stroke volume was not limited, neither at rest nor at exercise. There are other factors which are able to adapt the stroke volume, to increase it even when the vessels are stiffer.

Steinhagen-Thiessen: You have shown the results of the Baltimore Longitudinal Study. Are these aging individuals doing regular exercise work and, if so, does it mean a certain stress to them?

Lakatta: In some ways, the population I studied responded to stress like conditioned athletes would. The big difference is, however, that in addition to conditions at younger age, maximum heart rate is not attained. The men and women who were just working in the community and who did participate in a regular exercise program were highly motivated to do so. There were no athletes on this program.

Carlsson: β-blocking agents are able to prolong survival after heart infarct. Is it good or bad for the old heart to get less responsive to adrenergic stimulation?

Lakatta: I really do not know. As there is substantial scatter among individuals and also within the young and the old age group, it is hard to predict whether their response to catecholes would be high or low. Some believe that one should not give β-blockers to old people as they are already hyporesponsive. On the other hand, anti-hypertensives work in old people, but it is hard to predict whether there is an influence on their living together.

Stähelin: I was quite impressed how similar the effects in the old rat heart and in the human heart are. What theory of aging would you think suits best to explain this fairly distinct deficit?

Lakatta: It is difficult to ascribe the observed changes to one particular theory on aging on the molecular level. We studied function and changes in function in relation to time and were not, when we begun, bothered with theories. I doubt whether one of the theories discussed earlier successfully explains our observations. In a very general sense, one might say that different parts of the cardiovascular system and different parts of the heart have to communicate with each other and this manifestation of aging could be conceptualized as a break-down of communication.

Influence of Age and Training on Bone and Muscle Tissue in Humans and Mice

Elisabeth Steinhagen-Thiessen

Medizinische Kern- und Poliklinik, University Hospital, Hamburg, Federal Republic of Germany

Keywords
Exercise; Skeletal/heart muscle; Bone mineral content.

INTRODUCTION

The normal aging process in different organisms is influenced by extrinsic and intrinsic factors. The influence of physical training as an external factor is still considered to be controversial. Among the elderly the diseases which affect the locomotor system are some of the most important. To understand the physiology and the biochemistry of the locomotor system, we have to keep in mind that it is formed of muscle and bone tissue. The muscle represents a postmitotic tissue while bone is always a regenerating tissue. More and more attention is paid to physical activity and its influence on the muscle and bone tissue especially in the elderly population.

MUSCLE TISSUE

Human striated muscle exhibits a considerable age-dependent loss of specific activity in different muscle enzymes (Steinhagen-Thiessen and Hilz 1976). In order to analyse whether this is a result of extrinsic factors such as decreased physical activity in the elderly or whether this is an intrinsic phenomenon, mice

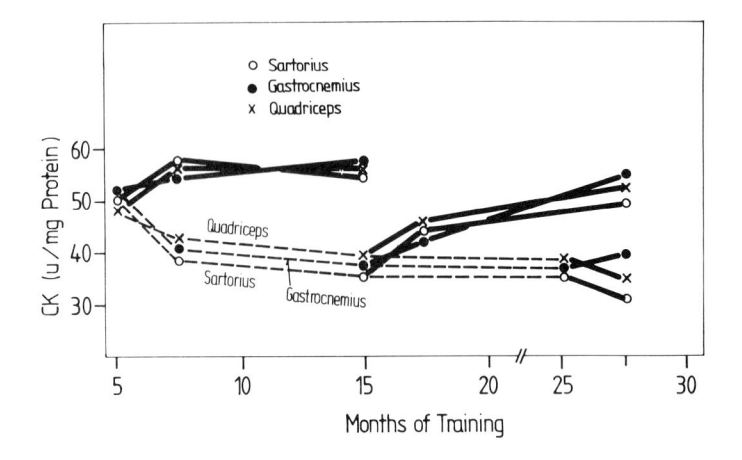

Fig. 1. CK activity/unit soluble protein in the different hind leg muscles of C57BL mice. ——— = trained animals; ------ = untrained animals.

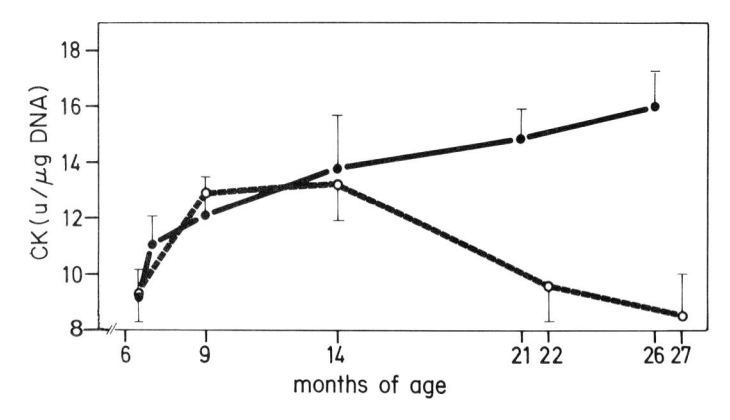

Fig. 2. CK activity/DNA in the hind leg muscles of C57BL mice. ——— = trained animals; ------ = untrained animals.

of two different strains and of various ages were trained for 5 weeks, 30 min/day on electrically driven running wheels (short-term training programme), and similar strains of mice were trained according to the same schedule but over their entire lifespan (long-term training programme). All experiments were carried out with two genetically different strains of mice to avoid results being strain dependent (for details see Steinhagen-Thiessen et al. 1980, 1981). The enzymes creatine kinase (CK), aldolase, superoxide dismutase (SOD) and catalase were chosen because of their different independent metabolic pathways in muscle tissue. Furthermore, the enzyme CK was chosen because it is a key enzyme in the initial production of ATP in muscle contraction. SOD was chosen because it is involved

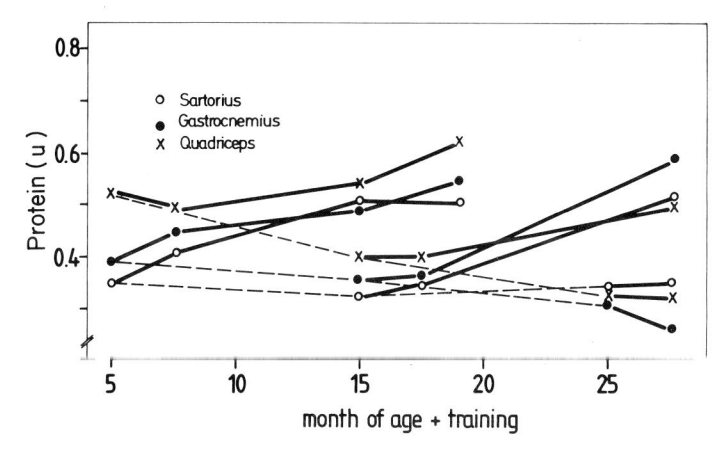

Fig. 3. Aldolase activity/unit soluble protein in the different hind leg muscles of C57BL mice. ——— = trained animals; ------ = untrained animals.

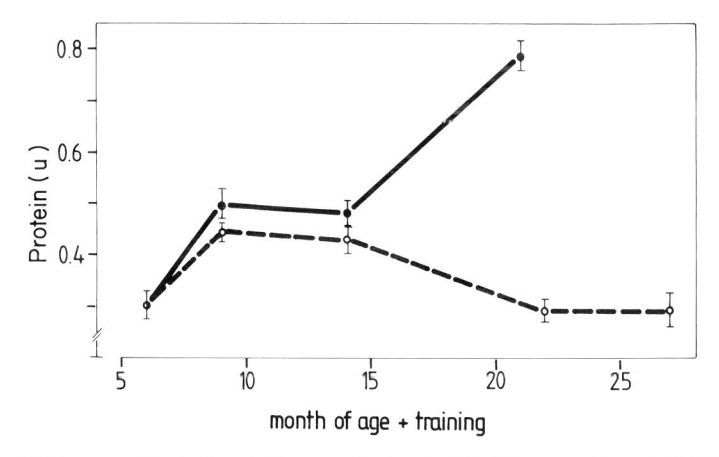

Fig. 4. Aldolase activity/unit soluble protein in the hind leg muscles of CW I mice. ——— = trained animals; ------ = untrained animals.

in the free radical protection of cells which may play an important role in cell senescence.

The 6-month-old mice in both strains in general showed an increase in all enzyme parameters during the short-term training period of 5 weeks (Steinhagen-Thiessen et al. 1980, 1981). But old animals — CW I and C57BL strains — showed a marked reduction of specific activities in the different enzymes after this 5-week training programme. We refer to this observed effect as a "negative adaptation" to aging and training. The same results were observed for these enzymes in the heart muscle tissue (Gershon et al. 1982, Reznick et al. 1982, Steinhagen-Thiessen et al. 1984)

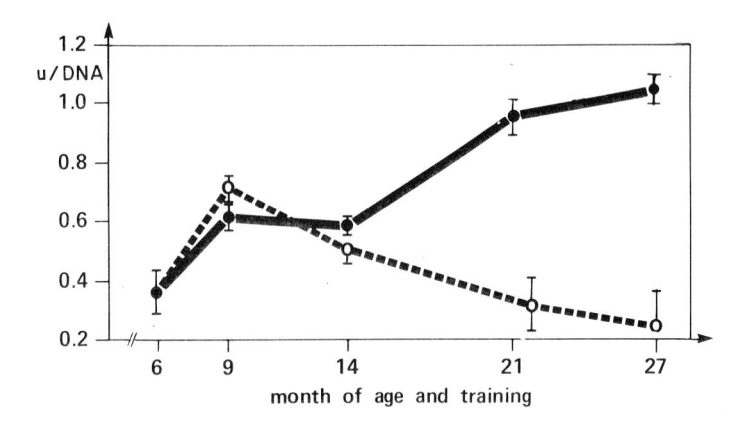

Fig. 5. SOD activity/DNA in the heart muscle tissue of CW I mice. ——— = trained animals;
------ = untrained animals.

In order to investigate how muscle adapts to a long-term training regimen, the CW I and C57 BL strains of mice were trained throughout their lifespan and, in addition, one group started their lifelong training programme at the age of 15 months. Figures 1 and 2 show the results of CK after the long-term training programme in the hind leg muscle of the different strains of mice. For the C57BL mice the specific activity of CK was measured in the following separate hind leg muscles: musculus sartorius, musculus quadriceps and musculus gastrocnemius. For the CW I mice the results are given in the whole hind leg muscle based on DNA. In both strains we measured a "positive adaptation" to training and aging. Even when mice started this training regimen at the age of 15 months they reached the same values of enzyme activity in the hind leg muscle as compared with those animals which started the training at 6 months of age. Identical results were observed for the enzyme aldolase in skeletal muscle (Figs 3 and 4).

Figure 5 shows the activity for SOD in heart muscle tissue of the same CW I mice after this long-term training period (for other enzymes see Steinhagen-Thiessen *et al.* 1984). In skeletal as well as in heart muscle tissue there is a significant difference of specific enzyme activities between the trained and the untrained groups of animals. The untrained animals also show the well known age-dependent loss of enzyme activity, but in the long-term trained animals the enzyme activities showed a "positive adaptation" to training in aging.

These results observed in different muscle enzymes (striated and heart muscle tissue) in two genetically different strains of mice demonstrate that external factors can influence the normal aging process; long-term training is obviously beneficial for the skeletal and heart muscle.

BONE TISSUE

Skeletal pain and fractures in the elderly are due to the loss of bone mineral content. One of the aetiological factors is the physical inactivity of the elderly. We also analysed the extrinsic effect of controlled physical activity on the bone mineral content in our mice model. The femura of the long-term trained mice (CW I) were analysed for different parameters: dry weight, mean volume, mean specific weight, calcium, phosphorous and magnesium content.

A significant increase in bone weight was observed throughout the duration of the training period. The calcium, phosphorus and magnesium contents in the bones of the untrained animals showed a decrease of these minerals with age. In the control animals we observed an age-dependent loss of bone mineral content which is similar to that seen in humans. But the significant increase in calcium, phosphorus and magnesium in the trained animal groups showed a positive effect on the bone (Fig. 6 and Table 1). Since this training programme involves the whole

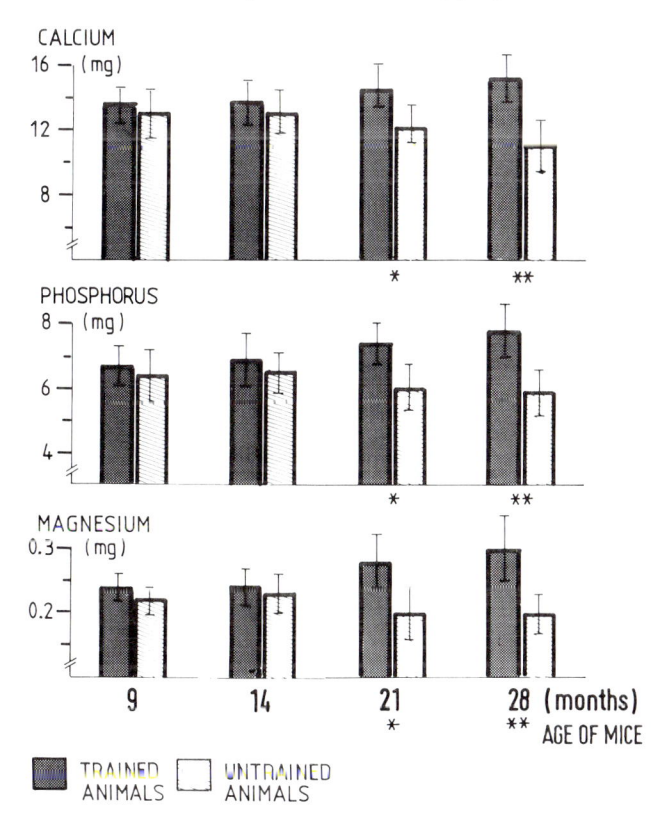

Fig. 6. Mean values of bone mineral content in the femura of CW I mice, long-term training programme. $*P < 0.01$, $**P < 0.001$.

Table 1

Age (months)	Mice n	Time of training (months)	Mean dry weight mg SD	Mean volume μl SD	Mean specific weight mg/μl SD
9	10	—	59.4±5.8 49.9±3.9	1.19±0.06	
	9	3	60.2±5.5 50.8±5.4	1.19±0.05	
14	10	—	58.4±4.9 49.5±5.9	1.18±0.06	
	9	8	60.9±5.7 50.1±4.8	1.21±0.06	
21	11	—	54.7±6.7 50.2±4.6	1.08±0.07	
	10	15	61.1±6.1 51.8±6.0	1.18±0.06	
27	11	—	51.8±8.0 50.5±4.9	1.03±0.05	
	11	21	62.4±5.8 52.5±6.1	1.19±0.08	

Table 2
Temporomandibular joint (CW I)

Age (months)	Thickness of the cartilage (μm) Control	Training	Cartilage cells/area (1/μm²) Control	Training	Bone cells/area (1/μm²) Control	Training
9	196.13±19		2.19±0.35		1.116±0.14	
20		154.3±47		2.532±0.66		1.12±0.09
24	144.6±7.5	157.7±19	1.19±0.019	1.52±0.16	0.96±0.002	1.14±0.1
27	140±17	167.4±14	1.159±0.18	1.24±0.07	0.903±0.1	0.898±0.083
32	115±1.3		0.679±0.02		0.791±0.0074	

locomotor system these results are likely to be representative of the whole skeleton.

In addition to our observations of the mineral content of the femura we analysed the temporomandibular joints of our trained and untrained mice. This joint was chosen because it is not primarily involved in physical exercise. In the long-term trained animals the cartilage in this joint was significantly thicker. The number of cartilage and bone cells in the trained animals was higher. The temporomandiubular joints of the aged trained animals showed no change in the parameters represented in Table 2 in comparison with the untrained aging animals. The results of the bone mineral content measurements in the long-term trained animals and the results of the temporomanidbular joints of the trained animals show that controlled physical activity initiated prior to a certain threshold of age can prevent age-dependent osteoporosis and degenerated arthritis.

All these parameters were evaluated in order to attempt to form a basis for an exercise programme for humans. Figure 7 gives the results of the bone mineral content of the forearm in humans. Most of the cross-sectional studies stop at the age of 65. We therefore extend our studies beyond the age of 65 in order to obtain more information about the age-dependent bone mineral content. After

Bone and Muscle Tissue 139

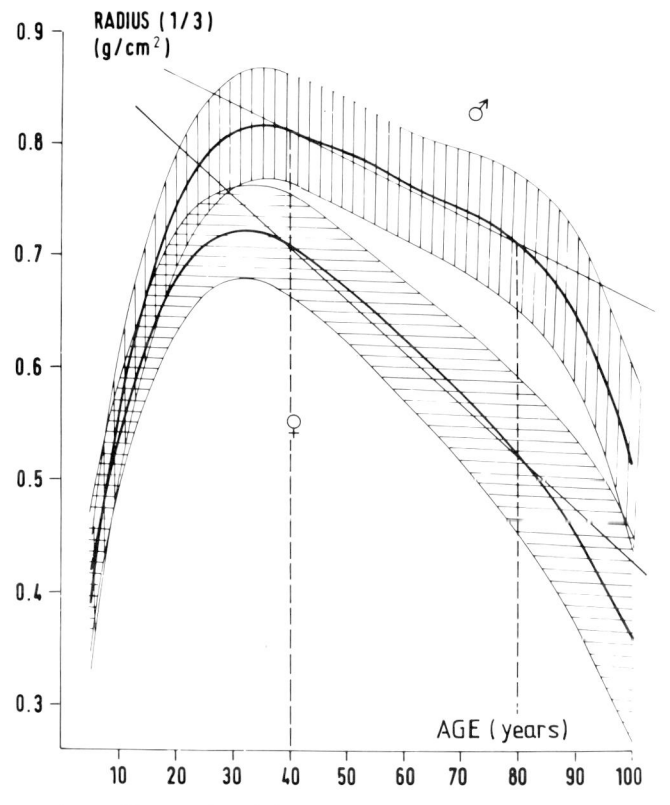

Fig. 7. Mean values of bone mineral content on the radius shaft in humans measured by the ^{125}J absorptiometry method. Males, $n=612$; females, $n=688$.

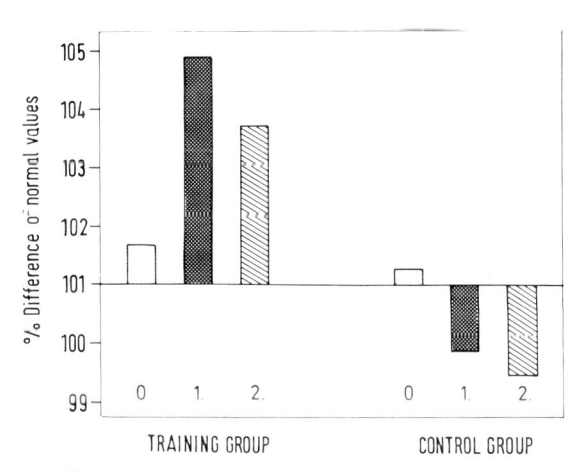

Fig. 8. Differences of bone mineral content in the radius shaft (⅓) after (1.) and 14 (2.) months of physical exercise in humans over 65 years.

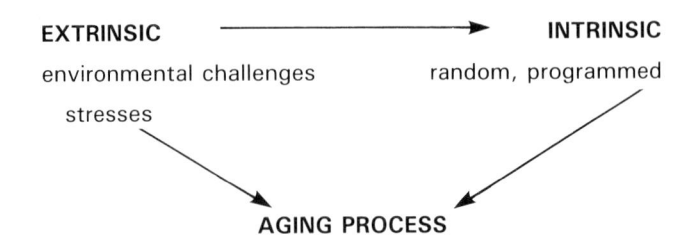

```
EXTRINSIC  ─────────────▶  INTRINSIC
environmental challenges    random, programmed
    stresses
           ╲              ╱
            ▶ AGING PROCESS ◀
```

Fig. 9. Influence of extrinsic and intrinsic factors on the aging process.

the age of 40 in both sexes there is a continuous decrease which accelerates until 80 years of age. In females the rate of bone loss in the 1/3 sites is an average of 4.4% between the ages of 30 and 70 years and then increases to 11% for the last three decades.

Based on this cross-sectional data we started a longitudinal exercise programme with elderly people. Preliminary results after 7 and 14 months of training showed an increase of bone mineral content compared to the untrained control group (Fig. 8). The control group shows an age-dependent loss of bone mineral content. Performing controlled mild exercise with the elderly — over 65 years of age — shows that even when the loss of bone mineral content has already started between 35 and 40 years of age, there is still a possibility of preventing age-dependent osteoporosis by physical activity. Physical exercise should play an important therapeutic role in the concept of treating elderly people suffering from osteoporosis.

These data in humans and mice on muscle and bone tissue under training conditions show that extrinsic factors like physical exercise can influence the aging process (Fig. 9). Furthermore, these results show that physical activity, if started early in life, can significantly slow down age-dependent destruction of the entire locomotor system. This is probably an important factor in health and socioeconomic aspects of the elderly.

REFERENCES

Gershon, D., Silbermann, M., Coleman, R., Finkelbrand, S., Steinhagen-Thiessen, E. and Reznick, A. (1982). The effect of age and exercise on some biochemical and morphological parameters in striated and cardiac muscles. *In* "Advances in pathology", (E. Levi, ed.) Vol. 2, pp. 257-260. Pergamon Press, Oxford and New York.

Reznick, A., Steinhagen-Thiessen, E. and Gershon, D. (1982). The effect of exercise on enzyme activities in cardiac muscles of mice of various ages. *Biochem. Med.* **28**, 347-352.

Steinhagen-Thiessen, E. and Hilz, H. (1976). The age-dependent decrease in creatine kinase and aldolase activities in human striated muscle is not caused by an accumulation of faulty proteins. *Mech. Age. Dev.* **5**, 447-457.

Steinhagen-Thiessen, E., Reznick, A. and Hilz, H. (1980). Negative adaptation to physical training in senile mice. *Mech. Age. Dev.* **12**, 231-236.

Steinhagen-Thiessen, E., Reznick, A. and Hilz, H. (1981). Positive and negative adaptation of muscle enzymes in aging mice subjected to physical exercise. *Mech. Age. Dev.* **16**, 363-369.

Steinhagen-Thiessen, E., Reznick, A. and Ringe, J. D. (1984). Age dependent variations in cardiac and skeletal muscle during short and long term tread-mill running of mice. *Eur. Heart J.* **5**(E), 27-30.

Discussion

Verdonk: Did you do any studies on the role of calcium uptake; this could make a difference to bone tissue in your two groups of resting and trained animals as well as in aged people.

Steinhagen-Thiessen: We tried to ask our study group about their food but we did not get very good answers — I have very little trust in this kind of questionnaire, I prefer exact measurements in the laboratory. Food plays an important role, e.g. age-dependent osteoporosis in Japan is completely different from in Europe. People in Japan drink less milk and eat much less cheese than people in Western countries.

Mombelloni: Did you find any difference in survival in trained and untrained mice?

Steinhagen-Thiessen: To give a conclusive answer, one should have a much larger number of animals. We took ten mice out of the whole group and we had the impression that the trained group died earlier, but the results were not significant.

Lucke: Are you absolutely convinced that the elderly people who you could encourage to do exercise are comparable with the control group? Everybody treating old patients knows that some like to do exercise and others do not. Apart from that, is your method of measuring mineral contents accurate enough to determine a bone loss of 3% with the rather high SD?

Steinhage-Thiessen: To your first question, I admit that one cannot really compare those two groups. When you experiment with humans, you always have the difficulty of getting people to do exercise voluntarily; but it is really better than doing nothing. Concerning your second question about the exactitude of our method: we must use non-invasive methods, especially when you have to convince people to come to the hospital. I agree with you that our method is not the best nor the most accurate one, but when we compare our results with those obtained with CT, there is a rather good correspondence.

Erminii: Your data from old animals after short-term exercise refer to enzymes of the energy metabolism, i.e. CK and aldolase decline in specific activity. Now, what about the structural proteins, i.e. the myofibrillar proteins, do they change too, perhaps in the sense of structural and functional deterioration? Can you perhaps observe some concomitant muscle wasting? In other words, are the observed biochemical changes indicative of noxious effects of short-term exercise in the aging?

Steinhagen-Thiessen: These biochemistry measurements in the muscle have been done at the same time as microscopical and electronmicroscopical studies. When you compare the microscopical and electronmicroscopical pictures of the aged short-term trained animals you see that the whole muscle architecture shows destruction. For example, the whole architecture of the mitochondria was very often lost in those aged short-term trained animals.

Häusler: Looking at your data in mice one gets the impression that the aging process is faster in bones than in muscles. When you look at your 20 to 21-month-old animals, they are similar to the old ones; but when you look at the data from the muscles, then they look similar to those of the younger animals. Is that correct?

Steinhagen-Thiessen: No, I would not agree. If you remember, there was also not always the same answer in the different enzyme activities either e.g. in the "intermediate" animals which were training for 2 months. Sometimes the 22-month-old animals showed the same picture as the 6-month-olds, but in other enzymes, they had the same picture as the 27-month-old.

Roth: Would you care to speculate on the mechanism responsible for exercise-induced protection against bone loss?

Steinhagen-Thiessen: I would propose that every environmental change has an influence on the body and how it is able to adapt to these changes. Maybe, behind all this are much more important mechanisms at the molecular basis and at the nervous system which is involved very much in this training procedure, too.

Roth: I would suggest measurement of parathyroid hormone, calcitonine and a general assessment of the endocrine profile.

Steinhagen-Thiessen: The endocrine system is certainly involved, there is no doubt about that.

Bruder: If one transfers these results to one's own life for practical purposes, the idea arises as to whether a shorter daily exercise time would also lead to an avoidance of loss of minerals and decrease of enzymes?

Steinhagen-Thiessen: Shorter periods have not been tested.

Functional Repair of the Nervous System: A Focus on Aging

Richard Jed Wyatt, Luis de Medinaceli, and William J. Freed

Neuropsychiatry Branch, National Institute of Mental Health, Saint Elizabeths Hospital, Washington, D.C., USA

Keywords
Regeneration; Brain grafts; Parkinson's disease.

INTRODUCTION

Probably the worst fear people have of growing older is of diminished nervous system function. While normal aging is associated with a known decrease in many bodily functions, there is considerable uncertainty about the affects of normal aging on the nervous system.

In the absence of disease and physical impairment, studies in aging individuals indicate slowing of normal human brain function (Welford 1977, Jarvik 1983). There does not seem to be any decrement in ability, however, until the loss of speed itself impairs function. This is particularly true of cognition. A gradual decrease in nervous system reserve (similar to cardiac reserve), however, may make a person more vulnerable to disease or trauma, producing a functional loss that would not occur in a younger person. Thus, determining functional deterioration may require stressing the system, at times in an extraordinary manner. In order to understand the aging process better, in our experiments we have often severely stressed the nervous system, trying to define basic principles relating both to degeneration and repair. We have consistently used measures of behavioural function as this is ultimately about what the individual is concerned. Although we have primarily focussed our attention on repair and promotion of recovery once function is lost, it is our expectation that some of the principles learned can be used for prevention of deterioration. In addition, we wish to give patients with loss of nervous system function some realistic hope of recovery.

We have used two basic models in our attempts to promote functional recovery of the nervous system. One is a model of a traumatic lesion—severing a peripheral nerve. The second is an animal model of a human degenerative disorder—Parkinson's disease.

LESSONS LEARNED FROM SEVERING AND REPAIRING THE SCIATIC NERVE

The central nervous system (CNS) is a network of three-dimensional interconnections with a consistency of warm gelatin. These qualities make mechanical intervention and repair difficult. To begin to understand how to repair traumatic lesions in the CNS we have used the comparatively simple rat peripheral nerve. Like the rest of the nervous system a peripheral nerve is fragile, but its fibres run a linear course from spinal cord to end organ. The cable-like nature of peripheral nerves together with the absence of interneurons considerably simplifies experimental studies.

Scarring

A simple crush of a peripheral nerve destroys the neurites, but leaves intact the basic structure because the basal lamina is not destroyed. The surviving basal lamina appears to provide enough longitudinal structure to act as a guide tube as the neurites cross the site of the crush and subsequently grow toward their physiological targets. Similarly, the structure of the basal lamina guides the migration of displaced Schwann cells that remyelinate the growing neurites and provide further support for the neurites. It is the retention of the basic structure of the peripheral nerve after a crush that often allows for full functional recovery (Gutmann 1942). Thus, the alcoholic with Saturday night palsy will regain most if not all function of his hand even though he has crushed his radial nerve from prolonged pressure; restoration of function will take only as long as it takes new neurites to grow from the site of the crush to the muscles.

The CNS does not retain its structure in an area where there has been significant disruption. Not only are the neurons disrupted, but unlike the peripheral nerve there is no basal lamina in the CNS, so there is no basic guidance after injury; the consequence is a massive glial and connective tissue scar (Tator and Rivlin 1983). To produce a less complicated experimental situation than the total disarray that occurs following a CNS lesion but which does not occur with a crush in the peripheral nervous system, we have used the completely severed peripheral nerve as a model. While there are many substantial differences between the severed peripheral nerve and a lesion in the CNS, they have some common elements.

Important similarities include scar formation, partial loss of orientation for the sprouting neurites and lasting motor and sensory deficits (Young 1942, Sunderland 1968).

Preventing the Scar

When a peripheral nerve is cut there is a macroscar that is apparent to the naked eye. Components of this scar include blood, fat and other debris from the cut ends. The macroscar has been apparent to most investigators and a number of elimination methods have been devised. Elimination of the macroscar, however, has done little to improve functional recovery.

A microscar also forms immediately at the point of separation. This scar includes the disruption or tangle in fibre alignment that comes from the shearing forces at the time of transection as well as the disruption that occurs from ionic changes between the intracellular and extracellular fluid at the time of transection. In addition to eliminating the macroscar, the microscar must be removed before the neurites in the proximal stump can cross the transection and have a relatively continuous, unbroken pathway to their target.

To remove the microscar (and the macroscar) the tips of the stumps must be removed in a manner that does not also produce a new microscar. A clean cut can be achieved by making the nerve tips firm by bringing the temperature of the stumps to near freezing (freezing of the nerve will cause damage). To harden the nerve further, polyvinyl alcohol is used to make the bathing fluid viscous. Preventing further ionic disruption at the time of scar removal is achieved by using a bathing medium with an ionic strength similar to that of intracellular fluid. One means of doing the latter is to bathe the nerve endings in a modified Collins fluid designed to mimic intracellular fluid (Collins et al. 1969). To further counteract the disruptive effect (thought to begin the process of Wallarian degeneration (de Medinaceli and Church 1984) and disrupt neurofilaments (Guth et al. 1965)) of intracellular calcium, EGTA or chlorpromazine is used in the medium. The scar can be cut from the stumps with a vibrating knife. Once the scar is cut from the damaged nerves, the nerve is gradually returned to room temperature and the medium surrounding the nerve restored to normal extracellular fluid (de Medinaceli et al. 1983).

Microsutures placed into the ends of the stumps, in order to aid realignment, will produce further disruption of the stump ends and new scar formation from the accumulation of blood and other products of clotting. Thus, reconnection and alignment of the cut stump ends must occur away from the ends of the stumps.

Reorientation and Reconnection

Following transection of a peripheral nerve there is vigorous regrowth of the neurites (Goldberg et al. 1984). Elimination of the scar requires preventing wandering of the growing neurites and aiming them in the direction of the proper guide tube in the distal stump. Once they reach the undisturbed tissue in the distal stump they continue to grow and there is nothing to cause further deviation.

While prevention of scar formation allows the neurites of a severed nerve to grow unimpeded, proper orientation of the growing fibres is necessary to insure that they progress into the distal stump and that they are appropriately orientated into that stump. Since mechanical intervention at the stump end will cause further scar formation, any manipulation must of necessity occur away from the end (de Medinaceli and Freed 1983). To prevent further scar formation, a nerve connector was designed that provides support and allows for manipulation of a cut nerve with no force applied directly to the nerve end. The nerve connector is a flat sheet made from a thin elastic material. The nerves are laid onto the approximating device and then sutured to it with epineural microsutures placed at some distance from the nerve ends. The distance of the sutures from the site of trauma allows for repositioning and alignment of the nerve without further scar production. Mechanical stress is displaced away from the actual site of transection. The flat support of the approximating device allows farther for cutting of the repositioned stumps after cooling. Finally, because the approximating device is made from an elastic substance, its natural tension can be used to bring the cut nerve ends to an accurate repositioning.

Functional Tests of Recovery

The procedures described above have been used to reunite the sciatic nerve of rats after complete transection. Functional recovery was determined by an empirically derived sciatic function index (SFI), that is determined from comparing hind limb walking tracks from the injured side with the uninjured side. Perineural suturing, the procedure used by the microsurgeon in the clinic, of the severed rat sciatic nerve rarely produces functional recovery. A crush injury, on the other hand, that destroys the neurites but not their guidance will invariably be followed by almost complete functional recovery in about 2 weeks and complete recovery in less than 2 months.

None of the procedures described above produced by themselves any increase in function from perineural suturing. Animals that received a combination of treatment (support cuff, freezing and modified Collins fluid), however, always recovered. The functional recovery returned to about two-thirds of baseline (de Medinaceli et al. 1982, 1983). It was unimportant whether the connection was performed immediately after the lesion or in the clinically more relevant time of 2 h.

Role of Trauma as a Cause of Lost Function with Age

It is well recognized that injury to the nervous system, whether it be physiological or structural, can cause loss of nervous system function. It is possible that multiple small injuries (microtrauma) might also play an important role in loss of brain function over time. Examples of repetitive trauma, such as boxers undergo with the subsequent development of Parkinsonism or decreased cognitive function, are being increasingly recognized (Stiller and Weinberger 1985). It is far less clear, however, if other individuals who undergo repeated microtraumas to the nervous system accumulate enough damage to produce loss of function. Does the soccer player who uses his head hundreds of thousands of times in his career suffer microtrauma, decreasing CNS function long after he is no longer playing soccer? Similarly, what happens to the truck or tractor driver who repeatedly goes over bumps? Although not usually considered a form of trauma, cerebral vascular accidents also are traumatic in nature. The occurrence of multiple transient ischaemic attacks is known to produce a step-like reduction in function over time, but are there less dramatic vascular occurrences that also take their toll?

Even though the nervous system appears to be outside the normal buffeting of the immune system, repeated trauma to the nervous system, as must happen in normal life, may over time induce autoimmune responses. To begin investigating this possibility we again used the peripheral nerve as a model. Repetitive injuries to the rat sciatic nerve were accompanied by local autoimmune reactions (de Medinaceli *et al.* 1985a,b,c). In our experimental conditions, these reactions had only a moderately adverse effect on function. It is possible, however, that the repetition of microtrauma occurring through life could lead to a progressively increased immunosensitivity. If this were the case, microtrauma sustained in old age could have more serious consequences than an identical trauma in youth.

Applications of Principles Learned from the Peripheral Nerve to the CNS

Success in producing functional recovery in the transected rat sciatic nerve depended on providing adequate support that could be used to manipulate the position of the nerve ends without causing further microscarring. The microscar that developed at the time of the transection had to be removed, again in a manner that would not produce a new microscar. Finally, the nerve ends had to be reconnected so that the axons would have accurate reorientation. At the very least, these same principles will be necessary for repair of the CNS.

Undoubtedly other factors will also need to be considered. From the preliminary studies on the peripheral nerve, immunological considerations may also have to be taken into account.

Lessons from the Peripheral Nerve used for the CNS

The part of the CNS that most closely resembles the peripheral nervous system is the spinal cord. Like the peripheral nerve, it is made up primarily of longitudinal fibres, but unlike the peripheral nervous system there are numerous fibres that run horizontally. The spinal cord also contains interneurons that play an important role in function and that are destroyed by any traumatic lesion. In addition, the support of the spinal cord is different from the peripheral nerve and a crush injury will lead to a massive glial and connective tissue scar. A number of techniques have been tried to decrease spinal cord scarring. Although some have been at least partially effective, none has resulted in complete spinal cord regeneration (Windle 1956, Puchala and Windle 1975, Bernstein *et al.* 1978).

We are beginning to explore methods of repair of the damaged spinal cord by developing the surgical procedures in which the spinal cord of rats can be used as a model for surgical repair (de Medinaceli and Wyatt 1986).

BRAIN GRAFTS AS A FORM OF NERVOUS SYSTEM REPAIR

Since the early part of this century (Dunn 1917) it has been known that small pieces of immature donor rat brain can be grafted into a host brain of another rat, not be rejected, and retain some of its structure. During the 1940s workers demonstrated better survival of grafts (Le Gros Clark 1940, Gless 1940), but it was not until recently that grafts were found to establish connections (Bjorklund and Stenevi 1977) with the host brain as well as improve functional deficits (Perlow *et al.* 1979).

Because of their ability to accept grafts from immunologically different mammals, the brain, anterior chamber of the eye, cheek pouch of the hamster and, of course, uterus of pregnant animals are sometimes referred to as "privileged sites". This privilege appears to be granted because graft-associated antigens do not have the opportunity to sensitize the immune system of the host animal, in the case of the brain because of the blood–brain barrier and perhaps lack of lymphatic drainage.

During the 1970s a number of investigators (Olson and Seiger 1972, Lund and Hauschka 1976, Bjorklund and Stenevi 1977, Das *et al.* 1979) developed techniques for grafting small pieces of embryonic rat brain into the brain of a host. The grafted tissue was often found to survive. It occurred to us that grafting might also be useful for correcting functional deficits (Perlow *et al.* 1979).

Fetal Grafts Used to Correct a Rat Model of Parkinson's Disease

Most of the symptoms of Parkinson's disease — slowing of voluntary movements, difficulty starting and stopping a movement, tremor, muscular rigidity, mask-like faces and flexion posture — are caused by the degeneration of dopaminergic neurons in substantia nigra of the brain. The primary target of processes of these neurons is the striatum (Ungerstedt 1971a). The neurons project ipsilaterally; when the substantia nigra on one side is destroyed, dopamine denervation takes place in the striatum on the same side as the lesion.

In the rat, the substantia nigra can be destroyed by stereotaxic injection of the neurotoxin, 6-hydroxydopamine, which when injected into the vicinity of dopamine neurons, is taken into the neurons by the dopamine reuptake system. Once in the neurons, 6-hydroxydopamine is autooxidized into a poison that destroys that neuron. With loss of dopamine at the target, the striatum (in the rat the striatum consists of the caudate and putamen), there is a compensatory increase in dopamine receptor number (Creese and Snyder 1979, Staunton et al. 1981).

Because there are more dopamine receptors in the striatum where the dopamine system has been destroyed there is a relative imbalance between the two sides. The disparity in number of receptors becomes functionally apparent when the rat is given a dopamine agonist such as apomorphine (Ungerstedt 1971b). The rat rotates away from the lesion (Ungerstedt 1971c).

Fetal Substantia Nigra Grafts

Two groups (Freed et al. 1985b, Dunnett et al. 1985) have actively studied grafting procedures in this system over a sustained period of time. Our studies began (Perlow et al. 1979, Freed et al. 1980) by producing unilateral substantia nigra lesions in the rat and counting the number of apomorphine-induced rotations over a standard time period; a postlesion baseline was established. In our initial studies, substantia nigra were dissected from 17-day gestational rat embryos. The host animal was anaesthetized and a small burr hole was placed in its skull. Through the burr hole an 18-gauge needle was stereotaxically placed into the lateral ventricle and the embryonic brain tissue containing the substantia nigra was gently washed into the ventricle (Freed 1985b). For controls, similar animals were grafted with sciatic nerve or parts of the brain that did not contain dopamine (Freed 1983).

Following placement of the graft the rats were again tested for apomorphine-stimulated rotation. Animals with sciatic nerve or other non-dopamine containing nervous tissue grafts had little or no reductions in turning. The substantia nigra grafted animals, however, had a mean reduction in turning of approximately 50%. This reduction in turning lasted for at least 6 months and was consistent with the notion that exposure to dopamine from the graft would decrease the number of dopamine receptors in the striatum.

To determine if the receptor number was actually altered by dopamine depletion and grafting, slices of the striatum were incubated with the radiolabelled dopamine receptor ligand, spiroperidol (Freed et al. 1985c). The slices were then examined using autoradiography (Niehoff et al. 1979) and spiroperidol binding quantified with computerized densitometry and image enhancement. In lesioned animals that had no change in turning following grafting there was 5.5 fmol/mg protein difference in bound spiroperidol in the dorsomedial quadrant of the striatum (the area adjacent to the graft) between the lesioned and unlesioned side. In animals in which the graft produced a change in rotation there was essentially no difference between the two sides. Thus, loss of dopamine because of destruction of the substantia nigra increased dopamine receptor number and the graft, in turn, decreased the number of receptors.

Histologically, fetal substantia nigra grafts placed into the lateral ventricle were found attached to the striatum, laterally and to the septum, medially. Some grafts were also attached to the corpus callosum above. Using histochemical fluorescence techniques that identify dopamine-containing cells, the grafted cells had the typical colour and form of dopamine-containing neurons in the normal substantia nigra pars compacta. The cell bodies had processes extending from them that not only filled the graft but also crossed for about a millimeter into the host brain. These processes were beaded and tortuous and resembled normal dopamine axons. Even after 22 months all animals were found to have surviving grafts (Freed *et al.* 1985a).

In addition to demonstrating the presence of dopamine in the graft histochemically, this was shown chemically (Freed *et al.* 1980). Frozen brain slices through the graft were punched with a needle and the punch tissue analysed with gas chromatography mass fragmentography (Karoum *et al.* 1975). The tissue punched from the graft itself had a greater concentration of dopamine than normal substantia nigra. There was a gradient of dopamine in the host brain from the punches that were furthest away from the graft.

The dopamine-containing neurons of the fetal grafts were also found to be spontaneously electrically active, thus providing appropriate input to the denervated striatum (Wuerthele *et al.* 1981). With extracellular unit recordings from the graft, the spontaneous waveform response to neuroleptics as well as a dopamine agonist was similar to that of normal substantia nigra neurons. Thus, the neurons were not only active but had the potential for autoregulation.

Adrenal Medulla Grafts

To test the diversity of graft tissues that might be used in the model of Parkinson's disease, we examined several donor tissues in addition to the fetal substantia nigra (Freed 1983). One tissue that is especially appealing is the adrenal medulla. The chromaffin cells of adrenal medulla normally make the catecholamines, epinephrine and norepinephrine. As part of the synthetic pathway in the production of catecholamines, dopamine is also synthesized. Following the finding by Olson *et al.* (1980) that chromaffin cells from the adrenal medulla could innervate fetal brain pieces grafted into the anterior chamber of the eye (also a privileged site), we began a series of experiments grafting adrenal chromaffin cells into the brains of unilaterally 6-hydroxydopamine-lesioned rats (Freed *et al.* 1981).

Adrenal chromaffin cells grafted into the lateral ventricle in the same manner as fetal substantia nigra produced identical functional results. The apomorphine-induced rotations that were prominent after the 6-hydroxydopamine lesion decreased by about 50%. Histologically the grafts survived. Nevertheless, unlike fetal substantia nigra grafts that had processes which crossed from the body of the graft into the host, the processes of the adrenal grafts formed only a network in the graft itself and only rarely invaded the host. Mass fragmentographic studies indicated that the grafts were making predominately dopamine, rather than epinephrine and norepinephrine. This suggests that synaptic formation is not necessary for dopaminergic innervation to be functional, at least in the rotational model, and in all probability dopamine is capable of altering brain function by diffusion.

On the other hand Olson *et al.* (1985) have found that use of nerve growth factor increases the number of surviving chromaffin cells as well as promoting the growth of fibres into the host parenchyma. Use of growth promoting factors (di Porzio *et al.* 1980) may ultimately prove useful to increase the influence each graft has on the brain and decrease the number of grafts necessary to correct function. This may be particularly useful in primates where it will be important to influence larger brain areas than is necessary in the rat (Wyatt and Freed 1985).

Age-related issues

Since the majority of people who develop Parkinson's disease are middle-aged or older, it is important to know if age is a relevant factor in producing functional grafts. Freed (1983) found that although intraventricular grafts from donors 6–8 weeks of age decreased apomorphine-induced rotation, adrenal grafts from 1- to 2-year-old donors were ineffective. Freed *et al.* (1986) found that while adrenal grafts from 4- to 5-week-old rats placed directly into the striatum of 6 hydroxy dopamine-lesioned rats tended to decrease apomorphine induced rotation, grafts from aging (22- to 24-months-old) donors were without effect. Using another behaviour that is affected by 6-hydroxydopamine lesions, sensory neglect (Marshall and Gotthelf 1979), both grafts from young and aging animals were effective. The results of this study indicate that age of donor may effect some behaviours and not others.

GRAFTS IN NON-HUMAN PRIMATES

Fetal substantia nigra and adrenal medulla grafts have been very successful in correcting behaviour in lesioned rats. Since one aim of this work is to use grafts clinically, it is important to determine if grafts can be equally successful in the primate. We have used the non-human primate, *Macaca mulatta* or rhesus monkeys. Adult animals were the host either for grafts into the striatum or the lateral ventricle adjacent to the striatum as well as grafts placed into the frontal cortex.

Striatal and Lateral Ventricular Grafts

To find landmarks for the stereotaxic lesioning of the substantia nigra, skull X-rays were taken. Following a trephine of the skull, the dura was cut and a 22-gauge needle stereotaxically lowered to the substantia nigra. 6-Hydroxydopamine was injected into the substantia nigra in a manner that was likely to produce a complete lesion of the substantia nigra. These lesions were ultimately verified at autopsy by examining the striatum for native dopamine fluorescence.

Our first series of six animals was unsuccessful in demonstrating graft survival, except for one animal that had a graft in the lateral ventricle (unpublished). In our second series—A1 and A2—substantia nigra were used from 59-day and 21-day fetuses, respectively. For animals A3 through A8, adrenal medulla grafts were divided into approximately 0.25 mm pieces and injected into the caudate. In the first of these animals the injections were made with the needle travelling through the corpus callosum. In the remainder of the animals a window in the corpus callosum was made for travel of the injection needle (Morihisa et al. 1984).

Bone flaps of 2 cm^2 were removed over the left cerebral cortex and an incision made in the dura. An injection needle was lowered into the head of the caudate using stereotaxic measures guided by X-ray. The needle was lowered 4 mm into the depth of the caudate and then withdrawn 1 mm. The suspended implant was injected in 10-15 μl spurts. For animals A3 through A8, adrenal medulla pieces the same size as the substantia nigra grafts were injected. These grafts were taken from the host animal and grafted within 1 h.

With the exception of animals A1 and A2, which were examined by Falck–Hillarp fluorescence histochemistry (Falck et al. 1962), all animals were examined by the glyoxylic acid method (de la Torre 1980). Over time the procedure has become somewhat more successful, as evidenced by a gradual increase in the number of surviving cell bodies, identified by hisotfluorescence, that could be found in the caudate. Most graft sites were deep within the body of the caudate along the implant tract. Some grafts appeared to be fused with the brain parenchyma. In the most successful animal, A7, over 600 cells were found in the caudate.

Cortical Grafts

Because of the low yield of the caudate grafts we decided to place the grafts in a surgically more accessible location. Grafts were placed into the frontal cortex without impairing the monkey and required relatively simple surgical procedures. The first series of cortical grafts using adrenal medulla, similar to the A series, produced animals with questionable cell survival—when there appear to be only a few cells present it is difficult to determine if they are real or an artifact. In addition, dissociated cells (Patel-Vaidya *et al.* 1985) fared no better than small pieces of graft.

The next experiments consisted of a series of monkeys who had a pocket placed in their cortex prior to placement of the graft. Under anaesthesia after removal of about 1 cm² of bone and cutting through the dura each animal had a 3-6 mm deep hole removed from its frontal cortex. The hole was 4-5 mm in diameter. Dura was laid over the hole and Gelfoam® was laid on top of the dura. The fascia and muscle were pulled over the hole in the skull and the skin closed with sutures. Ten days later the skull was opened again and autografts of the adrenal medulla placed into it. The animals were again closed as previously described. After 6-11 weeks the animals were sacrificed and the area of the cortex containing the graft examined both for catecholamine-specific fluorescence and immunochemically for tyrosine hydroxylase.

The five animals had clear evidence of graft survival. The majority of cells were just under the dura or attached to it. The cells had relatively few fibres stemming from them, but were somewhat elongated. In the most recent monkey (210S) in addition to placing tissue in the pocket, pieces of adrenal medulla were placed into the frontal cortex on the opposite side from the pocket with a fine forceps. These grafts remained embedded deep in the brain parenchyma and contained 54 cells and over 1000 cells in the two sites.

Over a period of about 5 years we have slowly increased the yield and consistency of successful grafts into the monkey brain. Our yield of surviving cells is not, however, as great as it is in the rat ventricle but is now similar to the rate of survival of chromaffin cells in the rat striatum, where an average of about 200 chromaffin cells per animal are found to survive permanently (Freed *et al.* 1986). The progress, although quite gradual, is encouraging.

Limitations of Brain Grafting in Humans

Although the future of any technique that is in its infancy, such as brain grafting, is unpredictable, given our current limited knowledge some barriers to its widespread use in the aging brain are apparent (Freed *et al.* 1984, 1985a).

The mature brain is the most complex three-dimensional object known. Its weave of fibres and cells interconnecting with one another is largely produced while the nervous system is developing. It is crucial to the production of the mature brain that tracts are formed at precise developmental stages. The dimension of time is lost to the would-be repairer. The brain repairer has limited ability to use the dynamics that are present during development and, like trying to rewire an old building, it can not easily be accomplished without tearing down a part of the original structure. Although a graft may be capable of making relatively simple repairs, it can not be expected to rewire large areas requiring complex schemata. Where a graft can be placed close to its terminal fields, better success would be expected than where its processes must find their way to distant targets. Even if a graft were placed adjacent to or in the target it would be surprising if point-to-point connections could be made between graft processes and the specific targets they need to innervate. For example, precise point-to-point wiring is necessary for fine motor movement in the pyramidal system. Such reconnections would not be expected to occur from a graft. On the other hand, where the influence of the neural tissue needs to be less precise, as in neurohormonal systems, grafts would be expected to, and do, work well (Gash *et al.* 1980, Krieger *et al.* 1982). Fortunately, most neurohormonal system disorders can be effectively treated with less invasive procedures.

With aging there appears to be a decline in cholinergic function (Bartus *et al.* 1982, Gibson *et al.* 1981). Aged rats who have difficulty in using environmental cues for spatial learning improve their performance when fetal septal tissue, rich in cholinergic neurons, are implanted bilaterally into the hippocampus (Gage *et al.* 1985). Alzheimer's disease is associated with a loss of brain acetylcholine. Grafting fetal acetylcholine-rich tissue into the hippocampus of rats with fimbria-fornix lesions, which deafferentates the hippocampus from acetylcholine inputs, aided the rats in learning new tasks (Gage *et al.* 1984, 1985). Alzheimer's disease, however, affects great regions of a brain and at least with current procedures it is difficult to conceive of how we could spread enough pieces or dispersed cells into the brain over a large enough area to have a beneficial effect. It is possible, however, that by placing tissue only in the hippocampus, that there would be enough functional recovery to be worthwhile.

The advantage of using grafts in Parkinson's disease over other degenerative diseases is the relatively discrete nature of the dopamine loss and relatively limited target range requiring influence for return of function. Even Parkinson's disease, however, is not as focal as it is often presented and complete recovery from a graft would not be expected. On the other hand, until such time as degenerative disorders such as Parkinson's disease can be prevented, grafting techniques offer the possibility of improving a patient's life after standard treatments have failed.

HOPE

Until recently, it was a commonly held belief that the adult mammalian nervous system was functionally static; severed tracts did not regrow and animals did not recover from lesions or destruction produced by disease. When recovery of function did occur following brain lesions, explanations such as alternate pathways, denervation supersensitivity or other attributions of the brain's capacity to circumvent the lesion were invoked. A host of studies now indicate that the nervous system, even in the mature adult, is relatively plastic. Natural repair is possible. And, as indicated previously, medically aided repair, under certain circumstances will also probably be gradually made possible.

The hope for repair of a damaged nervous system is particularly important to our aging society. During the first half of this century the death rate from infectious disease plummeted. In the last decade, the death rate from heart disease and stroke have dramatically decreased. Understanding of the associations between our environment and cancer give us clues to prevention, and treatments are becoming increasing successful. Perhaps by the turn of the century, the major medical problem of our aging population will be loss of brain function. It is thus fitting that we begin to explore how to prevent and treat nervous system disorders that will otherwise become increasingly debilitating.

SUMMARY

Probably the worst fear people have of growing old is of diminished nervous system function. Such loss of function can come from trauma, disease or possibly the process of normal aging. Until recently, it was a commonly held belief that the adult, and specifically the geriatric, mammalian nervous system was functionally static; severed tracts did not regrow and animals did not recover from lesions or destruction produced by disease. When recovery of function did occur following brain lesions, explanations such as alternate pathways, denervation supersensitivity or other attributions of the brain's capacity to circumvent the lesion were invoked. Because of this pessimism, interest in neuronal plasticity was directed mainly towards the study of lower animals, immature systems and peripheral nerves.

Since the 1979 demonstration that grafts of brain tissue from one animal to another could restore lost function, neural regeneration research has received increased attention. It is possible to produce functional recovery in a brain-lesioned rat by grafting brain tissue from a fetal animal to a mature host. The most intensely studied clinical model for brain tissue transplanation involves the destruction of the substantia nigra as it projects to the ipsilateral striatum. In human, such damage results in Parkinson's disease.

When a rat, with a unilateral substantia nigra lesion, is given a dopamine agonist such as apomorphine, the rat will rotate away from the lesion in an easily quantifiable manner. Embryonic cells can be grafted into the ventricle adjacent to the striatum or into the body of the striatum. Such grafts are not rejected even when made between histoincompatible strains of rats. Like L-dopa treatment of Parkinson's disease, the grafted substantia nigra provides dopamine to the striatum and corrects the apomorphine-stimulated turning behaviour.

Autografts coming from the rat's own adrenal medulla are not rejected and are capable of producing dopamine. The *in situ* adrenal medulla produces a preponderance of epinephrine, but when taken out of the environment of the steroid-producing adrenal cortex produces a relative excess of dopamine. Similar work has begun with monkeys with partial success.

While grafting techniques may ultimately be used for clinical CNS problems with discrete lesions, it is highly like that other regeneration techniques will have to be used in more complex situations. To discover the principles of nervous system regeneration, we have used the model of the severed rat sciatic nerve. By using this relatively simple peripheral system, we have delineated factors that we are not applying to the CNS.

This work is based on a simple hypothesis: because axons are extensions of cells, any attempt to repair axons should follow the requirements of cellular surgery, rather than conventional surgical procedures developed for tissues. This hypothesis has been borne out by our determination of various factors necessary to produce functional neural regeneration. Among these factors, the major ones are proper alignment of the stumps, sharpness of surgical cut, and above all, prevention of physical and chemical damage. Prevention of physical damage has been achieved by using a cooling process. Chemical damage is avoided by use of fluids mimicking the intraaxonal composition. The fluids are designed also to fight the adverse effect of free calcium ions on axoplasmic structures and to maintain an appropriate colloid osmotic pressure. The clinical results of this work have been the demonstration of functional recovery from nerve lesions, obtained consistently when the necessary conditions are met.

REFERENCES

Bartus, R. T., Dean III, R. L., Beer, B. and Lippa, A. S. (1982). The cholinergic hypothesis of geriatric memory dysfunction. *Science* **217**, 408-417.

Bernstein, J. J., Wells, M. R. and Bernstein, M. E. (1978). Effect of puromycin treatment on the regeneration of hemisected and transected rat spinal cord. *J. Neurocytol.* **7**, 215-228.

Bjorklund, A. and Stenevi, U. (1977). Reformation of the severed septohippocampal cholinergic pathway in the adult rat by transplanted septal neurons. *Cell Tiss. Res.* **185**, 289-302.

Collins, G. M., Bravo-Shugarman, M. and Terasaki, P. I. (1969). Kidney preservation for transplantation. *Lancet* **ii**, 1219.

Creese, I. and Snyder, S. H. (1979). Nigrostriatal lesions enhance striatal [^{3}H]apomorphine and [^{3}H]spiroperidol binding. *Eur. J. Pharmacol.* **56**, 227-281.

Das, G. D., Hallas, B. H. and Das, K. G. (1979). Transplantation of neural tissue in the brains of laboratory mammals: technical details and comments. *Experientia* **35**, 143-153.

de la Torre, J. C. (1980). An improved approach to histofluorescence using the SPG method for tissue monoamines. *J. Neurosci. Meth.* **3**, 1-5.

de Medinacelli, L. (1986). An anatomical landmark for procedures on rat thoracic spinal cord. *Exp. Neurol.* (in press).

de Medinaceli, L. and Church, A. C. (1984). Peripheral nerve reconnection: inhibition of early degenerative processes through the use of a novel fluid medium. *Exp. Neurol.* **84**, 396-408.

de Medinaceli, L. and Freed, W. J. (1983). Peripheral nerve reconnection: immediate histologic consequences of distributed mechanical support. *Exp. Neurol.* **81**, 459-468.
de Medinaceli, L. and Wyatt, R. J. (1986). Experimental shortening of rat thoracic spine with conservation of cord function. (Submitted for publication.)
de Medinaceli, L., Freed, W. J. and Wyatt, R. J. (1982). An index of the functional condition of rat sciatic nerve based on measurements made from walking tracks. *Exp. Neurol.* **77**, 634-643.
de Medinaceli, L., Freed, W. J. and Wyatt, R. J. (1983). Peripheral nerve reconnection: improvement of long term functional effects under simulated clinical conditions in the rat. *Exp. Neurol.* **81**, 488-496.
de Medinaceli, L., Church, A. C. and Wang, Y.-N. (1985a). Posttraumatic autoimmune reaction in peripheral nerve: effect of a single injury. *Exp. Neurol.* **88**, 372-384.
de Medinaceli, L., Church, A. C. and Wang, Y.-N. (1985b). Posttraumatic autoimmune reaction in peripheral nerve: effect of two successive injuries at different sites. *Exp. Neurol.* **88**, 396-404.
de Medinaceli, L., Church, A. C. and Wang, Y.-N. (1985c). Posttraumatic autoimmune reaction in peripheral nerve: effect of two successive injuries at the same site. *Exp. Neurol.* **88**, 385-395.
di Porzio, U., Daguet, M.-C., Glowinski, J. and Prochiantz, A. (1980). Effect of striatal cells on *in vitro* maturation of mesencephalic doapaminergic neurones grown in serum-free conditions. *Nature (London)* **288**, 370-373.
Dunn, E. H. (1917). Primary and secondary findings in a series of attempts to transplant cerebral cortex in the albino rat. *J. Comp. Neurol.* **27**, 565-582.
Dunnett, S. B., Bjorklund, A., Gage, G. H. and Stenevi, U. (1985). Transplantation of mesencephalic dopamine neurons to the striatum of adult rats. In "Neural grafting in the mammalian CNS" (A. Bjorklund and U. Stenevi, eds) pp. 451-470. Elsevier, New York.
Falck, B., Hillarp, N.-A., Thieme, G. and Torp, A. (1962). Fluorescence of catecholamines and related compounds condensed with formaldehyde. *J. Histochem. Cytochem.* **10**, 348-354.
Freed, W. J. (1983). Functional brain tissue transplantation: Reversal of lesion-induced rotation by intraventricular substantia nigra and adrenal medulla grafts with a note on intracranial retinal grafts. *Biol. Psychiatr.* **18**, 1205-1267.
Freed, W. J. (1985a). Repairing neuronal circuits with brain grafts: where can brain grafts be used as a therapy? *Neurobiol. Aging* **6**, 153-156.
Freed, W. J. (1985b). Transplantation of tissues to the cerebral ventricles: methodological details and rate of graft survival. In "Neural grafting in the mammalian CNS" (A. Barklund and U. Stenevi, eds) pp. 31-40. Elsevier, New York.
Freed, W. J., Perlow, M., Karoum, F., Seiger, A., Olson, L., Hoffer, B. and Wyatt, R. J. (1980). Restoration of dopaminergic function by grafting of fetal rat substantia nigra to the caudate nucleus: long-term behavioral, biochemical and histochemical studies. *Ann. Neurol.* **8**, 510-519.
Freed, W. J., Morihisa, J., Cannon-Spoor, E., Hoffer, B., Olson, L., Seiger, A. and Wyatt, R. J. (1981). Transplanted adrenal chromaffin cells in rat brain reduce lesion-induced rotational behavior. *Nature* **292**, 351-352.
Freed, W. J., Cannon-Spoor, H. E. and Wyatt, R. J. (1984). Embryonic brain grafts in an animal model of Parkinson's disease: criteria for human application. *Appl. Neurophysiol.* **47**, 16-22.
Freed, W. J., Cannon-Spoor, H. E. and Krauthamer, E. (1985a). Factors influencing the efficacy of adrenal medulla and embryonic substantia nigra grafts. In "Neural grafting in the mammalian CNS" (A. Bjorklund and U. Stenevi, eds) pp. 491-504. Elsevier, New York.

Freed, W. J., de Medinaceli, L. and Wyatt, R. J. (1985b). Promoting functional plasticity in the damaged nervous system. *Science* **227**, 1544-1552.

Freed, W. J., Olson, L., Ko, G. N., Morhisa, J. M., Niehoff, D., Stromberg, I., Kuhar, M., Hoffer, B. J. and Wyatt, R. J. (1985c). Intraventricular substantia nigra and adrenal medulla grafts: mechanisms of action and [^{3}H] spiroperidol autoradiography. *In* "Neural grafting in the mammalian CNS" (A. Bjorklund and U. Stenevi, eds) pp. 471-489. Elsevier, New York.

Freed, W. J., Cannon-Spoor, H. E. and Krauthamer, E. (1986). Intrastriatal adrenal medulla grafts from young and aging donors: long-term survival and behavioral effects. *J. Neurosurg.* (in press).

Gage, F. H., Bjorklund, A., Stenevi, U., Dunnett, S. B. and Kelly, P. A. (1984). Intrahippocampal septal grafts ameliorate learning impairment in aged rats. *Science* **225**, 533-536.

Gage, F. H., Bjorklund, A., Stenevi, U. and Dunnett, S. B. (1985). Grafting of embryonic CNS tissue to the damaged adult hippocampal formation. *In* "Neural grafting in the mammalian CNS" (A. Bjorklund and U. Stenevi, eds) pp. 559-573. Elsevier, New York.

Gash, D., Sladek, J. R. and Sladek, C. D. (1980). Functional development of grafted vasopressin neurons. *Science* **210**, 1367-1369.

Gibson, G. E., Peterson, C. and Jenden, D. J. (1981). Brain acetylcholine synthesis declines with senescence. *Science* **213**, 674-676.

Gless, P. (1940). The differentiation of the brain and other tissues in an implanted portion of embryonic head. *Am. J. Anat.* **75**, 239-247.

Goldberg, N. H. et al. (1984). Disparity between neurophysiologic measurements and clinical reality following peripheral nerve transection and microneurorraphy. *Surg. Forum* **35**, 608-610.

Guth, P. S., Amaro, J., Sellinger, Z. and Elmer, L. (1965). Studies *in vitro* and *in vivo* of the effects of chlorpormazine on rat liver lysosomes. *Biochem. Pharmacol.* **14**, 769-775.

Gutmann, E. J. (1942). Factors affecting recovery of motor function after nerve lesions. *Neurol. Psychiatr.* **5**, 81-95.

Jarvik, L. F. (1983). Age is in—Is the wit out? *In* "Aging of the brain" (D. Samuel, S. Algeri, S. Gerson, V. E. Grimm and G. Toffano, eds) "Aging" Vol. 22, pp. 1-8. Raven Press, New York.

Karoum, F., Gillin, J. C., McCullough, D. and Wyatt, R. J. (1975). Vanilmandelic acid (VMA), free and conjugated 3-methoxy-4-hydroxyphenylglycol (MHPG) in human ventricular fluid. *Clin. Chim. Acta* **62**, 289-297.

Krieger, D. T., Perlow, M. J., Gibson, M. J., Dames, T. F., Zimmerman, E. A., Ferin, M. and Charlton, H. M. (1982). Brain grafts reverse hypogonadism of gonadotropin-releasing hormone deficiency. *Nature* **298**, 468-471.

Le Gros Clark, W. E. (1940). Neuronal differentiation in implanted foetal cortical tissue. *J. Neuro Psychiat.* **3**, 263-284.

Lund, R. D. and Hauschka, S. D. (1976). Transplanted neural tissue develops connections with host rat brain. *Science* **193**, 582-584.

Marshall, J. F. and Gotthelf, T. (1979). Sensory inattention in rats with 6-hydroxydopamine-induced degeneration of ascending dopaminergic neurons: apomorphine-induced reversal of deficits. *Exp. Neurol.* **65**, 398-411.

Morihisa, J. M., Nakamura, R. K., Freed, W. J., Miskin, M. and Wyatt, R. J. (1984). Adrenal medulla grafts survive and exhibit catecholamine specific fluorescence in primate brain. *Exp. Neurol.* **84**, 643-653.

Niehoff, D. L., Palacios, J. M. and Kuhar, M. J. (1979). *In vivo* receptor binding: attempts to improve specific/non-specific ratios. *Life Sci.* **25**, 819-826.

Olson, L. and Seiger, A. (1972). Brain tissue transplanted to the anterior chamber of the eye. 1. Fluorescence histochemistry of immature catecholamine and 5-hydroxytryptamine neurons innervating the rat iris. *Z. Zellforsch* **195**, 175-194.

Olson, L., Seiger, A., Freedman, R. and Hoffer, B. (1980). Chromaffin cells can innervate brain tissue: evidence from intraocular double grafts. *Exp. Neurol.* **70**, 414-426.

Olson, L., Stromberg, I., Herrera-Marschitz, M., Ungerstedt, U. and Ebendal, T. (1985). Adrenal medullary tissue grafted to the dopamine-denervated rat striatum: histochemical and functional effects of additions of nerve growth factor. *In* "Neural grafting in the mammalian CNS" (A. Bjorlund and U. Stenevi, eds) pp. 505-518. Elsevier, New York.

Patel-Vaidya, U., Wells, M. R. and Freed, W. J. (1985). Survival of dissociated rat and monkey adrenal chromaffin cells transplanted into rat brain. *Cell Tiss. Res.* **240**, 281-295.

Perlow, M. J., Freed, W. F., Hoffer, B. J., Seiger, A., Olson, L. and Wyatt, R. J. (1979). Brain grafts reduce motor abnormalities produced by destruction of nigrostriatal dopamine system. *Science* **204**, 643-647.

Puchala, E. and Windle, W. F. (1975). The possibility of structural and functional restitution after spinal cord injury. A review. *Exp. Neurol.* **65**, 1-42.

Staunton, D. A., Wolfe, B. B., Groves, P. M. and Molinoff, P. B. (1981). Dopamine receptor changes following destruction of the nigrostriatal pathway: lack of a relationship to rotational behavior. *Brain Res.* **211**, 315-327.

Stiller, J. W. and Weinberger, D. R. (1985). Boxing and chronic brain damage. *Psychiat. Clin. North Am.* **8**, 339-345.

Sunderland, S. (1968). "Nerves and nerve injuries" Baltimore, 2nd ed. E & S Livingstone Ltd.

Tator, C. H. and Rivlin, A. S. (1983). Elimination of root regeneration in studies of spinal cord regeneration. *Surg. Neurol.* **19**, 255-259.

Ungerstedt, U. (1971a). Stereotaxic mapping of the monoamine pathways in the rat brain. *Acta Physiol. Scand.* **367**(Suppl.), 1-48.

Ungerstedt, U. (1971b). Postsynaptic supersensitivity after 6-hyroxydopamine induced degeneration of the nigro-striatal dopamine system. *Acta Physiol. Scand.* **367**(Suppl.), 69-93.

Ungerstedt, U. (1971c). Striatal dopamine release after amphetamine or nerve degeneration revealed by rotational behavior. *Acta Physiol. Scand.* **367**(Suppl.), 49-68.

Welford, A. T. (1977). Motor performance. *In* "Handbook of the psychology of aging" (J. E. Birren and K. W. Schaie, eds) pp. 450-496. Van Nostrand Reinhold, New York.

Windle, W. F. (1956). Regeneration of axons in the vertebrate central nervous system. *Physiol. Rev.* **36**, 427-440.

Wuerthele, S. M., Freed, W. J., Olson, L., Morihisa, J., Spoor, E., Wyatt, R. J. and Hoffer, B. J. (1981). Effect of dopamine agonists and antagonists on the electrical activity of substantia nigra neurons transplanted into the lateral ventricle of the rat. *Exp. Brain Res.* **44**, 1-10.

Wyatt, R. J. and Freed, W. J. (1985). Central nervous system grafting. *In* "Neurosurgery" (R. H. Wilkins and S. S. Rengachary, eds) Vol. 3, pp. 2546-2551. McGraw-Hill, New York.

Young, J. Z. (1942). The functional repair of nervous tissue. *Physiol. Rev.* **22**, 318-374.

Discussion

Mandel: Did you look at the morphology of the grafted neurons?

Wyatt: We certainly looked at the morphology of the tissues and tried to differentiate, but the adrenal neurons looked very similar to the dopaminergic neurons in the substantia nigra.

Mandel: Is there gliosis around the graft?

Wyatt: There is surprisingly little gliosis around the graft, maybe one or two cells, usually not more.

Karobath: The graft has a certain size. Has anybody calculated how much the immunological damage to the cortical spinal tract could be if you spike the striatum with about 1,500 transplants?

Wyatt: Obviously, 1,500 grafts would mean much damage. Our current calculation in the monkey is that six or seven penetrations are sufficient to introduce correctly enough grafts along each penetration. It is still possible, however, that we cause damage.

Ulrich: If I am well informed, similar transplantation has been tried in humans. Do you have more information?

Wyatt: I could cite the work from Karolinska Institute, where in four Parkinson patients the adrenal medulla was transplanted into the brain. Initially, there was some improvement in the movements, but no long-term success.

Ermini: The animals used for demonstrating the positive effects of tissue grafts into the brain are basically healthy ones with an acute lesion. The practical goal of brain tissue grafting, however, is currently the treatment of patients suffering from some sort of degenerative disease condition (Parkinsonism, Alzheimer's disease etc.). Should one, therefore, not rather try to study the effects of brain tissue grafting in animals which are themselves suffering from some sort of progressive degenerative brain disease? Or, the other way around, since up to now no such animal model exists, should one not try to use brain tissue grafts in patients suffering from acute traumatic brain lesions? This would more closely resemble the animal model situation.

Wyatt: There are two points in your question. The first is whether we are going to be successful if we deal with elderly, generally sick animals. Though our monkeys were on the elderly side they were not very sick; therefore I was not concerned about age, at least in terms of the host. Our next experiments will probably be with neurotoxic doses on rather sick animals. The second point you raised was — if one is thinking about Alzheimer's disease or Parkinson's disease or any other degenerative disease — whether there is something which causes degeneration of the normal host cell and also attacks the cells we replace. I do not think we know the answer, but presumably there is a neurotoxin which produces Parkinson's disease and which does not come from the dopaminergic neuron itself. That may be so. I do not know whether it is justifiable from my point of view or from the physician's or the patient's point of view to prolong the older patient's life perhaps by 5 or 10 years by such an uncertain operation. Most older patients to whom I have talked about this would not care to volunteer!

Rinne: As far as transplantation in Parkinson's disease is concerned, it is better to put the graft in the putamen than in the caudate nucleus because there is much evidence suggesting that the putamen is more related to motor dysfunction than is the caudate nucleus. Maybe this is the reason why the Karolinska group did not achieve good results in Parkinsonian patients as they put the graft in the caudate nucleus.

Mechanism of Age-related Alterations in Response to α- and β-Adrenergic Stimulation in Rat Hepatocytes and its Reverse in Primary Culture

Gozoh Tsujimoto,[1] Aiko Tsujimoto,[2] Salman Azhar[3] and Brian B. Hoffman[3]

[1]*Department of Pharmacology,* [2]*Department of Pediatrics, Yamanashi Medical College, Tamaho, Nakakoma-gun, Yamanashi, Japan, and* [3]*Department of Medicine, Stanford University School of Medicine and Geriatric Research, Education and Clinical Center, Palo Alto Veterans Administration Medical Center, Palo Alto, California, USA*

Keywords
Aging; Catecholamines; Glycogen phosphorylase; Adrenergic receptors; Rat hepatocytes.

INTRODUCTION

The regulation of liver glycogen metabolism is one of the factors which plays an important role in the control of carbohydrate metabolism (Stalmans 1976). The rate-limiting enzyme for the regulation of glycogenolysis is glycogen phosphorylase. This enzyme exists in interconvertible active and inactive form and is controlled by a variety of hormones and neural stimulations (Fisher *et al.* 1970, Villar-Palasi and Larner 1970). In particular, catecholamines are the major activators of glycogenolysis in the livers of a variety of species (Exton 1980).

Hepatic glycogenolysis induced by catecholamines occurs through both α- and β-adrenergic receptor mediated pathways (Exton 1980, Schmelck and Hanoune 1980). The β-adrenergic activation of glycogen phosphorylase is blocked by

Dimensions in Aging
ISBN 0 12 090162 5

Copyright ©1986 Academic Press, London
All rights of reproduction in any form reserved.

propranolol and is presumed to result from an increase of intracellular adenosine 3′,5′-cyclic monophosphate (cAMP). The α-adrenergic pathway, on the other hand, activates phosphorylase without detectable increases in intracellular cAMP levels or the activation of cAMP-dependent protein kinase, and is effectively blocked by phentolamine, phenoxybenzamine and prazosin, but is unaffected by propranolol. According to current evidence, the α-receptors governing hepatic glycogenolysis in isolated rat hepatocytes belong to the α_1-subclass (Hoffman et al. 1980, Aggerbeck et al. 1980), and this α-adrenergic receptor mediated pathway involves a rise in cytosolic Ca^{2+} which will stimulate phosphorylase kinase and lead to the activation of glycogen phosphorylase (Assimacopoulos et al. 1977, Keppens et al. 1977, Blackmore et al. 1982).

Modulation of the relative contribution of the hepatic α- and β-adrenergic receptors occurs in various physiological or pathologic conditions (for a general review, see Schmelck and Hanoune 1980). Developmental maturity and the aging process have been associated with a reduced responsiveness of the β-adrenergic receptor/adenylate cyclase system in rat liver (Bitensky et al. 1970, Moncany and Plas 1980, Blair et al. 1979, Morgan et al. 1983). In addition, the α-adrenergic receptor mediated pathway has been known to predominate in the activation of hepatic glycogen phosphorylase in the adult male rats (Assimacopoulos et al. 1977, Hutson et al. 1976, Blackmore et al. 1978). However, it is still uncertain what kind of alteration may develop during aging in the relative functional significance of α- and β-adrenergic receptor pathways in regulation of glycogenolysis, and there is very little information available for the mechanism of this age-related functional alteration.

Regarding this age-related modulation of hepatic adrenergic regulation of glycogenolysis, an interesting observation has been recently reported (Ichihara et al. 1980, Okajima and Ui 1982). The relative activities of α- and β-adrenergic agents were progressively reversed during culture of adult rat hepatocytes; the primary role of α-adrenergic receptors in activating phosphorylase decreases, whereas an effective β-adrenergic response which is absent *in vivo* and in freshly isolated cells emerges after primary culture. As this conversion of adrenergic regulation of glycogen phosphorylase from an α- to a β-type during primary culture can be regarded as one of "adult-to-fetal cell-like change" models, studying the mechanism of this phenomenon might give some clue for the age-related alteration. Thus, utilizing freshly isolated heptocytes from three different age groups of rats, our studies were designed to characterize the age-related change of the relative contribution of α- and β-adrenergic receptor pathways in the control of hepatic glycogenolysis. As an initial effort to elucidate the mechanism of the age-related functional change, the role of adrenergic receptors was examined. Furthermore, having succeeded in growing isolated hepatocytes in defined serum-free medium, we further investigated the mechanism(s) for the reciprocal change of adrenergic regulation during culture.

MATERIALS AND METHODS

Materials

Unlabelled (±)cyanopindolol was a generous gift from Dr G. Engel of Sandoz (Basel, Switzerland). (^{125}I)Iodocyanopindolol (ICYP) was prepared essentially as described by Engel et al. (1981). Carrier-free Na^{125}I (catalog no. IMS 30) was purchased from Amersham (Arlington Heights, IL). Alpha-D-(U-^{14}C) Glucose 1-phosphate, and (^{3}H)prazosin were purchased from New England Nuclear (Boston, Mass.). Anti-cAMP rabbit antiserum were obtained from Becton Dickinson. Prazosin was a gift from Pfizer Pharmaceutical Company. Commercial sources of other chemicals are collagenase (Type II) from Worthington Biochemical Company (Freehold, N.J.); new born calf serum, tissue culture medium 199 (Earl's salt), DMEM and MEM (minimum essential media) from Gibco company. Other chemicals and reagents were purchased from standard commercial sources.

Animals

Three groups of male Sprague-Dawley rats representing different ages were used. The first group, representing immature juveniles, weighed between 140 and 160 g and were 35-42 days old (6 weeks). An intermediate group, representing young adults, were 50-60 days old (8 weeks) and weighed 240-260 g; this group of rats were also used for studies in cultured hepatocytes. The oldest group, representing fully mature adults, weighed from 490 to 510 g and were 180 to 240 days old (30 weeks). The rats were fed a standard laboratory diet *ad libitum* and were kept on a 12 h light-12 h dark schedule. All rats were kept on this schedule for at least 7 days. Isolation of hepatocytes was routinely initiated 3-4 h into the light period.

Isolation of Hepatocytes

Hepatocytes were isolated by the collagenase perfusion method of Berry and Friend (1969) as modified by Bissel (1980). Briefly, the liver was perfused at 37.0 C with 150 ml of Ca^{2+} free-MEM buffered with bicarbonate containing 0.06%(W/V) collagenase. Medium alone was infused over a period of 6-7 min. Collagenase then was introduced. After 10-15 min, the liver was carefully cut from its ligaments and transferred to a sterile bottle, opened with scissors and shaken in MEM containing 0.002%(W/V) deoxyribonuclease in a rotary-action shaking water bath at 37.0°C for 10 min. After filtration through a double layer of sterile cotton gauze, the suspension was centrifuged at 50g for 2.5 min. Two cycles of washing with medium 199 or Hepes(4-(2-hydroxyethyl)-1-piperazine-ethanesulphonic acid)-buffered medium (134 mM NaCl, 4.7 mM KCl, 1.2 mM KH$_2$PO$_4$, 1.2 mM MgSO$_4$, 2.5 mM CaCl$_2$, 5 mM NaHCO$_3$ and 10 mM Hepes, pH 7.4) were carried out and cells were suspended finally in Hepes-buffered medium supplemented with 40 mM glucose. The yield of cells from one liver averaged 1.5×10^8, with 90-95% viability as estimated by trypan blue exclusion.

Fresh Hepatocytes

Freshly isolated hepatocytes (6 to 15×10^6 cells) were incubated in plastic tubes in a total volume of 1 ml of Hepes-buffered medium supplemented with 40 mM glucose and shaken in an orbital water bath shaker at 150 to 200 rpm at 37.0°C under an atmosphere of O_2/CO_2 (95:5). Hepatocytes were preincubated for 30 min before the stimulation by agonists, while prazosin or propranolol were added as required after 20 min of preincubation. At the end of incubation, 200 μl aliquots of the cell suspension were transferred to a plastic tube containing 50 μl of drugs as indicated. The tubes were then shaken in a bath at 37°C for 2 min, and immediately immersed in the liquid nitrogen to terminate the reaction. The frozen hepatocytes were stored at −70°C until assay. For the glycogen phosphorylase assay, the frozen hepatocytes were first mixed with a half volume of 30 mM MOPS (3-(N-morpholino)-propanesulphonic acid), 150 mM NaF, 15 mM EDTA (ethlenediaminetetracetic acid) and 3 mM dithiothreitol (pH 7.0). The samples were homogenized with a Polytron cell disrupter (Brinkman Instruments, Westbury, NY) at setting of 8 for 20 s. The homogenates were centrifuged at 12,000 g for 5 min at 4°C and the supernatant used for the assay of glycogen phosphorylase and cAMP as described below.

Cultured Hepatocytes

For culturing hepatocytes, medium 199 supplemented with the following: 100 units/ml penicillin G; 100 μg/ml streptomycin sulphate; 26 mM $NaHCO_3$; an additional 10 mM glucose (final concentration 15.6 mM); 3×10^{-8} M crystalline insulin; and 1×1^{-6} M corticosterone. Approximately 4×10^6 cells in a final volume of 3.0 ml were placed in a 60 mm culture dish coated with collagen which was purified and solubilized by the method of Wood and Keech (1960). The cultures were maintained at 37°C in an atmosphere of 95% air and 5% CO_2. The cultured media was changed to the Hepes-buffered medium described above supplemented with 40 mM glucose at the end of 24 h. Culture dishes were then incubated at 37°C in an atmosphere of 95% air and 5% CO_2 for 30 min. After this preincubation, 50 μl aliquots of various drugs or water (as control) were added to the culture dishes and incubated for 2 min at 37°C. At that point, the medium was immediately discarded and the dishes were placed on the dry ice to terminate the reaction. The frozen hepatocytes attached to the dish were stored at −70°C until assay.

To prepare the samples for assay, the frozen cultured hepatocytes were thawed on ice and 5 ml of ice cold buffer (0.5 mM Mops, 2.5 mM NaF, 0.25 mM EDTA,

0.05 mM dithiothreitol, pH 7.0) were added to the dish. The cells were scraped from the dish and homogenized with a Polytron cell disruptor at setting of 8 for 20 s. The homogenates were centrifuged at 12,000 g for 5 min at 4°C. The supernatant was then frozen in liquid nitrogen and lyophilized. The resulting sample was resuspended in 250 µl of ice cold 60 mM MES (2-(N-Morpholino) ethanesulphonic acid) buffer (pH 6.1). Lyophilization of the samples did not affect either cAMP levels or glycogen phosphorylase activity.

Assays of Glycogenolysis and cAMP Formation

Glycogen phosphorylase *a* activity was measured using a filter disc assay similar to that of Gilboe *et al.* (1972) as modified by Birnbaum and Fain 1977. Briefly, the total incubation volume was 0.06 ml and consisted of 50 mM MES, pH 6.1, 1% glycogen, 15 mM (^{14}C) glucose 1-phosphate (specific activity approximately 0.005 µCi/mmol), and either 0.5 mM caffeine or 0.5 M Na_2SO_4 and 1 mM AMP. Rabbit liver glycogen was purified by passing over an Amberlite MB-1 column followed by precipitation with ethanol. Caffeine was included in the assay to suppress phosphorylase *b* activity, thus generating a truer measure of the phosphorylase *a* content. All phosphorylase assays were performed at 30°C for 20 min; the reactions were terminated by pipetting 0.05 ml aliquots of incubation mixture onto filter discs and dropping them into cold 66% ethanol. Disks were washed twice in ethanol. Data are expressed as micromoles (µmol) of (^{14}C) glucose from α-D-(U-^{14}C)glucose 1-phosphate incorporated into total assay glycogen/min/mg of protein.

For the assay of cAMP, 100 µl of the supernatant described above were added to 50 µl of 0.4 N HCl. Samples were heated in a boiling water bath for 1 min, and neutralized with 4 N NaOH. Cyclic AMP was measured by radioimmunoassay (Steiner *et al.* 1972). Data are expressed as pmol/mg protein/2 min.

Hepatocytes Membrane Preparation for Radioligand Binding Assays

We measured α- and β-adrenergic receptors in a particulate fraction from freshly isolated and cultured rat hepatocytes using (^{3}H) prazosin and ICYP respectively. Freshly isolated and cultured cells (about 7×10^7 cell each) were suspended in 20 ml of ice-cold buffer (0.25 M sucrose; 5 mM Tris-HCl, and 1 mM $MgCl_2$, pH 7.5) and homogenized with a Polytron at setting 8 for 20 s. The homogenates were centrifuged at 1,000 g for 10 min and the resulting supernatant was centrifuged at 20,000 g for 30 min. The pellet was resuspended in 50 mM Tris-HCl (pH 7.4) containing 10 mM $MgCl_2$ and used immediately in the receptor binding assays.

α_1-Receptor number was determined by incubating 100 µl of the membrane suspension ($\simeq$ 1 mg protein) in a total volume of 150 µl containing (^{3}H)prazosin

(0.1-4 nM). Incubations were continued for 30 min at 37°C by which equilibrium had been achieved. Bound ligand was separated from free (^{3}H)prazosin by vacuum filtration and counted in a liquid scintillation spectrometer at an efficiency of 40%. Non-specific binding was defined as binding remaining in the presence of 10 μM phentolamine. The specific binding of (^{3}H)prazosin was shown to have appropriate specificity (Hoffman et al. 1981). The specific binding of (^{3}H)prazosin was routinely 80-90% of the total binding at radioligand concentration near the dissociation constant (K_D).

β-Adrenergic receptor assays using ICYP (40-600 pM) were in a total volume of 150 μl at a protein concentration of 400-600 μg; the incubation was 60 min at 25°C by which time binding was at equilibrium. Incubation was terminated by a vacuum filtration procedure (Whatman GF/C glass fibre filter) with a 20 ml of room temperature buffer. The radioactivity retained on the filters was counted in a gamma counter at 70% efficiency. The specific binding was defined as the difference in the amount of bound ICYP obtained in the absence and in the presence of 1 μM ($\pm$)-propranolol. Specific ICYP binding sites had the expected β-adrenergic specificity and stereospecificity. Decay of (^{125}I) was taken into account in all calculations.

Protein concentration was determined by the method of Lowry et al. (1951) using bovine serum albumin as standard.

Data Analysis

The data from saturation curves of radioligand studies were analysed using non-linear regression on a HP9816 computer. These data were fit based on the law of mass action using a general program for the analysis of data in terms of models (Peck and Barrett 1979). The experimental data given in the text are expressed as the mean$\pm$SEM. Statistical differences between two means ($P<0.05$) were determined by Student's t test for unpaired observations.

RESULTS

Studies on Freshly Isolated Heptocytes

The effect of age on the magnitude of stimulation of glycogen phosphorylase in isolated heptocytes by epinephrine, phenylephrine and isoproterenol is shown in Fig. 1. The phosphorylase a responses to epinephrine (a mixed α- and β-adrenergic agonist) and phenylephrine (an α-adrenergic agonist) decreased moderately with advancing age. On the other hand, the response to isoproterenol (a β-adrenergic agonist) markedly declined during aging, and almost disappeared in isolated hepatocytes from 500 g rats.

This age-related alteration in relative contribution of α- and β-adrenergic regulation of phosphorylase was further characterized by the experiments with

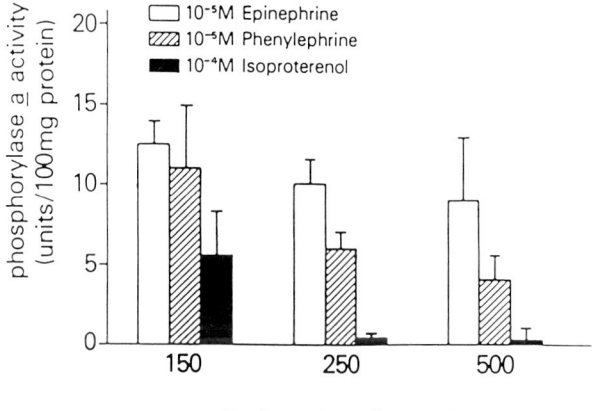

Fig. 1. Stimulation of glycogen phosphorylase by epinephrine, phenylephrine and isoproterenol in isolated hepatocytes from male rats of 150 g, 250 g and 500 g body weight. Freshly isolated hepatocytes were preincubated with 40 mM glucose, then incubated for 2 min with either 10^{-5} M epinephrine, 10^{-5} M phenylephrine or 10^{-4} M isoproterenol. Other details are described in the Material and Methods section. The data are shown as stimulation above basal activity. Basal activity (units/100 mg protein) was 3.0 ± 0.3 (150 g), 1.1 ± 0.2 (250 g) and 1.8 ± 0.2 (500 g), respectively. The results are presented as the mean ± SEM of results obtained from three to six separate experiments.

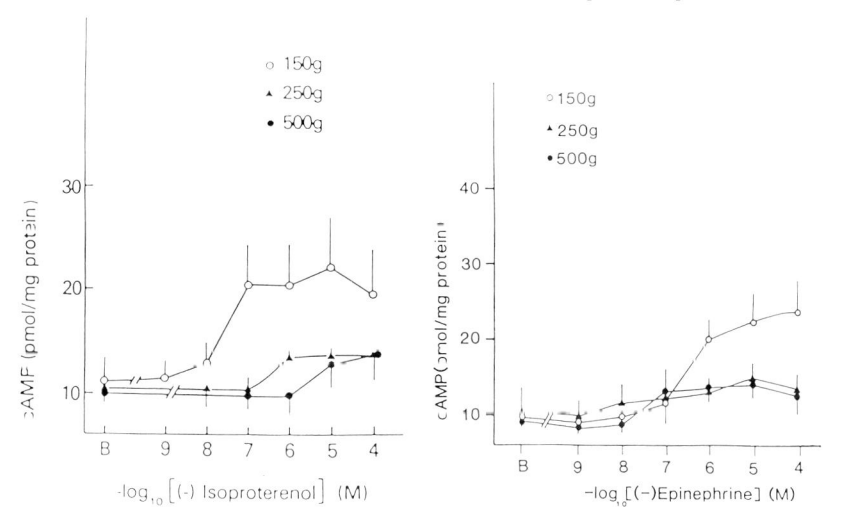

Fig. 2. Dose-response curves for isoproterenol (A) and epinephrine (B) stimulation of cAMP accumulation in hepatocytes from male rats of 150 g, 250 g and 500 g body weight. Experimental conditions were identical with those of Fig. 1, except that cAMP accumulation was measured in the presence of 0.2 mM IBMX (3-isobutyl-1-methylxanthine). Results are the mean ± SEM of three to five different experiments. (From Tsujimoto et al. 1986c, with permission.)

Table 1

Effect of α- and β-adrenergic blockade on epinephrine- phenylephrine- and isoproterenol-stimulated glycogen phosphorylase activation in isolated hepatocytes from male rats of 150 g, 250 g and 500 g body weight*

Animal weights (g)	Stimulants	%Inhibition[†] 10^{-6} M Prazosin	10^{-6} M Propranolol
150	Epinephrine	45.7±14.9	34.3±13.3
250		83.2± 2.8	21.5±11.3
500	(10^{-5} M)	84.6± 7.1	3.5± 3.4
150	Phenylephrine	92.1± 5.8	18.3±17.0
250		80.9± 5.7	19.6± 9.6
500	(10^{-5} M)	89.7± 4.9	0
	Isoproterenol		
150	(10^{-5} M)	40.9± 3.7	63.1±11.5
250	(10^{-4} M)	83.8± 4.8	38.7± 3.3
500	(10^{-4} M)	84.0±10.8	12.9± 6.9

*Experimental conditions were identical with those of Fig. 1 except that the hepatocytes were preincubated with each antagonist for 10 min at the time of addition of the indicated concentration of agonist.
[†]Results are means±SEM from four different experiments.
(From Tsujimoto et al. 1986c, with permission.)

specific antagonists, propranolol (10^{-6} M) and prazosin (10^{-6} M) (Table 1). In these experiments, phenylephrine (10^{-5} M) was preferentially antagonized by prazosin (10^{-6} M) rather than propranolol (10^{-6} M) in all age groups. The stimulation of isoproterenol was effectively blocked by both propranolol and prazosin in juvenile animals, whereas in older rats that was preferentially blocked by prazosin rather than propranolol. These data confirm that the α-adrenergic response predominates over β-adrenergic activation of glycogen phosphorylase as rats age. In addition, the dramatic decrease of β-adrenergic activation of glycogen phosphorylase was found to be associated with blunted cAMP accumulation in response to isoproterenol (Fig. 2A) or epinephrine (Fig. 2B) in hepatocytes from older rats.

In an initial effort to elucidate the mechanism of these observed age-associated changes in glycogen phosphorylase responsiveness to α- and β-adrenergic activation, we measured α_1 and β-adrenergic receptors in membranes prepared from isolated hepatocytes of the various ages of rats. Figure 3 summarizes α- and β-adrenergic receptor density in the different age groups. A progressive decrease in the total number of (^{3}H) prazosin (α_1 receptors) and ICYP (β-receptors) binding sites with increasing age was found. The loss of β-adrenergic sites in heptocytes from the older rats was more dramatic; indeed, we were unable to detect β-adrenergic receptors in the 490–510 g rats. The K_D's of (^{3}H) prazosin and ICYP bindings were not significantly different between three groups. The results of these receptor measurements were well correlated with the physiological

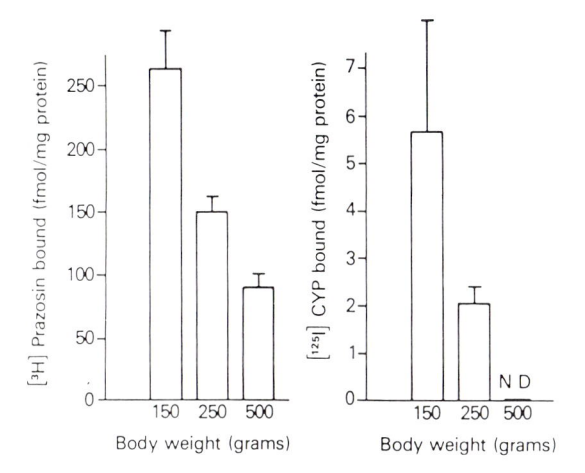

Fig. 3. Specific binding sites of (³H)prazosin and ICYP in membranes from isolated hepatocytes of 150 g, 250 g and 500 g body weight rats. Details of the membrane preparation and of the radioligand assay conditions appear in the Material and Methods section. Data for figure are the mean ± SEM of four to five separate experiments. ND: non-detectable. (From Tsujimoto et al. 1986a, with permission.)

data shown above, suggesting that the decrease in both α- and β-adrenergic receptors in rat hepatocytes may contribute to the age-related change in responsiveness of these cells to catecholamines.

Studies on Cultured Hepatocytes

We compared activation of glycogen phorphorylase in freshly isolated hepatocytes vs hepatocytes that had been cultured for 24 h. As indicated above, in hepatocytes freshly isolated from mature male rats α-adrenergic stimulation of glycogen phosphorylase predominates over β-adrenergic stimulation, whilst, in hepatocytes that had been cultured for 24 h the pattern of responsiveness changed markedly. In the cultured cells, isoproterenol activated glycogen phosphorylase whereas phenylephrine was relatively ineffective. The stimulation by isoproterenol was blocked by propranolol but not by prazosin (Fig. 4A,B). The activation by phenylephrine and epinephrine was partially blocked by both propranolol and prazosin suggesting that these agonists were activating glycogen phosphorylase through both α- and β-receptors in the cultured cells. There was a greater stimulation above basal value by phenylephrine in the freshly isolated heptocytes than in the cultured cells (5.9 ± 1.0 vs 1.8 ± 0.2 units/100 mg protein, respectively), indicating a loss in α-stimulation. Conversely, β-receptor mediated stimulation by isoproterenol increased from 0.3 ± 0.1 units/100 mg protein in the fresh cells to 3.9 ± 1.1 units/100 mg protein in the cultured hepatocytes.

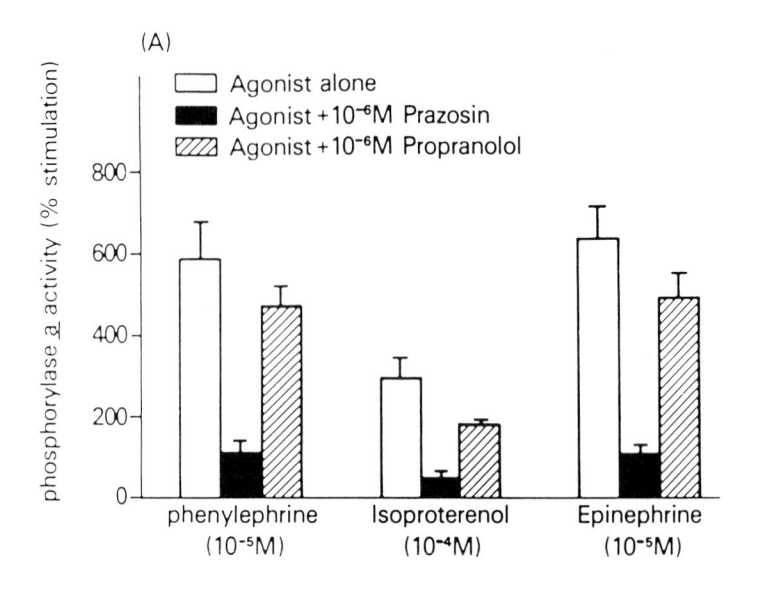

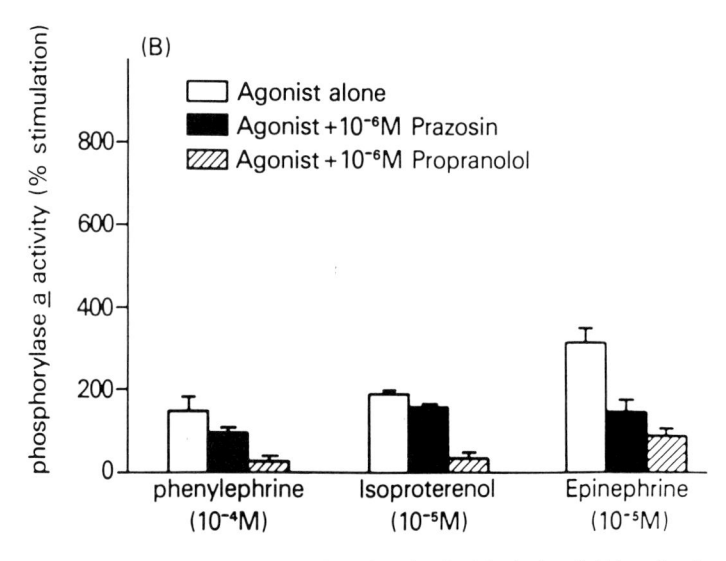

Fig. 4. Stimulation of glycogen phosphorylase in freshly isolated (A) and cultured (B) hepatocytes from adult male rats (250 g body weight) by phenylephrine, isoproterenol and epinephrine, and the influence of α- and β-adrenergic antagonists. Hepatocytes were preincubated for 10 min with 10^{-6} M prazosin or 10^{-6} M propranolol. Then agonists were added as indicated. Other details are described in the Material and Methods section. The results are presented as the mean of results obtained from at least three separate experiments. The error bar represents one SEM. No significant influence of prazosin or propranolol alone was noted in these experiments, and these data have been omitted for clarity. (From Tsujimoto et al. 1986b, with permission.)

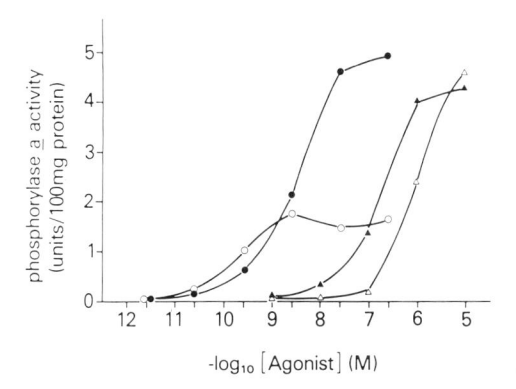

Fig. 5. Dose-response curves for arginine-vasopressin (○,●) and calcium ionophore A23187 (△,▲) activation on phosphorylase in fresh (open symbols) and cultured (closed symbols) hepatocytes. Experimental conditions were identical with those of Fig. 1 except that 10-min incubation was used for A23187 based on preliminary time-course experiments. Phosphorylase a activity is expressed as in Fig. 1. Basal activity (units/100 mg protein) was 2.1 in fresh hepatocytes and 5.8 in cultured hepatocytes in the vasopressin experiments, and 6.8 in fresh hepatocytes and 6.8 in cultured hepatocytes in the A23187 studies. The results are the mean of at least three separate experiments.

We next investigated the mechanism for the altered pattern of responsiveness to catecholamines. Firstly, α-stimulation of glycogen phosphorylase declined in culture. The mechanism of α-stimulation appears to be cAMP independent (Exton 1980, Schmelck and Hanoung 1980). Consequently we examined the activation of glycogen phosphorylase by vasopressin (Keppens and DeWulf 1976) and the ionophore A23187 (Joseph and Williamson 1983) in fresh and cultured hepatocytes, since both agents activate the enzyme by the mechanism involving increases in intracellular Ca^{2+}. As shown in Fig. 5, the ability of vasopressin to activate glycogen phosphorylase actually increased in the cultured cells. There was no change in the maximal responsiveness to A23187. These data indicate that there is no evidence for a general decline in cAMP independent activation of glycogen phosphorylase and suggest some specificity in the loss in responsiveness to α-adrenergic stimulation. Consequently, we measured α-receptors in membranes prepared from fresh and cultured hepatocytes with (^{3}H) prazosin. A marked decrease was found in the number of α-adrenergic receptors in the membranes prepared from cultured hepatocytes. The density of α-receptors decreased from 148 ± 14 fmol/mg protein in the membranes from fresh cells to 52 ± 5 fmol/mg protein in the membranes prepared from cultured hepatocytes ($P < 0.01$). There was no change in the K_D of (^{3}H) prazosin in the two groups (0.65 ± 0.13 nM vs 0.82 ± 0.10 nM, respectively). These data suggest but not definitely establish that the loss in responsiveness to α-agonists is caused by a loss in α-receptors.

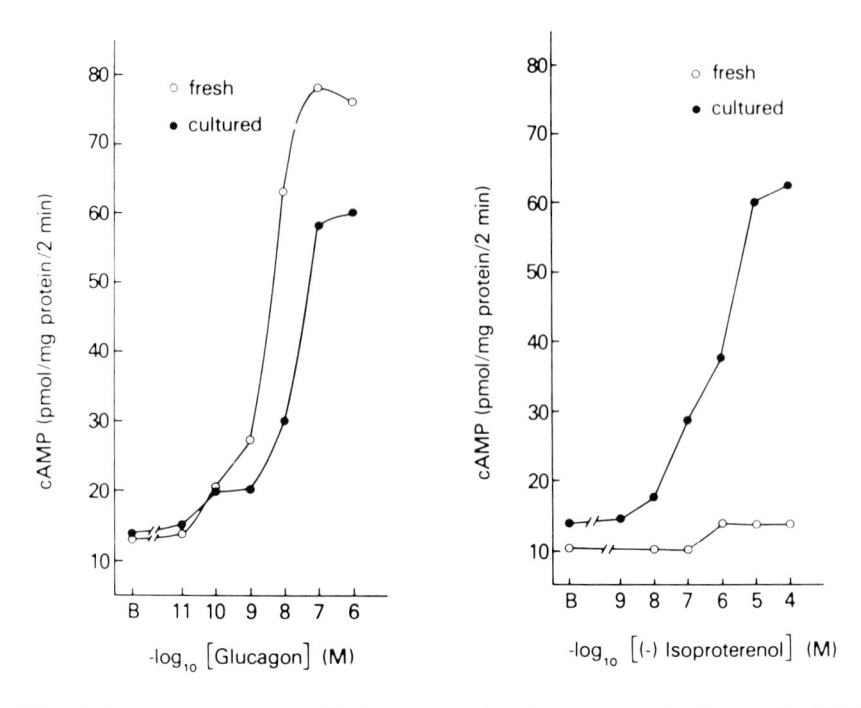

Fig. 6. Dose-response curves for isoproterenol and glucagon stimulation of cAMP accumulation in fresh (open symbols) and cultured (closed symbols) hepatocytes. Experimental conditions were identical with those of Fig. 1 except that cAMP accumulation was measured in the presence of 0.2 mM IBMX. Results are mean of 3-4 experiments.

With culture, there is a marked development in the ability of β-adrenergic agonists to stimulate glycogen phosphorylase as described above. As shown in Fig. 6, isoproterenol did not activate cAMP accumulation in the fresh cells whereas it caused a marked stimulation in the cultured hepatocytes. These findings suggest that the development of the ability of isoproterenol to activate glycogen phosphorylase in culture is due to the appearance of cAMP accumulation in response to the drug. There was also a modest decline in both maximal responsiveness and potency of glucagon in stimulating cAMP accumulation: the EC_{50} of glucagon increased from 5×10^{-9} M to 2×10^{-8} M ($P<0.05$) whereas maximal response decreased from 67.2 ± 10.9 to 43.7 ± 4.3 pmol/mg protein/2 min ($P<0.05$) in fresh hepatocytes compared with cultured cells respectively. These results are similar to those reported previously (Okajima and Ui 1982). In an effort to determine the mechanism for the development of the β-adrenergic response, we measured β-adrenergic receptors in membranes from fresh and cultured hepatocytes with the antagonist ICYP. We found that there was no change in the number of β-receptors (2.1 ± 0.4 vs 2.1 ± 0.3 fmol/mg protein) nor in their affinity for ICYP (K_D: 114 ± 8 vs 118 ± 15 pM) in the membranes from fresh and cultured hepatocytes respectively. Consequently, the development of β-adrenergic stimulation of cAMP accumulation and glycogen phosphorylase activation cannot be explained by a simple change in β-adrenergic receptor number.

DISCUSSION

Much interest has focussed on the altered responsiveness to catecholamines that occurs with aging (Roth and Hess 1982). Diminished responsiveness to both α- and β-adrenergic receptor stimulation has been found in a number of tissues (for general review, see Roth and Hess 1982). The exact mechanism responsible for these changes remains uncertain although some evidence suggests that altered responsiveness with age may be due, in some cases, to changes at the receptor level. In the present study, we have found that the pattern of glycogenolytic response of isolated rat hepatocytes to catecholamines varies with increasing age. Juvenile male rats exhibit both α- and β-adrenergic receptor activation of glycogen phosphorylase whereas in older rats the α-adrenergic response becomes greatly predominant. This result is in general agreement with earlier studies (Blair et al. 1979, Morgan et al. 1983). However, we found that the aging process is associated with an attenuation of both α- and β-adrenergic responses. Interestingly, the decrease in α-adrenergic activation with age is more modest than the marked fall in β-adrenergic activation that also occurs. These changes in α- and β-adrenergic responsiveness was paralleled by a fall in both α- and β-receptors in the hepatocytes. Thus, our results suggest that age-related alteration of hepatic glycogen phosphorylase activation by catecholamines may be in part explained by the changes in adrenergic receptors.

Our results extend the findings of McMillan et al. (1983) who examined changes in α- and β-adrenergic receptors in hepatocyte membranes from prenatal and young postnatal rats. Those workers found that β-adrenergic receptors decreased with early development (up to 100 days) while α-receptors increased from birth to 26 days postnatal. Our results indicate that there is a further loss in β-adrenergic receptors with increasing age. Also, we have shown that there is a fall in α-adrenergic receptor density with age although this decrease is much less marked than that seen for β-adrenergic receptors.

As shown above, catecholamines activate glycogen phosphorylase in hepatocytes from mature rats primarily by stimulating α-adrenergic receptors. Ichihara et al. (1980) made a surprising observation that, after primary culture, hepatocytes became more responsive to β-adrenergic agonists. Okajima and Ui (1982) showed that after a short period in primary culture, not only was there an increase in β-receptor stimulation but also a decline in α-receptor efficacy. We have designed further studies to investigate the mechanisms for these "Adult-to-fetal cell-like change". We have largely confirmed those observations regarding the change in pattern of catecholamine activation of glycogen phosphorylase in cultured hepatocytes.

There is a decline in the ability of α_1-receptors to activate glycogen phosphorylase in hepatocytes cultured for 24 h. We also examined the ability of vasopressin and A23187 to activate glycogen phosphorylase, since both agents regulate the enzyme in the same fashion as α_1-adrenergic stimulation probably by changing the intracellular Ca^{2+} concentrations. As the response to both these agents did not decline in culture, there is some specificity to the loss in responsiveness to α-stimulation and suggests that a receptor alteration might at least partially explain the observation. Indeed, we found a parallel decline in α_1-receptor number in cultured hepatocytes. However, one cannot conclude that the loss in α-receptors is the actual cause of the blunted response since other factors might also be involved such as coupling of the α_1-receptors to their effector.

The explanation for the acquisition of the β-adrenergic response after culture is much less clear. Our data and those of others (Ichihara et al. 1980, Okajima and Ui 1982, Nakamura et al. 1983, Refsnes et al. 1983) indicate that in adult hepatocytes β-agonists cause only a small increase in cAMP accumulation and glycogen phosphorylase activation whereas, after primary culture, the cAMP and glycogen phosphorylase responses are greatly increased. Presumably, it is the augmented cAMP response which enables β-agonists to stimulate glycogen phosphorylase. The mechanism for the enhanced cAMP response is uncertain. Nakamura et al. (1983) found no change in the amount of Ns labelled by cholera toxin in cultured hepatocytes. An obvious hypothesis to explain the augmented β-response is that there is an increase in β-adrenergic receptors in the cultured hepatocytes. Indeed, three groups (Nakamura et al. 1983, Refsnes et al. 1983, Schwarz et al. 1985) have found an increase in β-adrenergic receptors in cultured hepatocytes and concluded that this increase was the cause of the augmented cAMP response. However, in our present experiments, we found no change in the number of β-adrenergic receptors. Possible explanations for the differences in results may include certain methodological differences between our work and those recently reported by others (Nakamura et al. 1983, Refsnes et al. 1983, Schwarz et al. 1985) such as the use of serum rather than defined media in the hepatocyte culture. Those groups utilized serum in their cultures whereas we had utilized defined media in our initial experiments. When we conducted cultures in 10% newborn calf serum we found a similar augmentation in cAMP response to β-agonists that we had seen in cells grown in defined media (data not shown). However, the cells grown in serum containing media had a significant increase in β-receptor number without any change in the K_D of ICYP (β-receptors increased from 2.1 ± 0.4 fmol/mg protein in membranes from hepatocytes grown in defined media to 5.3 ± 0.4 fmol/mg protein in membranes from hepatocytes cultured in media containing serum, $P < 0.05$, $n = 4$; K_D's of ICYP in the two groups were 116 ± 12.0 pM vs 112 ± 11.8 pM). These data suggest that the increase in β-receptors are not necessary for the development of the enhanced cAMP response. Our results suggest that the increase in β-receptor number is a separate process due to factor(s) present in serum. The possibility that serum may modify β-adrenergic receptors has been previously documented in transformed cells in culture (Dibner *et al.* 1981, Darfler *et al.* 1981).

We have fortuitously found experimental conditions where the augmented cAMP response in culture hepatocytes can be disassociated from an increase in β-adrenergic receptor number. Consequently, our results suggest that an alteration in some other property of the hepatocytes is responsible for the enhanced response to isoproterenol. A more detailed characterization will be required to determine the specific alteration involved. One could conjecture a change in the stimulatory regulation of adenylate cyclase or conceivably a release of inhibitory effects on adenylate cyclase. Itoh *et al.* (1984) have recently reported that there is a parallel loss over time in a component of Ni (labelled by ADP-ribosylation in the presence of pertussis toxin) and the development of β-adrenergic receptor stimulated cAMP accumulation in cultured hepatocytes. Furthermore, Kunos *et al.* (1984) have shown after 4 h in culture in serum-free media, there is a development of enhanced β-adrenergic responsiveness in hepatocytes with no change in receptor number. The workers conjecture that the increased efficacy of the β-receptors is due to changes in membrane phopholipase A_2 activity (Kunos *et al.* 1984).

In conclusion, our studies characterized the age-related alterations in adrenergic regulation of glycogen phosphorylase in rat liver and provide an important insight into the mechanism for this phenomenon. Furthermore, studying the switch in the adrenergic control from adult-type to fetal-type during primary culture, we have learned diversity of mechanisms in modulating hepatic glycogenolysis. Although the physiological significance of these changes is unclear at present, the date suggest that the hepatocyte is an interesting model system to examine the age-related alterations in signal transduction.

ACKNOWLEDGEMENTS

Dr G. Tsujimoto was a Merck Sharp and Dohme International Fellow in Clinical Pharmacology and a Fellow of the California Heart Association during the course of these studies. Dr B. B. Hoffman is a recipient of a Hartford Foundation Fellowship. Miss Mie Yamada expertly prepared the manuscript.

REFERENCES

Aggerbeck, M. G., Guellaen, G. and Hanoune, J. (1980). Adrenergic receptor of the alpha-subtype mediates the activation of the glycogen phosphorylase in normal rat liver. *Biochem. Pharmacol.* **29**, 643-645.

Assimacopoulos-Jeannet, F. D., Blackmore, P. F. and Exton, J. H. (1977). Studies on alpha-adrenergic activation of hepatic glucose output. Studies on role of calcium in alpha-adrenergic activation of phosphorylase. *J. Biol. Chem.* **252**, 2662-2669.

Berry, M. N. and Friend, D. S. (1969). High-yield preparation of isolated rat liver parenchymal cells. *J. Cell. Biol.* **43**, 506-520.

Birnbaum, M. J. and Fain, J. N. (1977). Activation of protein kinase and glycogen phosphorylase in isolated rat liver cells by glucagon and catecholamines. *J. Biol. Chem.* **252**, 528-535.

Bissell, D. M. and Guzelian, P. S. (1980). Phenotypic stability of adult rat hepatocytes in primary monolayer culture. *Ann. N.Y. Acad. Sci.* **349**, 85-98.

Bitensky, M. W., Russell, V. and Blanco, M. (1970). Independent variation of glucagon and epinephrine responsive components of hepatic adenyl cyclase as a function of age, sex and steroid hormones. *Endocrinology* **86**, 154-159.

Blackmore, P. F., Brumley, F. T., Marks, J. L. and Exton, J. H. (1978). Studies on alpha-adrenergic activation of hepatic glucose output. Relationship between alpha-adrenergic stimulation of calcium efflux and activation of phosphorylase in isolated rat liver parenchymal cells. *J. Biol. Chem.* **253**, 4851-4858.

Blackmore, P. F., Hughes, B. P., Shuman, E. A. and Exton, J. H. (1982). Alpha-adrenergic activation of phosphorylase in liver cells involves mobilization of intracellular calcium without influx of extracellular calcium. *J. Biol. Chem.* **257**, 190-197.

Blair, J. B., James, M. E. and Foster, J. L. (1979). Adrenergic control of glucose output and adenosine 3':5'-monophosphate levels in hepatocytes from juvenile and adult rats. *J. Biol. Chem.* **254**, 7579-7584.

Darfler, F. J., Hughes, R. J. and Insel, P. A. (1981). Characterization of serum-induced alterations in the cyclic AMP pathway in S49 lymphoma cells. *J. Biol. Chem.* **256**, 8422-8428.

Dibner, M. D., Wolfe, R. A. and Insel, P. A. (1981). Replacement of serum with a defined medium increases beta-adrenergic receptor number in cultured glioma cells. *Exp. Cell Res.* **131**, 424-427.

Engel, G., Hoyer, D., Bethold, R. and Wagner, H. (1981). (±)-[^{125}Iodo] cyanopindolol, a new ligand for beta-adrenoceptors: Identification and quantitation of subclasses of beta-adrenoceptors in guinea pig. Naunyn-Schmiedeberg's *Arch. Pharmacol.* **317**, 277-285.

Exton, J. H. (1980). Mechanism involved in alpha-adrenergic phenomena: role of calcium ions in actions of catecholamines in liver and other tissues. *Am. J. Physiol.* **238**, E3-E12.

Fisher, E. H., Pocker, A. and Saari, J. C. (1970). The structure, function, and control of glycogen phosphorylase. *Essays Biochem.* **6**, 23-68.

Gilboe, D. P., Larson, K. L. and Nuttall, F. Q. (1972). Radioactive method for the assay of glycogen phosphorylases. *Anal. Biochem.* **47**, 20-27.

Hoffman, B. B., Michel, T., Millikin Kilpatrick, D., Lefkowitz, R. J., Tolbert, M. E. M., Gilman, H. and Fain, J. N. (1980). Agonist versus antagonist binding to alpha-adrenergic receptors. *Proc. Natl. Acad. Sci. USA.* **77**, 4569-4573.

Hoffman, B. B., Dukes, D. F. and Lefkowitz, R. J. (1981). Alpha-adrenergic receptors in liver membranes: delineation with subtype selective radioligands. *Life Sci.* **28**, 265-272.

Hutson, N. J., Brumley, F. T., Assilmacopoulos, F. D., Harper, S. and Exton, J. H. (1976). Studies on the alpha-adrenergic activation of hepatic glucose output. Studies on the alpha-adrenergic activation of phosphorylase and inactivation of glycogen synthase in isolated rat liver parenchymal cells. *J. Biol. Chem.* **251**, 5200-5208.

Ichihara, A., Nakamura, T., Tanaka, K., Tomita, Y., Aoyama, K., Kato, S. and Shinno, H. (1980). Biochemical functions of adult rat hepatocytes in primary culture. *Ann. N.Y. Acad. Sci.* **349**, 77-84.

Itoh, H., Okajima, F. and Ui, M. (1984). Conversion of adrenergic mechanism from an alpha- to a beta-type during primary culture of rat hepatocytes. *J. Biol. Chem.* **259**, 15464-15473.

Joseph, S. K. and Williamson, J. R. (1983). The origin, quantitation, and kinetics of intracellular calcium mobilization by vasopressin and phenylephrine in hepatocytes. *J. Biol. Chem.* **258**, 10425-10432.

Keppens, S. and De Wulf, H. (1976). The nature of the hepatic receptors involved in vasopressin-induced glycogenolysis. *Biochim. Biophys. Acta.* **588**, 63-69.

Keppens, S., Vandenheede, J. R. and De Wulf, H. (1977). On the role of calcium as second messenger in liver from the hormonally induced activation of glycogen phosphorylase. *Biochim. Biophys. Acta* **496**, 448-457.

Kunos, G., Hirata, F., Ishac, E. J. N. and Tchakarov, L. (1984). Time-dependent conversion of alpha- to beta-adrenoceptor-mediated glycogenolysis in isolated rat liver cells: Role of membrane phospholipase A_2. *Proc. Natl. Acad. Sci. USA.* **81**, 6178-6182.

Lowry, O. H., Rosebrough, N. J., Farr, A. L. and Randall, R. J. (1951). Protein measurement with the folin phenol regent. *J. Biol. Chem.* **193**, 265-275.

McMillan, M. K., Schanberg, S. M. and Kuhn, C. M. (1983). Ontogeny of rat hepatic adrenoceptors. *J. Pharmacol. Exp. Ther.* **227**, 181-186.

Moncany, M. L. J. and Plas, C. (1980). Interaction of glucagon and epinephrine in the regulation of adenosine 3':5'-monophosphate-dependent glycogenolysis in the cultured fetal hepatocyte. *Endocrinology*, **107**, 1667-1675.

Morgan, N. G., Blackmore, P. F. and Exton, J. H. (1983). Age-related changes in the control of hepatic cyclic AMP levels by alpha$_1$ and beta$_2$-adrenergic receptors in male rats. *J. Biol. Chem.* **258**, 5103-5109.

Nakamura, T., Tomomura, A., Noda, C., Shimoji, M. and Ichihara, A. (1983). Acquisition of a beta-adrenergic response by adult rat hepatocytes during primary culture. *J. Biol. Chem.* **258**, 9283-9289.

Okajima, F. and Ui, M. (1982). Conversion of adrenergic regulation of glycogen phosphorylase and synthase from an alpha to a beta-type during primary culture of rat hepatocytes. *Arch. Biochem. Biophys.* **213**, 658-668.

Peck, C. C. and Barrett, B. B. (1979). Nonlinear least-squares regression programs for microcomputers. *J. Pharmcokin. Biopharm.* **7**, 537-541.

Refsnes, M., Sandnes, D., Melien, O., Sand, T. E., Jacobsen, S. and Christofferson, T. (1983). Mechanism for the emergence of catecholamine-sensitive adenylate cyclase and beta-adrenergic receptors in cultured hepatocytes. *FEBS Lett* **164**, 291-298.

Roth, G. S. and Hess, G. D. (1982). Changes in the mechanisms of hormone and neurotransmitter action during aging: current status of the role of receptor and post-receptor alterations. *Mech. Age Dev.* **20**, 175-194.

Schmelck, P.-H. and Hanoune, J. (1980). The hepatic adrenergic receptors. *Mol. Cell. Biochem.* **33**, 35-48.

Schwarz, K. R., Lanier, S. M., Carter, E. A., Homcy, C. J. and Graham, R. M. (1985). Rapid reciprocal change in adrenergic receptors in intact isolated hepatocytes during primary cell culture. *Mol. Pharmacol.* **27**, 200-209.

Stalmans, W. (1976). The role of the liver in the homeostasis of blood glucose. *Curr. Top. Cell. Regul.* **11**, 51-97.

Steiner, A. L., Wehmann, R. E., Parker, C. W. and Kipnis, D. M. (1972). Radioimmunoassay for the measurement of cyclic nucleotides. In "Advances in Cyclic Nucleotide Research" Vol. 2 (P. Greengard and G. A. Robinson, eds) pp. 51-61. Raven Press, New York.

Tsujimoto, A., Tsujimoto, G. and Hoffman, B. B. (1986a). Age-related change in adrenergic regulation of glycogen phosphorylase in rat hepatocytes. *Mech. Age Dev.* **33**, 167-175.

Tsujimoto, A., Tsujimoto, G., Azhar, S. and Hoffman, B. B. (1986b). Mechanism of altered responsiveness to alpha and beta adrenergic stimulation in cultured hepatocytes. *Biochem. Pharmacol.* **35**, 1400-1404.

Tsujimoto, A., Tsujimoto, G., Kato, K. and Hashimoto, K. (1986c). Developmental alteration in adrenergic regulation of hepatic glycogen phosphorylase. *Japan J. Pharmacol.* **40**, 161–168.

Villar-Palasi, C. and Larner, J. (1970). Glycogen metabolism and glycolytic enzymes. *Annu. Rev. Biochem.* **39**, 639–672.

Wood, G. G. and Keech, M. (1960). The formation of fibrils from collagen solutions. *Biochem. J.* **75**, 588–598.

Discussion

Roth: I am rather surprised that you could not detect β-adrenergic receptors in liver from > 30-week old rats, since you detect a response. This result is apparently opposite to changes reported by Drs Dax and Gregerman at our Institute who found an increase in whole liver of β-adrenergic receptors between 6 and 24 months. Would you care to comment on this?

Tsujimoto: We have recently examined β-adrenergic receptors in isolated rat hepatocytes up to 24 months old, and we could not detect any β-receptors by radioligand binding study with ICYP. The different observations by your group and ours may partly be due to the different membrane preparations used. Whole liver contains heterologous types of cells including not only hepatocytes but also vasculature, blood cells and so on. Those cells are known to have β-receptors.

Carlsson: These interesting data show the greatest differences between immature and young mature rats. I wonder if one should not make a distinction between maturation and aging?

Tsujimoto: I think, you are right, one should do so.

Mombelloni: Could the difference in weight between the 6- and 8-week old rats explain the difference in the altered responsiveness?

Tsujimoto: This is possible. But the same can be observed when using a different strain of rats.

Lakatta: Does the effectiveness of the α-modulation of phosphorylase activity vary with age between 30 weeks and 24 months?

Tsujimoto: Yes, it decreases.

Aging at the Organ Level—Implications and Outlook

T. Franklin Williams

Director, National Institute on Aging, Baltimore, Maryland, USA

The five preceding papers have certain important themes in common, two of which may be summarized as follows:

1. There appear to be certain "intrinsic" changes in cellular responses associated with aging, as seen in various organ systems (myocardium, vascular smooth muscle, skeletal muscle, fat tissue, liver, central nervous system, skin, bone);

2. Most of these apparently age-associated changes can be modified or abolished with prolonged exercise regimens or transplantation of fetal neurons into damaged areas of the brain.

Thus the apparently "immutable" changes of aging are, strikingly, not so immutable after all.

Since there is no universal definition of aging, the aging process has to be studied with regard to a given function which may be altered by age, or by disease, and often by both. Each of these scientists has made imaginative and painstaking contributions to our understanding of various functions.

Dr Ebbesen has demonstrated the intrinsic nature of the aging and dying process as it correlates with the susceptibility to diseases. Again, these events are modifiable since social stress and gender lead to differences in survival.

Drs Lakatta and Tsujimoto have demonstrated that the physiologically important blunted response, evidenced with aging, of myocardium or other organs to β-adrenergic stimulation is at the postreceptor level, probably involving the protein kinase, Ca^{2+} transport, or binding. Dr Lakatta has made many advances in elucidating the role of Ca^{2+} in myocardial muscular contraction and, among other things, has shown that exercise tends to negate age-related changes. The blunted response of the aging human heart to catecholamines is confined to the stimulus transfer and not the result of a diminished contractility. Thus the aging heart may, when spared disease, maintain a high cardiac output with exercise.

Based upon Dr Tsujimoto's studies of young animals, it seems possible that the mechanisms which lead to decreased responsiveness in the aging heart may develop early in the adult and not just in the senescent animal. In his paper, Dr Tsujimoto reports results for 2-month-old and 12-month-old rats, with the implied assumption that the older rats would add nothing to the findings. Inasmuch as various studies have indicated a prolonged stability in both animals and humans after what might be called "maturation" has been achieved, one could postulate that the changes between 2 and 12 months simply represent a growing process from early life to maturity. Without data from the late months of rats' lives, e.g. 24 months or so, it is impossible to say whether the changes seen at 12 months simply represent maturity, or represent changes which will be progressive with age and thus might be termed "senescent". This is a problem common to many studies aimed at understanding aging.

Turning to the experiments done by Dr Steinhagen-Thiessen, it becomes clear that taking up exercise after maturation does successfully slow down age-related declines in enzyme activities in aging skeletal muscle. Exercise can also abolish or reverse the loss of bone mineral content which often accompanies aging. One particularly interesting observation is the positive effect exercise has on bones not involved in the actual exercise, indicating a general metabolic effect. These findings have very important implications both for revising our definition of "aging"—which may be simply progressive disuse—and for continued encouragement of activity which may minimize the changes often associated with aging.

The studies of Drs Wyatt, Freed and de Medinaceli illustrate that central nervous system function can be restored through transplants of fetal nervous tissue and adrenal medullary tissue. This work offers exciting prospects for some of the losses seen in neurological diseases suffered by older people, such as dementia.

In summary, these studies forcefully call our attention to the need of having an open mind to new findings about aging which may change concepts believed earlier. We need to be very cautious in attributing changes to aging *per se*, and must look for potentially modifiable processes with the expectation that we will often find them. In all of these approaches we are seeing research dealing with organ and cell function advancing to the chemical and molecular levels. We may anticipate further exciting results from the work of these scientists.

Part III

Human Competences in Aging

Neurochemical, Genetic and Clinical Aspects of Alzheimer's Disease

B. Winblad, W. Wallace, J. Hardy, C. Fowler, G. Bucht,
I. Alafuzoff and R. Adolfsson

Umeå Dementia Research Group, Department of Geriatric Medicine, University of Umeå, Umeå, Sweden

Keywords
Alzheimer's disease; Clinical and histopathological criteria; Brain biochemistry; Molecular biology

BACKGROUND

Alzheimer's disease (AD, which in this paper, unless otherwise stated, includes senile dementia of Alzheimer's type, SDAT) is a brain disorder characterized by a progressive dementia that occurs in middle or late life. It is the most prevalent disease causing dementia in old age and is probably one of the most common causes of death in persons over 65 years. Dementia refers to a global deterioration in all aspects of mental function, including memory, general intellect, emotional attributes and distinctive features of personality. The prevalence is about 5% for definite cases of dementia in the elderly population 65 years and older but rises dramatically in the eighth and ninth decades. The pathological characteristics are the degeneration of specific nerve cells and the presence of senile plaques and neurofibrillary tangles. The patterns of neurotransmitter pathway losses in AD show established deficits of the cholinergic pathways from the nucleus basalis, the noradrenergic pathways from the locus coeruleus and the serotonergic pathways from the raphe nuclei. In addition, cortical somatostatin interneurons and corticotropin-releasing factor neurons are affected as well, possibly, as dopaminergic neurons, although these changes may be late or secondary phenomena in the disease process.

So far clinical and biochemical investigations in AD have identified a group of patients with a typical history of signs and symptoms. They are characterized by a progressive course, a global deterioration of mental functions, and distinctive histopathological features and biochemical changes.

The association between aging and AD is complex but both conditions show some common features. Similarities in symptomatology between normally aged individuals and persons with "mild dementia" have not been fully elucidated but certainly exist empirically. However, most reports favour the assumption that the degenerative changes found in the brain of the elderly are considered to result from a disease and not inevitable consequences of advancing chronological age.

Few longitudinal studies have been presented and therefore the natural course of the disease is not well described. Some of the difficulties with cross-sectional as well as with longitudinal studies are obvious. The various attempts to follow the progress of the disease are hampered by the lack of diagnostic tests which cover the whole span of the disease.

Like any disease, the dementia disorders are multifaceted in nature. Different investigators study clinical, histopathological, neurochemical or genetic aspects, but often in relative isolation from one another. However, at Umeå a multidisciplinary approach has been put together that facilitates comparisons between various different aspects of the disease within each individual case, for example, by correlating clinical symptoms with histopathological changes. Such an integrated approach will illuminate the nature of the dementia disorders by following the entirety of changes which the demented brain undergoes from onset until death.

CLINICAL AND HISTOPATHOLOGICAL PROFILES OF THE DEMENTIA DISORDERS

Of the irreversible dementias, the most common type is the primary dementia, commonly referred to as Alzheimer's disease/senile dementia of Alzheimer type (AD/SDAT), where AD is the early onset form (before age 65) and SDAT the late onset form. AD/SDAT constitutes 50-70% of the total number of dementia cases seen at autopsy (Tomlinson 1980). Taken together, the essential features of AD/SDAT are the presence of an insidious onset and gradual progression involving loss of intellectual abilities, such as memory, judgement, abstract thinking and other advanced cortical functions, as well as change in personality and behaviour (Roth 1955, 1985, Slater and Roth 1970). On the other hand, there is no clouding of consciousness (DSM III 1980). With progression of the disease, the patient often becomes completely mute and inattentive.

Vascular dementia, also called multi-infarct dementia (MID), has been suggested to account for about 15% of the total number of dementia cases seen at autopsy (Tomlinson 1980), although other studies have suggested a higher incidence of this disorder (Adolfsson and Forsgren 1984). Contrary to AD/SDAT cases, MID cases show an abrupt onset, a stepwise and fluctuating progression with rapid changes that, early in the course of the disease, leave some of the intellectual function relatively intact (Hachinski et al. 1974, 1975). Disturbances in memory, abstract thinking, judgement, impulse control and personality are common. Patterns of deficits depend upon which regions of the brain are affected (Fisher 1968, Hachinski 1979, de Reuck et al. 1982). Focal neurological signs and symptoms are present. In addition, cerebrovascular diseases have been related to the aetiology of this disorder (Hachinski et al. 1975, Rosen et al. 1980, Birkitt and Raskin 1982).

In recent years, there have been attempts to standardize the clinical criteria for classifying the dementia patients. The most widely used clinical classification criteria for dementia, the DSM III criteria, were introduced in 1980 by the American Psychiatric Association (DSM III 1980). Use of such a clinical classification system can result in the designation of patients into five groups, namely: AD/SDAT, probable AD/SDAT, MID, probable MID and possible MID, depending upon how well the symptoms presented conform to the DSM III criteria (Adolfsson et al. 1986) (see Table 1).

The diagnostic hallmarks of AD/SDAT are the presence of abundant neurofibrillary tangles (Tomlinson 1980, Terry and Davies 1980) and senile/neuritic plaques (Tomlinson 1980, Gibson 1983). The tangles and plaques are observed in both cortical and subcortical areas with an accentuation in the temporoparietal lobe and the posterior cingulate gyrus (Brun and Englund 1981, Brun 1983). Plaques and tangles are usually also present in the normally aged brain, but in much lower numbers. The number of these lesions has been found in several studies to increase with the progress and severity of the dementia (see e.g. Blessed et al. 1968, Gibson 1983).

Table 1
Simplified presentation of (part of) the DSM III criteria as used in the study of Adolfsson et al. (1986)

Parameter	AD/SDAT	Probable AD/SDAT	MID	Probable MID	Possible MID
Progression of disease	Uniform decline	Uniform decline	Stepwise decline	Stepwise decline	Uniform decline
Cerebrovascular risk factors?	No	Yes	Variable	Variable	Yes
Neurological signs or symptoms?	No	No	Yes	No	Yes

Table 2
Simplified presentation of (part of) the histopathological diagnostic criteria used in the study of Adolfsson et al. (1986)

Parameter	Histopathological diagnosis			
	AD/SDAT	MID	AD/MID	Normal
Tangles score[a] in cortex and hippocampus	1-3	0-1	1-3	0-1
Plaques score[b]	1-3	0-3	0-3	0-3
Histopathological dementia score[c]	>4	≤4	>4	≤4
Microscopic infarcts[d] in:				
frontal cortex	0-2	0-2	0-2	0-2
hippocampus	0-1	2	2	0-1

[a]Counted in five randomly selected fields using Bodian PAS stained sections. Mean absolute number and scores: score 0: not observed; score 1: 0.1-5.0; score 2: 5.1-10.0; score 3: ≥10.1.
[b]Counted as for the tangles. Mean absolute number and scores: score 0: not observed; score 1: 0.1-10.0; score 2: 10.1-20.0; score 3: ≥20.1.
[c]Sum of plaques and tangles scores in the frontal cortex and hippocampus.
[d]Noted on haematoxylin-eosin stained sections. Score 0: not observed; score 1: occasional; score 2: widespread.

The diagnostic hallmark for MID is the presence of macro- and microscopic infarcts in cortical and subcortical areas. Such infarcts, both haemorrhagic and ischaemic, of a total volume greater than 100 ml (Tomlinson et al. 1968, 1970), infarcts localized in periventricular white matter or the thalamus (de Reuck et al. 1982) or involving the hippocampus (Fisher 1968, Corsellis 1976), have been pointed out as a cause of at least some of the clinical symptoms of MID.

The histopathological changes found in both AD/SDAT and MID are sometimes co-existent in certain cases of dementia. Whether these cases (termed AD/MID) are merely cases which started with AD/SDAT and then developed MID at a later stage (or vice versa) or whether AD/MID is a separate disease group is not fully elucidated.

In addition to the above-mentioned histopathological findings, there are a number of other structural changes of the brain associated with both aging and dementia, including brain atrophy, neuronal loss, dendritic atrophy, accumulation of lipofuscin, Hirano bodies and granulovascular degeneration (Tomlinson 1980, Brun 1983). The main criteria, however, used for the differential histopathological diagnosis of autopsy cases into AD/SDAT, MID and AD/MID, as employed in Umeå, are given in Adolfsson et al. (1986), and summarized in Table 2.

The definitive diagnosis of AD requires both a clinical diagnosis and a histopathological diagnosis (McKhann et al. 1984). One of the many difficulties associated with dementia research is that the clinical diagnoses (upon which the research findings are based) are often not confirmed at autopsy. In a recent study,

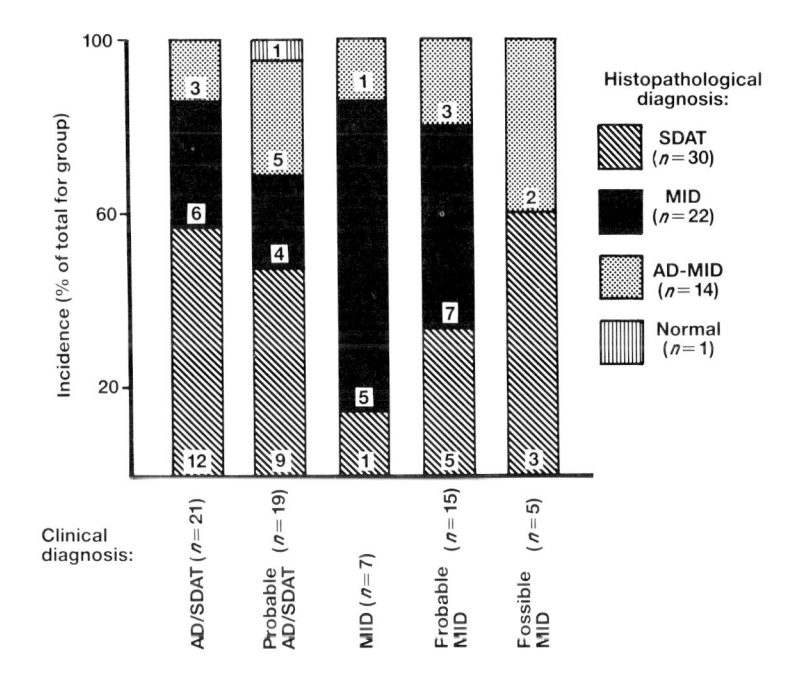

Fig. 1. Comparison of clinical and histopathological diagnoses.

Adolfsson et al. (1986) compared the clinical diagnoses of a non-selected series of patients using the DSM III criteria outlined in Table 1 with the histopathological diagnoses found later at autopsy. Comparison of the clinical and histopathological diagnoses indicated that the correlation between the two was rather poor (Fig. 1), a result in agreement with the study of Todorov et al. (1975). Whilst it is possible that a very restricted use of the DSM III criteria may result in a higher clinical:histopathological correlation rate for AD/SDAT, this can only be achieved at the cost of "selecting out" a large fraction of the patient material from the research, raising the spectre that the findings made may not be representative of the AD/SDAT group as a whole. Thus, it can be concluded from the findings of Todorov et al. (1975) and Adolfsson et al. (1986) that histopathological confirmation of the clinical diagnoses is essential when analysing data obtained from dementia patients.

Whilst AD/SDAT and MID are undoubtedly two separate conditions with different clinical criteria and different neuropathological bases, uncertainty persists as to whether or not subgroups exist and as to whether AD and SDAT are the same or different disorders (for discussion, see Winblad et al. 1986). Due to the lack of prospective studies based on early detected cases with later histopathological confirmation, this question is still unanswered. To date, most studies have been cross-sectional, and subgroups reported in the literature on the basis of either clinical, histopathological, neurochemical, or genetic findings are either valid disease subgroups or might represent artifacts due to the use of cross-sectional data. Therefore, a comprehensive longitudinal study is necessary to ascertain the significance of these reported subgroups.

NEUROTRANSMITTER CHANGES IN AD

The neurochemical changes present in AD have been studied for two reasons:
1. With the intention of finding a "primary lesion" which can lead in turn to transmitter replacement therapy (analogous to L-DOPA therapy in Parkinson's disease);
2. With the hope that the determination of such changes will lead to an understanding of the pathogenesis of the disorder.

Reported Transmitter Deficits in AD

Acetylcholine

A considerable loss of activity of choline acetyltransferase, a presynaptic marker for cholinergic neurons, particularly in the hippocampus and temporal cortex, has been reported by a number of authors (e.g. Davies and Maloney 1976). The extent of the reported loss varies considerably between groups but reaches significant levels in all reports. Choline acetyltransferase in other brain regions may also be affected, although this finding is less consistent (for review, see Rossor 1982, Hardy *et al.* 1985). Losses in other presynaptic markers for cholinergic neurons appear to be similar in general terms to the loss in choline acetyltransferase indicating that the decrement is not enzyme-specific. Thus, synaptosomal choline uptake is reduced in AD (Rylett *et al.* 1983) as is acetylcholinesterase activity (Pope *et al.* 1965). These findings have been confirmed and extended in biopsy studies (Sims *et al.* 1983) which have shown that acetylcholine synthesis and release from tissue prisms is also reduced in AD. The histological correlate of the biochemical loss is reduced cell numbers in the nucleus basalis complex (Pilleri 1966, Whitehouse *et al.* 1982, see also Rossor *et al.* 1982b) and the presence of tangles in this nucleus (Ishii 1966).

The losses in presynaptic markers do not appear to be mirrored by losses in muscarinic receptors. Reports have shown these to have either normal levels (Wood *et al.* 1983, Reisine *et al.* 1978) or reduced only in a subpopulation of AD sufferers (Wood *et al.* 1983). The possibility of receptor compensation has been raised (Nordberg *et al.* 1983).

Noradrenaline

A noradrenergic deficit in AD has been found by several independent groups (Table 3) (for review, see Hardy *et al.* 1985). Thus, noradrenaline

Table 3

	Cholinergic neurons	Noradrenergic neurons	Serotonergic neurons	Dopaminergic neurons	Glutamate neurons
Cell loss, reduced nucleolar volume and neurofibrillary tangles	Nucleus basalis of Meynert (1-3)	Locus coeruleus (2-4)	Raphe (dorsal tegmental) nucleus (2,3,5)	Ventral tegmentum (20)	Pyramidal cells (21)
Loss of neurotransmitter marker	ChAT ir. many regions (5); ACh in temporal cortex (7)	NA in many regions (8), DBH in cerebral cortex (9,10), reduced NA uptake in temporal cortex (11)	5-HT in several regions (12); loss of imipramine binding (13), and reduced 5-HT uptake in temporal cortex (11)	DA in several regions (8,12)	D-aspartate uptake and binding (22,23)
Changes in receptor number	↓Muscarinic (M) receptors (14,15) (hippocampus) ±0 M receptors (16) (hippocampus) ↓M$_2$, ±0 M$_1$ receptors (17) (frontal and infratemporal cortex) ±0 Nicotinic receptors (16) (hippocampus)	±0 β-Adrenoceptors (13) (temporal cortex) ±0 α$_1$-, α$_2$- and β-adrenoceptors (18) (hippocampus, occipital cortex)	↓S$_2$ receptors[a] (frontal cortex, hippocampus) (18,19) ↓S$_1$ receptors[a] temporal cortex (13)	—	Changes in excitatory amino acid receptors (24,25)

Abbreviations: ChAT = choline acetyltransferase; ACh = acetylcholine; NA = noradrenaline; DBH = dopamine-β-hydroxylase; 5-HT = 5-hydroxytryptamine.
Representative references are given in the table (for a more complete list, see Hardy et al. 1985):
(1) Pilleri 1966; (2) Mann et al. 1984; (3) Ishii 1966; (4) Forno 1978; (5) Mann and Yates 1983; (6) Davies and Maloney 1976; (7) Richter et al. 1980; (8) Arai et al. 1984; (9) Cross et al. 1981; (10) Perry et al. 1981; (11) Benton et al. 1982; (12) Winblad et al. 1982; (13) Bowen et al. 1983; (14) Reisine et al. 1978; (15) Nordberg et al. 1983; (16) Rinne et al. 1985; (17) Mann et al. 1985; (18) Cross et al. 1984; (19) Reynolds et al. 1984; (20) Mann et al. unpublished observations; (21) Hardy et al. unpublished observations; (22,23) Cross et al. unpublished observations; (24) Greenamyre et al. 1985; (25) Geddes et al. 1985.
[a] This decrease may, however, be due in part to a localization of these binding sites on cholinergic nerve terminals (see Cross and Deakin 1985, Quirion et al. 1985).

concentrations and dopamine β-hydroxylase levels have been reported to be reduced in AD (Adolfsson *et al.* 1979, Cross *et al.* 1981, Perry *et al.* 1981) and cell losses in the locus coeruleus have been documented (Mann 1983, Bondareff *et al.* 1982). In addition, large numbers of tangles have been reported in the locus coeruleus neurons (Ishii 1966). Noradrenaline uptake is also reduced in biopsy samples from AD patients (Benton *et al.* 1982) indicating that the noradrenaline deficit is not an artifact of the end stage of the disease. The distribution of the loss of noradrenergic innervation is not well established although the hypothalamus appears to be severely affected and the hippocampus less so (Gottfries *et al.* 1983). The only direct comparisons of cell numbers and relative losses in the substantia innominata and the locus coeruleus in AD revealed a larger although more variable loss in the latter (Mann *et al.* 1984). Neither α- nor β-noradrenergic receptors appear to be affected by the disorders (Bowen *et al.* 1983, Cross *et al.* 1984).

Serotonin

Losses of serotonin innervation in AD have been documented by measurement of serotonin and 5-hydroxyindoleacetic acid concentrations (Adolfsson *et al.* 1979) and imipramine binding (Bowen *et al.* 1983) to post-mortem human brain tissue (Table 3) (for review, see Hardy *et al.* 1985). In addition, a reduction of serotonin uptake into biopsy specimens of AD when compared with other surgical material has been reported (Benton *et al.* 1982, Bowen *et al.* 1983), again suggesting that the results obtained with post-mortem material are not artifacts of the final stages of the disease. These biochemical observations correlate with reports of reduced cell counts and the presence of tangles in the raphe nuclei (Mann and Yates 1983, Ishii 1966). S_2 receptors and probably S_1 receptors are also reduced in the disorder (Bowen *et al.* 1983, Cross *et al.* 1984) although this may be a result of their partial localization on cholinergic cell bodies (see Cross and Deakin 1985, Quirion *et al.* 1985).

Dopamine

Reduced dopamine concentrations in striatal and extrastriatal regions have been reported in some patients (Adolfsson *et al.* 1979, Gottfries *et al.* 1983). Reductions in dopamine metabolite concentrations have also been reported in both brain and spinal fluid studies (Adolfsson *et al.* 1979, Gottfries *et al.* 1983, Gottfries and Roos 1973, Soininen *et al.* 1981, Palmer *et al.* 1984). There have been no investigations, however, of cell counts in the substantia nigra in AD. It may be that a dopamine deficit is found in a subgroup of patients with AD; certainly a rather high proportion of AD patients develop Parkinson-like symptoms. Whether it is these patients who have reduced dopamine and homovanillic acid levels is not known. Recently, however, histological observations in the ventral tegmental area have shown profound cell loss (Mann *et al.* 1986, unpublished observations). These studies indicate that the dopamine innervation of the cortex may indeed be affected in this disorder.

Whilst the above-mentioned neurotransmitter deficits are of undoubted importance in determining the symptomatology of AD, these neuronal systems make up only a small proportion of the total number of cortical neurons. The severe cortical neuronal loss found in AD must therefore encompass other transmitter systems, of which the two obvious candidates are GABA and glutamatergic neurons, since they constitute the bulk of cortical neurons. These systems are discussed below.

GABA

Most studies have suggested an intact GABA system in AD (see Rossor *et al.* 1982b). However, since somatostatin and GABA are co-transmitters in some cortical neurons (Smechel *et al.* 1984) and since somatostatin is lost in the disease (Davies *et al.* 1980), a subpopulation of the GABA neurons may well be affected.

Glutamate

Glutamatergic function has not been assessed in AD. However, it is the transmitter for many pyramidal neurons (Fonnum and Walaas 1978) and there is a loss of such neurons in this disorder (Mann *et al.* 1984). Recent studies investigating the uptake site for glutamate as a neuronal marker have shown a large loss in AD (Cross *et al.* 1986, Hardy *et al.* 1986, both unpublished observations).

Peptides

Most peptidergic neurons appear to be little affected in AD (for review, see Hardy *et al.* 1985). However, both somatostatin and corticotropin-releasing factor seem to be reduced in this disorder (Davies *et al.* 1980, Bisette *et al.* 1985). Furthermore, somatostatin neurons have been shown to be tangle bearing (Roberts *et al.* 1985).

Transmitter Specificity—General Points

Early optimism suggesting there was a specific cholinergic deficit analogous to the dopamine deficit in Parkinson's disease has been largely dissipated. This theory was progressively widened to include other neurons (Rossor 1981), but it would seem to us that the idea of transmitter specificity in AD appears more and more to resemble the pot of gold at the end of the rainbow—the closer you approach the theory, the more the evidence for it seems to disappear. This makes the search for a replacement therapy appear daunting but does yield clues as to the pattern of transmitter deficits involved in the pathogenesis of the disease.

The Site of the Pathogenesis of AD

The site of the pathogenesis would seem to be cortical since all the affected neurons are either within the cortex/hippocampus or innervate these areas. Thus, whilst the cholinergic innervation of the cortex is damaged (see above), cholinergic neurons in the striatum are unaffected (Rossor *et al.* 1982a). Similarly the ventral tegmentum is damaged whereas the substantia nigra is spared (see above).

Neurofibrillary tangles are not only found in AD but also in other pathological conditions, such as dementia pugilistica and viral infections (for a review of the pathology of dementia, see Corgellis *et al.* 1973). Since in these cases the cause of the disease is established, it is hard to argue conclusively that the tangles are the primary event in AD; rather (as for the neurotransmitter losses) they are merely a secondary event. On the other hand, plaques are found almost exclusively in the cortical and hippocampal regions in AD and are not found in dementia pugilistica. Thus, it is tempting to speculate that plaques may be the site of the pathogenesis of AD.

Some recent reports have suggested that plaques are always associated with blood vessels (see e.g. Miyakawa *et al.* 1982). This, and reports suggesting that the plaque core protein is similar in structure to the cerebrovascular amyloid frequently found in AD (Masters *et al.* 1985, Glenner and Wong 1984), point to a blood vessel-related pathogenesis and suggest that the neurons affected degenerate secondarily to this in a non-specific manner. In this respect, it is particularly interesting that many of the affected neurons appear to be involved in the innervation of blood vessels. Thus, a serotonergic innervation of cortical blood vessels from the raphe has been established (Edvinsson *et al.* 1983), a noradrenergic innervation from the locus coeruleus has long been suspected (Mann 1983), and a cholinergic innervation of central but unknown origin reported (Estrada *et al.* 1983). This suggests a further link between the affected neurons and blood vessels and may explain the early and severe loss in these systems in AD. Furthermore, this scheme may explain the frequently reported changes in blood flow in AD.

Regardless of whether or not the above hypothesis is correct, the transmitter deficits observed are secondary to the neuron loss. It is important to determine whether such neuron loss, however caused, is genetically predetermined and whether the genes responsible for such degeneration can be identified. These questions are discussed below.

MOLECULAR GENETIC INVESTIGATIONS

The contribution of a genetic component in AD has been difficult to assess. Population analyses of families in which a member manifests this disease have been hindered by several factors. These problems include: the definition of AD by histopathological examination of autopsy tissue, the lack of definitive diagnosis in living patients, the expression of the disease late in life and the possibility that the current manifestations of the disease may simply be the results of various different aetiologies.

The evidence implicating a genetic component has come from identification of families exhibiting the disease (e.g. Nee *et al.* 1983), population genetic analysis of selected samples (Larsson *et al.* 1963, Heston *et al.* 1981, Breitner and Folstein 1984, see also Heston 1983), and relating Down's syndrome to AD (Heston and Mastri 1977).

The mode of transmission underlying the genetic basis of the disease is still uncertain. Certain families in which AD is prevalent exhibit a simple autosomal dominant mode of transmission (see e.g. Nee *et al.* 1983). However, the results of investigations which have examined AD families within a general population indicate a more complicated segregation of the disorder. Larsson *et al.* (1963) noted a familial aggregation of the disease and suggested a dominant inheritance with incomplete penetrance due to the age-dependent expression of the genotype. Later Heston *et al.* (1981) using selected, histopathologically confirmed AD probands and their families concluded that siblings of early onset AD probands had a risk approaching 50% of manifesting a dementia by age 90. Similarly, Breitner and Folstein (1984), using a clinical definition of the disease and a nursing home population, concluded the same risk to siblings. A 50% risk is consistent with an autosomal dominant transmission of the disease. However, the later two studies disagreed on the prevalence of the familial form of AD; Heston suggesting 33% while Breitner and Folstein suggested 78% of all AD cases were familial. The prevailing view is that the genetic basis of AD is a simple autosomal dominant transmission with an incomplete penetrance due to the late onset of the disease.

The results of the studies of Larsson *et al.*, Heston *et al.* and Breitner and Folstein are, however, consistent with other modes of genetic transmission and expression. For example, the differences between the results expected from the model of a single gene with incomplete inheritance and a model of multifactorial inheritance may not be significant (Edwards 1960). Likewise, polygenic models may be consistent with the observed deviation from simple Mendelian segregation of the disease.

Thus, AD may be considered a disorder which is inherited as a threshold character (Wright 1934, Roth 1985), in which genetic and environmental factors are required for the expression of the AD gene(s). The threshold model has been proposed for other age-dependent disorders such as diabetes mellitus (Falconer 1967) and schizophrenia (Gottesman and Shields 1967). The threshold model assumes that some inherited underlying disorder causes the clinically and histopathologically defined AD only when the underlying disorder has accumulated sufficiently. Such a threshold concept has also been proposed for AD from histopathological and clinical considerations (Roth 1985, Tomlinson *et al.* 1970). The inheritance of AD may then be considered as the inheritance of the underlying disorder or predisposition (called threshold character).

Identification of the Gene(s) Responsible for AD

The clearest and most direct way to determine a genetic component of AD is the identification of the gene(s) whose abnormality is responsible for the disease.

At Umeå this problem is being investigated in two ways: (1) identifying alterations in RNA content in Alzheimer post-mortem tissue and (2) identifying restriction fragment length polymorphisms of DNA sequences in AD families.

Alterations in Alzheimer Tissue Characterization of RNA

Abnormalities in gene function will be detectable as a corresponding alteration in messenger RNA (mRNA) as either a change in levels or in structure. Thus, the determination of alterations in RNA content during the disease may be used to identify the abnormal gene(s). In addition, the characterization of such alterations may be used to characterize the pathogenesis of gene expression in Alzheimer tissue.

The search for such changes of RNA content have begun with the isolation and characterization of mRNA and polysomes from control and Alzheimer post-mortem brain tissue. Initially, it has been determined that the RNA which reflects the mRNA present within the living brain could be isolated from normal and Alzheimer post-mortem brain tissue (Wallace, Eriksson and Winblad, unpublished results). RNA was isolated from various regions (including cerebral cortical areas, hippocampus and several subcortical regions) of normally aged brains using a method that allows the simultaneous extraction and characterization of many samples (Auffray and Rougeon 1980). A surprising but reproducible regional variability of RNA content was found. However, a few regions (including the postcentral gyrus, occipital cortex, putamen and cerebellum) contained a significantly greater amount of RNA while the medulla oblongata and globus pallidus contained a significantly lower content of RNA.

The RNA that was isolated from the normal post-mortem tissue was shown to be intact by four separate observations. First, the total RNA included levels of polyadenylated sequences comparable to those observed in tissues from other sources. Second, the total RNA which was separated by formaldehyde gel electrophoresis exhibited identical patterns of ethidium bromide staining with undegraded rat brain RNA ((1) similar electrophoretic mobilities of the 28S and 18S ribosomal RNA, (2) a greater preponderance of the 28S over the 18S species, and (3) the absence of any discrete lower molecular weight RNA species). Third, equal yields were reproducibly obtained from the same region from brain to brain. Finally, mRNA was found to be biologically active by being able to programme protein synthesis in an *in vitro* translation assay.

Because the RNA appeared to be intact, it is likely to be representative of the RNA which is present in the living brain. Therefore, it was concluded that under these conditions, the post-mortem human brain, with all its inherent advantages, may be used as a source of RNA to investigate the heterogeneity of gene expression in the normal and Alzheimer brain. mRNA has also been isolated from Alzheimer tissue and studies are underway to characterize the observed changes in the diseased tissue.

Table 4
Polysomes from control, MID and Alzheimer frontal cortex

	Yield (A_{260} units/g wet weight brain) (± 1 SD)	Translation activity ($\times 10^3$ dpm ^{35}S-met/ A_{260} unit, ± 1 SD)
Control	2.07 (± 0.49) ($n=7$)	695 (± 212) ($n=10$)
Alzheimer	0.73 (± 0.42)★ ($n=6$)	345 (± 82)★ ($n=8$)

★$P \leqslant 0.01$ from control by ANOVA test.

In addition to total and mRNA, differences in polysome content between control and Alzheimer tissue have been investigated (Wallace, Långström, Lindroos and Winblad, unpublished results). Because polysomes contain mRNA in the process of synthesizing new proteins, changes in polysome function represent disruptions in the gene expression within the Alzheimer brain.

Cytosolic polysomes were prepared from the cortices of control and histopathologically diagnosed AD brains as described by De Gennaro et al. (1983). The yields of polysomes from AD frontal cortices were reduced 65% compared to the yields from control tissue (Table 4). However, control and AD polysomes exhibited virtually identical distributions within a sucrose gradient after centrifugation, indicating that the structural integrity of the two sets of polysomes were similar (Fig. 2a).

The polysomes were characterized for biological activity with a rabbit reticulocyte *in vitro* translation assay (De Gennaro et al. 1983). The amount of translation products obtained from AD polysomes was only 50% of that obtained from control polysomes (Table 4). By a combination of lower polysome content and reduced translational activity per polysome, the AD frontal cortex may be estimated to contain approximately 16% of the protein synthetic activity per gram of tissue compared to control frontal cortex. The polypeptides synthesized by control and AD polysomes exhibited no obvious differences in size as examined by SDS-PAGE and fluorography (Fig. 2b).

The polysomes were further examined to determine whether the reduced capability of protein synthesis by AD polysomes was due to the absence of a translation factor or to the presence of an inhibitor of translation. In order to discriminate between these two possibilities, AD and control polysomes were mixed and translated together. Thus either control polysomes were initially translated alone for 15 min in the *in vitro* translation assay after which an equal amount of AD polysomes were added, or control polysomes were added to translating AD polysomes. From these experiments it was observed that more translation products were obtained from control polysomes alone than AD polysomes alone throughout the translation incubation (Fig. 2c). The addition of either an equal amount of AD polysomes to control polysomes or control

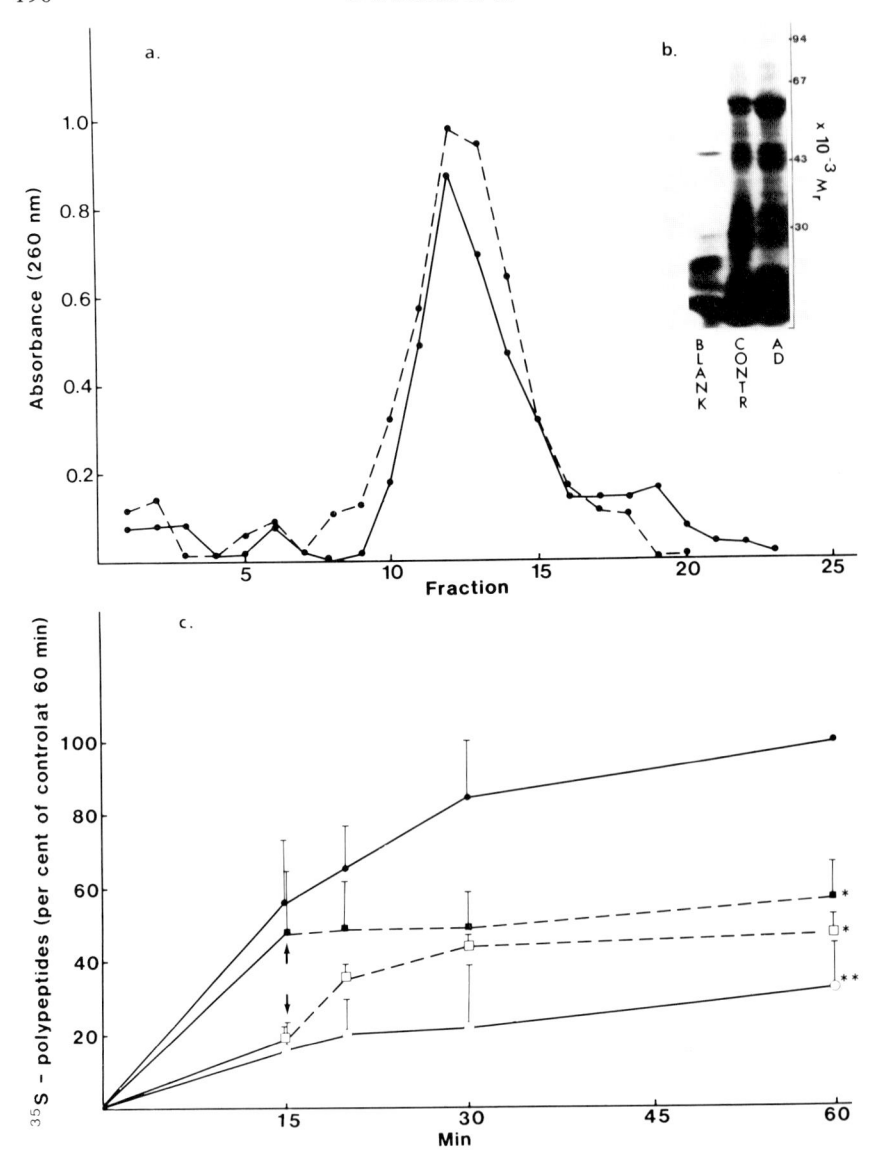

Fig. 2. (a) Sucrose gradient analysis of polysomes isolated from control (———) and AD (----) frontal cortices. (b) Fluorogram of polypeptides synthesized by control and AD polysomes in an *in vitro* translation assay. (c) Time course of protein synthesis by both control and AD polysomes in the presence or absence of additional control or AD polysomes. An aliquot of either control (●———●) or AD (○———○) polysomes were added to a reticulocyte *in vitro* translation system. In the mixing experiments, either an aliquot of AD polysomes was added to control polysomes (■ ——— ■) or control polysomes were added to AD polysomes (□ --- -□) 15 min after beginning the translation with the one type of polysome alone (indicated by the two arrows). Shown above are the mean results of three experiments (±1 SD).

polysomes to AD polysomes greatly reduced the continuation of protein synthesis (Fig. 2c). Finally, the translation of twice the amount of control polysomes under the same assay conditions doubled the level of protein synthesis indicating that the observed reductions in AD plus control polysome translations were not due to the depletion of translation factors.

Gene expression in AD tissue may be disrupted at one or more of several levels of control, including transcriptional activity, stability of RNA, protein synthetic activity and posttranslational modifications. These reductions in polysome content and translational activity indicate that the translational control of gene expression is specifically disrupted in AD tissue. The reduced translational activity per unit of polysome and the inhibition of control polysome translation by AD polysomes indicate that these translational disruptions are separate events from reduction in RNA concentrations (Sajdel-Sulkowska and Marotta 1984). Thus, the presence of less and poorly translating polysomal mRNA in AD frontal cortex suggests that an impairment in gene expression of the brain from an individual suffering AD occurs at the level of translational control.

Identification of Restriction Fragment Length Polymorphisms in AD Families

The problem of determining the genetic component of AD is also being investigated in Umeå with pedigree and molecular genetic analyses of families in which AD is prevalent. The identification of restriction fragment length polymorphisms (RFLP) which co-inherit with a disease has become a powerful method for the determination and localization of genes responsible for various diseases (see Gusella *et al.* 1984). An RFLP is an alteration of the base sequence of the genome detectable as a variation in the size of gene fragments produced by digestion of the genome with a restriction endonuclease. Such RFLPs can be detected with specific DNA probes that can also localize the position of the RFLP within the genome. Thus, when an RFLP is found to be linked genetically with a disease, the gene responsible for the disease may be co-localized with the RFLP.

The determination of such a genetic linkage for any marker RFLP to AD is intimately dependent upon the availability of genetic material from a large sample of well characterized, confirmed AD families. Such an investigation has been initiated with the identification of Alzheimer families in northern Sweden and the establishment of permanently transformed lymphocytic cell lines as permanent sources of DNA from members of these families.

CONCLUSIONS

In the above article, it has been demonstrated that despite a number of hypotheses concerning AD, many problems remain to be solved. Some of these problems can be summarized as follows:

Clinical/histopathological: The lack of agreement between clinical diagnosis and histopathological examination highlights the need for improved diagnostic resolution. Furthermore, the uncertainty as to whether AD and SDAT represent a continuum or heterogenous disorders needs further investigation.

Neurochemical: The patterns of neurotransmitter deficits have not conclusively shown any one pathogenesis to be responsible for the demented brain. The examination of AD, SDAT, MID and mixed cases separately seems to be warranted, preferably in longitudinal studies.

Molecular genetics: The genetic basis of AD is not fully characterized. The identification of the gene(s) responsible for AD would definitively indicate that this disease is a separate entity from the normal aging process. The characterization of these genes and their products would allow a better understanding of the pathogenetic processes involved. In addition, the identification of such a gene would facilitate early diagnosis and treatment.

From the above discussion, it is apparent that our understanding of AD has come a long way in recent years. It would seem to us, however, that an integrated approach to this disease is vital in future studies. Thus, the examination of patients from a longitudinal and comprehensive point of view may yield hitherto hidden aspects of this disease.

ACKNOWLEDGEMENTS

This study was supported from the Swedish Medical Research Council, Gustaf V and Queen Victoria's, Hansson's, Osterman's, Stohne's, Thuring's and "Gamla Tjänarinnors" foundations. We thank as always Karin Gladh for editorial assistance.

REFERENCES

Adolfsson, R. and Forsgren, L. (1984). Kliniska synpunkter på diagnoserna Alzheimers sjukdom och multiinfarkt demens. *Läkartidningen* **81**, 3919-3924.

Adolfsson, R., Gottfries, C. G., Roos, B. E. and Winblad, B. (1979). Changes in brain catecholamines in patients with dementia of Alzheimer type. *Br. J. Psychiat.* **135**, 216-223.

Adolfsson, R., Alafuzoff, I. and Winblad, B. (1986). Histopathological validation of the DSM-III criteria in Alzheimer type dementia and multi-infarct dementia. (Submitted for publication.)

Arai, H., Kosaka, K. and Iizuka, T. (1984). Changes in brains from patients with Alzheimer's type dementia. *J. Neurochem.* **43**, 388-393.

Auffray, C. and Rougeon, F. (1980). Purification of mouse immunoglobulin heavy-chain messenger RNAs from total myeloma tumor RNA. *Eur. J. Biochem.* **107**, 303-314.

Benton, J. S., Bowen, D. M., Allen, S. J., Haan, E. A., Davison, A. N., Neary, D., Murphy, R. P. and Snowden, J. S. (1982). Alzheimer's disease as a disorder of the isodendritic core. *Lancet* **i**, 456.

Birkett, D. B. and Raskin, A. (1982). Arteriosclerosis, infarcts and dementia. *J. Am. Geriatr. Soc.* **30**(4), 261-266.

Bissette, G., Reynolds, G. P., Kelts, C. D., Widerlov, E. and Nemeroff, C. B. (1985). Corticotrophin-releasing factor-like immunoreactivity in senile dementia of the Alzheimer type. *J.A.M.A.* **254**, 3067-3069.

Blessed, G., Tomlinson, B. E. and Roth, M. (1968). The association between quantitative measures of dementia and of senile change in the cerebral grey matter of elderly subjects. *Br. J. Psychiat.* **114**, 797-811.

Bondareff, W., Mountjoy, C. Q. and Roth, M. (1982). Loss of neurons of origins of the adrenergic projection to cerebral cortex (nucleus locus coeruleus) in senile dementia. *Neurology* **32**, 164-168.

Bowen, D. M., Allen, S. J., Benton, J. S., Goodhardt, M. J., Hann, E. A., Palmer, A. N., Sims, N. R., Smith, C. C. T., Spillane, J. A., Esiri, M. M., Neary, D., Snowdon, J. S., Wilcock, G. K. and Davison, A. N. (1983). Biochemical assessment of serotonergic and cholinergic dysfunction and cerebral atrophy in Alzheimer's disease. *J. Neurochem.* **41**, 266-272.

Breitner, J. C. S. and Folstein, M. F. (1984). Familial Alzheimer dementia: a prevalent disorder with specific clinical features. *Psychol. Med.* **14**, 63-80.

Brun, A. (1983). An overview of light and electron microscopic changes. In "Alzheimer's disease: the standard reference" (B. Reisberg, ed.) Vol. 4, pp. 37-47. Macmillan Inc., New York.

Brun, A. and Englund, E. (1981). Regional pattern of degeneration in Alzheimer's disease: neuronal loss and histopathological grading. *Histopathology* **5**, 549-564.

Corsellis, J. A. N. (1976). Ageing and dementia. In "Greenfield's neuropathology" (W. Blackwood and J. A. N. Corsellis, eds) p. 798. Edward Arnold, London.

Corsellis, J. A. N., Bruton, C. J. and Freeman-Browne, D. (1973). The aftermath of boxing. *Psychol. Med.* **3**, 270-303.

Cross, A. J. and Deakin, J. F. W. (1985). Cortical serotonin receptor subtypes after lesion of ascending cholinergic neurones in rat. *Neurosci. Letters* **60**, 261-265.

Cross, A. J., Crow, T. J., Perry, E. K., Perry, R. H., Blessed, G. and Tomlinson, B. E. (1981). Reduced dopamine-beta-hydroxylase activity in Alzheimer's disease. *Br. Med. J.* **282**, 93-94.

Cross, A. J., Crow, T. J., Johnson, J. A., Perry, E. K., Perry, R. H., Blessed, G. and Tomlinson, B. E. (1984). Studies on neurotransmitter receptor systems in neocortex and hippocampus in senile dementia of Alzheimer type. *J. Neurol. Sci.* **64**, 109-117.

Davies, P. and Maloney, A. F. J. (1976). Selective loss of central cholinergic neurons in Alzheimer's disease. *Lancet* **ii**, 1403.

Davies, P., Katzman, R. and Terry, R. D. (1980). Reduced somatostatin-like immunoreactivity in cases of Alzheimer's disease and Alzheimer senile dementia. *Nature* **288**, 279-280.

De Gennaro, L. J., Kanazir, S., Wallace, W. C., Lewis, R. M. and Greengard, P. (1983). Neuron-specific phosphoproteins as models for neuronal gene expression. *Cold Spring Harbor Symp. Quant. Biol.* **48**(Z), 337.

de Reuck, J., Sieben, G., de Coster, W. and van der Eecken, H. (1982). Dementia and confusional state in patients with cerebral infarcts. A clinicopathological study. *Eur. Neurol.* **21**, 94-97.

DOM III (1980). Organic dementia disorders. In "Diagnostic and statistical manual of mental disorders" 3rd edn, pp. 101-161. American Psychiatric Association, Washington, D.C.

Edvinsson, L., Degueurce, A., Duverger, D., Mackenzie, E. T. and Scatton, B. (1983). Central serotonergic nerves project to the pial vessels of the brain. *Nature* **306**, 85-87.

Edwards, J. H. (1960). The simulation of mendelism. *Acta Genet. Statist. Med.* **10**(1-3), 63-70.

Estrada, C., Hamel, E. and Krause, D. N. (1983). Biochemical evidence for cholinergic innervation of intracerebral blood vessels. *Brain Res.* **266**, 261-270.

Falconer, D. S. (1967). The inheritance of liability of diseases with variable age of onset, with particular reference to diabetes mellitus. *Ann. Hum. Genet.* **31**, 1-20.

Fisher, C. M. (1968). Dementia and cerebral vascular disease. *In* "Cerebral vascular disease" (J. E. Toole, R. G. Sickert and V. P. Vishnant, eds) pp. 232-236. 6th Printington Conference, New York.

Fonnum, F. and Walaas, I. (1978). The effect of intrahippocampal kainic acid injections and surgical lesions on neurotransmitters in hippocampus and septum. *J. Neurochem.* **31**, 1173-1181.

Forno, L. S. (1978). The locus coeruleus in Alzheimer's disease. *Neuropathol. Exp. Neurol.* **37**, 614.

Geddes, J. W., Monoghan, D. T., Cotman, C. W., Lott, I. T., Kim, R. C. and Chui, H. C. (1985). Plasticity of hippocampal circuitry in Alzheimer's disease. *Science* **230**, 1179-1181.

Gibson, P. H. (1983). Form and distribution of senile plaques seen in silver impregnated sections in the brains of intellectually normal elderly people and people with Alzheimer-type dementia. *Neuropathol. Appl. Neurobiol.* **9**, 379-389.

Glenner, G. G. and Wong, C. W. (1984). Alzheimer's disease: initial report of the purification and characterization of a novel cerebrovascular amyloid protein. *Biochem. Biophys. Res. Commun.* **120**, 885-890.

Gottesman, I. I. and Shields, J. (1967). A polygenic theory of schizophrenia. *Proc. Nat. Acad. Sci. USA* **58**, 199-205.

Gottfries, C. G. and Roos, B. E. (1973). Acid monoamine metabolites in cerebrospinal fluid from patients with presenile dementia (Alzheimer's disease). *Acta Psychiat. Scand.* **49**, 257-263.

Gottfries, C. G., Adolfsson, R., Aquilonius, S. M., Carlsson, A., Eckernäs, S. Å., Nordberg, A., Oreland, L., Svennerholm, L., Wiberg, Å. and Winblad, B. (1983). Biochemical changes in dementia disorders of Alzheimer type (AD/SDAT). *Neurobiol. Aging* **4**, 261-271.

Greenamyre, J. T., Penney, J. B., Young, A. B., D'Amato, C. J., Hicks, S. P. and Shoulson, I. (1985). Alterations in glutamate binding in Alzheimer's and Huntington's diseases. *Science* **227**, 1496-1499.

Gusella, J. F., Tanzi, R. E., Anderson, M. A., Hobbs, W., Gibbons, K., Raschtchian, R., Gilliam, T. C., Wallace, M. R., Wexler, N. S. and Conneally, M. (1984). DNA markers for nervous system diseases. *Science* **225**, 1320-1326.

Hachinski, V. C. (1979). Relevance of cerebrovascular changes to mental function. *Mech. Age. Dev.* **9**, 173-183.

Hachinski, V. C., Lassen, N. A. and Marshall, J. (1974). Multi-infarct dementia, a cause of mental deterioration in the elderly. *Lancet* **ii**, 207-210.

Hachinski, V. C., Iliff, L. D., Zilhka, E., DuBoulay, G. H., McAllister, V. L., Marshall, J., Russell, R. W. and Symon, L. (1975). Cerebral blood flow in dementia. *Arch. Neurol.* **32**, 632-637.

Hardy, J., Adolfsson, R. Alafuzoff, I., Bucht, G., Marcusson, J., Nyberg, P., Perdahl, E., Wester, P. and Winblad, B. (1985). Transmitter deficits in Alzheimer's disease. *Neurochem. Int.* **7**, 545-563.

Heston, L. L. (1983). Dementia of the Alzheimer type: a perspective from family studies. "Banbury report 15. Biological aspects of Alzheimer's disease" (R. Katzman, ed.) pp. 183-190. Cold Spring Harbor Laboratory, Cold Spring Harbor, USA.

Heston, L. L. and Mastri, A. R. (1977). The genetics of Alzheimer's disease. Association with hematologic malignancy and Down's syndrome. *Arch. Gen. Psychiat.* **34**, 976.

Heston, L. L., Mastri, A. R., Anderson, V. E. and White, J. (1981). Dementia of the Alzheimer type: genetics, natural history, and associated conditions. *Arch. Gen. Psychiat.* **38**, 1085-1090.

Ishii, T. (1966). Distribution of Alzheimer's neurofibrillary changes in the brain stem and the hypothalamus of senile dementia. *Acta Neuropathol.* **6**, 181-187.

Larsson, T., Sjögren, T. and Jacobson, G. (1963). Senile dementia. *Acta Psychiat. Scand.* **39**(Suppl. 167), 1-259.

Mann, D. M. A. (1983). The locus coeruleus and its possible role in aging and degenerative disease of the human central nervous system. *Mech. Age. Dev.* **23**, 73-94.

Mann, D. M. A. (1985). The neuropathology of Alzheimer's disease: a review with pathogenic, aetiological and therapeutic considerations. *Mech. Age. Dev.* **31**, 213-255.

Mann, D. M. A. and Yates, P. O. (1983). Serotonin nerve cells in Alzheimer's disease. *J. Neurol. Neurosurg. Psychiatry* **46**, 96.

Mann, D. M. A., Yates, P. O., and Marcyniuk, B. (1984). Alzheimer's presenile dementia, senile dementia of Alzheimer type and Down's syndrome in middle age form an age related continuum of pathological changes. *Neuropathol. Appl. Neurobiol.* **10**, 185-207.

Mash, D. C., Flynn, D. D. and Potter, L. T. (1985). Loss of M2 muscarine receptors in the cerebral cortex in Alzheimer's disease and experimental cholinergic denervation. *Science* **228**, 1115-1117.

Masters, C. L., Multhaup, G., Simms, G., Pottgeisser, J., Martins, R. N. and Beyreuther, K. (1985). Neurofibrillary tangles of Alzheimer's disease contain the same protein as the amyloid of plaque cores and blood vessels. *EMBO J.* **4**, 2757-2763.

McKhann, Z., Drachman, D., Folstein, R., Katzman, R., Price, D. and Stadham, E. M. (1984). Clinical diagnosis of Alzheimer's disease: report of the NINCDS-AFRDA work group under the auspices of the Department of Health and Human Service task force of Alzheimer's disease. *Neurology* **34**, 939-944.

Miyakawa, T., Shimoji, A., Kuramoto, R. and Higuchi, Y. (1982). The relationship between senile plaques and cerebral blood vessels in Alzheimer's disease and senile dementia. *Virchows Arch.* **40**(B), 121-129.

Nee, L. E., Polinsky, R. J., Eldridge, R., Weingartner, H., Smallberg, S. and Eberg, M. (1983). A family with histologically confirmed Alzheimer's disease. *Arch. Neurol* **40**, 203-208.

Nordberg, A., Larsson, C., Adolfsson, R., Alafuzoff, I. and Winblad, B. (1983). Muscarinic receptor compensation in hippocampus of Alzheimer patients. *J. Neural. Neurosurg. Transm.* **56**, 13-19.

Palmer, A. M., Sims, N. S., Bowen, D. M., Neary, D., Palo, J., Wikstrom J. and Davison, A. N. (1984). Monoamine metabolite concentrations in lumbar cerebrospinal fluid of patients with histology verified Alzheimer's dementia. *J. Neurol Psychiatry* **47**, 481-484.

Perry, E. K., Perry, R. H., Tomlinson, B. E., Blessed, G. and Gibson, P. H. (1980). Coenzyme A acetylating enzymes in Alzheimer's disease: possible cholinergic compartments of pyruvate dehydrogenase. *Neurosci. Letters* **18**, 105-110.

Perry, E. K., Tomlinson, B. E., Blessed, G., Perry, R. H., Cross, A. J. and Crow, T. J. (1981). Neuropathological and biochemical observations on the noradrenergic system in Alzheimer disease. *J. Neurol. Sci.* **31**, 279-287.

Pilleri, B. (1966). Kluver-Bucy syndrome in man—a clinical-anatomical contribution to the function of the medial temporal lobe structures. *Psychiat. Neurol.* **152**, 65-103.

Pope, A., Hess, H. H. and Levin, E. (1965). Neurochemical pathology of the cerebral cortex in presenile dementias. *Trans. Am. Neurol. Ass.* **80**, 15-16.

Quirion, R., Richard, J. and Dam, T. V. (1985). Evidence for the existence of serotonin type-2 receptors on cholinergic terminals in rat cortex. *Brain Res.* **333**, 345-349.

Reisine, T. D., Yamamura, H. I., Bird, E. D., Spokes, E. and Enna, S. (1978). Pre- and postsynaptic neurochemical alterations in Alzheimer's disease. *Brain Res.* **159**, 477-481.

Reynolds, G. P., Arnold, L., Rossor, M. N., Iversen, L. L., Mountjoy, C. Q. and Roth, M. (1984). Reduced binding of (^{3}H)ketanserin to cortical 5HT2 receptors in senile dementia of the Alzheimer type. *Neurosci. Letters* **44**, 47-51.

Richter, J. A., Perry, E. K. and Tomlinson, B. E. (1980). Acetylcholine and choline levels in postmortem human brain tissue: preliminary observations in Alzheimer's disease. *Life Sci.* **26**, 1683-1689.

Rinne, J. O., Laakso, K., Lönnberg, P., Mölsä, P., Paljärvi, L., Rinne, J. K., Säkö, E. and Rinne, U. K. (1985). Brain muscarinic receptors in senile dementia. *Brain Res.* **336**, 19-25.

Roberts, G. W., Crow, T. J. and Polak, J. M. (1985). Location of tangles in somatostatin neurons in Alzheimer's disease. *Nature* **314**, 92-94.

Rosen, W. C., Terry, R. D., Fuld, P. A., Katzman, R. and Peck, A. (1980). Pathological verification of ischaemic score in differentiation of dementias. *Ann. Neurol.* **7**, 486-488.

Rossor, M. N. (1981). Parkinson's disease and Alzheimer's disease as disorders of the isodendritic core. *Br. Med. J.* **283**, 1588-1591.

Rossor, M. N. (1982). Dementia. *Lancet* **i**, 1200-1203.

Rossor, M. N., Emson, P. C., Mountjoy, C. Q., Roth, M. and Iversen, L. L. (1982a). Neurotransmitters of the cerebral cortex in senile dementia of Alzheimer type. *Exp. Brain Res.* Suppl.5, 153-157.

Rossor, M. N., Svendsen, C., Hunt, S. P., Mountjoy, C. Q., Roth, M. and Iversen, L. L. (1982b). The substantia innominata in Alzheimer's disease: an histochemical and biochemical study of cholinergic marker enzymes. *Neurosci. Letters* **28**, 217-222.

Rossor, M. N., Garret, N. J., Johnson, A. L., Mountjoy, C. Q., Roth, M. and Iversen, L. L. (1982c). A postmortem study of the cholinergic and GABA systems in senile dementia. *Brain* **105**, 313-330.

Roth, M. (1955). The natural history of mental disorder in old age. *J. Ment. Sci.* **101**, 281-301.

Roth, M. (1985). Some strategies for tackling the problems of senile dementia and related disorders within the next decade. *Danish Med. Bull.* **32** (Suppl.1), 92-111.

Rylett, R. T., Ball, M. J. and Colhoun, E. H. (1983). Evidence for high affinity choline transport in synaptosomes prepared from hippocampus and neocortex of patients with Alzheimer's disease. *Brain Res.* **289**, 169-175.

Sajdel-Sulkowska, E. M. and Marotta, C. A. (1984). Alzheimer's disease brain: alterations in RNA levels and in a ribonuclease-inhibitor complex. *Science* **225**, 947-948.

Sims, N. R., Bowen, D. M., Allen, S. J., Smith, C. C. T., Neary, D., Thomas, D. J. and Davison, A. N. (1983). Presynaptic cholinergic dysfunction in patients with dementia. *J. Neurochem.* **40**, 503-509.

Slater, E. and Roth, M. (1970). Ageing and the mental diseases of the aged. *In* "Clinical psychiatry" (W. Mayer-Gross, E. Slater and M. Roth, eds) Vol. 3, Ch. 8, pp. 533-560. Bailliere, Tindall and Cassell Inc., London.

Smechel, D. E., Veikney, B. G., Fitzpatrick, D. and Elde, R. P. (1984). GABAergic neurons of mammalian cerebral cortex. Widespread subclass defined by somatostatin content. *Neurosci. Letters* **47**, 227-232.

Soininen, H., MacDonald, E., Rekonen, M. and Riekkinen, P. J. (1981). Homovanillic acid and 5-hydroxyindoleacetic acid levels in cerebrospinal fluid of patients with senile dementia of Alzheimer type. *Acta Neurol. Scand.* **64**, 101-107.

Terry, R. D. and Davies, P. (1980). Dementia of the Alzheimer type. *Ann. Rev. Neurosci.* **3**, 77-95.
Todorov, A. B., Go, R. C. P., Constantinidis, J. and Elston, R. C. (1975). Specificity of the clinical diagnosis of dementia. *J. Neurol. Sci.* **26**, 81-98.
Tomlinson, B. E. (1980). The structural and quantitative aspects of the dementias. *In* "Biochemistry of dementia" (P. J. Roberts, ed.) pp. 15-51. John Wiley & Sons Inc., Chichester.
Tomlinson, B. E., Blessed, G. and Roth, M. (1968). Observation on the brains of non-demented old people. *J. Neurol. Sci.* **7**, 331-356.
Tomlinson, B. E., Blessed, G. and Roth, M. (1970). Observation on the brains of demented old people. *J. Neurol. Sci.* **11**, 205-242.
Whitehouse, P. J., Price, D. L., Struble, R. G., Coyle, J. T. and DeLong, M. A. (1982). Alzheimer's disease and senile dementia—loss of neurons in the basal forebrain. *Science* **215**, 1237-1239.
Winblad, B., Adolfsson, R., Carlsson, A. and Gottfries, C. G. (1982). Biogenic amines in brains of patients with Alzheimer's disease. *In* "Alzheimer's disease: a report of progress" (S. Corkin, ed.) "Aging" Vol. 19, pp. 25-33. Raven Press, New York.
Winblad, B., Bucht, G., Fowler, C. J. and Wallace, W. C. (1986). Beyond the transmitter-based approach to dementia of Alzheimer type. *In* "Treatment Development Strategies for Alzheimer's Disease" (T. Crook, ed.). Mark Powers Associates Inc., New Canaan (in press).
Wood, P. L., Etienne, P., Lal, S., Nair, N. P. V., Finlayson, M. H., Gauthier, S., Palo, J., Haltia, M., Paetou, A. and Bird, E. D. (1983). A postmortem comparison of the cortical cholinergic system in Alzheimer's disease and Pick's disease. *J. Neurol. Sci.* **62**, 201-207.
Wright, S. (1934). The results of crosses between inbred strains of guinea pigs differing in number of digits. *Genetics* **19**, 537-551.

Discussion

Karobath: You have postulated that the primary event in the degeneration in AD starts with changes in cortical blood vessels, which works its way up via plaques and tangles to neurons. How can it be explained with this hypothesis that in AD a number of cortical neuronal systems are spared, like the GABA or CCK-containing neurons?

Winblad: I think that the three systems mentioned (acetylcholine, noradrenaline and sentorin) are the first affected. Whether other systems like somatostatin and corticotropin-releasing factor are affected secondarily or are also actively damaged, I don't know.

Rinne: First, our group in Turku has also carried out an epidemiological study on the validity of clinical diagnosis verified by post-mortem neuropathological examination. The results were published in the *Journal of Neurological Sciences*, 1985. Our results seem to be in good agreement with those you presented. Now my question: in your material, are there cases of combined dementia with — at the same time — clear-cut Alzheimer changes together with vascular changes?

Winblad: The bad agreement between clinical diagnosis and histopathology is partly due to the fact that in pathology one deals with mixed or combined groups which do not exist in the clinic. Therefore, there cannot be a 100% agreement. Further, I am not sure whether this is a separate entity or not. We have looked closely at the mixed group and by using multivariate data analysis it seems that the mixed group is separate from the AD group and from the MID group.

Reisberg: I found your longitudinal investigations with their clinical and pathological correlation most interesting. I wonder if you could say a few words regarding your neuropathological criteria for AD and MID?

Winblad: We just used conventional microscopic techniques: routine staining to look for infarcts, silver staining to look for plaques and tangles; we have classified the patients according to our score which allowed discrimination between AD and MID. In MID cases, there is no abundance of tangles in the cortical area, and especially not in the frontal cortex. We used our simplified score on four areas of the brain, three cortical regions and the hippocampus. However, we think the relevant areas are the frontal cortex and the hippocampus. The difference from Tomlinson's classification is that we do not require infarctions of at least 100 ml as necessary for the diagnosis of MID. Some of our MID cases have only lost about 2 ml, but there were microscopic infarctions. Furthermore, when we use immunocytochemical stainings, we found that around the blood vessels in the cortex, in MID, there appears to be a deposit of serum proteins. This might be an indication of a damaged blood-brain barrier in MID, which is not so pronounced in AD.

Bergener: If I understand you correctly, you can find infarction anywhere in the brain.

Winblad: Even in Alzheimer's disease.

Brion: What evidence is there for senile plaques being located near blood vessels? Generally, there is no close relationship between vessels and plaques. Furthermore, dishoric angiopathy shows an absence of plaques in the vicinity of the striate cortex. If, as you seem to think, senile plaques are primitive, how can you explain zones where there are neurofibrillary tangles but no senile plaques, such as in basal nuclei and especially in the nucleus basalis of Meynert (or in a particular disease e.g. Steele-Richardson's disease)?

Winblad: I regard tangles as secondary to the primary event in the cortex. I think it is a reaction of the neuron to any damage rather than to a specific event. As to your second question: we find tangles in the nucleus basalis because, we think, it is a kind of retrograde degeneration, a sign of a degenerating neuron. Anatomically, the nucleus coeruleus consists of the same type of cells, but it innervates different parts, e.g. the cortical areas. Here you find tangles in those cells that mainly innervate the temporoparietal lobe, while the abundance of plaques is most convincing. But you find no tangles in the locus coeruleus cells which innervate the spinal cord, consistent with the idea that the tangles in such regions are the result of retrograde degeneration.

Sir Martin Roth: If you regard plaques as the primary lesion, would you diagnose AD pathologically in the presence of plaques and no tangles? What quantitative criteria do you use in order to separate AD patients with plaques from normal subjects who may die with plaques, but will very rarely exhibit tangles in the cerebral cortex?

Winblad: Our patients usually die at the end stage where we have both plaques and tangles. One piece of evidence for the importance of the plaques is as follows: if you consider Down's syndrome as a good model, the patients start to show dementia at the age of 30–35 when they only have plaques. Mann and coworkers have looked at cases of 30- to 40-year-olds and even when they show progressive dementia, only plaques are present. However, when they have passed 40, they also show tangles.

Sir Martin Roth: If you quote the Down's syndrome issue, one has to quote Guam's Parkinson's dementia in which there is an indubitable dementia associated with tangles alone and never plaques. And these tangles are to be found in the cortex and in the corpus striatum.

Viidik: Could you suggest a unification between the hypothesis you proposed and the biochemical data you presented: (1) the vascular one, possibly suggesting an immunological mechanism (plaque core similarity to serum amyloid protein) and (2) Alzheimer polysome changes (especially their inhibition of normal polysomes) which favour an aberration in the genome in the AD cases.

Winblad: This is not possible at present, but I just wanted to be a little provocative, to give new ideas and new ways of thinking in order to review the literature and our own data. However, my idea is still that in normal aging there is a loss of neurons in locus coeruleus. This will in turn lead to a derangement in the innervation of the vessels, which in consequence will increase with age the blood–brain barrier permeability. This will give some agents access towards the nerve endings, what will certainly have some influence on the vessel walls. Whether this is genetically determined or not, I don't know.

Holliday: Have any studies been carried out on cultured glial cells from AD patients? If consistent differences from controls were seen (e.g. in growth or *in vitro* longevity) these cells might give excellent material for experimental studies in the molecular basis of the disease.

Winblad: Dr Gottfries might know more about that. We have looked into monoamine oxidase type B which could be a marker. In AD, very little has been done.

Nosological Aspects of Differential Typology of Dementia of Alzheimer Type

C. G. Gottfries

Department of Psychiatry and Neurochemistry, St Jörgen's Hospital, Gothenburg University, Hisings Backa, Sweden

Keywords
Classification of dementias; Cerebrovascular disease and dementia; Alzheimer's disease; Senile dementia of Alzheimer type.

INTRODUCTION

Historically, dementia means an acquired, irreversible, global deterioration of mental functions. The disorder is supposed to be due to organic brain damage and to be progressive. In this definition, different aspects of the disease are brought together in a way, which in the light of present knowledge, is difficult to accept. Dementia is better defined as a disorder characterized by mental impairment acquired in later life, independent of cause, extent or aetiology. To be considered as dementia the mental impairment should be of such a degree that it interferes with the social life or health of the patient and should not be explained by confusion or depression.

NORMAL AGING AND DEMENTIA DISORDERS

Before trying to classify different dementias the question of distinguishing normal aging from dementing disorders must be raised. Great importance is attached to clarification of the relationship between dementia and the **natural processes**

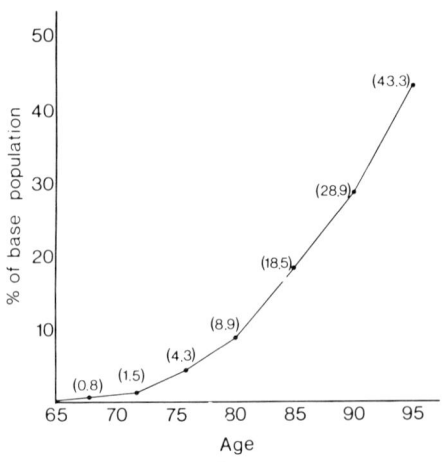

Fig. 1. The frequency of dementias in different age groups expressed as percent of total population. Data are from investigations of institutionalized individuals in a Swedish county.

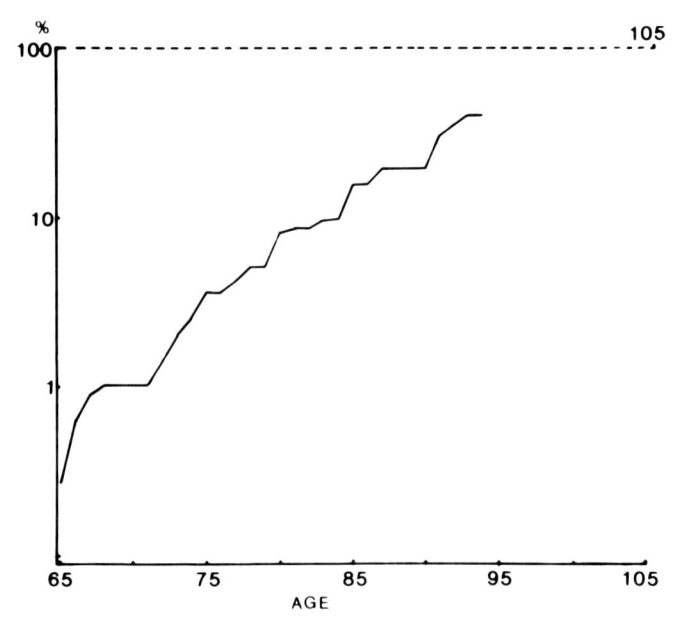

Fig. 2. The prevalence of dementia in institutions expressed as percentage of total population estimated by isotonic regression.

of senescence, in terms of structural changes in the brain, neurochemical damage and behavioural disturbances. It is uncertain whether the two are qualitatively or merely quantitatively different. If Alzheimer's disease (AD) or senile dementia (SD) are analogous to aging then one set of hypotheses can be formulated about causation, whereas if they are different quite other hypotheses must be formulated.

Epidemiological data indicate that there is a very high correlation between age and dementia disorders (Fig. 1) (Adolfsson *et al.* 1981, Gottfries 1985). As is evident from the figure there is a very low frequency of dementias below the age of 80 which after the age of 80, rises considerably. In ages above 95 the frequency is at least 43%. In the epidemiological study performed, dementia was diagnosed by a rating scale and was so severe that the demented individuals had to be kept in institutions. The strong relationship between age and the frequency of dementia disorders indicates that dementia is inevitable (Fig. 2). As is evident from the figure, 100% dementia is expected around the age of 105 years.

From a theoretical point of view it is possible to differentiate normal aging from age-related diseases. The normal aging process has an insidious onset, is slowly progressive and the process is assumed to take place on a subcellular level without giving rise immediately to signs or symptoms. Slowly, however, when the reserve capacity of the brain is destroyed the cumulative effect will give rise to symptoms of insufficiency.

At present it clinically is not possible to distinguish mental impairment due to normal aging from that due to pathological processes in the brain, by psychological tests or rating scales. The clinical status and the course of the disorder delimit dementias with early onset from normal aging but dementias with late onset can not be delimited from the mental impairment caused by the normal aging process.

Nor do morphological changes clearly delimit normal aging from SD. Atrophy of the brain can be seen as well in advanced age as in SD. The same is true for the neuron loss. Senile plaques and neurofibrillary changes are also seen as well in normal aging as in SD, although there are quantitative differences.

Post-mortem human brain studies have been performed for studying the neurotransmitter metabolism. In these investigations some interesting findings have appeared indicating differences between the normal aging process and dementia disorders. In several investigations it is shown that some of the neurotransmitters of the brain and the enzyme activity involved in the neurotransmitter metabolism are reduced with age (McGeer and McGeer 1976, Carlsson and Winblad 1976, Gottfries *et al.* 1983). In an ongoing post-mortem investigation we have confirmed earlier observations (Gottfries *et al.* 1986). In the ongoing investigation (Table 1) we found an age-related reduction of 5-hydroxytryptamine (5-HT), noradrenaline (NA), dopamine (DA), 3 methoxy-tyramine (MT), neutral phospholipids and cholesterol. The investigation was made in the caudate nucleus, the hippocampus and for the myelin components also in centrum semiovale. However, when studying the metabolites to the neurotransmitters there were no reductions with age. This was true for 5-hydroxyindolacetic acid (5-HIAA), 3-methoxy 4-hydroxyphenylglycol (HMPG) and homovanillic acid (HVA). This indicates that although there are reduced concentrations of the active amine possibly being due to a neuron loss, the remaining neurons in the normally aged brain may increase release of the neurotransmitter and by doing so the metabolites are kept on a normal level.

Table 1
The product moment correlation (r) between age and biochemical variables in brains from patients with normal aging

	Nucleus caudatus r	n	Hippocampus r	n	White matter r	n
Age/						
5-HT	−0.60***	22	−0.09	22		
5-HIAA	−0.02	22	0.15	22		
NA	0.34	22	−0.45*	22		
HMPG	0.27	22	0.23	22		
DA	−0.24	22	−0.65***	22		
DOPAC	−0.16	22	0.12	22		
HVA	−0.28	22	−0.05	22		
MT	0.15	22	−0.66*	10		
CAT	0.45	10	0.68*	10		
Neutral phospholipids	−0.75***	17	−0.76***	17	−0.49*	17
Acidic phospholipids	−0.09	17	−0.33	17	−0.16	17
Cholesterol	−0.59*	14	−0.83***	17	−0.66***	17
Cerebrosides					−0.10	17
Sulphatides					−0.22	14

* = $P<0.05$; *** = $P<0.005$; n = number of cases

Table 2
Neurochemical variables in brains from controls and from patients with Alzheimer's disease and senile dementia (AD/SD)

	Nucleus caudatus								
	Controls			AD/SD					
	n	M	SD	n	M	SD	t	P	% of controls
5-HT ng	22	250	96	20	200	74	1.91	0.07	80
5-HIAA nmol/g	22	590	329	20	319	113	3.64	0.002	54
NA ng	22	28	15	20	22	19	1.19	<0.20	77
HMPG nmol/g	22	0.35	0.21	20	0.36	0.11	−0.08	<0.20	102
DA ng	22	1879	774	20	1454	699	1.86	0.008	77
DOPAC ng	22	655	265	20	524	261	1.61	0.12	80
MT ng	22	1141	370	20	777	299	3.49	0.002	68
HVA nmol/g	22	17.96	5.64	20	12.76	5.01	3.14	0.004	71
Neutral phospholipids	17	37.9	3.5	16	34.0	4.0	2.97	0.005	90
Acidic phospholipids	17	9.17	1.50	16	8.28	1.50	1.74	0.09	90
Cholesterol	17	33.34	6.26	16	29.19	5.75	1.98	0.06	88

n = number of cases; M = mean; SD = standard deviation; t = Student's t.

Table 3
Neurochemical variables in brains from controls and from patients with Alzheimer's disease and senile dementia (AD/SD)

	Hippocampus Controls			Hippocampus AD/SD					% of controls
	n	M	SD	n	M	SD	t	P	
5-HT ng	22	51.7	24.8	19	31.2	15.3	3.22	0.003	60
5-HIAA nmol/g	22	285	113	19	164	69	4.18	0.0002	58
NA ng	22	19.0	6.3	19	15.2	6.4	1.91	0.06	80
HMPG nmol/g	22	0.36	0.16	20	0.39	0.17	−0.63	<0.20	106
DA ng	22	21.0	15.8	19	9.1	10.8	2.78	0.008	43
DOPAC ng	22	21.7	8.3	19	16.9	6.7	2.02	0.05	78
MT ng	10	46.3	21.9	13	26.7	22.2	2.11	0.05	58
HVA nmol/g	22	1.80	0.70	20	1.60	1.34	0.58	<0.20	89
Neutral phospholipids	17	36.0	4.9	16	30.5	5.5	3.05	0.005	85
Acidic phospholipids	17	8.5	1.4	16	7.8	1.7	1.31	<0.2	92
Cholesterol	17	35.9	7.1	16	29.7	6.5	2.57	0.02	83

n = number of cases; M = mean; SD = standard deviation; t = Student's t.

In AD and SD 5-HT, 5-HIAA, DA, MT and HVA are reduced in the caudate nucleus (Table 2) and 5-HT, 5-HIAA, DA, DOPAC and MT in the hippocampus (Table 3). As is evident from the tables not only the neurotransmitters but also their metabolites are reduced. Thus the neurons in the demented brains have not increased their speed of turnover. The feedback mechanism that seems to operate in the normally aged brain does not function in the demented brain.

ALZHEIMER'S DISEASE AND SENILE DEMENTIA

One important question is whether AD and SD is one disease or two (Fig. 3). Alzheimer originally described the presenile form in which he found the typical brain lesions. Later on neuropathologists have described the same type of lesions in the primary dementias with onset after the age of 65 and the name senile dementia of Alzheimer type (SDAT) has been suggested for this group. In several scientific investigations the two forms are brought together into one called dementia of Alzheimer type (DAT). There is, however, still no justification for grouping these two forms together. In studies of familial aggregation in the AD-SD complex Heston (1977) found that relatives of AD-patients had markedly increased risks for AD. Sjögren et al. (1952) and Sourander and Sjögren (1970) found, that there is a four-fold increased risk for SD in siblings to SD-patients. No instances

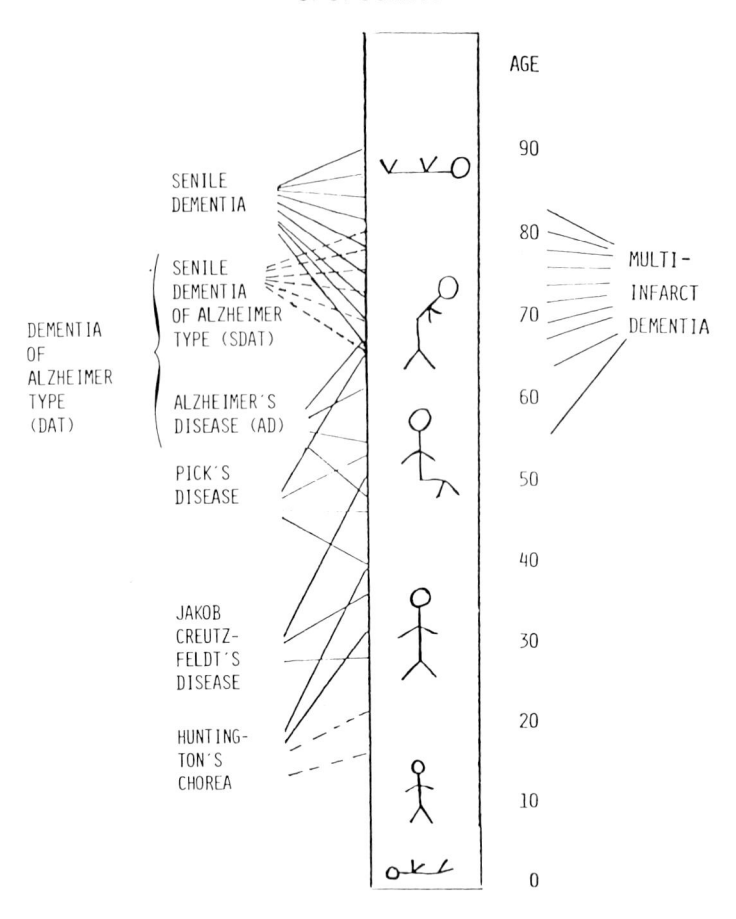

Fig. 3. Dementia disorders related to their age of onset.

of AD were found in the 2,675 family members investigated. These family studies thus indicate that the two disorders are separated from each other. Biochemical investigations of neurotransmitters, their metabolites and enzyme activities involved in the metabolism of neurotransmitters indicate that the changes recorded, are more severe in cases with an early onset when compared to those with a late onset (Gottfries et al. 1983, Rossor et al. 1984).

Brun and Gustafson (1978) discussed white matter changes in brains from patients with dementia. They found these changes mostly in patients with a high age dementia that is SD but to a lesser extent in patients with AD.

In an investigation by Mayeux et al. (1985) the distribution of frequency of age at onset of symptoms was recorded for patients with AD and SD. In this investigation a bimodal distribution was found, again indicating that there are two disorders with different age of onset.

IS SENILE DEMENTIA A HOMOGENOUS GROUP?

In fact SD is a dementia disorder delimited by the age of onset and the absence of evident explanations to the mental impairment. It is obvious that this way of diagnosing dementia delimits a heterogenous group of disorders. In Fig. 4 the author has given examples of disorders that may be included in the concept SD. I will not discuss in detail here the different disorders suggested, only comment on one suggestion and that is avitaminosis. In preliminary findings from our institute (Regland and Gottfries 1986) we have found that some patients with a late onset dementia have reduced concentrations of vitamin B12. At present we are further studying the eventual etiological importance of this reduced vitamin concentration.

Regarding the concept of SD, the most important thing to my mind is to analyse to what extent this group includes individuals with normal aging where forms of treatment strategies can perhaps be applied.

SENILE DEMENTIA

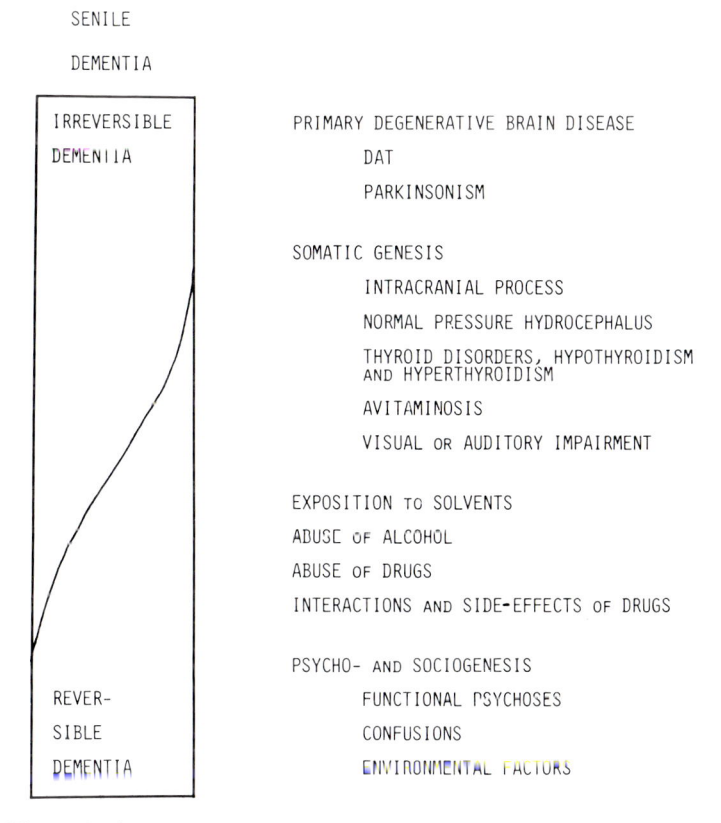

IRREVERSIBLE DEMENTIA	PRIMARY DEGENERATIVE BRAIN DISEASE
	DAT
	PARKINSONISM
	SOMATIC GENESIS
	INTRACRANIAL PROCESS
	NORMAL PRESSURE HYDROCEPHALUS
	THYROID DISORDERS, HYPOTHYROIDISM AND HYPERTHYROIDISM
	AVITAMINOSIS
	VISUAL OR AUDITORY IMPAIRMENT
	EXPOSITION TO SOLVENTS
	ABUSE OF ALCOHOL
	ABUSE OF DRUGS
	INTERACTIONS AND SIDE-EFFECTS OF DRUGS
	PSYCHO- AND SOCIOGENESIS
REVER-	FUNCTIONAL PSYCHOSES
SIBLE	CONFUSIONS
DEMENTIA	ENVIRONMENTAL FACTORS

Fig. 4. The author's suggestion to different disorders that can be included in the present concept senile dementia.

IS ALZHEIMER'S DISEASE A HOMOGENOUS GROUP?

In an investigation by Mayeux *et al.* (1985) the heterogeneity in dementia of the Alzheimer type has been carefully studied. In this investigation the patients with dementia of Alzheimer type were subdivided into four groups: patients with extrapyramidal symptoms, patients with myoclonic symptoms, patients with a benign form of dementia and the typical form. The subdividing of the dementias was not related to the age of onset. The group with extrapyramidal symptoms were found in 21% of the individuals investigated and these patients had a higher prevalence of psychotic behaviour and a greater mental reduction. In 9.9% myoclonus was found. Seven patients of the total number 110 had a benign form of dementia, yet those patients met the criteria for dementia at the first assessment. Of interest was that the benign form did not progress to the same extent as the others. The small rather exclusive group of patients with the presenile form of Alzheimer's disease thus may not be a homogenous group.

DEMENTIA OF ALZHEIMER TYPE AND MULTIINFARCTION DEMENTIA

It may seem simple to delimit AD and SD from multiinfarction dementia (MID). However, a mixed group of dementias is often discussed in which Alzheimer lesions are found together with encephalomalacias. It is obvious that in studying the structural changes in these dementia disorders there is a rather great overlap.

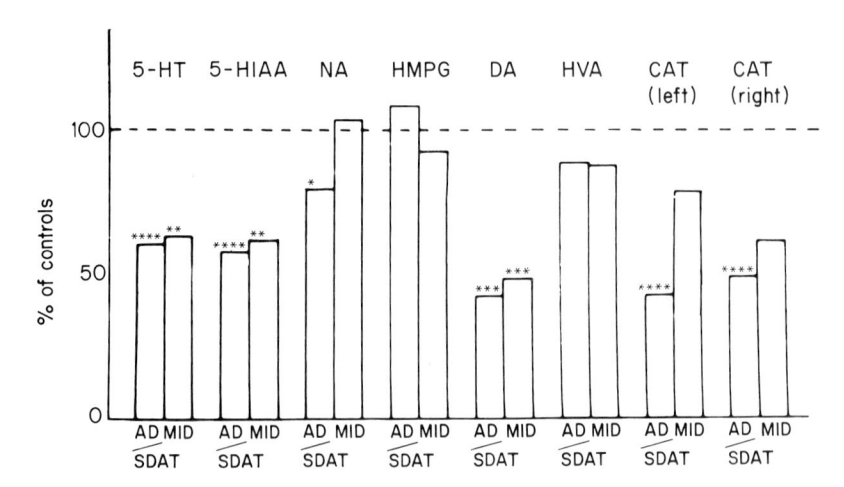

Fig. 5. Changes in hippocampus expressed as percentage of controls ($n=21$) in a group of Alzheimer dementias ($n=22$) and a group of multiinfarction dementias ($n=9$). $*=P<0.10$; $**=P<0.05$; $***=P<0.01$; $****=P<0.005$; group differences using Student's t-test.

A question is whether biochemical variables can better distinguish the different forms of dementias. In preliminary investigations this seems not to be the case (Carlsson and Gottfries 1986). In MID there seem to be rather general biochemical disturbances in the brain, and these disturbances are very similar to the disturbances found in the AD/SDAT brains (Fig. 5) (Gottfries 1986, Gottfries et al. 1986). As is seen from Fig. 5 5-HT, 5-HIAA and DA are significantly reduced in brains from AD/SDAT as well as in brains from MID. The choline-acetyl transferase (CAT) level in the hippocampus was, however, significantly more decreased in the brains from the AD/SDAT patients than in those from the MID patients. The biochemical disturbances found in the MID brain can hardly be related to the localization and the amount of degenerated brain tissue. These findings have made us question the aetiological importance of the macroscopic infarctions in MID.

The biochemical similarities between AD/SD and MID are perhaps of greater importance than the structural differences.

DISCUSSION

It seems to be necessary to try to delimit better the mental impairment due to normal aging, from mental impairment due to degenerative disorders. In this field epidemiological, clinical, neuropathological and neurochemical studies are necessary.

It is also necessary to investigate further the homogeneity of the presenile form of AD. The neuropathological and the biochemical findings reported in this disorder, may be only secondary phenomena to aetiological factors of which we still do know nothing.

Senile dementia can not be included in the Alzheimer dementia group. It must be assumed that this is a very heterogenous group including different forms of dementia as well as mental impairment due to normal aging.

The concept MID is at present difficult to accept. In neurology many patients have strokes and neurological symptoms without dementia. In the brains of patients with infarctions as well as dementia the biochemical damage to the brain often is so extensive that it can not be explained only by the damage due to the macroscopic infarctions.

SUMMARY

Mental impairment due to the normal aging process can clinically hardly be distinguished from mental impairment due to dementia disorders. Epidemiological data indicate that there is a high correlation between age and dementia disorders and these data support the assumption that dementia is inevitable

Neurochemically there are qualitative differences between changes seen in the normally aged brain compared to brains from patients with dementia disorders. The neurons in the normally aged brain can respond to feedback systems while the neurons in the demented brains can not.

Family studies, clinical investigations and results from neurochemical studies of brain tissue indicate that Alzheimer's disease and senile dementia are two different disorders.

The presenile form, Alzheimer's disease, seems to be the most homogenous group. Some subgroups have however been discussed e.g. a subgroup of patients with extrapyramidal symptoms. Senile dementia can be assumed to be a more heterogenous group including several forms of degenerative disorders together with normal aging and pseudodementia.

The differentiation of Alzheimer's disease/senile dementia from multiinfarction dementia offers problems. There is an overlap in morphological changes in the two groups. In Alzheimer's disease and in senile dementia widespread biochemical disturbances are described in the brain. It seems, however, as also in multiinfarction dementia there are extensive disturbances that can hardly be explained by the macroscopic infarctions. The value in using biochemical instead of morphological variables in differentiating dementia groups must be considered.

REFERENCES

Adolfsson, R., Gottfries, C. G., Nyström, L. and Winblad, B. (1981). Prevalence of dementia disorders in institutionalized Swedish old people. The work load imposed by caring for these patients. *Acta Psychiat. Scand.* **63**, 225-244.

Alzheimer, A. (1907). Ueber eine eigenartige Erkrankung der Hirnrinde. *Cbl. Nervenheilk Psychiat.* **18**, 177-179. Cited in: Torack, R. (1971). *In* "Dementia" (C. Wells, ed.) F. A. Davis Co., Philadelphia.

Brun, A. and Gustafson, L. (1978). Limbic lobe involvement in presenile dementia. *Arch. Psychiatr. Nervenkr.* **226**, 76-93.

Carlsson, A. and Gottfries, C. G. (1986). Neurotransmitter abnormalities in old age dementias. *In* "Proceedings of the Vth South-East European Neuropsychiatric Conference, Graz 1983" (H. Leichner and A. Parasctios, eds) pp. 634-645. University Study Press, Thessaloniki, Greece.

Carlsson, A. and Winblad, B. (1976). Influence of age and time interval between death and autopsy on dopamine and 3-methoxytyramine levels in human basal ganglia. *J. Neural Transm.* **38**, 271-276.

Gottfries, C. G. (1985). Review. Alzheimer's disease and senile dementia: Biochemical characteristics and aspects of treatment. *Psychopharmacol.* **85**, 245-252.

Gottfries, C. G. (1986). Clinical management of the European patients with dementia. Presented at the XIIIth World Congress of Neurology, Hamburg, September 1-6, 1985. To be published.

Gottfries, C. G., Adolfsson, R., Aquilonius, S. M., Carlsson, A., Eckernäs, S. E., Nordberg, A., Oreland, L., Svennerholm, L., Wiberg, A. and Winblad, B. (1983). Biochemical changes in dementia disorders of Alzheimer type (AD/SDAT). *Neurobiol. Aging* **4**, 261-271.

Gottfries, C. G., Alafuzoff, I., Carlsson, A., Svennerholm, L., Wallin, A. and Winblad, B. (1986). (In preparation.)

Heston, L. L. (1977). Alzheimer's disease, trisomy 21 and myeloprofilerative disorders: Associations suggesting a genetic diathesis. *Science* **196**, 322-323.

Mayeux, R., Stern, Y. and Spanton, S. (1985). Heterogeneity in dementia of the Alzheimer type. Evidence of subgroups. *Neurology* **35**, 453-461.

McGeer, E. G. and McGeer, P. L. (1973). Some characteristics of brain tyrosine hydroxylase. *In* "New concepts in neurotransmitter regulation" (A. J. Mandell, ed) pp. 53-69. Plenum Press, New York.

McGeer, E. G. and McGeer, P. L. (1976). Neurotransmitter metabolism in the aging brain. *In* "Neurobiology of Aging" (R. D. Terry and S. Gershon, eds) pp. 389-403. Raven Press, New York.

Regland, B. and Gottfries, C. G. (1986). Vitamin B12—MAOB in thrombocytes—dementia. A preliminary report. Presented at the 8th Nordic Congress on Gerontology, Tammerfass, Finland May 25-28, 1986.

Rossor, M. N., Iversen, L. L., Reynolds, G. P., Mountjoy, C. Q. and Roth, M. (1984). Neurochemical characteristics of early and late onset types of Alzheimer's disease. *Brit. Med. J.* **288**, 961-964.

Sjögren, T., Sjögren, H. and Lindgren, A. G. H. (1952). Morbus Alzheimer and morbus Pick. A genetic, clinical and patho-anatomical study. *Acta Psychiatr. Neurolog. Scand.* (Suppl.) **82**.

Sourander, P. and Sjögren, H. (1970). The concept of Alzheimer's disease and its clinical implications. *In* "Alzheimer's disease and related conditions" (G. E. W. Wolstenholme and M. O'Connor, eds) pp. 11-36. Churchill, London.

Discussion

Bergener: What is your explanation or interpretation for the higher ratio of senile dementia in the group of 'very old'? Is there a correlation to other somatic disorders? Is the senile dementia process a disorder of or in old age?

Gottfries: We think that there may be an involution process in the brain. Dr Hayflick's paper pointed out that there is a limit, when the cells do not divide or live any longer. Before we reach that limit, there are several changes taking place in the neuron. From the age of 65 and onwards, we think there takes place an involutionary process in the brain. As the brain has a very large reserve capacity, the symptoms will not appear until the age of 80 or 85. When one reaches the limit of this reserve capacity, mental impairment appears.

Verdonk: You showed the difficulties to differentiate mental impairment from Alzheimer's disease and from normal aging. Are there no therapeutic measures which would ameliorate the normal aging impairment and so differentiate these cases from Alzheimer?

Gottfries: This would be important for the clinician, but I am afraid, I cannot give you an answer. From the clinical point of view, we cannot differentiate these disorders. We have tried to differentiate with CFS studies, but we have not got any results that clearly delimit the disorders.

Hildebrand: Like others, we also looked for Vitamin B12 in demented patients. Especially in elderly patients we find in a substantial number of slightly reduced level of B12. Usually these patients do not respond to the administration of vitamins. Do you have any figures which you would suggest that below this level vitamin B12 really is involved in dementia?

Gottfries: I cannot give you a figure. We have the same findings as you. But we have also found that these lower B12 levels are correlated to changes in platelet mono-amino-oxydase. This makes the story rather more interesting. This is a very preliminary finding and one has to really study further the role of low B12 levels. It may indicate a disturbed absorption from the gut, but also a direct influence on brain function.

Spiegel: Could you say a little more on drug therapy? You said that the normal aging brain responds to pharmacotherapy and that the dementia brain does not. There are, of course, many approaches to drug therapy. Would you say e.g., that a normal old person should be treated with a precursor like lecithin or with a postsynaptic agonist, a presynaptic blocker or something of this type?

Gottfries: In the pharmacological treatment of DAT there are at present many investigations going on. I can only say that the precursor treatment of the cholinergic and the monoaminergic system is a failure. There is a marginal effect with enzyme blockers in the synaptic area, but you cannot use them clinically. The same is true with monoaminooxidase inhibitors. We have also tried some agonists of the dopaminergic system without great success. What we must think about these failures is that there is a neurochemical damage to the neurons so that they cannot respond in the proper way. In normal aging perhaps the neurons can respond in a better way to pharmacological challenges.

Brion: For a long time it has been proven that there is a total difference between Alzheimer's disease and SDAT. Do you not think that these terms are creating confusion with people who do not exactly understand the picture?

Gottfries: I agree with you. It is very bad to label human beings with the diagnose of senile dementia and SDAT is still worse. In a normal aging process you are much more eager with rehabilitation, activation, stimulation, than if you think it is a degenerative process. Also from the scientific point of view one should differentiate in order to get homogeneous groups. It is a good idea what Bengt Winblad proposed, to study Alzheimer patients with hereditary pattern.

Reichenfeld: I agree that the patients we label as demented are a very heterogeneous group, but how to differentiate between different groups of demented patients?

Gottfries: It is very difficult to differentiate and I have no special rating scales or psychological tests to offer you. I think one should try to define target symptoms and then try to treat these pharmacologically.

Karobath: Concerning your remark that neurons of demented patients may not respond properly to drug treatment, I would like to comment that those therapeutic trials have not been made with the appropriate drugs to test hypotheses. It requires great faith to believe that orally administered lecithin is indeed a precursor of acetylcholin. I am not aware of fundamental differences in receptors in demented brains, although our knowledge about receptor-effector systems in dementia is limited. Thus the failure of drug treatment up to now may be explained by the limitation of the drugs used and by the possibility that the neuronal system altered by these drugs may not be therapeutically relevant.

Gottfries: I think, especially when we discuss receptor agonists, there are not enough data to say that they do not respond. We do not have good cholinergic agonists, we still have to wait for them. I believe you are right here.

Antonini: From the gerontological point of view we see that with increasing age everybody becomes senile demented. Is there any rare case that has no defect in the sense of dementia at high age? Everybody is demented, but one exception may exist — can you find anybody who is not demented at high age?

Gottfries: I would like to meet that man! We tried to do so, in 1975, when we selected a group of individuals in highest age and intended to follow them up in order to see whether all of them were demented. As the ethical committee did not allow us to do so, we had to abandon this plan.

Applied Pharmacology in the Elderly: An Overview of the Dunedin Program

Ronald B. Stewart

Department of Pharmacy Practice, College of Pharmacy, University of Florida, Gainesville, Florida, USA

Keywords
Geriatrics; Drug use; Adverse drug reactions; Epidemiology.

INTRODUCTION

Elderly persons have repeatedly been shown to receive more medications per capita than any other age group (Simonson 1984). Persons over 65 years of age represent about 12% of the population in the USA, but account for almost 30% of the health care expenditure and receive 31% of all prescribed medications (Lamy 1985, Rowe 1985). In view of this high level of drug use one would expect the efficacy and safety of medications to have been carefully and methodically evaluated in this age group, but such is not the case.

When treating elderly persons with medications, physicians are often forced to travel an uncharted therapeutic course. They must evaluate the cost-benefit of drug treatment although very few drug efficacy studies have been conducted in the elderly. Doctors are expected to dose medications accurately when, in fact, only general guidelines are available for most drugs in this age group. Drug treatment must often be carried out in a setting where the patient receives multiple drugs that have often been prescribed by several doctors. Furthermore, the symptoms or disease being treated usually exist admist other diseases and symptoms in the elderly. Therefore, the physician must treat every therapeutic adventure in elderly patients as a new pharmacological experiment and carefully assess the therapeutic outcome.

One could ask, "How have we painted ourselves into this corner of therapeutic ignorance for the elderly?" One reason is that we have carefully excluded elderly subjects from drug trials over the years because of their age and pathology. Treatment of hypertension provides an excellent example of how the elderly have been largely excluded from drug efficacy studies. Koch-Weser (1979) reviewed 100 reports of hypertensive studies conducted since 1972 involving 3,063 patients (Koch-Weser 1979). The mean age of patients in these studies was 47.9 years and the mean age of the oldest patient in each series was 63 years. Only 16 studies included any patients over 69 years of age. Furthermore, not one of these studies stratified results by age and, therefore, provided no information concerning the efficacy of antihypertensive treatment specifically in the elderly. Physicians are now left with a dilemma of treatment *vs* non-treatment of this condition (Applegate *et al.* 1984).

Most information about drug side-effects has initially been gained from relatively short-term exposure to medications in clinical trials using relatively young patients where the major objective is evaluation of efficacy. Once a drug is released for general use by the public, information on side-effects is obtained from an often poorly co-ordinated system of voluntary physician reporting. Since most elderly persons suffer from chronic disorders such as hypertension, diabetes or arthritis, drug therapy is often prescribed for months or even years. Chronic toxicity from prolonged treatment with drugs is likely to be expressed differently and is more difficult to detect than acute side-effects.

In recent years we have come to recognize the paucity of information on drugs in the elderly. The National Institute of Aging and the Food and Drug Administration in the USA have recently launched programs to gain additional information on pharmacology in the elderly. The US Food and Drug Administration has proposed that every drug intended for use in the elderly should undergo pharmacokinetic evaluation in the elderly (Temple 1985). Additionally, the drug must be evaluated for interaction potential when prescribed with other drugs. These stopgap measures will not produce results for many years and we must attempt to gain useful information on drugs in the elderly from other available sources. This includes, but is not limited to reassessment of available medical and drug literature, post-marketing surveillance, and evaluating large drug use data bases from third party and government payment programs.

THE DUNEDIN PROGRAM

Since 1978, we have used information collected from a health screening program to conduct applied pharmacology studies in the elderly. The purpose of this paper is to describe the methods employed in this program and briefly review results obtained over the last 5 years. Information derived from this program can be divided into studies of drug utilization, cross-sectional evaluation of drug effects, and longitudinal analysis of drugs and diseases.

METHODS OF THE DUNEDIN PROGRAM

Dunedin is a retirement community on the mid-west coast of Florida. In 1975, Dr William E. Hale conceived of an idea to begin a community service program that would screen elderly residents on an annual basis for undetected medical disorders (Hale et al. 1980).

Questionnaire — Medical disorders, Personal data

Laboratory values — Haemogram, SMAC-25, Urinalysis

Drug use — Prescribed, Non-prescribed

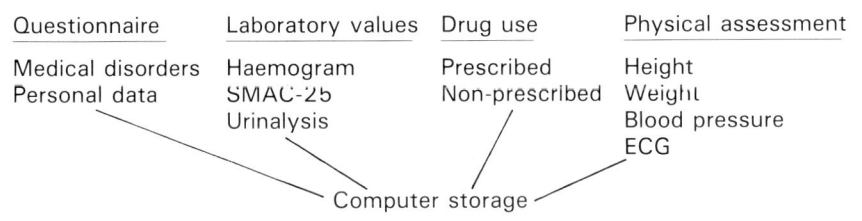

Physical assessment — Height, Weight, Blood pressure, ECG

Computer storage

Fig. 1. Information collected on Dunedin participants.

Table 1
Information collected from questionnaires

Family history	Sleep habits
Previous illnesses	Hair colour
Present illnesses	Eye colour
Drug history	Current symptoms
Smoking history	Frequency of medical examinations
Alcohol intake	Social activities
Emotional status	Exercise
Coffee consumption	Attitude toward current health care
Diet habits	Dental examinations

Table 2
Drug dictionary — example for Aldoril®

Drug number	Drug name	Therapeutic use	Pharmacological category
12366	Methyldopa	H400-Hypertension	C700 Serotonin antagonist
			E530 Catecholamine false transmitter
	Hydrochlorothiazide	H100-CHF drug	H300 Antihypertensive drug
		H400-Hypertension N100-Diuretic	N121 Thiazide

Table 3
Laboratory measurements of Dunedin subjects

Biochemical	Haemogram	Urinalysis (qual.)
Glucose	Leukocyte count	Blood
Sodium	Erythrocyte count	Protein
Potassium	Haemoglobin	Glucose
Chloride	Haematocrit	
Carbon dioxide	Mean corpuscular volume	
BUN/creatinine ratio	Mean corpuscular haemoglobin	
Uric acid	Mean corpuscular haemoglobin concentration	
Total calcium		
Ionized calcium		
Phosphorus		
Total protein		
Globulin		
Total bilirubin		
Alkaline phosphatase		
Lactic dehydrogenase (LDH)		
SGOT (transaminase)		
SGPT (transaminase)		
Cholesterol		
Triglycerides		
Iron		

When the study was begun, Dunedin had a population of 23,288 residents and 6,826 persons were over 65 years of age. Dr Hale was able to enlist over 4,300 (64%) persons to participate in the annual screening process.

Participants in the program are scheduled for annual screening by telephone or personal visit about 5 months prior to their appointments. One week before the scheduled visit, a letter is mailed to remind subjects of their appointments. Also enclosed is a detailed questionnaire and a form for listing all prescribed and non-prescribed drugs used on a regular basis. Information collected on each participant is summarized in Fig. 1. The questionnaire is designed to collect information about heredity, past medical history, current symptoms and disorders, habits and diets. The questionnaire changes from year to year although some questions have not changed (Table 1).

For each medication listed the subject is asked to specify the product's intended therapeutic use (e.g. angina, hypertension, arthritis) and how frequently it is used (e.g. daily, several times a week, occasionally). Participants are also asked to indicate the duration of use as, less than 1 month, 1 month-1 year, 1-2 years, or longer than 2 years. Medications are coded for computer storage using a modification of the therapeutic and pharmacological classification of the World Health Organization (Helling and Venulet 1974). This system allows one to identify all ingredients used in the population (Table 2).

When a participant arrives for evaluation, initial blood pressure measurements are obtained in both arms. An electrocardiogram is obtained and a venepuncture is performed. Haemogram and SMAC-23 biochemical determinations are performed on the blood sample (Table 3). The entire examination procedure requires about 1 h. All information collected since 1975 has been coded and stored for computer analysis.

Since the program began in 1975, 45% of the original 3,164 subjects screened have returned and completed all nine visits. Information obtained on subjects who have not returned revealed that 25% moved from the area, 25% have dropped out and 50% have died.

DRUG USE STUDIES

Since little information existed on drug use patterns in the elderly (particularly non-prescription drugs), our first objective was to describe in detail the nature and extent of drug use in this population. To accomplish this, drug use was studied in 3,192 participants screened in the program during the period from 1 August 1978 to 31 July 1980. Drug histories were obtained on 2,009 women (63%) and 1,183 men (37%) (May et al. 1982). In this population, 9.8% of the women were taking no medication while 14.1% of the men reported no medications and the number of drugs ranged from 0 to 17 for women and from 0 to 16 for men. Approximately 70% of medications used by these subjects were either prescribed or were used under the direction of a physician.

One study objective was to determine whether drug usage changed with increasing age. Using a multiple regression model it was found that the number of drugs taken increased with age and women took significantly more drugs than men. The average number of drugs used by participants was 3.2, with women using an average of 3.5 and men 2.8 drugs. Although the number of drugs used increased with age in men and women, the increase was due to prescribed medication. Non-prescription medication use did not appear to increase with advancing age (Fig. 2).

Most medications (64.7%) used by these subjects had been taken for longer than 2 years, reinforcing the need for chronic toxicity studies of drug-induced illness in this population. The majority of medications (71.6%) were administered on a daily basis while 18.7% of the drugs were used only as needed.

For each medication used, participants were asked to specify its therapeutic indication. Antihypertensives (30.5%), analgesics (18.9%), antirheumatics (16%), cathartics (15.4%) and multiple vitamins (12.9%) were the five most common therapeutic indications.

Prescribed drugs used most frequently by Dunedin participants are listed in Table 4. The five most commonly used drugs were digoxin, hydrochlorothiazide, hydrochlorothiazide-triamterene, propranolol and diazepam. The most common

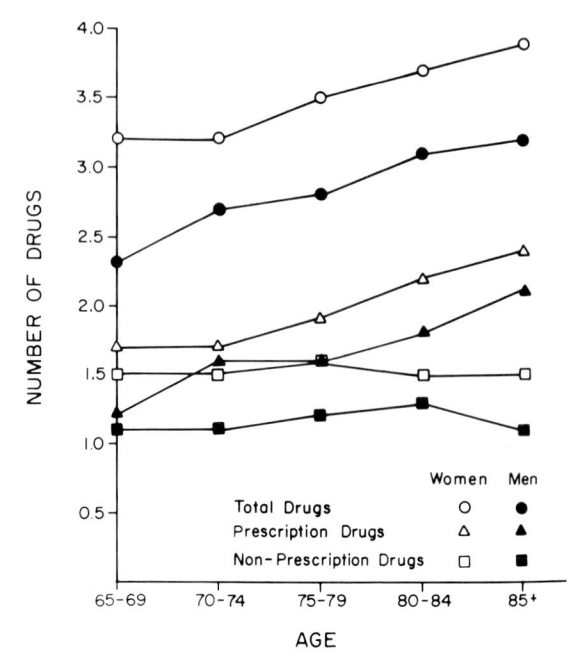

Fig. 2. Prescribed and non-prescribed drug use by age and sex. (From May et al. 1982, with permission.)

Table 4
The most common prescription drugs and percentage of total participants taking these drugs

Prescription drugs	Women	%	Men	%	Total	%	Significance level (P)
Digoxin	168	8.4	124	10.5	292	9.1	0.042
Hydrochlorothiazide	201	10.0	89	7.5	290	9.1	0.020
Hydrochlorothiazide-triamterene	195	9.7	78	6.6	273	8.6	0.003
Propranolol	123	6.1	70	5.9	193	6.0	0.828
Diazepam	136	6.8	46	3.9	182	5.7	0.001
Nitroglycerin	89	4.4	70	5.9	159	5.0	0.060
Furosemide	108	5.4	47	4.0	155	4.9	0.078
Potassium chloride	110	5.5	41	3.5	151	4.7	0.010
Flurazepam	100	5.0	45	3.8	145	4.5	0.128
Isosorbide dinitrate	58	2.9	59	5.0	117	3.7	0.002
Ibuprofen	88	4.4	28	2.4	116	3.6	0.003
Thyroid	98	4.9	13	1.1	111	3.5	0.001
Chlorthalidone	77	3.8	27	2.3	104	3.3	0.018
Methyldopa	62	3.1	31	2.6	93	2.9	0.457
Allopurinol	25	1.2	57	4.8	82	2.6	0.001

*Modified from May et al. (1982).

Table 5
The most common non-prescription drugs and percentage of total participants taking these drugs

Non-prescription drug	Women	%	Men	%	Total	%	Significance level (P)
Aspirin	370	18.4	220	18.6	590	18.5	0.872
Multiple vitamins	321	16.0	123	10.4	444	13.9	0.001
Vitamin E	301	15.0	129	10.9	430	13.5	0.001
Multiple vitamins with minerals	232	11.5	109	9.2	341	10.7	0.042
Vitamin C	230	11.4	103	8.7	333	10.4	0.015
Psyllium hydrophilic mucilloid	131	6.5	67	5.7	198	6.2	0.341
Aspirin, aluminium glycinate, magnesium hydroxide	152	7.6	39	3.3	191	6.0	0.001
Acetaminophen	127	6.3	40	3.4	167	5.2	0.001
Vitamin B complex	89	4.4	35	3.0	124	3.9	0.039
Magnesium hydroxide	62	3.1	38	3.2	100	3.1	0.833
Nicotinic acid	62	3.1	33	2.8	95	3.0	0.643
Aluminium, magnesium hydroxide plus simethicone	73	3.6	22	1.9	95	3.0	0.005
Aluminium, magnesium hydroxide	57	2.8	27	2.3	84	2.6	0.350
Aspirin, caffeine	56	2.8	24	2.0	80	2.5	0.189
Vitamin B_{12} (oral)	49	2.4	19	1.6	68	2.1	0.190

*Modified from May et al. (1982).

non-prescription drugs used were aspirin, multiple vitamins, vitamin E, multiple vitamins with minerals and vitamin C (Table 5).

All of the most commonly prescribed drugs used by Dunedin participants were for chronic ailments and none were curative. This fact must always be considered when the physician is weighing the cost-benefit of drug treatment. These medications can all produce adverse effects and the benefit of treating symptoms must be carefully weighed against the possibility that the patient may experience an adverse effect.

Specific Therapeutic Categories

Once we had described overall drug use patterns in Dunedin participants a plan was developed to analyse use characteristics of specific drug classes and, wherever possible, assess their impact on biochemical measurements and symptoms reported by these subjects. Since the elderly are believed to be predisposed to constipation because of physical inactivity, inadequate fluid intake and preoccupation with bowel function, we began our analysis with laxatives.

In Dunedin participants 16.4% of women and 12.2% of men reported using at least one laxative product and there was an increasing trend of laxative use in both men and women with increasing age (Stewart *et al.* 1982). Nearly one-half of all laxatives were being used on a daily basis and nearly two-thirds had been used for longer than 2 years. The three most common laxatives were psyllium hydrophyllic mucilloid, magnesium hydroxide and phenophthalein.

Habitual reliance on laxatives by the elderly has been an area of great concern for gastroenterologists and therefore it was expected that differences in biochemical measurements would be observed between daily laxative users and persons not using these products. There were no significant differences in biochemical measurements in laxative users when compared to non-users, except laxative users had a lower concentration of blood urea nitrogen (19.1 mg/dl *vs* 18.6 mg/dl). This finding raises an interesting question concerning chronic use of laxatives in the elderly. Although the practice of frequent laxative use has been condemned in younger age groups, one might question this extrapolation in the elderly. In this study no attempt was made to stratify subjects by the type of laxatives used and results may have been different if subjects using phenophthalein were analysed separately.

Frequency of nutritional supplement use in this ambulatory elderly population came as a major surprise to our research group. Interestingly, 45.5% of women and 34.0% of men reported the regular use of vitamins (Hale *et al.* 1982). Additionally, 22.4% of women and 15.0% of men reported regular use of mineral supplements. The most commonly used vitamin products were multiple vitamins, multiple vitamins with minerals, vitamin E and vitamin C, while for minerals the ranking was potassium chloride, calcium salts and ferrous sulphate. More than 90% of nutritional products taken by these participants were administered on a daily basis.

Great reliance on nutritional supplements demonstrated in this age group presents several interesting research questions for both the behaviouralist and nutritionist. Why do these elderly persons take so many vitamins? Furthermore, why do 13% of these subjects use vitamin E, a substance with no proven value in the elderly, whereas less than 3% reported the use of iron supplements, a substance that is clearly indicated in anaemic elderly persons. There is a great need for research to determine specific nutritional requirements in the elderly.

Diuretics are also among the most common drugs prescribed for the elderly, largely because of the prevalence of hypertension and heart failure in this age group. Therefore, we next studied the nature and extent of diuretic use and assessed diuretic effects on biochemical and haematological profiles.

Subjects using diuretics were divided into eight groups based on the type of diuretic taken and a control group was composed of subjects not using these drugs (Stewart *et al.* 1983). About 40% of women and 30% of men reported the use of at least one diuretic drug. The four most common diuretic products used were hydrochlorothiazide (9.1% of the study population) a hydrochlorothiazide-triamterene combination (8.6%), furosemide (4.9%) and chlorthalidone (3.3%).

Mean biochemical test values for subjects in the diuretic use groups were compared with the control group. Interestingly, the mean serum potassium concentration was lowest in participants using chlorthalidone (3.47 mEq/l), followed by thiazides (3.74 mEq/l), a hydrochlorothiazide-triamterene combination (3.99 mEq/l) and furosemide (4.05 mEq/l). Mean serum potassium concentration in participants not using diuretics was 4.18 mEq/l. This finding supported the accuracy of the Dunedin data base since Morgan and Davidson had recently reviewed published literature to evaluate the fall in serum potassium concentrations resulting from diuretic therapy. They found the average fall was less after furosemide (0.3 mEq/l) than after a thiazide (0.6 mEq/l) (Morgan and Davidson 1980). In Dunedin subjects, use of potassium supplements were not adequate to maintain serum potassium concentration in the normal range. The use of potassium-retaining diuretics rather than supplements appears to be a more rational method of maintaining potassium balance in the elderly.

ADVERSE DRUG REACTIONS

Information from the Dunedin Program has also been used in an attempt to verify reports of adverse drug reactions that have appeared in the medical literature. For instance, vitamin E is widely used by the American population where it is considered by many to be a panacea for medical disorders, while others believe it is no more than a grand placebo. The vitamin has been recommended for many disorders such as anaemia, angina, hypercholesterolaemia, infertility and diabetes, but only two conditions have been shown to benefit from treatment with vitamin E after controlled double-blind trials (Hale *et al.* 1986a). On the otherhand, some clinicians have argued that regular use of vitamin E can cause adverse effects including hypertension, thrombophlebitis, vaginal bleeding and diarrhoea (Roberts 1981).

In an attempt to answer these questions, we used information available on 369 participants using vitamin E and 1,861 subjects who had not used this vitamin, to evaluate both adverse and beneficial effects of the drug. There was no statistically significant difference in the age, mean weight, systolic or diastolic blood pressure between vitamin E users compared with non-users. However, the average number of drugs used by the vitamin E group for women was 5.50 compared with 2.75 in the non-vitamin E group, while in men it was 5.23 compared with 2.26, respectively. Higher medication use in the vitamin E group was largely due to use of other nutritional supplements.

Eleven clinical disorders that had possibly been attributed to vitamin E use (i.e. hypertension, headache, shortness of breath) were evaluated. The only difference observed was that men using vitamin E reported a greater prevalence of shortness of breath (24.5%) compared with controls (15.2%), while 23.3% of men using vitamin E reported angina symptoms compared with 13.8% of controls

($P < 0.03$). For these two symptoms it is likely that there was a higher prevalence of these symptoms in the vitamin E group because participants were using vitamin E to treat the condition.

To determine if vitamin E use affected biochemical or haematological parameters, the subjects were separated by sex into user and non-user groups. There were no significant differences between vitamin E users or controls for any haematological values and only one biochemical value, SGOT in men, was different from controls. Men using vitamin E had higher SGOT concentrations (21.2 iu/l) than non-users (19.0 iu/l), although both were within the accepted normal range. It appears, therefore, that the use of vitamin E in the elderly exerts little influence on haematological or biochemical parameters, or symptom prevalence.

Studies similar to the above were conducted by our research group on psychotropic, analgesic and antacid drugs. These investigations all employed a similar data base of 3,192 subjects.

In 1984 our group received funding from the AARP Andrus Foundation to completely computerize the remaining 4 years of our drug data base. This new data base provided a mechanism to plan and conduct longitudinal studies of drug utilization and adverse effects of medication. Several disease states and physiological parameters have now been examined longitudinally.

SYMPTOMS IN THE ELDERLY

In the practice of geriatrics one often hears that the elderly are very stoic and do not readily complain of aches and pains. In view of these often expressed principles we used our data base to examine the prevalence of 28 reported symptoms in 1,927 women and 1,140 men over 65 years of age. This study was conducted in a cross-sectional fashion at the time of their fourth visit to the program. A comparison was made of the prevalence of specific symptoms by sex, age, disease states and drug use patterns (Hale et al. 1986b).

Women reported a mean of 3.99 symptoms compared to 3.22 reported by men ($P < 0.0001$). Since reporting of symptoms and presence of disease should be closely related, an analysis was performed to compare symptom prevalence with disease prevalence. The number of symptoms reported is strongly related to the number of reported diseases and there is a difference in sexes in reported symptoms. Based on our findings, elderly women do not report more diseases than men but as the number of diseases reported increases, women tend to report more symptoms. The most common symptoms reported by women were nocturia (80.4%), swollen feet or ankles (30.5%), cold feet and/or legs (28.6%) and irregular heartbeat (23.2%), while men complained most often of nocturia (79.8%), irregular heartbeat (24.8%), cold feet and/or legs (23.6%) and tinnitus (23.1%).

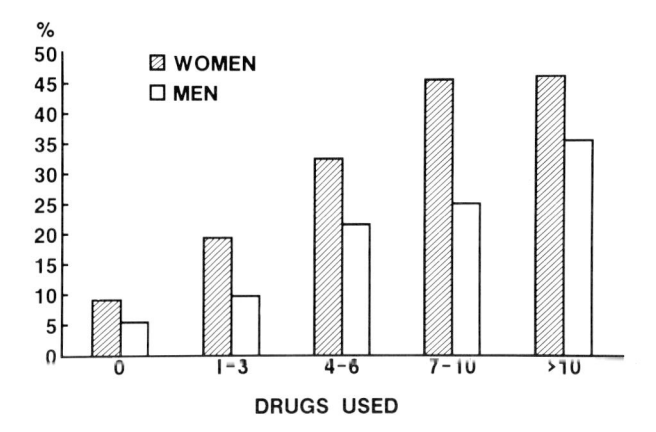

Fig. 3. Relationship of recurrent constipation reported by Dunedin participants to the number of medications used.

Table 6
Prevalence of anaemia at all eight visits

Visit	Anaemic (n)	Anaemic (%)	Total participants
1*	833	25.3	3,299
2*	292	21.2	1,377
3	591	19.8	2,993
4	655	20.9	3,133
5	557	21.3	2,621
6	518	22.0	2,351
7	413	21.6	1,910
8	372	22.6	1,646

*Visits one and two do not include all values since data from approximately 1,000 patients were categorically coded at the time of analysis.

The relationship of drug use and reported symptoms was also examined. For most symptoms there is a highly significant relationship between the use of any medication and reporting of a symptom. Women using medications for example, were more likely to complain of dizziness, chest pain and swollen ankles. Figure 3 shows the relationship of reported constipation symptoms to increasing drug use. One must use care in attributing symptoms in the elderly to use of a drug since a high percentage of subjects reporting specific symptoms were taking no medications.

This study documented a high prevalence of symptoms and diseases in elderly Dunedin participants. When all symptoms are combined there is a strong correlation between symptom prevalence and the number of diseases, drugs used and, less importantly, age of elderly participants. These results reinforce the principle of geriatric medicine that senescence alone is not sufficient to explain the occurrence of a symptom.

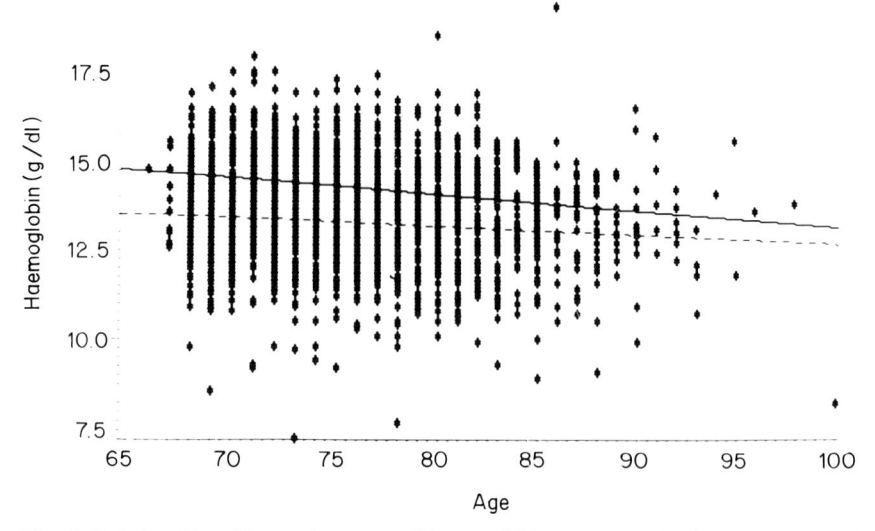

Fig. 4. Relationship of increasing age and haemoglobin concentration in men —— and women -----.

Most studies conducted in geriatric patients have shown a decline in haemoglobin values with age. Our data base was used to examine the effect of age, sex, medication and disease on anaemia (Celestin-Roux et al. 1986). Anaemia was defined as a haemoglobin of less than 14 g/dl for men and less than 12 g/dl for women.

Prevalence of anaemia for participants across all eight visits to the program is shown in Table 6. Prevalence ranged from 19.8% of the population at visit three to a high of 25.3% at visit one. The prevalence of anaemia for all visits and age groups was 3.7 times greater in men than women, and a consistent increase in prevalence of anaemia was observed with increasing age in both men and women. By their eighth visit to the program 70% of men over 85 years of age were classified as anaemic compared with 20% of women in this age group.

The mean number of medical disorders reported by men and women with anaemia and those without anaemia were compared at the fourth visit. Women with anaemia reported a mean 2.7 diseases compared with 2.4 medical disorders in women without anaesmia. Men reported a slightly lower prevalence of medical disorders with a mean of 1.8 for both anaemic and non-anaemic individuals.

Twenty-three specific medical disorders were studied to determine if they were associated with anaemia. Three conditions, diverticulosis, kidney infection and cancer were associated with a significantly higher prevalence of anaemia in women, while in men there was a significant relationship with osteoarthritis. However, after adjusting for age using the Mantel-Haensel test, no significant differences were observed between any disease reported and anaemia.

A multiple regression analysis was used to determine the relationship of haemoglobin with the number of medications taken by these subjects and an inverse relationship was found between haemoglobin and the number of drugs used ($P<0.005$). Although several drugs were found to be used more often in anaemic subjects (psyllium, ibuprofen and allopurinol) no significant association between drugs and anaemia was found after adjusting for age differences.

It was found that from 65 to 85 years of age, a change in mean predicted haemoglobin from 14.8 to 13.8 g/dl occurs (Fig. 4). Although a decrease of 1 g/dl was found to be statistically significant, the clinical significance of this remains to be determined in a geriatric group. Interpretation of laboratory values must be made in context with the clinical setting.

FUTURE APPROACHES

In the past many randomized controlled clinical trials have systematically excluded elderly persons from studies designed to answer therapeutic questions. Many questions about drug treatment that are important to the elderly could be best answered through clinical trials, but this type of research involves special problems.

There are numerous ethical considerations involved in clinical trials in the elderly (Miller *et al.* 1985, Weintraub 1984). For instance, how does the investigator obtain informed consent from elderly confused subjects. In addition, personal physicians may be hesitant to refer elderly subjects for study because of a strong desire to protect them. It is also exceedingly difficult to enrol frail, elderly subjects into studies when the methods and risks are clearly communicated (Weintraub 1984).

Although there are many obstacles to conducting clinical trials in geriatric patients often a therapeutic answer can only be obtained through this type of research design. Therefore, renewed efforts must be directed at innovative approaches to controlled clinical trials. In addition to these traditional research methods, non-traditional research methods must be increasingly used including consensus panels, observational studies and case controlled studies. Careful review and analysis of the existing body of literature can lead to more rational therapy. For example, Helms (1985) reviewed 21 studies dealing with the efficacy of antipsychotics in treating behavioural complications of dementia to justify judicious use of these drugs.

Lastly, a substantial body of information is already available on many drugs and treatment in the elderly and better methods are needed to improve the drug use process in the elderly. We know that in many instances drugs are overprescribed for elderly subjects leading to drug-drug interactions and drug-disease interactions. Compliance patterns are poor in the elderly which often leads to ineffective treatment or drug intoxication. Better methods are needed to manage medication regimens received by the elderly to prevent overlapping treatment and therapeutic misadventures.

I believe that computers can be increasingly called upon to periodically analyse drug regimens of the elderly. When properly programmed a computer can identify drug interactions, doses outside the accepted range and inappropriate prescribing. Computers can also be programmed to provide feedback on drug therapy to prescribing physicians and health professionals caring for the patient.

The Dunedin Program is only one example of an approach to evaluate drug therapy in the elderly. It is clear that many different approaches and disciplines will be needed to make drug therapy for the elderly safer, more effective and less costly.

ACKNOWLEDGEMENTS

This study was supported in part by the James Hilton and Emma Austin Manning Foundation, the AARP Andrus Foundation and the American Heart Association, Florida Affiliate, Suncoast Chapter.

REFERENCES

Applegate, W. B., Dismuke, S. E. and Runyan, J. W. (1984). Treatment of hypertension in the elderly: a time for caution. *J. Am. Geriatr. Soc.* **32**, 21-23.

Celestin-Roux, C., Hale, W. E., Perkins, L. L. and Stewart, R. B. (1986). Anemia: an evaluation of age, sex, disease and medications in a geriatric population. *J. Geriatr. Drug Ther.* (in press).

Hale, W. E., Marks, R. G. and Stewart, R. B. (1980). The Dunedin Program, a Florida geriatric screening process: design and initial data. *J. Am. Geriatr. Soc.* **27**, 377-380.

Hale, W. E., Stewart, R. B., Cerda, J. J., Marks, R. G. and May, F. E. (1982). Use of nutritional supplements in an ambulatory elderly population. *J. Am. Geriatr. Soc.* **30**, 401-403.

Hale, W. E., Perkins, L. L., May, F. E., Marks, R. G. and Stewart, R. B. (1986a). Vitamin E effects on symptoms and laboratory values in the elderly. *J. Am. Diet. Assoc.* **86**, 625-629.

Hale, W. E., Perkins, L. L., May, F. E., Marks, R. G. and Stewart, R. B. (1986b). Symptom prevalence in the elderly: an evaluation of age, sex, disease and medication use. *J. Am. Geriatr. Soc.* **34**, 333-340.

Helling, M. and Venulet, J. (1974). Drug recording and classification by the World Health Organization research center for international monitoring of adverse reactions to drugs. *Meth. Inf. Med.* **13**, 169-178.

Helms, P. M. (1985). Efficacy of antipsychotics in the treatment of the behavioral complications of dementia: a review of the literature. *J. Am. Geriatr. Soc.* **33**, 206-209.

Koch-Weser, J. (1979). Treatment of hypertension in the elderly. In "Drugs and the elderly" (J. Crooks and I. H. Stevenson, eds) Ch. 23, p. 247. University Park Press, Baltimore.

Lamy, P. P. (1985). Patterns of prescribing and drug use. In "The aging process, therapeutic implications" (R. N. Butler and A. G. Bearn, eds) p. 57. Raven Press, New York.

May, F. E., Stewart, R. B., Hale, W. E. and Marks, R. G. (1982). Prescribed and nonprescribed drug use in an ambulatory elderly population. *South. Med. J.* **75**, 522-528.

Miller, S. T., Applegate, W. B. and Perry, C. (1985). Clinical trials in elderly persons. Editorial. *J. Am. Geriatr. Soc.* **33**, 91-92.

Morgan, D. B. and Davidson, C. (1980). Hypokalaemia and diuretics: an analysis of publications. *Br. Med. J.* **280**, 905-908.

Roberts, H. J. (1981). Perspective on vitamin E as therapy. *JAMA* **246**, 129-131.

Rowe, J. W. (1985). Health care of the elderly. *N. Engl. J. Med.* **312**, 827-835.

Simonson, W. (1984). "Medications and the elderly" p. 7. Aspen Publications, Rockville, Maryland.

Stewart, R. B., Hale, W. E. and Marks, R. G. (1983). Diuretic use in an ambulatory elderly population. *Am. J. Hosp. Pharm.* **40**, 409-413.

Stewart, R. B., May, F. E., Hale, W. E. and Marks, R. G. (1982). Laxative use among an ambulatory elderly population: a Report from the Dunedin Program. *Contemp. Pharm. Pract.* **5**, 166-169.

Temple, R. (1985). FDA guidelines for clinical testing of drugs in the elderly. Paper presented at DIA Workshop on Geriatric Drug Testing and Development-Practical Applications, April 2, 1985, Bethesda, Maryland.

Weintraub, M. (1984). Ethical concerns and guidelines in research in geriatric pharmacology and therapeutics. *J. Am. Geriatr. Soc.* **32**, 44-48.

Discussion

Steen: Your city has a high proportion of elderly (30%), it is obviously a retirement community. To what extent, would you say, are your drug consumption figures representative for the elderly in the USA? What information do you have from the relatively high number of non-responders?

Stewart: The number of our elderly population is in fact higher than the average for the USA. Half of the individuals have come to Dunedin from the north-east of the USA, about 28% from central, 15% from the south-east and the rest from places scattered about the other parts. The only means of comparison comes from the National Institute of Aging which studied two rural communities in Iowa. The drugs used in rural communities in Iowa are almost identical with those taken in our group.

Alloza: Did you conduct audits to assess the consumption of drugs *vs* the real need for medication?

Stewart: We did not, because we would not interfere with treating doctors, we did not want to institute educational programs nor audit the doctors about the reason for their prescriptions.

Sorensen: According to literature there is quite a high intake of oestrogens among menopausal women in the USA. How many of your females had an oestrogen intake and did they differ in any way from the other women?

Stewart: About 4% of our women reported the use of oestrogens and we have not compared these women to non users of oestrogen.

Crepaldi: Folate deficiency is one of the most common vitamin deficiencies in the elderly. A typical sign of this deficiency is the increased mean erythrocyte corpuscular volume. In your patients with multivitamin use is there a certain amount of folate deficiency? And are there differences in these parameters between users and non-users?

Stewart: I have no information. We have not looked for pernicious anaemia in this population.

Lakatta: The question of whether the drugs are really necessary is one of the most important raised in these papers. Recently, my colleagues and I did a double-blind cross-over study with digoxin and placebo in patients with an average age of 70. Neither the patients nor the physicians could tell from the effect whether digoxin or placebo had been taken. All the outpatients belonged to class II to III heart failure.

Neve: Have you any data about the mean calcium level of patients taking thiazide and of the prevalence of osteoporosis.

Stewart: In our population there was no difference in mean calcium level of patients taking thiazide diuretics compared to controls.

Sociological Perspectives on Aging, Families and the Future

Vern L. Bengtson

Andrus Gerontology Center, University of Southern California, Los Angeles, California, USA

Keywords
Family; Longitudinal studies; Demographic and social changes; Intergenerational attitudes; Aging.

Seldom, if ever, have sociologists been considered good prophets. Nor have they been particularly well received as historians. There may be good reason for this. From Marx and Spencer and Durkheim down to the present, sociologists' assessments of the mechanisms underlying social structure and behaviour have often run counter to conventional wisdom concerning the way things have been, are, or should be.

But whether popularly received or not, the "sociological imagination," as suggested by C. Wright Mills (Mills 1959), has proven useful in pointing out how wrong conventional wisdom can be in understanding social forces in changing societies. The purpose of this paper is to use both the sociological imagination and sociological facts to examine aspects of aging, the family and the future. The focus is on common assumptions reflecting family relations and aging in light of current social trends and projections to the twenty-first century.

While it is certainly not the intent of this paper to engage in social prophecy, I think it is useful to examine alternatives to common beliefs about aging and the future as suggested by current sociological data. We are all aware that because of expanded longevity and decreased mortality, most citizens of contemporary industrialized societies will live far longer than did their grandparents. We are also aware that another demographic trend, decreased fertility, has meant fewer children, and lower proportions of wage-earning taxpayers to care for the increased numbers and proportions.

Conventional wisdom suggests that these trends imply increasing vulnerability for the aged and increased intergenerational tensions associated with the dependencies of aging in the future. Are such projections accurate? What might twenty-first century society be like and what are its implications for gerontologists interested in quality of life issues for the elderly and for families with aging members?

This paper will begin with the future: possible configurations of twenty-first century society, scenarios originally proposed for medical care system planners who were exploring projections for the twenty-first century. The second section turns to the recent past, summarizing seven demographic trends which have an impact on the family life of the aged. The third section reviews some findings from current research on aging and the family, findings which may provide some perspective on the quality of future life for families with dependent elders. The conclusion presents some suggestions concerning how professionals and laypersons interested in aging can react to, and anticipate, these scenarios in addressing what I view as our highest humanitarian priority in gerontology: *enhancing the competencies of aged individuals and the supportive capacities of their social networks.*

FOUR VIEWS FROM THE POTENTIAL FUTURE

We begin with a look toward the twenty-first century. Many current social trends—medical, economic, technological, demographic—have been the topic of considerable debate in gerontology as we look to the future (see Binstock 1985a, Birren 1985, Schneider and Brody 1983, H. Brody 1985, Fries 1980, Haber 1985, Skolnick 1984, Collins 1985 and several chapters in volumes edited by Gaitz *et al.* 1984, Dunkle *et al.* 1984). Other trends are less easy to document: the increase of individualism in the post-1960s decades, the decline of some collective action (such as labour unions), the recent worldwide trend toward political conservatism and religious fundamentalism, the perception of decline in traditional social institutions such as the family, changes in the labour market leading to decreases in desirable jobs. Each, of course, has implications for the shape of society in the twenty-first century.

Since 1979, the Institute for Alternative Futures, a Washington based planning group led by Clement Bezold and his associates, has been developing possible scenarios for the twenty-first century (Bezold 1984, Bezold and Peck 1984). These futurists have described 40 "plausible futures" which they have employed in strategic consultation for a number of constituencies: state legislatures, agencies, professional organizations and health care planners in the USA. My colleagues and I have found these scenarios highly provocative in considering future implications of trends we have documented in family demography and relationships (Bengtson and Campbell 1985) and of the relationship between family, work and the rhythm of demographic flow (Dannefer and Bengtson 1987). Though prepared with the peculiar configurations of the USA in mind, these scenarios have general applicability to potential futures in other industrialized nations. The four selected for summary below reflect distinctly different views of what might happen in the next four decades, during which members of the "baby boom" cohorts will be growing old.

The "Continued Growth" Scenario*

This view of the early twenty-first century reflects the consequence of competent management, consensus and technological ingenuity beyond present levels. Rising affluence has encouraged high levels of consumption; there has been full employment. This is a world of new technology, with sophisticated communication and widely disseminated computers. Multinational corporations enjoy partnerships with regional world governments. Households have instant access to the world's best information sources, which in turn has reshaped education. More people are living longer, richer lives. This is something like the future Herman Kahn (1981) described in "The Coming Boom".

Health care technologies and expenditures continue to grow. Therapies are more complex and more effective than they were in the 1980s. Vaccines have been developed to prevent many diseases, including most forms of heart disease and most cancers, and definitive cures are found for many that cannot be prevented. Other chronic diseases, particularly those that are stress related, are still common because there has been little significant change in lifestyle. Life extension is made possible by organ and tissue transplants, which have become common. The "hospital-on-the-wrist" technology performs many of the diagnostic and therapeutic functions of the physician and hospital.

The "Decline and Stagnation" Scenario

Looking back, the 1990s can best be described as a period of increasing distress. There were deepening recessions, continuing international monetary concerns, much social unrest and difficult resource shortages. Climatic changes, blamed on the "greenhouse effect", made the weather increasingly unpredictable and severe, leading to food shortages. Throughout most societies there is a general sense of failure, but no dramatic change in the political order. Expanded immigration from developing nations further taxes overburdened health and social service systems. Pollution has caused significant environmental damage, and there have been disturbing outbreaks of disease. While some are able to insulate themselves, the poor and particularly the elderly suffer disproportionately. The

---

*The four scenarios are adapted from Bezold (1984).

Council of Rome sceptics who wrote "The Limits to Growth" (Meadows *et al.* 1972) and other similar reports in the 1970s were accurate.

In terms of health, a two-tier health care system has become accepted. The tier serving the poor and much of the middle class is severely underfunded. Health status diminishes as food shortages increase malnutrition, and the decaying infrastructure helps spawn an increase in infectious disease. The elderly have a particularly difficult time as their morbidity and mortality rates rise. Drugs are much sought after, but little innovation occurs. Alternative therapies and non-traditional providers grow in number.

The "Disciplined Society" Scenario

Most industrialized societies overcame a period of economic distress during the 1990s by abandoning some traditional individual freedoms for the sake of a tightly organized, disciplined political order. The goals of security, comfort and material success are met through rational management, enforced conservation and efficiency. Behavioural control, systems engineering and centralized management techniques are put to maximum use with the aid of effective communications and information processing techniques. Socioeconomic activity is regulated by a powerful (and generally popular) alliance between government and business. While a scarcity of energy and material resources has continued, there is effective distribution and adequate material well being for most citizens. And the trains run on time.

The health care system is well ordered, with clear-cut standards for applying and evaluating the cost-effective therapies that physicians and allied health personnel (who now have more responsibilities) are allowed to use. Public health programmes are very successful. Elders are encouraged to die comfortably, but without the utilization of death-delaying strategies which extended life in the 1980s beyond cost-effective limits. Destructive personal behaviour is not tolerated. Some have said society has finally achieved George Orwell's rendition of "1984"; others suggest this is too negative a view of the inevitable.

The "Transformed Society" Scenario

Western industrial society has indeed been "transformed" into another civilization by the year 2020. The values of voluntary simplicity and ecological balance have ended the overproduction and overconsumption that once drove industrial North America. Technology remains an important part of economic well-being, but economic well-being is subordinate to the inner growth of most individuals. New understandings of physics, chemistry and biology have led to new scientific paradigms which have created a much less labour-intensive society and which afford a very comfortable life for the vast majority of people. Since the healthiest members of society are recognized by their frugal material and rich spiritual lives, opulent lifestyles are far less popular. Alvin Toffler (1980) in "The Third Wave" and John Naisbitt in "Megatrends" (1982) made the basic forces of the transformation a familiar topic, though the shift to values of voluntary simplicity far outpaced their forecasts.

Health care has become an energetic marketplace, as the more equal access to practice for all health providers replaces the licensure systems that until the 1990s gave physicians their state sanctioned monopoly on care. Now, allied and non-conventional health providers compete with physicians. Community groups monitor and publicize the effectiveness of providers. Consumers also do much more selfcare and many have developed their own "body wisdom" that performs many of the functions of the "hospital-on-the-wrist".

Implications of the Scenarios

These visions assembled by the Institute for Alternative Futures evoke strong reactions. None of the four may be entirely pleasing; some are greatly dismaying. Each is individually based on assumptions that may be questionable. But note in passing three possible events which are absent from each: no nuclear holocaust, no worldwide war, and no international monetary collapse. While these are certainly possible, and deserve the concern given them in the mass media, they (along with the apocalypse described in the New Testament's "Book of Revelations") are probably less likely than other, more mundane futures. It may well be useful to be reminded that such catastrophic events have occurred very infrequently in human history; to plan for the future only with Armageddon in mind is hardly practical.

I think the principal value of these four visions of the future may indeed lie in the perspective of diversity they imply. We frequently think of the future in terms of extremes: either continuity or catastrophes. The truth likely falls in between. For gerontologists and policymakers, it is well to be reminded of the variety of factors—demographic, technological, economic, sociopolitical—which may lead to diverse outcomes in the near future. What is done between now and then, of course, will influence the likelihood of these futures—catastrophic or otherwise.

None of these four visions says much about the demographic metabolism of modern societies, especially in terms of age composition and stratification phenomena already having impact on worklife and personal fortunes of the baby boom cohort (see Dannefer and Bengtson 1987, for a discussion). None says much about the family or about potentials for enhancing the competencies of older individuals in aging societies, a point to which I will return shortly. It is beyond the scope of this paper to debate the plausibility or the desirability of any of the four scenarios, or the adequacy of the data and assumptions on which they are based. Rather, it seems useful to explore some findings from current research in the sociology of aging and the family which might have implications for any futuristic visions, in the light of conventional wisdom which suggests the vulnerability and incapacity of families to deal with social change regarding the dependencies of aging.

RECENT TRENDS IN THE DEMOGRAPHY OF FAMILY LIFE AND AGING†

There are at least seven demographic trends discernable in the late twentieth century which have significant implications for aging as well as family life in the future. These trends have special salience for any future scenarios of individual well-being and health care trends involving the aged. These have emerged in most industrialized societies since World War II to alter dramatically the demography of kinship and later life. While the discussion to follow is based primarily on US Census data, the trends are characteristic of most industrialized nations (Cherlin and Furstenberg 1983, Treas and Bengtson 1986, Hagestad 1984, Myers 1985, Uhlenberg 1986).

Growing Numbers and Increased Proportions of the Elderly Population

The first and most significant population trend of past decades is the rapid growth of the older population. This "greying of modern societies" is occurring both in terms of the absolute numbers of the elderly and in terms of their proportions to other age groups of society. In the USA, for example, at the beginning of this century those above the age of 60 numbered less than 5 million (one of every 16 in the population). Today the older population of the USA currently numbers 39 million — one in every six Americans is over age 60. By the year 2025, this figure is expected to double, reaching 80 million — or one in every four US citizens (Fowles 1984).

Moreover, the older population itself continues to get older, thus demonstrating what demographers refer to as the "fluid characteristics of America's elderly" (De Vos and Ruggels 1985). Those 85 and older currently represent the fastest growing age group in the USA, growing at a rate four times as high as the rate for the entire population 60 years and older (US Senate Committee on Aging 1985, p.15, Fowles 1984, Pedersen 1984). There are now some 32,000 centenarians in the USA alone, and their numbers — particularly among women — are climbing at the rate of 210 per week (Population Reference Bureau Report, as quoted by Pedersen 1984).

Ironically, the magnitude and scope of this revolution was unanticipated by most social scientists and policymakers alike. As recently as 1971, for example,

---

†This material is adapted from Bengtson and Campbell (1985).

the US Census Bureau projected that the US population of 65 and over would grow by about 17.6% during the coming decade. This is a rate only slightly faster than the population at large, which was expected to grow by 15%. Instead, however, between 1971 and 1981 the US population of 65 and over grew by 28.4% (Bengtson and Campbell 1985).

Increased Longevity

These unprecedented shifts in the age composition of the population have been produced by the interaction of two long-term population trends: increase in life expectancy and decrease in fertility. The increase in life expectancy is due largely to decline in infant mortality. Since the turn of the century life expectancy in the USA has jumped by almost 27 years, from less than 50 in 1900 to almost 75 in 1985 (US Senate Committee on Aging 1985, p. 22). In 1900, for example, only 63% of women surviving to childbearing age (20) were expected to reach the age of 60. Now, in comparison, almost 90% of all North American women who survive to childbearing celebrate their sixtieth birthday and beyond (US Senate Committee on Aging 1985, p. 24). In fact, 40% of contemporary women can expect to survive past the age of 85, and death rates are expected to decline further (NCHS 1982).

Decreased Fertility

A third trend, evident at the opposite end of the age distribution, concerns decreases in fertility rates. In 1957, the peak of the post-World War II baby boom, the total fertility rate in the USA was 3.7 children per woman. Just two decades later, fertility has fallen to almost half, or 1.8 children for every woman (Hagestad 1984). This trend reflects a shrinking family size (Preston 1984) and a growing incidence of childlessness (Sell and DeJong 1985), particularly among dual-career couples. In only four decades, between 1930 and 1970, the percentage of women aged 60-64 who had borne four or more children dropped dramatically, from 50% to only 21% (Hagestad 1985).

Gender Contrasts in Longevity

A prominent feature of the changing age pyramid of western societies is the growing imbalance in the sex ratio at the upper ends of the age distribution. Demographers use the term "mortality gap" in referring to the growing tendency for women to outlive men. The tendency for women to outlive men is evident at birth as well as at age 65. Life expectancy at birth for women in the USA is now 78.2 years compared to 70.9 for men, while at age 65 women on average can expect to live an additional 18.2 years compared to only 14.5 years for men (NCHS 1982, Riley 1985).

Gender differences in the mortality experiences of men and women are reflected in the age at which widowhood is experienced. While the average age at widowhood is approximately 68 and 71 for women and men respectively, the proportion of widowed persons increases differentially by sex until age 75, when four out of five women are widowed compared to only one out of five men (US Senate Committee on Aging 1985, p. 110, De Vos and Ruggles 1985). Gender differences like these in the experiences of later life have led some observers to claim that old age is increasingly becoming a "female problem" (Somers 1985).

Labour Force Participation

A fifth significant demographic development in recent decades, particularly since 1970, is the increased labour force participation of women. This increase has been most dramatic among women with children under 3 years of age. There is also evidence to suggest that older women (55 and over) are remaining in the labour force at a higher rate than their male counterparts, who are increasingly choosing early retirement (US Senate Committee on Aging 1985, pp. 76-77). The changing labour force participation of women has implications for their traditional kinkeeping functions within families (Rosenthal 1985).

Divorce and Remarriage

The sixth demographic development is the increase in divorce and remarriage at all stages of the life cycle (Cherlin and Furstenberg 1983). Marriage rates have remained fairly stable over the past 100 years, with more than 90% of all men and women who survive to middle age having married. Divorce rates, in contrast, have increased dramatically over these years. Whereas 10% of the marriages contracted around 1900 ended in divorce, it is projected that 50% of those marriages after 1970 will experience a divorce (Uhlenberg 1986, Cherlin 1981).

But divorce is no longer a situation facing only the young. Each year 10,000 Americans over the age of 65 are divorced. By the year 2000, over half of those entering old age will have been divorced at least once. Remarriage rates must also be considered. While equal numbers of men and women divorce, a greater percentage of men remarry at least once and many more go on to have second families (Preston 1984, Hagestad 1984). Treas and Van Hilst (1976) find that remarriage is rare for elderly women, however: less than one in 20 widows over age 60 remarry.

Dependency Ratios

A final trend, resulting from shifts in the age composition of population, concerns support ratios: the number of dependants, either children or elderly, to the number of individuals in the "working age" population (18-65). The "aged support ratio", as opposed to the "young ratio", is especially important to our discussion since more publicly funded health care programmes serve the needs of the elderly than they do those of children (Preston 1984).

For example, at the turn of the century, there were only about seven elderly persons for every 100 persons aged 18-64; by 1982, the ratio had increased to 19 elderly people per 100 persons of working age. For the next three decades, this ratio will remain stable. But by the year 2020, it is expected to rise again, to 29 per 100; by 2050 it will reach a high of 38 retirement age individuals for every 100 working age persons (US Senate Committee on Aging 1985, p. 20).

Implications for Aging and Family Life in the Future

Taken together, these seven age-related population trends of the twentieth century add up to nothing short of a demographic revolution. The impact of these trends for the future of aging within the family context is sobering (Cherlin and Furstenberg 1983, Dannefer and Bengtson 1987). For example, it is estimated that one in ten individuals over age 65 has a child who is also 65 or older. This suggests considerable strains on family support systems and raises difficult questions of "generational equity" between family members as well as age groups in the larger society (Longman 1985). The contemporary demographic revolution in kinship and later life has led at least one social historian (Hareven 1978) to question whether the family can survive the impact of these population changes. She suggests that while the family has survived the Industrial Revolution of the nineteenth century and the social and psychological revolution of the 1960s and 1970s, the question now may be whether families can survive the new demographic regime of its members.

The changing picture of intergenerational families suggested by the demographic trends is characterized by four major features. They include: (1) acceleration of generation turnover, due to decreased "reproductive span", smaller families, closer spacing of children and the trend toward earlier marriage evident for most of the twentieth century, (2) a rise in multigeneration families and the verticalization of their intergenerational structure (Knipscheer 1982); (3) extension of long-term intergenerational bonds reflecting what Hagestad (1981, 1985) refers to as "life overlaps", the tendency for parents and children to grow old together; and (4) increasing diversity and complexity in the wider kinship networks in which families are embedded due to chains of divorce and remarriage which are weaving through all generations (Hammel *et al.* 1981, Hagestad 1982, Cherlin 1978, Uhlenberg and Myers 1981, Uhlenberg and Chew 1984).

In light of these demographic trends, the four scenarios of the future presented earlier suggest somewhat different implications for the position of the aged. In the "continued growth" scenario there would be the fewest surprises: the situation of the aged tomorrow would be much as it is today, with future strains on the dependency ratio accommodated by slight increments in governmental support provisions. Gradual legislative changes to help families care for their elders may also increase, the outcome of continued prosperity and grudging social liberalism, with enlightened selfinterest acknowledging the desirability of provision to avoid the development of pockets of poverty— especially among the elderly. The continued reinforcement of traditional values may lead to a renewed emphasis on the family as the locus for social support, with tax incentives to assist this aspect of the private sector in providing services. Alternatively, the continuation of individualistic values may further erode the situation of the aged, as the "unproductive" status of those retired or medically dependent is perceived as a greater burden.

In the "decline and stagnation" scenario the aged are more obviously at risk. Eroding societal resources will leave those not economically productive more at the mercy of familial capabilities for assistance; an increasingly large number of families will be unable to give their elders economic assistance. Those elderly without families would be even more vulnerable. Euthanasia may become widely acceptable. On the other hand, in a society facing chronic uncertainty with technological innovation no longer providing the sure hope it did in the twentieth century, the "wisdom" of elders representing a brighter past may be more highly valued than today.

The "disciplined society" scenario depicts an outgrowth of rational planning to face unparalleled social and political failure. It is difficult to imagine that the aged in such a society would face any more than a grim future, as their families gird themselves to deal with rigid structuring of economic and social life. Yet there are alternative implications to this scenario as well. Under an enlightened despotism the collective contributions of the aged have often been affirmed, as Machiavelli observed; under other forms of totalitarian government, gerontocracy has emerged following rigid rules of seniority and succession to power. Indeed, such a development might be plausible following the "failure" of a younger cohort of leadership as occurred in Russia following the abortive 1871 revolution.

The "transformed society" future suggests two extremes in terms of the elderly and their families. On the one hand, a society which values personal worth in terms of contemplation and social bondedness (instead of defining personal worth as economic productivity and conspicuous consumption) would probably accord higher status to elderly or non-economically productive members than does contemporary society. On the other hand, in a society which has experienced a phenomenal shift in values from production/consumption to contemplation/ simplicity the elderly may be captive to their own cohort history, unable or unwilling to adapt; in such a case the elderly would appear superannuated, thoroughly old-fashioned, irrelevant.

This section has explored some aspects of social structure: demographic trends, their consequences for aging and the family, their implications for future scenarios. What these changes in structure mean for the quality of family relations is equally important. Much contemporary discussion centres on the issue of the availability of kin *vs* the capacity of kin to provide social and economic support to its older members (Hammel *et al.* 1981, De Vos and Ruggles 1985, Day 1984, Hagestad 1981). What about the sociopsychological aspects of family relations in rapidly changing societies? What does available research suggest about family stability and connectedness in light of these dramatic demographic shifts?

RECENT TRENDS IN THE SOCIAL PSYCHOLOGY OF FAMILY LIFE AND AGING

The family represents the oldest and most basic form of social organization; the intergenerational bond represents the classic manifestation of social security to address human dependencies. But the family, and especially the intergenerational dyad, also reflects the most basic paradox in human experience. On the one hand it represents security, continuity and some sense of identity in the context of social change and challenge. On the other hand it reflects obligations, guilt and frustration to independent action. It is no wonder that the history of western literature, from King David to Oedipus to Lear to Willy Loman, reflects the classic myth of intergenerational conflict. It is no wonder that contemporary analyses of demographic trends and social organization lead to myths about the decline of intergenerational bonds in fast changing societies.

Family Decline and Disorganization: Fact or Myth?

The sociological imagination begins, as C. Wright Mills suggested (Mills 1959), with an examination of commonly held beliefs about social processes. Myths and stereotypes are important, for they suggest belief structures from which behaviours and orientations toward action arise. But myths and stereotypes can also be misleading. If used as the sole basis for policy and behaviour, they may lead to socially dysfunctional consequences, as Binstock's (1985b) penetrating discussion of public policy regarding the "oldest old" demonstrates.

One trend in popular culture of the 1960s and 1970s was the tendency to characterize families as disorganized and decomposing under the strains of technological innovation, geographical mobility and the generation gap (Lasch 1979, Naroll 1983). One eminent sociologist, writing from his observation of the American experience, suggested that "the American middle-class family, already stripped of most non-essential duties, now faces an attack on its remaining last bastions" (Etzioni 1977, p. 4). Its elders, especially, were seen as the victims of family disorganization, isolated, abandoned by their offspring, heartsick at their childrens' divorces; grandparents were seen as casualties of modernization and the decline of traditional social structures. Ethel Shanas (1979) has called this stereotype of the abandoned elder the "Hydra-headed myth" of our era, so frequently did it emerge and was challenged, only to resurface again. Her research, and that of others, has helped to displace this myth, at least among professionals, with facts concerning intergenerational contact among aging individuals in modern societies.

There are several indications from studies conducted during the past few years which question the myth that the family is no longer viable and is irrelevant to problems of aging (for reviews of this vast literature, see Bengtson and Treas 1980, Sussman 1985). First, data show that four out of five elderly parents have at least weekly contact with offspring (Shanas 1979, Bengtson *et al.* 1984). Second, data show that most grandparents have regular contact with grandchildren and express high degrees of satisfaction in their role (Bengtson and Robertson 1985). Third, data show that, in the case of divorce, family intergenerational ties are often still important and sometimes involve the older generation in more intimate relationships than before (Johnson 1985, Cherlin and Furstenberg, 1985). Fourth, data show that there is a high degree of intergenerational care giving of dependent parents, even at high cost to the middle-aged child, usually but not always the daughter (Brody 1981, E. M. Brody 1981, 1985, Zarit *et al.* 1980). About 90% of primary care giving to Alzheimer's patients, for example, is contributed by family members, most often the spouse in conjunction with children. The kinds of feelings and the quality of interaction which accompanies such relationships may often reflect stress and produce adverse consequences for the care giver; but the commitment is still there and suggests the extreme case of family assistance in the dependencies of aging members.

Fifth, there is the more global myth concerning decline in the importance of the family as a social institution in modern society. This is more difficult to document. But one study, a 50-year follow-up of a classic sociological investigation of a mid-western American city (originally described by Lynd and Lynd 1929), concluded that the data evidenced "no appreciable decline in the Middletown family during the past 50 years", but rather "a strengthening of the institutional form and an increased satisfaction for participants". The researchers note that

> these conclusions obviously are contrary to the prevailing belief that the family has been declining for a long time, that its survival past the present generation is in doubt, and that massive intervention is required to save it—so contrary, indeed, that we are likely to be accused of bias no matter how much we insist that the conclusions were forced on us by our data and were as surprising to us as they may be to our readers (Caplow *et al.* 1982, p. 327).

Middletown certainly may not represent a cross-section of American life, and its families may not be typical; but the respondents' statements concerning the strength of family ties is instructive.

Into each of the scenarios for consequences of aging in the twenty-first century, therefore, we must insert the demonstrated viability of the family as a social institution and the importance of intergenerational bonds, as against the myths of familial abandonment which appeared so often in the last decade. Even Toffler

(1980) charts the reemergence of the family as a characteristic of "the Third Wave" in the 1980s society. But what do family members say about these intergenerational bonds? How much microstructure changes occur in aging families, reflecting the macrostructure changes in the demographic trends reviewed in the preceding section?

Longitudinal Trends Regarding Change in Family Intergenerational Structures

In the longitudinal study of family relations ongoing at the University of Southern California, my colleagues and I are examining the magnitude of change in various dimensions of intergenerational relations over a relatively long period of time (14 years), as well as the interpretations respondents have of these changes. We are only beginning to analyse these data (from the 1985 follow-up of the 2,044 individuals originally contacted in 1971). However, preliminary analyses provide suggestions of the magnitude of change in typical, non-clinical family networks including aged members, and of perceptions regarding stability and change in intergenerational relationships.

The data to be reported here come from 1,378 individuals representing the second wave of a panel study which began in 1971-1972. These respondents were originally sampled from a population of 870,000 members of a prepaid medical health plan, contacted via a random sample of older male subscribers (potential grandfathers) to the programme. The response rate for the Time-2 (1985) survey was 62%; this varied by generation, with the G1 (grandparent) response rate almost 69% and the G3 (grandchild) rate 60%. Average age of the G1 respondents in the Time-2 (T-2) assessment is almost 80 years; for the G2, 58 years; and G3, 33 years. Mortality rates were, of course, high in the 13-year time period between the two surveys, especially for the G1 respondents: 51% of the grandfathers in the original sample and 27% of the grandmothers have died since 1971.

One striking feature of the analyses to date concerns the extent to which the family composition and structure of this sample has changed since 1971. The first question in the survey asks respondents to list events or changes that have most affected them or their family in the past 14 years. Three out of four (over 75%) indicated changes in the composition of their families owing to birth and death, as well as to marriage, divorce or remarriage. From individual reports of change in marital status (Fig. 1) we see the extent of such change in this relatively middle-class, non-clinical population during a 14-year period. Since 1971 38% of the G1s and 62% of the G3s, have experienced at least one change in marital status. Most of the change has occurred via widowhood for G1s and via marriage for the G3s. One out of six of the middle generation (G2) have experienced change in marital status. Parental status has also changed: nine out of ten families indicate additions to generational structure, through birth of grandchildren to G1s and G2s and children to G3s; almost half the G3s have become parents, leading to

CHANGE IN MARITAL STATUS

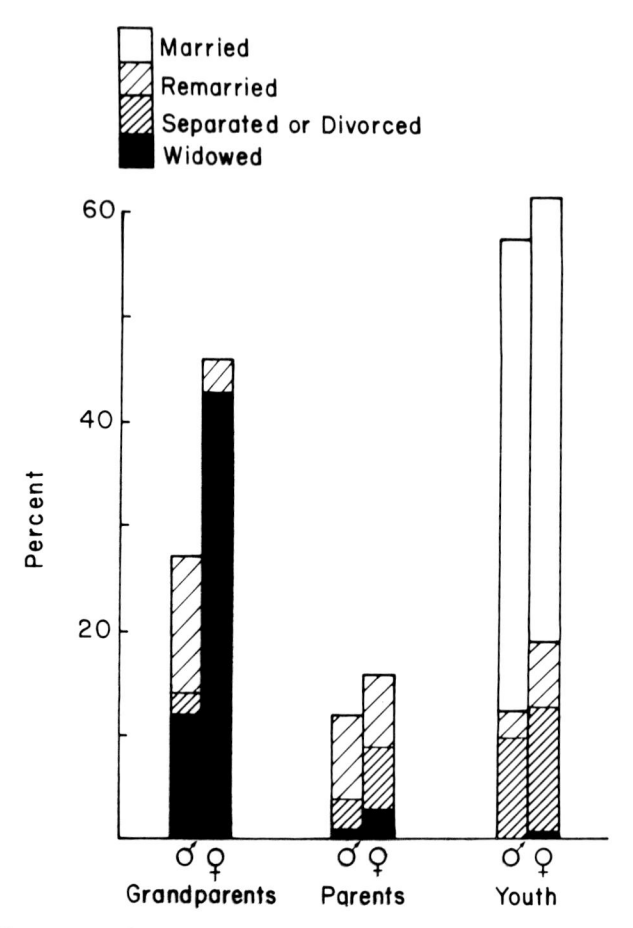

Fig. 1. Percentage of responders who have changed marital status since 1971. G1, grandparents; G2, parents; G3, grandchildren.

four-generation family structures for the majority of our respondents. In addition, almost one in six of the G3s have become step-parents, another type of familial change which has important intergenerational implications (step-grandparenting, for example).

In addition to these changes in family composition, many respondents recorded geographical moves and job changes which may have impact on intergenerational relationships. One in three G1s, 42% of the G2s and 93% of the G3s indicated a change in residence in the past 14 years. This does not include the almost 15% of the original 1971 respondents who were impossible to locate because of multiple geographical moves and out-of-date postal addresses.

Given these indicators of structural and geographical change, it would not be surprising if there were significant changes in the perception of intergenerational relations. However, the data in general point to substantial stability—not change—in the evaluations reported by these families of their intergenerational interaction.

Perceptions of Change
Regarding Intergenerational Relations

As family members age together, it can be anticipated that the nature of their interpersonal relationships will also change. Grandparents may become increasingly dependent on their children at the same time as grandchildren are moving away from the parental home and starting their own families. In 1971, the average age of the grandchildren was 19, with less than 25% of them married. At T-2 the majority of the grandchildren (average age 33) had married and started families. Many G3 respondents volunteered comments regarding changes they experienced in their relationships with parents, brought about by the birth of their own children, suggesting they had become more tolerant and understanding of their parents and grandparents, now that they too faced the problems and joys of raising a new generation.

The data on perceptions of change (Fig. 2) support these expectations, though there are some surprises. The most general trend in these data reflects what might be called an "optimistic reconstruction of intergenerational history". Summing over the six intergenerational relationships represented in this figure, over 40% of the total sample reported that the relationship had "improved considerably" or "improved somewhat", while only 12% perceived that it had "declined somewhat" or "declined considerably". Such optimistic reconstructions may or may not be related to reality, in terms of actual T-1 vs T-2 comparisons regarding the quality of the relationships (as will be discussed in the next section). But these assessments are nonetheless important as perceptions; the widespread belief that intergenerational relationships in these families have improved in the past 13-14 years suggests an important indication of these respondents' investment in intergenerational bonds, and their optimism concerning the family as an interpersonal resource.

The generational contrasts in these perceptions of change are of interest. As might be expected, the youngest generation perceived the greatest change in intergenerational relationships, in terms both of improvement and decline. From column 5 of Fig. 2, 61% of the G3s reported that the relationship with their parents (G2s) had improved, with less than 9% perceiving decline. With their grandparents, 28% reported improvement; an equal amount (28%) perceived some decline.

The G2 parents, like their children, perceived improvement in the G2-G3 relationship over the past 14 years (column 4 of Fig. 2); 55% of the G2s reported

PERCEPTIONS OF CHANGE IN RELATIONSHIP

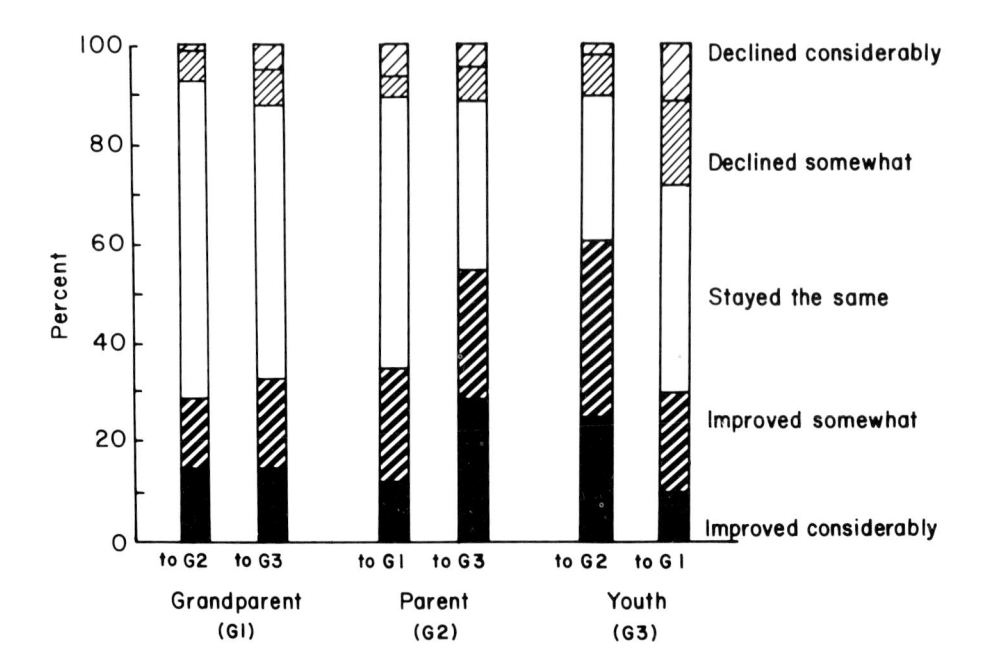

Fig. 2. Perception of improvement in relationship with other generation members; percentage figures report "improved considerably" or "improved somewhat". G1, grandparents' perception; G2, parents' perception; G3, grandchildren's perception.

that their relationship with their study child (G3) had improved either somewhat or considerably, compared to only 10% who said it had declined. This perception of improvement may reflect their experience of decline in intergeneration conflict following adolescence.

The majority of the G2s (column 3) also reported optimistically concerning change in their relationship with their aging parents (G1s) since 1971: nine out of ten (90%) perceived either improvement *or* no change, with 35% reporting improvement, and only 10% reporting decline. This may be an interesting example of perceptual distortion, as will be discussed later with regard to actual T-1 *vs* T-2 score comparisons.

The grandparents, by contrast, reported far less change in their relationships with their children and grandchildren. With regard to their own children (G2s, column 1), 60% noted that the relationship had stayed the same, *vs* 7% who reported a decline and 33% an improvement. They reported a similar lack of change in their relationships with study grandchildren (column 2). Despite the major social and developmental changes which have occurred over the past 14 years in the lives of the G3s, 57% of their grandparents said the relationship was about the same, compared to 30% who reported an improvement and 13% who perceived a decline.

Longitudinal Trends in Actual Reports of Intergenerational Affect

Respondents' *perceptions* of change can be compared, in this longitudinal design, with *actual* changes between T-1 and T-2 in scores reflecting the intergenerational relationship. These too are perceptions, but they are perceptions assessed at two points in time. The construct measured in this analysis is *affectual solidarity*, defined as the positive sentiments expressed by one generation member about the other (Bengtson and Schrader 1981). This is operationalized in the USC study as the sum of six questions: closeness, communication, perceived similarity, getting along with, understanding him/her, and he/she understanding you. Each question is answered on a six-point scale; the summated scale thus ranges from 6 to 36.

Figure 3 presents the 1971-1985 comparisons for the grandparents, parents and grandchildren in this sample. The major finding is that most respondents

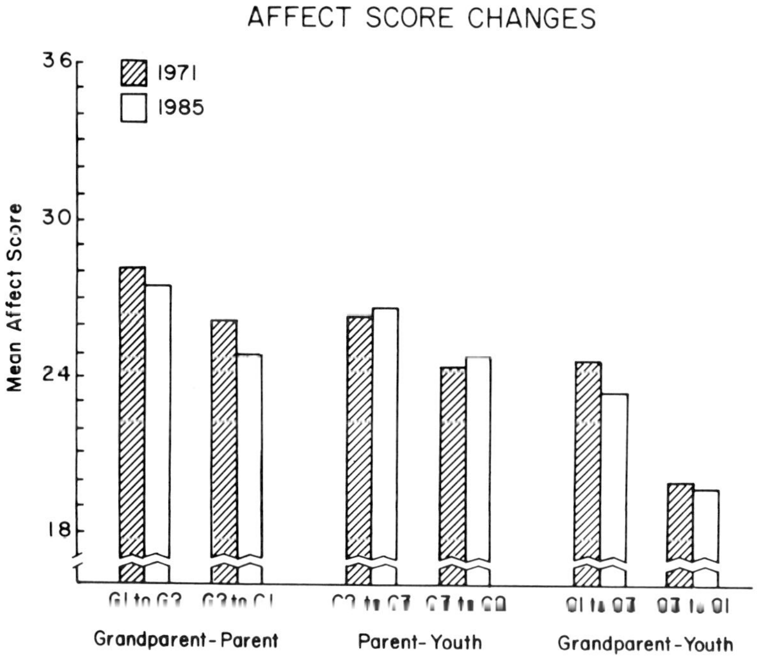

Fig. 3. Actual affect score changes between generational dyads, 1971 *vs* 1985. (1971: shaded column; 1985: unshaded column)

appeared to report about the same high levels of solidarity as they did more than a decade earlier. A score of 15 represents the mid-point of the scale; all the 1985 mean scores for each of the six intergenerational dyads were above this level.

However, some decreases in affectual solidarity scores should be noted. Most striking is the decrease in affect between G1 parents and G2 children over the 14-year time span (columns 1 and 2 of Fig. 2; t-test $P>.05$ and $P>.01$, respectively). Perhaps this decline in our sample groups reflects the effects of increased dependency of aging parents on the perceptions of affectual solidarity between generations. Feelings of "burden" (E. M. Brody 1985) which sometimes surface among caregiving children, and decreased health and independence among elder family members (Zarit *et al.* 1980) may adversely affect perceptions of the quality of affect. (On the other hand it could be argued that dependency would increase levels of affect, a rekindling of feelings reflecting filial piety; this interpretation is not supported by the data.)

In addition both grandparents and grandchildren (columns 5 and 6 of Fig. 3, $P>.01$ and $P>.05$, respectively) evidenced decreases between 1971 and 1985 in affect. We are examining whether this too may be related to the increased dependency of the oldest generation. However, another analysis of these data suggests that structural changes may also have had an adverse effect (Miller *et al.* 1985): one grandmother said, "My grandchildren do not visit me or have anything to do with me. I love them, but due to their father divorcing their mother, they shut me out of their lives." Another frequent comment was that geographical moves created long-distance relationships which were difficult to maintain.

There was a slight increase in G2-G3 affect scores for both generations over the 14-year period (columns 3 and 4) but neither was statistically significant. Contrary to our expectations, resolution of potential "adolescent rebellion" and effects of emerging adult independence are not reflected in the 1971-85 affect data comparisons.

The contrast between these "actual" affect comparisons over time and the perception of changes in intergenerational relationships (Fig. 2) is instructive. The "optimistic construction of intergenerational history", however real it may be in the perceptions of these respondents, is not supported by four of the six intergenerational dyads in comparing actual scale scores. This finding must be considered in the context of the generally high affectual intergenerational solidarity reported by respondents at both times of measurement: increment over already high scores may be unlikely.

Are these respondents "biased", engaging in wish fulfilment concerning the strength of their intergenerational bonds? Perhaps; but if so, the bias is consistent over time. And that, perhaps, is the major message of these preliminary findings.

In so far as these findings are generalizable, family members evaluate intergenerational bonds positively, perceive changes to be in the positive direction and—with two exceptions—are remarkably stable in their 14-year evaluations concerning intergenerational affect.

In evaluating these data in the light of alternate futures, it seems clear that the continuity of intergenerational bondedness is substantial, despite changes in marital status and residence; and that the evaluation of intergenerational affect is high—perhaps astonishingly so. Though conflict between generations may be inevitable, and though there are many pressures which appear to work against intergenerational bondedness in a highly mobile, individualistic society, extrapolation to the twenty-first century of these longitudinal data suggest that intergenerational solidarity is a factor which must be considered more seriously than it has been in the past.

Multiple Roles and Multiple Problems

Other recent research has emphasized the diversity of roles in contemporary multigenerational families, their functional and perceived importance to family members, and the way the timing of their entry and exit affects intergenerational interaction. Each of these issues suggests some problems faced by contemporary families, as well as the inevitability of negotiation in the unfolding biographies of families changing through time (Bengtson and Treas 1980).

One example is research carried out by Victor Marshall and Carolyn Rosenthal documenting the multiplicity of roles, often unacknowledged by members, in multigenerational kinship units. One important role is "kinkeeping" (Rosenthal 1985). Over two-thirds of their 458 families were able to name someone who carried out that function; 74% of those so designated were females. Another is the "head of the family" role (Rosenthal and Marshall 1986) which was assigned by 80% of families (mostly to a male). Other family roles as well were identified by their respondents: job broker; economic advisor; counsellor in advice and comfort. The pervasiveness of these roles, seldom explicitly acknowledged in discussions of modern families, and their salience to individuals interviewed, are indicators that contemporary family organization is a complex and engaging enterprise, providing important psychosocial meanings for individuals.

Another study, concerning grandparenthood and its negotiation in the context of non-normative timing, is suggestive of the consequences of increasing longevity, at least in some North American families (Burton and Bengtson 1985). The design of this study involved comparisons between "on-time" grandmothers (age 37-55) and "early" grandmothers (age 27-32), sampled among black families in south central Los Angeles. The "early" grandmothers were contacted through physician records of teenage pregnancies—the young mothers in this subsample ranged from 11 to 19 years, with a median age of 15. In one of the families six generations were interviewed, from the 14-year-old new mother to the 91-year-old great-great-great-grandmother. The results of this study indicate the complexity of role negotiation and identity in multigenerational families—from the 29-year-old who denied her new status on the grounds that she was "much too young" to be a grandmother, to the 54-year-old great-grandmother who took a much younger boyfriend in an attempt to demonstrate her youthfulness (to the dismay of her progeny). With four, five and six generations still living in interaction with each other—a trend which is increasingly prevalent, and which will likely be characteristic of the twenty-first century—both the opportunity for increased mutual support and the chance of age-role conflict are characteristics which must be considered in tomorrow's families.

Diversity in the grandparental role represents a third perspective on emergent family themes. A recent study by Cherlin and Furstenberg (1985) presents an analysis of grandparental styles in a nationally representative sample. The modal pattern among their 510 respondents involved "active" grandparenting—high on parent-like influence and high on intergenerational exchange of help. They further identify on the basis of their scales five types of grandparents: the passive (29% in their sample); the detached (26%); the influential (19%); the supportive (17%); and the authoritative (9%). This very diversity, in a social role which is more common than at any previous point in human history, suggests the need for greater examination of the consequences of this family bond.

Finally, research on the multigenerational effects of divorce (and remarriage) provides another indication of the complexity and strength of what Hagestad (1985) terms the "vertical bond" in family life. Studies by Johnson (1985), Aldous (1985) and Hagestad et al. (1982), as well as Cherlin and Furstenberg (1985), note the special salience of intergenerational relationships in the context of divorce, a factor not often considered in discussions of this topic. This is not to suggest that grandparent-grandchild relationships compensate for broken parent-child relations, or to ignore the plight of "non-custodial" grandparents who wish for more contact with grandchildren, a topic which has received deserving publicity recently (Bengtson and Robertson 1985).

Each of these analyses of roles, change and negotiation suggests the importance of kinship patterns in a rapidly changing society. Not only is the family "here to stay" (Baine 1976) as a societal institution, but also, its importance to individuals is becoming increasingly documented by contemporary social scientists, and most of the data accumulated to date points to the salience of intergenerational bonds in dealing with change.

This is not to deny that families have their troubles nor to say that the negotiation of changing roles, expectations and dependencies is a simple matter. Indeed, as Bengtson and Kuypers (1986) have suggested, problems facing the aging family, compared to other challenges to family functioning, may be especially difficult for members to resolve. The problems a family encounters in caring for a dependent parent may in part reflect decades of conflict between parent-child or sibling dyads. More research is needed to document the challenges families face and the strategies they attempt to employ (whether successful or unsuccessful) in dealing with problems of aging. This is an important research agenda for the 1990s and beyond.

But the point is that family resources *are* important in considering the consequences of any alternative future scenario. This is true particularly at the microsocial level, focusing on the effects on individuals and their immediate social world of social change. It may be equally true that families are buffers, cushioning the impact of technology, economic and political alterations, styles of thinking. It may be that families are sources of frustration, guilt, disappointment. Certainly they are symbolic mediators, influencing changing individuals in changing societies to construct meaning out of events beyond their control.

CONCLUSION

The purpose of this paper has been to explore some sociological perspectives on aging, families and the future. It was noted that seven demographic trends—primary among them increased longevity and decreased fertility—have led to something of a demographic revolution regarding the elderly in the twentieth century. These trends have led to conventional beliefs that the elderly are increasingly vulnerable to the forces of social change in the twenty-first century, and that their families may be overburdened in attempts to care for their dependencies. These conventional beliefs were examined in light of contemporary sociological data about intergenerational relations and aging, which suggest the viability of intergenerational relationships as perceived by family members, and the multiplicity of intergenerational roles which might mediate societal change.

What are the implications of these findings for policymakers and practitioners interested in enhancing the competencies of the aged and their support networks?

For better or for worse, the family is an important source of competence in aging. I suggested earlier that the most general humanistic goal of those of us interested in aging involves *enhancing the competence of aging individuals and their social support networks*. What do the trends, scenarios and research data as reviewed in this paper suggest about addressing this goal?

First, we should recognize the universal strain toward continuity, in the face of the equal ubiquity of change. In reviewing the four future scenarios summarized above, one can be impressed by the degree of continuity with the present which is evident, to varying degrees, in each. Their difference lies in the contrasting emphasis they place on four existing trends in today's social systems: continued growth, continued stagnation, continued authoritarianism, continued transformation. Before we withdraw in panic or distaste from any vision of the future, we should perhaps take solace in the fact that there will be continuity with the past, and with the present, as we experience it.

But second, and more importantly, we who are interested in aging and in families must acknowledge the continuity that is inherent in every individual, and exhibited by almost every family system, in the face of change. The elderly are survivors, if nothing else. They have coped. They have resources that have made them competent in the past and can enable them to make competent adjustments to change in the present and future. One of the emergent lessons from James Birren's (1985) recent research on autobiographies is the astonishing chronicle of coping with diversity that is evident from his respondents' reminiscences. As professionals we must acknowledge, and build upon, that continuity of competence. Even the most frail of our elderly can exhibit it; so too will we, as we age.

The same is true with families, as they negotiate the dependencies of an aged elder. At times the indignities of aging create a "Social Breakdown Syndrome", which as Bengtson and Kuypers (1986) have noted applies to families as well; but with proper support and/or intervention this vicious circle can be reversed, with the family learning to expand its competence in dealing with even the most traumatic dependency, as seen in Alzheimer's disease (Zarit *et al.* 1980).

Finally, we should not fail to recognize the opportunities and the delights of change. Of course, the twenty-first century will present challenges and readjustments. Facing an uncertain future makes it difficult to see the opportunities that may be presented. But, as my wife's 105-year-old grandfather, born in 1869, remarked once, "If I had known how easy it would be to drive a truck, I wouldn't have wasted all that time learning how to control a wagon with four horses."

ACKNOWLEDGEMENTS

This paper reflects contributions of many colleagues whom I want gratefully to acknowledge. Several sections are based on papers presented elsewhere, with Marlee Campbell (Bengtson and Campbell 1985) and Dale Dannefer (Dannefer and Bengtson 1987). I am especially indebted to Clement Bezold and his colleagues at the Institute for Alternative Futures. I am grateful to Richard Miller for assistance in data analysis, to Linda Hall for editorial and clerical assistance, and to Peter Uhlenberg, Victor Marshall, Carolyn Rosenthal, Patricia Passuth, David Featherman, Bert Adams, Charles Longino, Alice Rossi and Andrew Cherlin for comments on earlier drafts.

REFERENCES

Aldous, J. (1985). Parent–adult child relations as affected by the grandparent status. *In* "Grandparenthood" (V. L. Bengtson and J. Robertson, eds) pp. 117-132. Sage Publications, Beverly Hills.

Baine, M. J. (1976). "The family: here to stay". Duke University Press, Durham, North Carolina.

Bengtson, V. L. and Campbell, M. (1985). Aging within the family: current trends, future scenarios. Paper presented at the 14th Annual Meeting of the Canadian Gerontological Society, Hamilton, Ontario, Canada, October 19, 1985.

Bengtson, V. L. and Kuypers, J. A. (1986). The family support cycle: psychosocial issues in the aging family. *In* "Life span and change in a gerontological perspective" (J. M. A. Munnichs, P. Mussen and E. Olbrich, eds) pp. 61-77. Academic Press, New York.
Bengtson, V. L. and Robertson, J. (eds) (1985). "Grandparenthood". Sage Publications, Beverly Hills.
Bengtson, V. L. and Schrader, S. S. (1981). Parent-child relations. *In* "Handbook of research instruments in social gerontology" (D. Mangen and W. Peterson, eds) Vol. 2, pp. 115-185. University of Minnesota Press, Minneapolis.
Bengtson, V. L. and Treas, J. (1980). The changing family context of mental health and aging. *In* "Handbook of mental health and aging" (R. B. Sloane and J. E. Birren, eds) pp. 400-428. Prentice-Hall Inc., Englewood Cliffs, New Jersey.
Bengtson, V. L., Mangen, D. J. and Landry, P. H. Jr. (1984). The multi-generation family: concepts and findings. *In* "Intergenerational relationships" (V. Garms-Homolov, E. M. Hoerning and D. Schaeffer, eds) pp. 63-79. C. J. Holgreve, Inc., New York.
Bezold, C. (1984). "Pharmacy in the 21st century: planning for an uncertain future." Institute for Alternative Futures, Alexandria, Virginia.
Bezold, C. and Peck, J. (1984). Preparing for the 2nd pharmaceutical age. *Pharmaceutical Age* **71** (May), 21-23.
Binstock, R. H. (1985a). Health care of the aging: trends, dilemmas, and prospects for the year 2000. *In* "Aging 2000: our health care destiny" (C. M. Gaitz *et al.*, eds) pp. 3-16. Springer Verlag, New York.
Binstock, R. H. (1985b). The oldest old: A fresh perspective or compassionate ageism revisited? *Milbank Memorial Fund Quarterly* **63**, 420-451.
Birren, J. E. (1985). Health care in the 21st century: the social and ethical context. *In* "Aging 2000: our health care destiny" (C. M. Gaitz *et al.*, eds) pp. 381-390. Springer Verlag, New York.
Brody, E. M. (1985). Parent care as a normative family stress. *Gerontol.* **25**, 19-29.
Brody, H. M. (1981). Health and its social implications. *In* Aging: a challenge to science and social policy" (A. J. J. Gilmore, A. Svanberg, M. Marois, W. M. Beattie and J. Piotrowski, eds) "Medicine and Social Sciences", Vol. II, pp. 189-201. Oxford University Press, Oxford.
Brody, H. M. (1985). Tomorrow and tomorrow and tomorrow: toward squaring the suffering curve. *In* "Aging 2000: our health care destiny (C. M. Gaitz *et al.*, eds) pp. 371-380. Springer Verlag, New York.
Burton, L. C. and Bengtson, V. L. (1985). Black grandmothers: issues of timing and continuity in roles. *In* "Grandparenthood" (V. L. Bengtson and J. Robertson, eds) pp. 304-338. Sage Publications, Beverly Hills.
Caplow, T., Bahr, H. M., Chadwick, B. A., Hill, R. and Williamson, M. H. (1982). The myth of the declining family. "Middletown families: fifty years of change and continuity" pp. 320-327. The University of Minnesota Press, Minneapolis.
Cherlin, A. (1978). Remarriage as an incomplete institution. *Am. J. Sociol.* **84**, 634-650.
Cherlin, A. (1981). "Marriage, divorce, remarriage". Johns Hopkins Press, Baltimore.
Cherlin, A. and Furstenberg, F. Jr. (1983). The American family in the year 2000. *The Futurist* (June).
Cherlin, A. and Furstenberg, F. Jr. (1985). Styles and strategies of grandparenting. *In* "Grandparenthood" (V. L. Bengtson and J. Robertson, eds) pp. 97-116, Sage Publications, Beverly Hills.
Dannefer, D. and Bengtson, V. L. (1987). Families, work and aging: implications of disordered cohort flow for the 21st century. *In* "Health in aging: sociological issues and policy directions" (R. Ward and S. Tobin, eds) Springer Verlag, New York.

Day, A. (1984). Kinship networks and informal social support in the later years. Paper presented at the Berlin Conference in Canberra, Australia.
De Vos, S. and Ruggles, S. (1985). The demography of kinship and the life course. *Ann. Rev. Sociol.* **12**, 136-148.
Dunkle, R. E., Haug, R. and Rosenberg, M. (1984). "Communications technology and the elderly: issues and forecasts". Springer Verlag, New York.
Etzioni, A. (1977). The family: is it obsolete? *J. Curr. Social Iss.* **14** (winter), 4-9.
Fowles, D. (1984). The numbers game: a look at the future. *Aging* (Sept.-Oct.), 46-47.
Fries, J. F. (1980). Aging, natural death, and the compression of morbidity. *N. Engl. J. Med.* **303**, 130-135.
Gaitz, C. M., Niederehe, G. and Wilson, N. (eds) (1984). "Aging 2000: our health care destiny". Springer Verlag, New York.
Haber, P. A. L. (1985). Technology in aging. Donald P. Kent Award Lecture presented at the Gerontological Society of America Annual Meeting in New Orleans, November 25, 1985.
Hagestad, G. O. (1981). Problems and promises in the social psychology of intergenerational relations. *In* "Aging: stability and change in the family" (J. G. March, ed.) pp. 11-46. Academic Press, New York.
Hagestad, G. O. (1982). Divorce: the family ripple effect. *Generations* **6** (winter), 24-25.
Hagestad, G. O. (1984). Twentieth century family patterns: a guide for the twenty-first? Paper presented at the annual meetings of the Eastern Sociological Society, Boston.
Hagestad, G. O. (1985). Older women in intergenerational relations. *In* "The physical and mental health of aged women" (M. R. Hallig *et al.*, eds) pp. 137-151. Springer Verlag, New York.
Hagestad, G. O., Smyer, M. A. and Stierman, K. I. (1982). Parent-child relations in adulthood: the impact of divorce in middle age. *In* "Parenthood: psychodynamic perspectives" (R. S. Cohen *et al.* eds). Guilford Press, New York.
Hammel, E. A., Wachter, K. W. and McDaniel, C. K. (1981). The kin of the aged in AD 2000: the chickens come home to roost. *In* "Aging: social change" (S. B. Kiesler *et al.*, eds) pp. 11-39. Academic Press, New York.
Hareven, T. (1978). "Transition: the family and the life course in perspective". Academic Press, New York.
Johnson, C. L. (1985). Grandparenting options in divorcing families: an anthropological perspective. *In* "Grandparenthood" (V. L. Bengtson and J. Robertson, eds) pp. 81-97. Sage Publications, Beverly Hills.
Kahn, H. (1981). "The coming boom". Putnam, New York.
Knipscheer, C. P. M. (1982). Het Familie Vetband Als Kontekst Van De Levensloop. *Tydscht V. Gerontologie end Gerialtie* **13**, 232-242.
Lasch, C. (1979). "The culture of narcissism." Warner, New York.
Longman, P. (1985). Justice between generations. *Atlantic Monthly* (June), 73-78.
Lynd, R. S. and Lynd, H. M. (1929). "Middletown: a study in American culture". Harcourt Brace Jovanovich, New York.
Meadows, D. H., Meadows, D. L., Randers, J. and Behrens, W. W. III. (1972). "The Limits to Growth". Signet, New York.
Miller, R., Schneider, J. and Bengtson, V. (1985). Perceptions of change in parent-child relationships over 13 years. Paper presented at the annual meeting of the Gerontological Society of America.
Mills, C. W. (1959). "The sociological imagination". Oxford University Press, New York.

Myers, G. C. (1985). Aging and worldwide population change. *In* "Handbook of aging and the social sciences" (R. Binstock and E. Shanas, eds). Van Nostrand Reinhold, New York.
Naisbitt, J. (1982). "Megatrends: ten new directions transforming our lifes." Warner, New York.
Naroll, R. (1983). "The moral order". Sage Publications, Beverly Hills.
NCHS (1982). Vital Statistics of The United States, 1982. Life Tables. Vol. II, Section 6.
Pedersen, W. (1984). New report flags a revolution in demographics. *Public Relations Journal* **19** (October) 19-23.
Preston, S. (1984). Children and the elderly: divergent paths for America's dependents. *Demography* **21**(4), 435-457.
Riley, M. W. (1985). The changing older woman: a cohort perspective. *In* "The physical and mental health of aged women" (M. R. Haug *et al.*, eds) Ch. 1, pp. 3-15. Springer Verlag, New York.
Rosenthal, C. J. (1985). Kinkeeping in the familial division of labor. *J. Marriage Fam.* **47**(4), 965-974.
Rosenthal, C. J. and Marshall, V. W. (1986). The head of the family: social meaning and structural variability. *Can. J. Sociol.* **11**(2) (in press).
Schneider, E. L. and Brody, J. A. (1983). Aging, natural death, and the compression of morbidity. *N. Engl. J. Med.* **309**, 854-855.
Sell, R. R. and DeJong, G. F. (1985). Social structure and childlessness in the U.S.: 1970-1980. Paper presented at the Annual Meetings of the American Sociological Association in Washington D.C.
Shanas, E. (1979). Social myth as hypothesis: the case of family relations of old people. *Gerontologist* **19**(1), 3-9.
Skolnick, M. H. (1984). Technology in health care for and by the aged. *In* "Communications technology and the elderly: issues and forecasts" (R. E. Dunkle, *et al.*, eds) pp. 11-24. Springer Verlag, New York.
Somers, A. R. (1985). Toward a female gerontocracy? Current social trends. *In* "The physical and mental health of aged women" (M. R. Haug *et al.*, eds) pp. 16-26. Springer Verlag, New York.
Sussman, M. B. (1985). The family life of old people. *In* "Handbook of aging and the social sciences" (2nd edn) (R. H. Binstock and E. Shanas, eds) pp. 415-449. Van Nostrand Reinhold, New York.
Toffler, A. (1980). "The third wave". Bantam, New York.
Treas, J. and Bengtson, V. L. (1986). Family in later years. *In* "Handbook on marriage and the family" (M. Sussman and S. Steinmetz, eds). Plenum Press, New York.
Treas, J. and Van Hilst, A. (1976). Marriage and remarriage rates among older Americans. *Gerontologist* **16**, 132-136.
Uhlenberg, P. (1986). Aging: a demographic perspective. *In* "Modern pioneers: an interdisciplinary view of the aged" (P. Silverman, ed.). Indiana University Press, Indiana.
Uhlenberg, P. and Chew, K. S. (1986). The changing phase of remarriage in the life course. *In* "Family relations in life course perspective" (D. Kertzer, ed.) JAI Press, New York.
Uhlenberg, P. and Myers, M. A. P. (1981). Divorce and the elderly. *Gerontology* **21**, 276-290.
US Senate Special Committee on Aging in Conjunction with the AARP (1985). "Aging America: trends and projections".
Zarit, S. H., Reever, K. E. and Bach-Peterson, J. (1980). Relatives of the impaired elderly: correlates of feelings of burden. *Gerontologist* **20**(6), 649-655.

Discussion

Roth: Do you have anything to say to the biologist with respect to what might be the reason for the increase in the mortality gap between the genders?

Bengtson: Twenty years ago it was predicted that the mortality gap would grow smaller, because more women were smoking, more women were entering the work force, they would suffer more stress and so the gap between males and females would decrease. And that did not happen. I think that this is at present an example of a genetic effect which sociologists cannot explain.

Holliday: Are there no contradictions in the demographic trends? If more women are entering the work force, if they are entering a career, that often means that they delay having children, and that means that the gap between generations is increasing.

Bengtson: The issue of employment and delayed childbearing is an important trend and it reverses the trend towards early childbearing in the 1950s and 1960s. I think that we can say that for most of us our grandchildren will spend a longer period of their lives as great-grandparents than our grandparents lived as grandparents. I do not believe that this creates more of a socio-psychological "gap" between generations. On the contrary: my belief is that the greater timespan of protracted interaction between generations will result in greater psychosocial investment in the family. Delayed childbearing and decreased fertility are less relevant than increased longevity—though the number of grandchildren per surviving grandparent may indeed pose some problems.

Contributions to a Multi-level Model of Intervention in Psychogeriatrics

M. Bergener, E. U. Kranzhoff and J. Husser

Rheinische Landesklinik, Cologne, FRG

Keywords
Psychogeriatrics; Evaluation; Intervention; Therapy; Depression; Life events; Network; Social support.

In the 1970s, research in gerontology witnessed a shift of emphasis, moving away from more theoretical projects and closer towards the considerations of general practice: how should therapeutic interventions be designed, implemented and evaluated. This shift—referred to euphemistically by some as a revolution—basically took up a subject that has long been familiar in psychogeriatric research and in medicine in general. What was new was the extended time-frame of reference, which no longer focused just on crisis situations, and the associated need to single out specific content domains of intervention, which led to terms such as optimization, prevention, restoration, management (Fig. 1). There is general agreement on what elements should be considered when determining

1. Explicate objectives	Evaluation:
2. Designate target population	hypotheses
3. Posit theory of change effects	generating
4. Develop treatment plan	
5. Implement treatment programme	
6. Develop research design to study implementation and impact	Evaluation: hypotheses testing

Fig. 1. Elements of intervention strategy.

Dimensions in Aging
ISBN 0 12 090162 5

1. Evaluation as applied science
   (e.g. Guttentag and Struening)
2. Evaluation as systems management
   (e.g. Alkin, Provus)
3. Evaluation as decision theory
   (e.g. Edwards, Guttentag and Snapper)
4. Evaluation as assessment of progress toward goals
   (e.g. Tyler)
5. Evaluation as jurisprudence
   (e.g. Levine)
6. Evaluation as rational empiricism
   (e.g. Scriven)
7. Evaluation as description or portrayal
   (e.g. Stake)

Fig. 2. Alternative conceptions of evaluation.

strategies of medical and social intervention. Less well defined, in our opinion, is the role played by "evaluation" in the process of intervention: a role that is certainly determined by the researcher's specific conceptualization of evaluation. In order to illustrate the concept of evaluation on which the research efforts of our group are based, we shall introduce the systematization (Fig. 2) of Glass and Ellett (1980). The authors subsume their reviewed literature under seven different conceptualizations of evaluation.

EVALUATION AS APPLIED SCIENCE
(e.g. Guttentag and Struening 1975)

An experimental or quasi-experimental design is adopted in an attempt to make a causal analysis of the effects of an intervention.

EVALUATION AS SYSTEMS MANAGEMENT
(e.g. Provus 1971)

According to this definition of evaluation, the main objective should be to provide rational decision-making aids for executive and administrative bodies. Rational is defined much in the Weberian sense as that which serves the aims of the system. Critics of this approach have thus concentrated on this last characteristic, which tends, at least in practice—if not on theoretical grounds—to highlight the smooth and efficient running of programmes etc.

EVALUATION AS DECISION THEORY
(e.g. Edwards *et al.*, 1975)

The problems of this concept of evaluation as an applied statistical decision theory—in a sense the counterpart of the last approach—are first, that the expensive analyses are of a non-committal nature for decision-making bodies, and secondly, the evaluation is confused with terms like decision, measurement, planning.

EVALUATION AS ASSESSMENT OF PROGRESS TOWARD GOALS

Historically, this concept of evaluation reaches farthest back. It is particularly popular in educational sciences and was the favoured approach under the Kennedy administration as a result of the influence of Tyler (1949). Its main disadvantages are that it fails to evaluate the goals and thus does not consider alternative goals. In psychiatry, this approach gained popularity particularly through the Goal Attainment Scaling of Kiersuk and Lund (1975).

EVALUATION AS JURISPRUDENCE
(e.g. Levine 1978)

This conception of evaluation is
> patterned after juridical procedures. An evaluation question is posed as though it were a question submitted to a court of law. Advocats for both sides of the question are selected and made adversaries. The merits of both positions are argued in front of a jury or judge; rules of the common law control submission of evidence; and a verdict is rendered.

As far as we know, however, this conceptualization of evaluation has contributed little to the stimulation of empirical research in the psychosocial field. It reduces the problem of evaluation to simple yes or no decisions, which, as in the forensic model, are represented by pro and contra advocates; it is, apart from the cost intensity, extremely dependent on the competence of the respective advocates.

EVALUATION AS RATIONAL EMPIRICISM
(e.g. Scriven 1967)

This approach, which resembles most tightly to what is commonly thought of as evaluation, is best described by Scriven's own definition:

> [Evaluation] consists simply in the gathering and combining of performance data with a weighted set of criterial scales to yield either comparative or numerical ratings, and in the justification of (a) the data-gathering instruments, (b) the weightings, and (c) the selection of criteria. (Scriven 1967, p. 40).

In practical evaluation work this approach frequently results in an eclectic procedure, likewise applying comparative experimental design, need analysis, goals analysis, composite outcome measures and the like; the determination of the evaluation design itself is a meta-evaluation problem depending on fundamental purposes and situational possibilities.

EVALUATION AS DESCRIPTION OR PORTRAYAL
(e.g. Stake 1975, 1976)

According to the exponent of this approach (Stake 1975), this concept of evaluation aims at ensuring as complete as possible a description of the programme: its activities, its effects and of the associated expectations and appraisals. A programme is seen as a complex process and not as the sum of rather arbitrarily selected variables. Stake typifies most other evaluation approaches as "preordinate" and compares them with his approach, which he labels "responsive". Accordingly, most preordinate concepts of evaluation prefer:

A formal declaration of objectives;
Standardized tests;
Standards oriented to the programme personnel;
A classical research report.

In contrast, because of the constantly changing situation, a responsive evaluation allows the investigator to redetermine constantly what is to be described and which central question is to be investigated; Stake emphasizes:

The actual process;
Direct and indirect observation and ideas from participants in the programme;
The pluralism of the various groups' standards;
The constant consideration of the participants' informational needs;
An adequate adaptation of communication media and of reporting.

Some problematic aspects of this approach are the low accuracy of the measurements that can be made, the poor representativeness of the samples and the limited generalizability of the results. This approach, which is preferred by our working group, concentrates on finding ways of solving problems that occur with certain interventions and does not aim at making generalized statements on interventions or programmes in general. Stake visualizes his process of evaluation as 12 main terms forming the points of a clock; after one circuit the process can lead into a new circuit like a spiral (Fig. 3).

Multi-level Model of Intervention in Psychogeriatrics 267

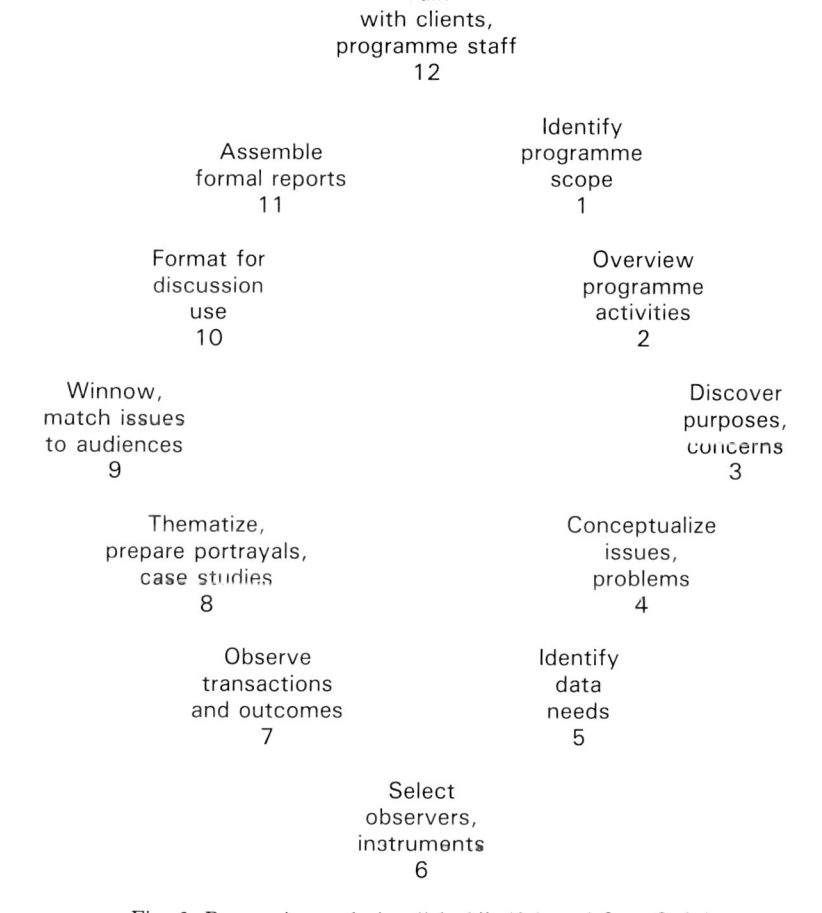

```
                    Talk
                 with clients,
                programme staff
                      12

                                        Identify
          Assemble                     programme
        formal reports                   scope
             11                            1

         Format for                      Overview
         discussion                     programme
            use                          activities
            10                              2

  Winnow,                                          Discover
 match issues                                      purposes,
 to audiences                                      concerns
      9                                               3

       Thematize,                       Conceptualize
   prepare portrayals,                     issues,
      case studies                        problems
           8                                 4

            Observe                    Identify
          transactions                   data
          and outcomes                  needs
              7                           5

                      Select
                    observers,
                   instruments
                        6
```

Fig. 3. Responsive evalution "clock". (Adapted from Stake).

Since a responsive evaluation is, by definition, closely related to a particular institution, it follows that it is more difficult to present excerpts from empirical investigations that are of more general interest than would be the case with a preordinate evaluation.

The general plan of the project ("Evaluation of Gerontopsychiatric Interventions" ("Evaluation gerontopsychiatrischer Interventionen") Bergener *et al.* 1984, unpublished research report) which is the subject of the following report, can be formulated as follows: While the primary objective of the project was to arrive at an unprejudiced—yet not unqualified—description and analysis of the therapeutic practice of a psychogeriatric unit, two main perspectives became evident in the process of analysing the objectives and interests of those who participated in, or were the subject of, the project (Fig. 4).

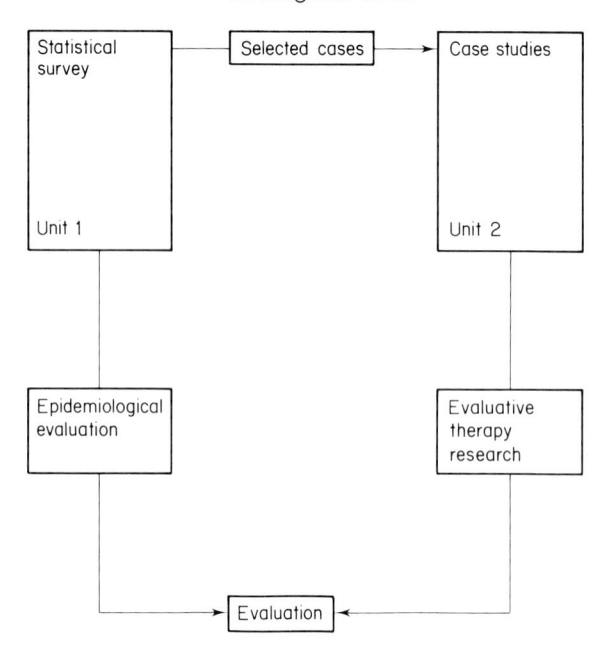

Fig. 4. General plan of project "Evaluation of psychogeriatric interventions".

Subject matter	Statistical analysis of total of patients 65 years and over
	Concerning 1. Personal data of subjective and objective life circumstances 2. Data relevant to treatment course
Instruments	Documentation of treatment process Social data Patient self-rating Rating of patient by assessor Psychiatric evidence Somatic evidence Neurological evidence
Data analysis	1. Cross-tabulation by main diagnostic groups 2. Analyses of life events, social support systems and self-rated changes in perceived psychopathology
Level of action	1. Amelioration of clinical documentation system 2. Interdisciplinary guide for first contacts with patient

Fig. 5. The factors constituting Unit 1.

1. The first concentrated on the hospital as a whole and how it caters for a standard patient population. Of particular interest were questions such as where the patients came from, what happened to them in the hospital (patient management), and where they were finally discharged to. In Fig. 4, these questions are subsumed under Unit 1.
2. The second focused on the work on the ward; the main interest was to find an instrument for monitoring the course of therapy with which one could make a definite and early enough decision about individual patients, particularly for assessing gradual changes of depressive disorders in the course of treatment. These objectives and interests are summarized in Fig. 4 under Unit 2.

Figure 5 shows the factors constituting Unit 1. Included in the record were all newly admitted patients aged 65 and over. A documentation form developed by our research group was used, and Fig. 6 shows the breakdown into groups of variables. Of particular interest—especially considering the expected high proportion of depressive patients—were the areas: critical life events, social support system and social network. In this paper we concentrate on the influence of these constructs on an indicator of perceived changes in psychopathologically relevant areas. The aim of the analyses was to improve the clinical documentation system and, in particular, to make a more careful record of information on the social situation which might be of relevance to later interventions in the social environment.

Figure 6 presents an overview of the final version of the documentation form, which was modified several times after discussing details with the social workers and ward psychiatrists who were to be primarily responsible for the recordings. It can be seen that the block of somatic and neurologic–psychiatric variables is almost equally as large as the block of data on the social situation. The first set of data contains a fluctuating number of variables insofar as it included patient

1. Data concerning admission, treatment, discharge, illness history (37–90 variables)
2. Demographic data (4 variables)
3. Socioeconomic data (13 variables)
4. Living situation (19 variables)
5. Family network (19 variables)
6. Larger social network and social activities (41 variables)
7. Psychiatric and somatic illness history (14 variables)
8. Activities of daily living (5 variables)
9. Self-rated psychopathological status (16 variables)
10. Global appraisal of current situation (16 variables)
11. Expert psychopathological description (84 variables)
12. Expert somatic description (19 variables)
13. Expert neurological description (8 variables)

Fig. 6. Variables included in Unit 1.

Subject matter	Case studies of selected patients diagnosed depressive
	Concerning Therapy-dependent behaviour, using standardized instruments
Instruments	BF-S (Befindlichkeitsskala/general well-being and mood)
	D-S (Depression Scale)
	HAMD (Hamilton Depression Scale)
	CGI (Clinical Global Impression)
	NOSIE (Nurses' Observation Scale for Inpatient Evaluation)
	LSI I (Lebenszufriedenheits-Index/present life satisfaction)
	LSI II (Lebenszufriedenheits-Index/global life satisfaction)
Level of Analysis	1. Assessment of behavioural changes during course of therapy
	2. Comparison of self- and expert ratings
	3. Comparison of different expert groups
Level of action	1. Establishing individualized treatment plans
	2. Optimization of patient allocation

Fig. 7. Overview of the objectives, instruments and levels of analysis in Unit 2.

management, which was dependent on a high interindividual variation in the number of ward transfers.

Figure 7 shows a corresponding overview of the objectives, the instruments and the levels of analysis and action of Unit 2. The selection of instruments was naturally confronted with the chronic problem—particularly common outside English-speaking countries—that practically all kinds of recording instruments require further development before they can be applied reliably for persons aged 65 and over. The selection is thus to a great extent random, but not arbitrary. The main criterion was the instruments' practicability for this age group as established after discussions with clinical psychologists from this field. In concordance with the evaluation model briefly described above, the data were analysed not so much to provide a general statement on how reliably and validly changes in the course of therapy were portrayed, the object was much more modest: we were interested in finding out which type of rating scale (self-rating global/specific, expert rating by psychiatrist, global/specific, expert rating by nursing staff, global/specific) most faithfully portrayed the general course of

Table 1
Relating ICD numbers to diagnostic syndromes

Depressive syndrome (n=118/98)*	Psychoorganic syndrome (n=195/95)*	Paranoid syndrome (n=42/35)*
296.1.3.4	290.0-4.8.9	295.0-9
298.0	291.1.2	297.0-3.8.9
300.4.7	293.0.1.8.9	298.3.4
308.0	294.0.1.8.9	
309.0.1		
311		

*First number: total sample; second number: sample which could be included in the evaluation.

treatment of depressive patients under the concrete conditions of a specific institution. (The evaluation process thus far conforms to position 4, 5, and 6 of Stake's model of evaluation (see Fig. 3)).

We have described above how we define the term evaluation and have given an outline of the general design of a project that was performed in line with this definition. We should like to present some results of the analyses, starting with the first block, which was conceived as an epidemiological study of persons who make use of the health service. In the 1-year recording, a total 491 new admissions of patients aged over 65 were registered. These included 73 readmissions i.e. 418 different patients were treated at least once. At the end of the data collection, 104 patients (21%) had not yet been discharged. The average age of the patients was 74 years; 28% were men, and 72% were women.

Of these patients, 28% were suffering primarily from a depressive syndrome, 47% from an organic brain syndrome and 10% from a paranoid syndrome. The remaining 15% were given other diagnoses. Table 1 shows how these main syndromes were operationalized. There has been a long history of endeavours to identify the aetiologically relevant factors in the social networks of psychiatric patients. Our primary interest in this respect was to look into differential syndromes with a view to specific interventions in the social environment of aged patients.

With regard to the analysis of the social situation, sufficient information was available for 271 of the 418 patients included in this investigation. There are two main reasons for this considerable proportion of missing data (in 35% of patients). First, the social workers responsible for collecting data could not devote the necessary hours, and secondly, the type or severity of many patients' disorders made it impossible to carry out the examination in the necessary detail. Table 1 shows that only 17% of the groups of depressive and paranoid syndromes were affected by these missing data, while this was true for 51% of the group of organic brain syndromes.

We had more than 100 variables with which to describe the social situation

Table 2
Comparison of adjusted and unadjusted probability levels (from a total of 27 variables)

	P	Significance P unadjusted < 0.05	Significance P adjusted < 0.0002
Age	< 0.001	+++	NS
Sex	< 0.010	++	NS
Family contacts (quantitative)	< 0.001	+++	NS
Family contacts (quantitative)	< 0.050	+	NS
Membership organization	< 0.050	+	NS
Visit of psychiatrist	< 0.010	++	NS

of our psychogeriatric patients; we selected 27 variables referring to seven different areas in order to build up a differential picture of the social situation of patients suffering from either depressive, paranoid or organic brain syndromes. Using conventional statistical procedures, six of the 27 selected variables proved to be significantly related with the three syndrome groups at different levels of significance (Table 2). However, since one consequence of the high number of simultaneous χ^2 tests ($n=250$) was that α had to be adjusted to 0.0002 to give a significance level of 0.05, not one of the relationships reached this level. Because of these technical and statistical problems and also because of our more general objections to a blindly accepted myth of significance levels, we decided to base our interpretation on a measure of association, in this case the Pearson's association coefficient C (corrected for rows and columns). A number of these coefficients (a total 16) reached a level of 0.250, which is generally regarded in the literature as a substantial relationship between psychosocial variables.

A higher incidence of organic brain syndromes with increasing age was paralleled by a reduction of other syndromes. Depressive syndromes were much more common in the youngest group of elderly patients (see Appendix, Table A1). One point of criticism here is that the relevance of this relationship might be overestimated for two reasons; first, problems with regard to a differential diagnosis of depressions and dementias have still to be solved, and secondly, one has still to investigate the diagnostic habits in the case of primary diagnoses in later life. There were more men than women among the patients with organic brain syndromes, and more women than men among patients with depressive syndromes.

The weak relationship between diagnostic syndromes and marital status confirms clinical observations (as a self-fulfilling prophecy?) that unmarried persons are more common in the group with paranoid syndromes, and married persons among the depressives.

Just less than half the patients who provided analysable data on their social situation gave details on their financial situation. (No other variable had a higher proportion of missing data; the problem is by no means unknown in gerontological literature!) Of this group, one in six had an income that made them dependent on social welfare. There were slightly more depressives in this group. As might have been expected of persons aged 65 and over, three-quarters were educated only to an elementary school-leaving level. Patients with organic brain syndromes were overrepresented in this group; the same is more evident in the otherwise small group of persons who experienced a deterioration of their financial situation in the year before being admitted to hospital.

As for occupational categories, the greatest part were ordinary employees without managerial status; patients with paranoid syndromes were overrepresented here. The proportion of housewives, however, was high in the group of patients with depressive syndromes (see Appendix, Table A2).

With regard to the living situation, the specific situation of the depressive patients was particularly noticeable. They included an unexpectedly high number who did not live in rented accommodation but in their own house or appartment. If it is assumed that the living situation plays a supportive or obstructive role in the making and maintaining of social contacts, then our data suggest that depressive patients were in a particularly favourable position to build up a supportive social network (see Appendix, Table A3).

Patients from the group with organic brain syndromes reported more frequently than patients from the other two groups that they had no (living) children and thus no children nearby who could come to their assistance in times of difficulty. The contacts with their children were few and far between, and were mainly rated as negative and a nuisance. Depressive patients, on the other hand, had good and numerous contacts with their children, yet also experienced — perhaps for that very reason — negative events in the familial sphere (deaths, serious illnesses etc.) more often than patients from the other syndrome groups (see Appendix, Table A4).

Patients with organic brain syndromes also stated more frequently than expected that they had no contacts whatsoever with friends and acquaintances. It was particularly difficult to evaluate such contacts in the group of patients with paranoid syndromes. In agreement with the tendencies described above, it is once again the depressive patients who more often reported negative changes in the extended social network. Note, however, that only 20% of the entire group reported such negative changes. While the proportion of patients who were active members of a club was highest among the depressive patients — an unexpected finding, particularly in the light of clinical experience — the three syndrome groups did not differ as far as visits to old people's clubs were concerned (see Appendix, Table A5).

According to many gerontological studies, the visit to the doctor is the most common — and often the only — source of communication in the life of an old person (e.g. Lehr 1979). This also becomes evident in our sample: a total 70% reported that they regularly visit their GP. There were, however, no group-specific differences in this respect. The picture changes when the visits to a psychiatrist are analysed. While depressive and paranoid patients visit a psychiatrist more frequently than might be expected on the marginal conditions, the opposite is true for the patients with organic brain syndromes. This might reflect the negative stereotype view that there is generally no treatment for organic brain syndromes in old age (see Appendix, Table A6).

Many of the above tendencies appear to illustrate no more than commonplace clinical experience. Yet we advise caution before making such a conclusion; first, because the very aspects that are so commonplace and well known ought to have shown numerous relationships between the social situation and the selected psychiatric syndromes, e.g. with regard to living alone, satisfaction with the living situation, regular visits to the doctor, yet even trends were not found in statistical analysis. Secondly, we reported tendencies that go against clinical experience.

Even though the character of this study was to generate hypotheses, we nevertheless regard the tendencies for differentiating between syndromes as sufficiently important to argue for the inclusion of corresponding variables in a clinical documentation system, since they provide at least preliminary evidence for differential interventions in the patients' social environment.

As briefly reported in the overview of Unit 2, we included a total of eight rating scales in the weekly examinations of selected depressive psychogeriatric patients: two specific self-ratings, two self-ratings of current and general life satisfaction, two observer-rating scales for psychiatrists, and two observer-rating scales for the nursing staff (Table 3).

As none of these instruments was developed for the explicit use with persons 65 years and over, we computed coefficients of internal consistency, using the Kuder–Richardson formula 21, as an indicator of the reliability of the instruments

Table 3
Reliability (internal consistency) of applied rating scales

Scale	Reliability
Depression Rating Scale D-S (D-S') (v. Zerssen)	0.89
Mood Scale BF-S (BF-S') (v. Zerssen)	0.93
Life Satisfaction Index LS1 I (actual) (Modified Cantril version)	0.71
Life Satisfaction Index LS1 II (global) (Modified Cantril version)	0.83
Hamilton Depression Rating Scale HAMD (Hamilton)	0.64
Clinical Global Impression CGI (NIMH)	0.77
Nurses' Observation Scale for Inpatient Evaluation NOSIE (Honigfeld and Klett)	
Scales 1+2	0.76
Scales 6+7	0.79

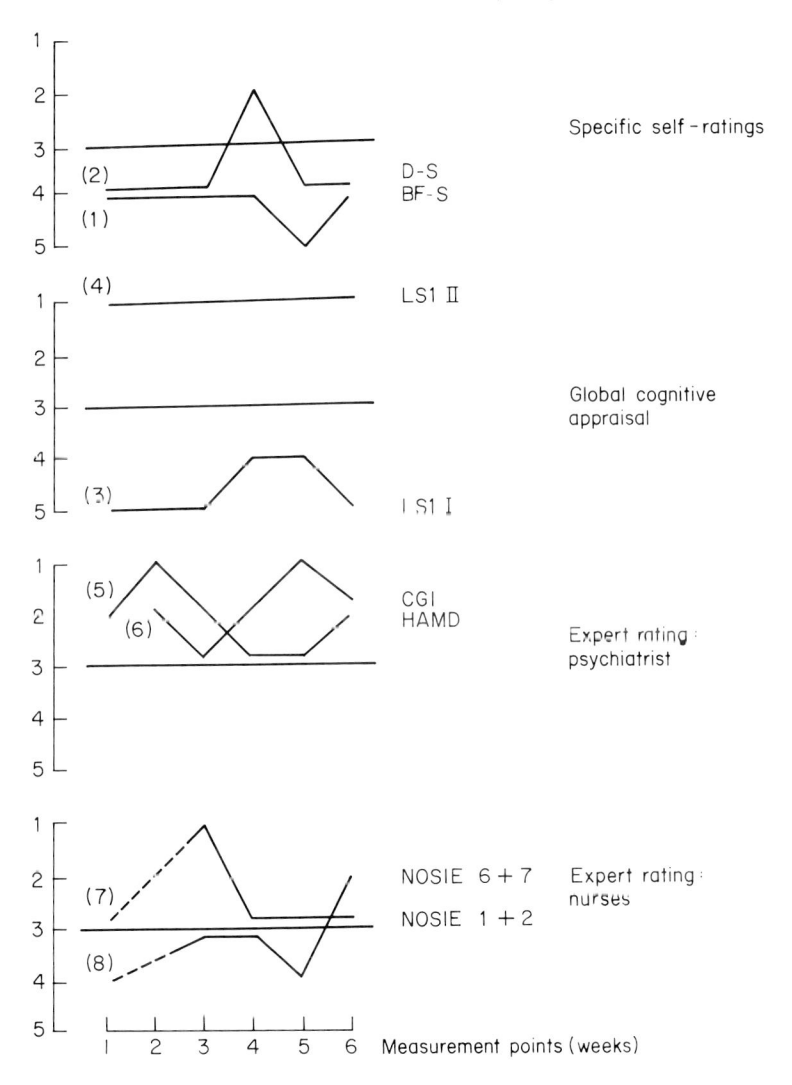

Fig. 8. Graphic representation of rating scales, case no. 26.

for our sample. Table 3 shows that the widely used Hamilton Rating Scale proved least reliable in our sample, which once again raises the question of the one-dimensionality of this instrument. The remaining coefficients are all of a tolerable, and some of an impressively high, numerical value.

After excluding cases with incomplete data (in particular concerning the HAMD and the NOSIE), the original 34 case studies were reduced to a sample of 24 cases that could be used for the analyses reported below. The graphic representation of the eight scales per person was guided by the principle of a concept-bound population-independent standardization as put forward by Schlosser (1976). Instead of comparing different scales by the usual normalized z-statistics, equalling means and standard deviations, the procedure proposed by Schlosser takes as its point of departure the theoretical parameters of the scales themselves independent of sample characteristics. As the different scales are of unequal lengths (ranging from 11 to 56 items) and do not display point symmetry, and as we wished to achieve the above-described standardization before taking the results as a basis for further graphic and statistical analysis, we reduced the different scale ranges to five scale points per scale, unifying the scale directions by attributing in each case "severely impaired" to scale point 5 and "unimpaired" to scale point 1.

Figure 8 gives an example of the data from six measurement points of one patient, transformed using the procedure described above. For the sake of greater comprehensibility and in order to facilitate comparisons, we separated four levels of evaluation

Specific self-rating (D-S, BF-S);
Global cognitive appraisal (LSI I, LSI II);
Expert rating/psychiatrist (HAMD, CGI);
Expert rating/nurses (NOSIE 1+2, NOSIE 6+7).

Broken lines indicate missing data.

In the next step, we developed a mean profile of each individual course of treatment, averaging the available transformed scale values per measurement point. The general individual profile thus integrated the unweighted appraisals from the four levels of evaluation.

Figure 9 displays the mean profile for the same patient as in Fig. 8. The figure contains some further interesting information. The two dots per measurement point indicate the two most discrepant judgements of this particular measurement point. Below the mean profile are the mean deviations from the mean profile per measurement point; this information gives an indication of how close to each other the raters were at each measurement point. Finally, there is a graphic representation of the mean deviation of each particular scale from the mean profile, grouped by levels of evaluation. In the case of the patient presented in Figs 8 and 9, we have an impressive example of a high conformity of nurses' ratings with individual mean profile compared with a remarkably low conformity of individual mean profile and global cognitive rating of life satisfaction. The goodness of portraying the individual global course of treatment thus is high in the former case and low in the latter.

This quality of a scale, namely its ability to portray the individual profile faithfully, was tested by applying a Friedman analysis of variance of ranks and a final evaluation of central tendencies according to Nemenyi. The analysis of variance of ranks resulted in a χ^2 of 20.39 which is significant at the 5% level, indicating that the different scales portrayed the individual mean profiles to significantly different degrees of faithfulness.

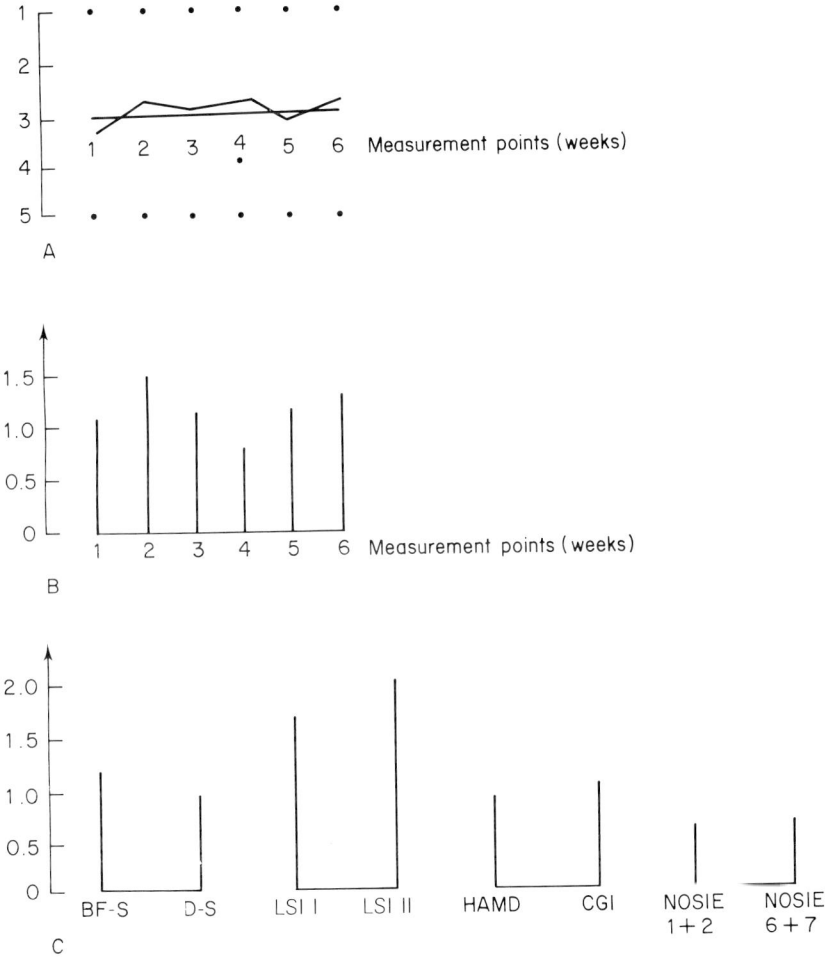

Multi-level Model of Intervention in Psychogeriatrics 277

Fig. 9. Mean profile and deviations, case no. 26. (A) Individual mean profile; (B) mean deviations from the mean profile for each measurement; (C) mean deviation of each scale from the mean profiles.

The statistical results lend themselves to the following conclusions (see Table 4):
1. The most specific self-rating scale (D-S) and the most unspecific expert-rating scale (CGI) most faithfully reflect the mean course of the depressive state.
2. Two other self-rating scales are second best at reflecting the individual mean profiles, proving that the self-rating scales in this analysis were intelligibly superior to expert-rating scales when it comes to portraying the average individual course of treatment.
3. Of the three remaining expert-rating scales, the HAMD reflected the individual mean profile the least faithfully.

Table 4
Multiple comparisons of ranks (Nemenyi)

Sum of ranks	Scale	Goodness of fit "cluster"
85.0	D-S	I
85.5	CGI	
104.0	LSI I	II
105.5	BF-S	
121.0	NOSIE 1+2	III
124.0	NOSIE 6+7	
126.5	HAMD	
146.5	LSI II	IV

4. The global appraisal of past life expectedly showed the least convergence with the individual mean profiles. At the same time, this result points to the fact that when evaluating their depressive state, the patients were quite able to differentiate past from present experiences, which may be one more indication of the widely depreciated validity of self-rating of psychiatric patients.

In our opinion, the results of this analysis constitute a clear argument for weighting the patients' self-ratings of changes of their condition much higher than is frequently the case.

The discussion of these analyses and of others, a description of which would be beyond the scope of this paper, with representatives of professions involved in the treatment of psychogeriatric patients (see Fig. 3) led to numerous points of departure for further analyses. We wish here to take up only one aspect which refers to the data material of Unit 1. There was clear dissatisfaction with the limited validity of the univariate analyses of the relationship between psychiatric syndromes and indicators of social situation, and particularly with their unsatisfactory theoretical base. Therefore, in a further analytical step, the data were integrated into a socioepidemiological paradigm recently described by Waltz (1981). The socioepidemiological paradigm includes two groups of independent variables — social stressors and psychosocial resources — and a dependent variable group, namely mental or somatic impairments (Fig. 10).

The differentiation of the individual model compartments has in the meantime been advanced a long way by different research groups. Here, however, it cannot be discussed, nor can the numerous unanswered terminological questions and the associated overlaps of particular aspects of the model components; this latter issue is illustrated in Fig. 10 in the splitting up of the construct of social support.

The extensive empirical literature introduces different concepts of the hypothetical relationship between the model components. They are listed below according to Waltz (1981).

A. Components of model

P S

    1. Psychosocial stressors: Critical life events; Environmental demands (e.g. Holmes and Rahe, Pearlin, Kaplan)

    2. Psychosocial resources
        2.1 External resources: structural network components; instrumental support (e.g. Kaplan, Henderson, Mueller)
        2.2 Internal resources
            2.2.1 Cognitive representation of social support (emotional support) (e.g. Cassel, Cobb, Lin)
            2.2.2 Coping strategies (e.g. Pearlin and Schooler, Haan, Lazarus, Thomae)

    3. Psychic/somatic impairments

B. Possible causal mechanisms

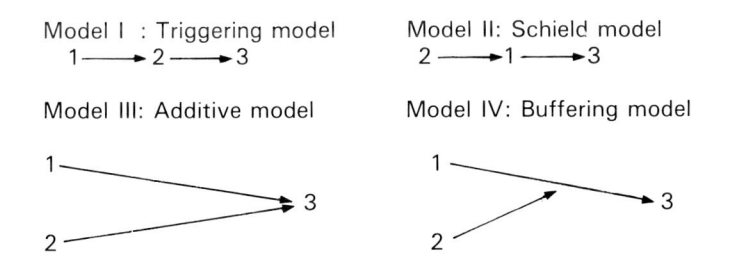

Model I : Triggering model
1 ⟶ 2 ⟶ 3

Model II: Schield model
2 ⟶ 1 ⟶ 3

Model III: Additive model
1 ⟶ 3
2 ⟶ 3

Model IV: Buffering model
1 ⟶ 3
2 ⟶ (arrow to middle of 1→3)

Fig. 10. Socioepidemiological paradigm. (Adapted from Waltz 1981.)

MODEL I

The scale of psychosocial stressors influences the size of resources (e.g. reduction or increase of coping possibilities, shrinking of the social network, decrease or increase of social support), which in turn influence the state of mental/physical health.

MODEL II

The psychosocial resources shield the individual from stressors and/or change the cognitive representation of the stressors, which in turn influence the state of mental/physical health.

MODEL III

Inadequate psychosocial resources impair the mental/physical state of health in the same way as a high level of psychosocial stressors. In an analysis of variance, these would be termed main effects.

MODEL IV

The impairment of the mental/physical state of health by psychosocial stressors is only found in this model if there is at the same time a certain amount of impairment of psychosocial resources. Otherwise, adequate psychosocial resources act as a buffer between the influence of the psychosocial stressors and the mental/physical state of health. In an analysis of variance, these would be termed interaction effects.

We are not aware of any attempts in the literature to prove a possible fifth model: inadequate psychosocial resources only have a negative influence on a person's mental/physical state of health when the person is subject to a serious amount of psychosocial stressors. Most of the cross-sectional empirical proof for model IV could in our opinion, be interpreted along the lines of such a model V; a particularly strong argument would be that the impairment of psychosocial resources goes further back in time than the influence of psychosocial stressors.

The often unreflected sociological or psychological position of the researcher clearly plays an important role here. Indeed, research carried out within the

Item No.	Item Content
1.	Death of partner
2.	Death of children
3.	Death of sibling
4.	Death of relative
5.	Serious illness of partner
6.	Serious illness of child
7.	Serious illness of sibling
8.	Serious illness of relative
9.	Divorce
10.	Conflicts with family
11.	Empty nest situation
12.	Death of friend or acquaintance
13.	Serious illness of friend
14.	Moving to new residence
15.	Worsened residential situation
16.	Dissatisfaction with residential situation

Fig. 11. List of critical life events.

framework of this socioepidemiological paradigm does give the impression of a professional pocketing of psychological aspects by the field of sociology — we refer to the increasing demands that one consider personality determinants and cognitive representations of aspects of the social network without being able to consider adequately the differentiated state of psychological knowledge — and the ignoring of essential sociological aspects by cognitively oriented psychologists. In contrast, the paradigm itself would be a classic example for stimulating interdisciplinary activities of physicians, psychiatrists, sociologists and psychologists.

The following figure and tables briefly show how we tried to operationalize some aspects of the paradigm's model components using the available data. This retrospective approach is admittedly open to critical objections, yet we must refer back to Stake's concept of evaluation.

In order to record the psychosocial stressors (model component 1), we took information collected in the interview on the presence or absence of the 16 critical life events (Fig. 11). As has been repeatedly demanded by researchers in this particular field, we attempted with a preliminary version of the documentation form to record how far back into the past the critical event took place and, particularly, how it was experienced by the subject. This technique, however, could not be put into practice with our patients and was rejected. In order to include at least an approximate time component, the final version of the documentation form expressly confined the question of these critical events to the year before being admitted to the hospital.

The critical life events were weighted (see Appendix, Table A7) on the basis of an expert rating and also taking into account the judgements of patients who could be questioned in an appropriately differentiated manner. Table A7 shows both the number of critical life events and the proportion of each weighted event in relation to the weighted total of critical life events. The death or serious illnesses of a partner or close relative appear to be the strongest psychosocial stressors for psychogeriatric patients according to the frequency and the weighting in this classification.

An overview of the occurrence of the four differently weighted categories of critical life events in the three syndrome groups shows a high concordance for depressive and organic brain syndromes. Paranoid patients tend to be affected more by serious critical life events. This effect is indeed statistically significant ($P<0.1$), yet the associative relationship is quite weak ($C_{cor.}=.192$) (Table 5).

An attempt to operationalize two aspects of psychosocial resources, or in more precise terms, the structural network aspect of external resources (model component 2) is presented in Table A8 of the Appendix. The leading variables of the variable bundles resulting in rank scales are the frequency of contacts. Since not all the possible permutations were occupied, there is a correspondingly reduced number of codes or scale gradations.

The corresponding scale of Table A9 of the appendix refer to aspects of internal resources, namely the cognitive representation of emotional support (model

Table 5
Weighted critical life events relative to three psychiatric syndrome groups

CLE-items	Weight	Depressive syndrome (%)	Psychoorganic syndrome (%)	Paranoid syndrome (%)
1-4	4	34.0	37.7	30.2
5-9	3	38.7	29.4	50.9
10-13	2	15.1	15.4	7.6
14-16	1	12.2	17.5	11.4

Table 6a
External and internal resources within family network

		Quantity High (5-9)		Quantity Low (1-4)		TOTAL	
Quality	Good (5-10)	47	53.4%	4	4.5%	51	58.0%
	Bad (1-4)	10	11.4%	27	30.7%	37	42.0%
		57	64.8%	31	35.2%	88	100.0%

Table 6b
External and internal resources within larger social network

		Quantity High (3-5)		Quantity Low (1-2)		TOTAL	
Quality	Good (4-5)	6	6.8%	8	9.1%	14	15.9%
	Bad (1-3)	15	17.0%	59	67.0%	74	84.1%
		21	23.9%	67	76.1%	88	100.0%

component 2.2.1). It can be seen that our operationalizations result in almost equally differentiated scales for the familial and extrafamilial network.

For the depressive psychogeriatric patients, who have been selected as an example in the following sections, there is a relationship between internal and external resources; in Table 6, the scales were dichotomized above the median of the total group. Slightly more than half of the depressive patients rated both the extent and quality of family contacts positively; only one in 15 patients rated the extrafamilial contacts positively. In contrast, one in three patients rated the extent and quality of the familial network negatively and three-quarters the extrafamilial network.

Nervous
Agitated
Absent-minded
Lack of concentration
Sleep disturbed
Anxious
Reduced appetite
Losing things
Confused
Misnaming
Black-outs
Misinterpret behaviour of others
Suicidal thoughts
Anxious of being robbed
Suspicious of being spoken about
Auditory hallucinations

0 = No answer, symptom not present,
    symptom not aggravated
1 = Slightly aggravated
2 = Severely aggravated

Fig. 12. Changes in perceived psychopathology.

With regard to both the familial and extrafamilial network, it was more common to find that the patients had a high number of contacts which, however, they rated negatively than a low number of contacts that were rated positively. Concordant ratings of internal and external resources were found in 84.1% and 73.8% respectively, which discordant ratings were found in 15.9% and 26.1%.

In order to operationalize the dependent variable, we examined the self-rating of perceived mental changes over the previous 6 months (model component 3), for which we drew up a list of 16 symptoms which could be rated as slightly or severely increased, not present, or not increased (Fig. 12). Assuming a markedly reduced life space in later life (Birren and Renner 1977), which has also been shown in our data, it was especially interesting to see to what extent the depressive patients can turn to their social network as a source of help in coping with critical life events. The index of perceived psychopathological changes was taken as an indicator of successful or less successful means of coping.

An analysis of variance (see Appendix, Table A10) of the influence of external and internal resources and the presence of critical life events on the subjective extent of negative changes of mental state in the year before being admitted to the hospital showed a significant interaction between internal resources and critical life events ($P \leq 0.05$), while the main effects did not reach significance. There were no significant main or interaction effects for the relationship between external resources and critical life events. Therefore, for this group of depressive psychogeriatric patients, we could determine no influence of the size of social resources *alone* on negatively experienced mental changes.

Likewise, we could find no influence of a history of critical life events *alone* on negatively experienced mental changes. With regard to the possible causal relationships as shown in the description of the socioepidemiological paradigm, the group of depressive psychogeriatric patients seems to support the buffering hypothesis: positively rated emotional support in the familial network markedly reduces the effects of a serious extent of critical life events on negative changes of mental state. Or in other words, emotional support from the familial network has an influence on the extent of negatively rated changes of mental state only when the depressive patient has been affected by many critical life events.

We have interpreted this interaction effect according to the above-mentioned hypothetical model V. The decision in favour of this model and against model IV (critical life events are only followed by an impairment of mental state if the emotional resources in the familial network are predominantly rated as negative) which is likewise compatible with the data, was made mainly for heuristic reasons. One way out of this dilemma would be to make a longitudinal investigation. Clinical observation that the way a person experiences emotional support in the familial network can be determined long before the occurrence of critical life events, comes up against the objection that a retrospective assessment of the quality of emotional support can be influenced by the impact of past critical life events and particularly by the affective impairments of patients in a way that cannot be controlled in cross-sectional analyses. Yet whether one opts for model IV or model V when interpreting the interaction effect, in each case we find support for an intervention approach that calls for greater attention to ways of influencing the emotional support system as it is perceived by the patient, insofar as the limits of the individual network permit.

REFERENCES

Birren, J. E. and Renner, W. J. (1977). Research on the psychology of aging: principles and experimentation. *In* "Handbook of the Psychology of Aging" (J. E. Birren and K. W. Schaie, eds) pp. 3-38. Van Nostrand Reinhold, New York.

Edwards, W., Guttentag, M. and Snapper, K. (1975). A decision-theoretic approach to evaluation research. *In* "Handbook of evaluation research" (M. Guttentag and E. L. Struening, eds) pp. 139-1981. Sage Publications, Beverly Hills.

Glass, G. V. and Ellett, F. S. (1980). Evaluation research. *Am. Rev. Psychol.* **31**, 211-228.

Guttentag, M. and Struening, E. L. (1975). *In* "Handbook of evaluation research." Sage Publications, Beverly Hills.

Kiersuk, T. J. and Lund, S. H. (1975). Process and outcome measurement using goals attainment scaling. *In* "Program evaluation: alcohol, drug abuse, and mental health services" (J. Zusman and C. R. Wurster, eds) pp. 213-228. Heath, Lexington, Massachusetts.

Lehr, U. (1979). "Psychologie des Alterns". UTB Quelle, Heidelberg.

Levine, M. (1978). Adapting the jury trial for program evaluation. *Eval. Program Plann.* **1**, 177-186.

Provus, M. (1971). "Discrepancy evaluation." McCutchan, Berkeley.
Schlosser, O. (1976). "Einführung in die soz.-wiss. Zusammenhangsanalyse." Rowohlt, Reinbek.
Scriven, M. (1967). The methodology of evaluation. *In* "AREA monograph series on curriculum evaluation" (R. E. Stake, ed.) pp. 39-83. Rand McNally, Chicago.
Stake, R. E. (1975). Program evaluation: particularly responsive evaluation. Occasional Paper No. 5, Kalamazoo, Michigan.
Stake, R. E. (1976). A theoretical statement of responsive evaluation. *Stud. Educ. Eval.* **2**, 19-22.
Tyler, R. W. (1949). "Basic principles of curriculum and instruction." University of Chicago Press, Chicago.
Waltz, E. M. (1981). Soziale Faktoren bei der Entstehung und Bewältigung von Krankheit—ein Überblick über die empirische Literatur. *In* "Soziale Unterstützung und chronische Krankheit—Zum Stand sozialepidemiologischer Forschung" (B. Bandura, ed.) pp. 40-119. Suhrkamp Verlag, Frankfurt.

Further reading on statistical analysis:
Lienert, G. A. (1973). "Verteilungsfreie Methoden in der Biostatistik I." Hain, Meisenheim.
Lienert, G. A. (1978). "Verteilungsfreie Methoden in der Biostatistik II." Hain, Meisenheim.

APPENDIX

Table A1
Sociodemographic data

Variable	%	Psychoorganic syndrome	Depressive syndrome	Paranoid syndrome	C_{cor}
Age ($n=271$)					0.449
65-69	29		+		
70-74	32				
75-79	24				
80+	15	+			
Sex ($n=271$)					0.290
Male	24	+			
Female	76		+		
Family status ($n=296$)					0.208
Single	10			+	
Married	32		+		
Widowed	49				
Divorced	9				

Table A2
Socioeconomic data

Variable	%	Psychoorganic syndrome	Depressive syndrome	Paranoid syndrome	$C_{cor.}$
Income (n=132)					0.261
200- 800	15		+		
801-1500	40				
1501-2000	26				
2001+	19				
Education (n=245)					0.218
"Volksschule"	72	+			
"Mittelschule"	18				
"Gymnasium"	10				
Occupation (n=238)					0.265
Housewife	22		+		
Labourer	23				
Employee (unqualified)	34			+	
Employee (qualified)	15				
Civil servant	6				
Reduced standard of living (n=217)					0.262
Yes	12	+			
No	88				

Table A3
Residential situation

Variable	%	Psychoorganic syndrome	Depressive syndrome	Paranoid syndrome	$C_{cor.}$
Type of residence (n=249)					0.254
Property	20		+		
Rent	68				
Home	12				
Duration (n=203)					0.137
Long	19		+		
Middle	42				
Short	39				
Satisfaction (n=215)					0.185
Very high	40				
Average	41				
Low	19				

Table A4
Family network

Variable	%	Psychoorganic syndrome	Depressive syndrome	Paranoid syndrome	$C_{cor.}$
Children ($n=258$)					0.307
None	33	+			
1-2	50				
3	10				
4+	7				
Children nearby ($n=254$)					0.234
None	44	+			
1-2	46				
3+	10				
Living situation ($n=172$)					0.129
Alone	74				
Not alone	26				
Negative changes ($n=241$)					0.273
None	47				
Few	30				
Average	17				
Many	5		+		
Contacts (quantitative) ($n=239$)					0.351
Few	13	+			
Average	66				
Many	21		+		
Contacts (qualitative) ($n=215$)					0.292
Bad	21	+			
Average	44				
Good	35		+		

Table A5
Larger social network

Variable	%	Psychoorganic syndrome	Depressive syndrome	Paranoid syndrome	$C_{cor.}$
Contacts (quantitative) ($n=202$)					0.238
Few	32	+			
Average	48				
Many	20				
Contacts (qualitative) ($n=216$)					0.163
Bad	41			+	
Average	39				
Good	19				
Negative changes ($n=203$)					0.126
Yes	18		+		
No	82				
Deaths ($n=197$)					0.139
Yes	13				
No	87				
Membership of organization ($n=208$)					0.259
Yes	18		+		
No	82				
Church attendance ($n=211$)					0.164
Regularly	37	+			
Rarely	37				
Never	26				
Old people's club ($n=208$)					0.093
Yes	17				
No	83				

Table A6
Medical care

Variable	%	Psychoorganic syndrome	Depressive syndrome	Paranoid syndrome	$C_{cor.}$
Regular visit of doctor (GP) ($n=228$)					0.078
Yes	71				
No	29				
Regular visit of psychiatrist ($n=226$)					0.322
Yes	40		+	+	
No	60	+			

Table A7
Critical life events relative to weighted total

Item	Weight	Content	n	Weighted total %
1	4	Death Partner	20	9.8
2	4	Child	1	0.5
3	4	Sibling	35	17.2
4	4	Relative	17	8.4
5	3	Serious illness Partner	41	15.1
6	3	Child	11	4.1
7	3	Sibling	30	11.1
8	3	Relative	13	4.8
9	3	Divorce	3	1.1
10	2	Conflicts with family	20	4.9
11	2	Empty nest	3	0.7
12	2	Death of friend	25	6.2
13	2	Illness of friend	9	2.2
14	1	Moving to the new residence	55	6.8
15	1	Worsened residential situation	29	3.6
16	1	Dissatisfactory residential situation	29	3.6

Table A8
External resources: 1. contacts within family network

Code	Children	Children nearby	Contact with children	Siblings nearby	Contact with siblings
1	No	No	None	Yes/no	Rarely-never
2	No	No	None	Yes	Regularly
3	Yes	No	Rarely-never	Yes/no	Rarely-never
4	Yes	Yes	Rarely-never	No	Rarely-never
5	Yes	Yes	Rarely-never	Yes	Regularly-never
6	Yes	No	Regularly	Yes/no	Regularly-never
7	Yes	Yes	Regularly	No	Rarely-never
8	Yes	Yes	Regularly	Yes	Rarely-never
9	Yes	Yes	Regularly	Yes	Regularly

Table A8
External resources: 2. contacts within larger social network

Code	Number of regular contacts	Regular visit of doctor	Organizations, clubs
1	None	No/yes	No/yes
2	1-2	No	No
3	3-5	No	No
4	1-2	Yes	Yes
5	3-5	Yes	Yes

Table A9
Internal resources: 1. emotional support within family network

Code	Perceived contact with children	Support by children	Perceived contact with siblings	Support by siblings
1	Bad	Rarely-never	Bad	Rarely-never
2	Bad	Rarely-never	Good	Rarely-never
3	Bad	Rarely-never	Good	Regularly
4	Bad	Regularly	Bad	Rarely-never
5	Good	Rarely-never	Bad	Rarely-never
6	Good	Rarely-never	Good	Rarely-never
7	Good	Rarely-never	Good	Regularly
8	Good	Regularly	Bad	Rarely-never
9	Good	Regularly	Good	Rarely-never
10	Good	Regularly	Good	Regularly

Table A9
Internal resources: 2. emotional support within larger social network

Code	Perceived contact outside family	Perceived support outside family
1	Bad	None
2	1-2/Good	None
3	3-5/Good	1-2
4	1-2/Good	1-2
5	1-2/Good	3-5

Table A10
ANOVA results

Variance	SAQ	FG	MQ	F ratio	Significance
Rows	3.54	1	3.54	2.04	NS
Columns	1.26	1	1.26	0.73	NS
Rows × columns	7.12	1	7.12	4.11	$P < 0.05$
Within	1042.76	54	1.73	–	–

Critical life events	Emotional support within family network	
	Good	Bad
Few	7.55	6.00
Many	6.76	10.55

Implications and Outlook

Sir Martin Roth

Department of Psychiatry, University of Cambridge Clinical School, Cambridge, UK

NEUROBIOLOGICAL ASPECTS

A wealth of observations has been presented in the course of the preceding section and the comments that follow are confined to select points that have general implications for future developments in scientific enquiry or clinical practice.

The work of Bengt Winblad and Carl Gottfries individually, and in collaboration over a long period, has made a significant contribution to the advances that have been seen in knowledge of Alzheimer's disease during the last 15-20 years. Although understanding of its aetiology is not yet within sight, a large body of new information has been recorded and a number of promising growing points have been defined. Clinical and neurobiological observations have been marked by a growing measure of cohesion. For example, counts of cortical neurons in columns have proved to be inversely correlated with plaque counts and estimates of neurofibrillary tangle (NFT) formation positively correlated with choline acetyltransferase activity. (Mountjoy et al. 1983, 1984). Dementia scores during life have also been found to be associated with plaque counts estimated post-mortem. As these associations have proved consistent and also in the direction predicted, they suggest that the neurobiological changes have a common association with the underlying degenerative process in Alzheimer's disease. To take one example, positive correlations between neuronal counts and plaque counts and negative ones with ChAT would have been uninterpretable and would have suggested that these and other associated variables were unimportant epiphenomena in Alzheimer's disease.

Dr Gottfries drew attention to the contrast between the detailed character of the transmitter deficits to be found in Alzheimer's disease and the age-related changes observed in normal controls. The decline in levels of dopamine and 5-hydroxytryptamine (5-HT) had been found in both groups. But whereas the metabolites homovanillic acid and hydroxyindoleacetic acid were decreased in

Dimensions in Aging
ISBN 0 12 090162 5

Copyright © 1986 Academic Press, London
All rights of reproduction in any form reserved.

Alzheimer's cases, normal persons showed no such decline. Dr Gottfries inferred that there had been some compensatory activity, perhaps in the form of increased turnover of the transmitters in question in the normal subjects; in Alzheimer cases this attempt to overcome deficiency may have reached the stage of failure. Now this raises the possibility that in the course of evolution of the pathology we find in Alzheimer's disease there may be a course of events similar to that now authenticated in relation to Parkinson's disease. In about 4% of patients who die of other causes and with no overt Parkinsonism Lewy bodies are present. These patients could well be suffering from a subclinical form of the pathological process in Parkinson's disease. For there is evidence that the number of neurons in the substantia nigra declines in the course of normal aging. (McGeer *et al.* 1977). About 80–85% of the neurons of the substantia nigra and about the same proportion of the dopamine content of the striatum have to be present before frank Parkinsonian symptoms appear (Marsden 1982). In the asymptomatic period there is evidence reminiscent of that tentatively suggested by Dr Gottfries, that the turnover of dopamine has increased. But in Parkinson's disease enhancement of postsynaptic receptor sensitivity is also known to occur.

Now in Alzheimer's disease certain lines of evidence have been adduced to suggest that pathological changes have to accumulate to beyond a certain point before symptoms make their appearance. The evidence is particularly clear in relation to plaque formation; the great majority of patients suffering from Alzheimer's disease are found post-mortem to have an average plaque count of more than 12 per light microscopic field, those without dementia have mean counts below this figure (Roth 1971). As the NFTs are so rarely seen in the cortex of normal old people (changes are largely confined to the hippocampus) threshold phenomena in respect of this change are more difficult to demonstrate. But choline acetyltransferase activity which is inversely related to plaque counts, both in cases of Alzheimer's disease and normal elderly people may prove to exhibit a similar threshold effect. And in the locus coeruleus a portion of the melanin-loaded cells lend an intensely pigmented appearance in Alzheimer's disease according to Bondareff (1986, unpublished observations), suggesting that they are overworking. As cellular fall-out follows they may be working themselves to exhaustion. But evidence suggesting heightened sensitivity of the postsynaptic receptor is not available.

There is a need for more intensive qualitative examination of the pathological and neurochemical changes in well preserved elderly people. What, for example, is the significance of the range of values in respect to plaque formation of between very few or no plaques, sometimes seen in mentally vigorous and productive old people who die at an advanced age, and mean plaque counts of 10–12, that are near threshold values? The same questions can be posed in relation to changes in the hippocampus. Is there any association with neuropsychological measures of cognitive and other mental functions?

The issue dicussed here has both scientific and clinical implications. Should an effective pharmacological agent become available for the treatment of Alzheimer's disease it might prove most potent in the preclinical phase of the disorder. From a scientific point of view it would be well worth exploring the possibility that the analogy with Parkinson's disease is closer than existing data permit us to conclude. From a neurochemical point of view, in addition to the more limited deficit in respect to choline acetyltransferase activity, Parkinson's disease resembles Alzheimer's syndrome in that there is a marked deficit both of noradrenaline and 5-HT. The most recent evidence (Quinn *et al.* 1986) suggests that the greater part of the excess prevalence of dementia reported in Parkinson's disease is in fact due to its fortuitous coincidence with common but distinct degenerative processes of late life including Alzheimer's disease. However, further exploration of the resemblance between the latter and Parkinson's disease in respect of threshold and other phenomena might well prove highly informative. Dr Winblad concluded that the senile plaque is the primary lesion in Alzheimer's disease and the NFT, a secondary one. But as senile plaques are common among mentally normal old people, there is continuity between normal mental aging and the Alzheimer syndrome in respect to what he regards as the primary lesion. This is not the case as far as the NFT is concerned. Abundant tangle formation in the cortex is accepted by most pathologists as indicative of Alzheimer's disease. These facts are difficult to reconcile with the view also expressed by Dr Winblad that Alzheimer's disease is a condition *sui generis* and quite distinct from normal senescence. The alleged non-specificity of the tangle which has been described in other conditions such as motor neuron disease and progressive supranuclear palsy is derived, as Wischik and Crowther (1986) have indicated, from a merely superficial resemblance between the structures in these conditions and the NFT of Alzhcimer's disease, and in none of these conditions is there the same body of evidence testifying to a fairly strict quantitative relationship between the extent of the mental impairment observed during life and the intensity of both plaque and tangle formation in Alzheimer's disease. I have discussed the evidence that favours the central importance of tangle formation for the pathology of Alzheimer's disease elsewhere (Roth 1986).

The data Dr Winblad presented from his studies with techniques derived from molecular biology are new and interesting. He compared the translation activity of polysomes derived from normal subjects with that of polysomes extracted from the brains of patients with Alzheimer's disease. The translation activity of the polysomes from the latter was only half that in the former, and the yield of protein in cerebral cortex derived from Alzheimer cases was only one-sixth of that from the cortex of controls. Moreover, polysomes added to normal polysomes inhibited protein synthesis by polysomes derived from normals. The details for the methods employed to isolate polysomes will be available in the full publication of the work. This should make it possible for other workers to attempt replication of these interesting observations.

UNITARY HYPOTHESES FOR THE AETIOLOGY OF ALZHEIMER'S DISEASE

A number of attempts have been made recently to formulate some unitary hypothesis which accounts for the whole range of structural changes and neurochemical deficits in Alzheimer's disease and their clinical manifestations in terms of a single lesion or basic functional disturbance. The decrease in protein synthesis Dr Winblad has found has been reported by others as the basic defect and the cause of the other changes. Recently Pearson and his colleagues (Pearson *et al.* 1985) raised the possibility of a viral infection giving rise to the selective severity of the lesions in anterior association cortex, leaving posterior cortex relatively intact. The distribution of lesions is herpes simplex encephalitis is similar, although the structural changes are of course quite different. However, evidence for an infective aetiology in Alzheimer's disease is lacking (Corsellis 1986).

One reason for focussing attention on the NFTs (that there are structural features in common with the plaque is well established) is the recent evidence which suggests that the paired helical filament (PHF), which is its main constituent arises through a *de novo* assembly of a structural subunit which may consist of an aberrant protein. If this proves to be the case, a unitary theory of causation in Alzheimer's disease will, perhaps, have been initiated.

The evidence was gathered in the course of a collaborative study between the Department of Psychiatry in Cambridge and the Laboratory of Molecular Biology, where structural analysis of the NFT was undertaken. The NFT presents on electron microscopy as a matted clump of PHF which is remarkably resistant to solution by protein solvents. Dr Claude Wischik has developed a preparation that isolates PHF in a form susceptible to structural analysis. This has revealed the PHF to consist of a double helical stack of transversely oriented subunits giving the overall shape of a ribbon twisted into a left-handed helix (Wischik *et al.* 1985, Wischik and Crowther 1986) (Fig. 1). Image construction with the aid of computer techniques provided a cross-sectional density map of the PHF. It reveals two C-shaped subunits which correspond to the helices and span the diameter of the filament each made up of three domains. This has provided an independent confirmation for the double helical character of PHF (Crowther *et al.* 1985). The fact that paired helical filaments show only transverse breaks occurring at random intervals with no evidence whatsoever of fraying into protofilaments even in the smallest fragments, is consistent with the view that the double helical stack of the PHF is made up of transversly oriented subunits. The biochemical nature of the subunit is unknown at the present time. But Wischik (1986, pers. comm.) has made good progress recently in isolating the protein of which it is constituted.

Further progress in relation to the neurobiology of Alzheimer's disease will depend in part upon the initiation of further clinical and epidemiological enquiries into certain problems. These will require more refined as well as valid and reliable

Implications and Outlook

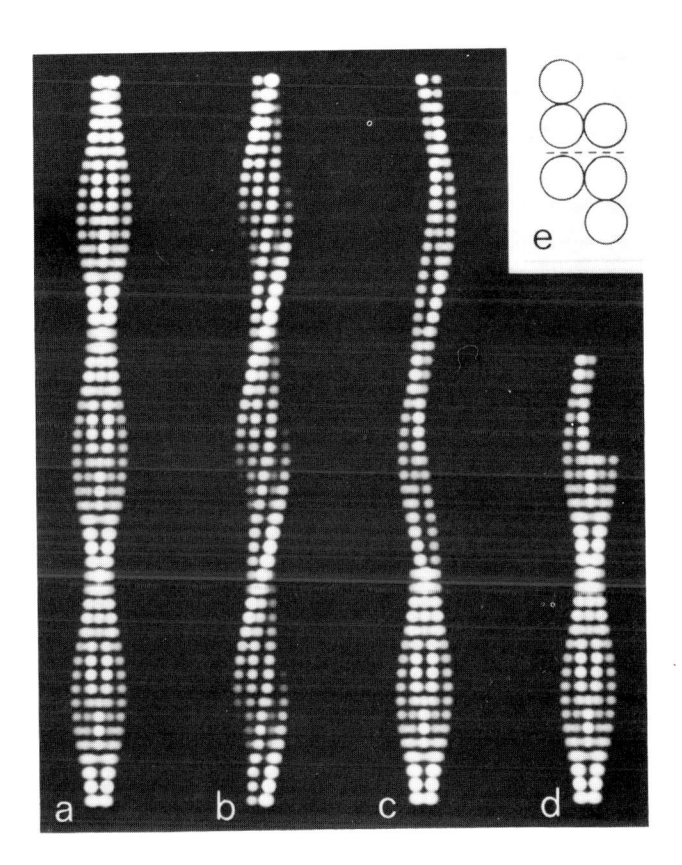

Fig. 1. Subunit structure of PHFs in Alzheimer's disease (reproduced with permission from Wischik and Crowther 1986). These images were generated by computer in order to model the main features seen in isolated PHFs. It was found that a double helical stack of C-shaped subunits, each with three domains (e), gave the best approximation to the striation patterns seen in images of isolated PHFs. The main patterns are shown in (a) and (b), and consist either of longitudinal striations where three white lines merge into four (a), or a pattern of oblique striations (b). The three to four pattern (a) arises when there is complete penetration of the filament by negative stain, whereas the oblique pattern (b) can be simulated by accentuating only the far side of the filament. This occurs in images where stain penetration is restricted to the side of the filament in contact with the carbon grid. Fragmentation patterns seen in isolated filaments show that half filaments retain structural integrity, and this is modelled in (c) and (d). The PHF model is seen in cross-section in (e). Two C-shaped subunits span the diameter of the PHF, and each subunit has three domains. This first approximation to the PHF cross-section has since been confirmed objectively by image reconstruction from diffraction patterns (Crowther *et al.* 1985).

diagnostic evaluation and psychological measurement for characterizing cases. For example, very little is known at present about the early stages of the disease, either in its clinical or pathological aspects. Until this gap in knowledge has been filled, understanding of its aetiology is likely to remain incomplete. It is also the early stages that are most likely to respond to any effective treatments that come to light and they may prove most effective at the stage before or soon after threshold values in respect of structural damage have been exceeded.

SOCIOLOGICAL ASPECTS

The contributions by Dr Bengtson's and Professor Bergener's groups in relation to social aspects and the care of the elderly with mental disorder in the community brings into focus the social networks made up of relatives and friends who play such a crucial role in maintaining the viability of old people in families or homes of their own. Four out of five patients with Alzheimer's disease are at present living outside institutions. They could not survive in the community without the active help and support of families and neighbours. No form of domiciliary or institutional care provided by health and welfare services could take the place of these indigenous helpers motivated by social concern alone.

Unfortunately, these networks are being slowly eroded. It is imperative that they should be reinforced and sustained. For if even one-quarter of the numbers at present being cared for outside hospitals and residential homes had, within a short time, to be accommodated in institutions, health and welfare services would be overwhelmed. Neither good scientific nor satisfactory clinical work can be undertaken in efficient and incoherent health and welfare services.

One message that comes across from Dr Stewart's contribution is the need for closer monitoring of the medication provided for elderly people. Clouded and delirious states, or "confusional" states as they are often called, are among the most common forms of organic mental disorder in the aged and they are liable to present in the form of a crisis. Intoxication with drugs is among the more common causes. On close investigation, medication often proves to have been taken from supplies accumulated in the home of the old person over the years. Frail, forgetful and confused old people, who live or spend much time alone, draw upon such supplies and are liable to forget that the medication prescribed has already been taken hours or minutes previously. Others will take them at random. When no clear histories are available, severe confusional states may be mistakenly diagnosed as dementia and opportunities for effective treatment missed. Effective therapy is often possible where a clouded state is due to a "silent" infection or a metabolic disorder. In some cases when such a complication is superimposed on dementia, this will appear more advanced than it really is until treatment of the temporary disturbance of consciousness reveals the true nature. It may then be seen to be a mild dementia with limited cognitive deficit.

These considerations are neither academic for the clinician or trivial for the scientist. Their practical importance is self-evident. And without accurate diagnosis and measurement, and exploration of the social and familial circumstances, research into dementia or aging of the brain may go astray through a shortfall of relevant information.

REFERENCES

Corsellis, J. A. N. (1986). The transmissibility of dementia. *Br. Med. Bull.* **42**(1), 111-114.
Crowther, R. A., Wischik, C. M. and Stewart, M. (1985). Analysis of the structure of paired helical filaments. *Proc. EMSA* **43**, 734-737.
Marsden, C. D. (1982). Basal ganglia disease. *Lancet* **ii**, 21-32.
McGeer, P. L., McGeer, E. G. and Suzuki, J. S. (1977). Ageing and extrapyramidal function. *Arch. Neurol.* **34**, 33-35.
Mountjoy, C. Q., Roth, M., Evans, N. J. R. and Evans, H. M. (1983). Cortical neuronal counts in normal elderly controls and demented patients. *Neurobiol. Aging* **4**, 1-11.
Mountjoy, C. Q., Rossor, M. N., Iversen, L. L. and Roth, M. (1984). Correlation of cortical cholinergic and GABA deficits with quantitative neuropathological findings in senile dementia. *Brain* **107**, 507-518.
Pearson, R. C. A., Esiri, M. M., Wilcock, G. H. and Powell, T. P. S. (1985). Anatomical correlates of the distribution of the pathological changes in Alzheimer's disease. *Proc. Natl Acad. Sci. USA* **82**, 4531-4534.
Quinn, N. P., Rossor, M. N. and Marsden, C. (1986). *Br. Med. Bull.* **42**(1), 86-90.
Roth, M. (1971). Classification and aetiology of mental disorders of old age. Some recent developments. *In* "Recent Developments in Psychogeriatrics" (D. Kay and A. Walk, eds). British Journal of Psychiatry Special Publication No. 6.
Roth, M. (1986). The association of clinical and neurobiological findings. Behrings class and aetiology of Alzheimer's disease. *Brit. Med. Bull.* **42** (no. 1), 42-50.
Wischik, C. M. and Crowther, R. A. (1986). Subunit structure of the Alzheimer tangle. *Br. Med. Bull* **42**(1), 51-56.
Wischik, C. M., Crowther, R. A., Stewart, M. and Roth, M. (1985). Subunit structure of paired helical filaments in Alzheimer's disease. *J. Cell Biol.* **100**, 1905-1912.

General Conclusions

Arvid Carlsson

Department of Pharmacology, University of Gothenburg, Gothenburg, Sweden

> Last scene of all,
> That ends this strange eventful history,
> Is second childishness, and mere oblivion,
> Sans teeth, sans eyes, sans taste, sans everything.
> (*As You Like It* II, vii.)

We have discussed in this volume a sad, unescapable process, which appears to be basically built into our genes and will ultimately extinguish our lives, unless other causes intervene. Before that we may well pass into that miserable condition already so aptly described four centuries ago by William Shakespeare. Why do we study it so carefully? What can we do about it?

When reviewing this multifaceted series of lectures, where several interesting epidemiological aspects have been discussed (see the papers by Drs Bengtson, Bergener *et al.* and Stewart), it is appropriate at the outset to mention the well known "squaring off" of population survival curves, implying a shift to the right of these curves, which may be expected to approach a theoretical maximum lifespan, presumably determined largely by the genetic factors so elegantly discussed by Drs Hayflick and Holliday. I suppose we can all agree that one important goal in our research field is to try to speed up the shift of the survival curve towards this hypothetical maximum. I think we can also agree that any attempts to push this curve beyond this maximum, which would then presumably involve manipulation of the genetic material, would probably be very difficult and perhaps not at all desirable.

While survival curves are obviously important, it is of course even more urgent to try to make the longer lifespan more worthwhile. Aging is obviously accompanied by a decreasing general vitality and an increasing number of health problems. One striking illustration is the age-related decline in the resistance to stressful events, such as trauma, infection, drug exposure and environmental changes, showing up, for example, as an increased liability to confusion, a phenomenon already discussed by Sir Martin Roth in the previous paper. In the experience of many clinicians the turning point at which this increased liability starts to show up, is at the age of about 50. Does this age-related decrease in vitality undergo a change similar to that of the survival curves? There is evidence that this is, in fact, the case. For example, Dr Svanborg, who unfortunately was unable to attend this meeting, has demonstrated the remarkably good health and vitality of 70-year-old people in Gothenburg, Sweden. In fact, a rather dramatic improvement seems to be going on, judging by the comparison of two cohorts of 70-year-old people, examined 5 years apart by Svanborg and his colleagues. The more recent cohort was found to be significantly more healthy than the previous one. It would indeed have been interesting to study a corresponding cohort in Shakespeare's days! Presumably those people presenting with the picture described by Shakespeare were shockingly young by our standards.

When observing these gratifying trends in terms of survival and vitality one wonders to what extent these and other age-related changes refer to the aging process in the strict sense or to factors related to age in a different way. For example, the changes observed by Dr Tsujimoto at puberty may have very interesting implications, though presumably unrelated to the degenerative phenomena that we usually associate with the aging process. Likewise, while we were encouraged by Dr Steinhagen's mouse experiment, showing that age-related bone atrophy can be largely avoided by physical exercise, we obviously have to raise the question as to whether bone atrophy in the elderly is linked to the aging of bone tissue or rather an example of disuse atrophy, as suggested by Dr Williams. Paradoxically, the more encouraging the results are from the practical point of view, the more distant, probably, are the mechanisms under study of the aging process *per se*.

Another example of this universal problem of interpretation is provided by Dr Ebbesen's interesting experiment, demonstrating that male mice, living together in cages of, presumably, somewhat limited size, have a shorter lifespan than (1) female mice under similar conditions, and (2) male mice living together with female mice. It would appear that it was not the absence of female mice but rather the aggregation of other male mice that constituted the negative environmental factor. It would be interesting to know whether the presumably stressful impact of other males had an influence on the aging process proper or merely represents an example of increased susceptibility to stress during aging as discussed above. In any event Dr Ebbesen's experiment demonstrates what I have suspected for a long time, namely that the female brain is superior to the male brain in a very important respect. It was obvious that the female mouse can cope with a variety of environmental changes much better than the male. A partial explanation may be that the serotonergic system, which among other things is instrumental in suppressing aggressive behaviour, is better developed in the female than in the male rat brain (Carlsson *et al.* 1985).

I found Dr Beregi's lymphocyte study very interesting. It appears that her lymphocyte model may be able to yield important information of the aging process at the cellular level.

Even if a phenomenon is genuinely related to the aging process, the question remains whether it is an expression of aging of the tissue under investigation or secondary to aging of another tissue. Dr Meites warned us that our neuroendocrine system undergoes profound changes during aging and that these changes may well have an impact on other tissues. For example, an age-related decrement of hypothalamic neurotransmitter systems, perhaps especially catecholamine systems, may lead to secondary changes in many other tissues.

Not all age-related changes are necessarily negative from the functional point of view. For example, if an elderly individual takes longer to respond to a certain stimulus, it may be partly due to a larger store of relevant information which has to be scanned through before a decision can be made. Dr Lakatta's finding, that the heart of the elderly is less responsive to a β-adrenergic stimulus, may protect the old heart from being pushed beyond its capacity.

I suppose we can all agree with Dr Wyatt that the worst fear people have of growing old is of diminished nervous system function. When studying the aging of this system we again encounter a bewildering complexity. A fundamental question, which of course is relevant for all areas of research on aging, is whether there is a distinct demarcation line between normal and pathological aging. Are there disorders, which are basically due to a pathological speeding up of the aging process? Alzheimer's disease might perhaps be an example.

The normal aging process seems to be associated with both morphological and neurochemical changes in the brain. Interestingly, the changes are not uniform but vary in different brain regions and in different types of neuron. Catecholamine-storing neurons exhibit a relatively strong age dependence. However, the profile of neurochemical changes is clearly different in Alzheimer's disease compared to normal aging. Whereas the cholinergic system does not seem to be particularly sensitive to the normal aging process it is obviously affected in Alzheimer's disease. This difference in profile argues against the notion that Alzheimer's is an exaggeration of the normal aging process.

As pointed out by several speakers the concept that Alzheimer's disease/senile dementia of Alzheimer's type (AD/SDAT) is essentially due to degeneration of central cholinergic pathways, is not tenable. Several other systems are obviously involved, e.g. the noradrenergic, dopaminergic and serotonergic systems. Also certain neuropeptides are reduced in AD/SDAT e.g. somatostatin. Moreover, changes in the white matter, involving several lipid constituents, have been reported (see Dr Gottfries' paper).

The morphological changes observed in AD/SDAT continue to attract considerable attention, despite the fact that they are not specific but are also observed in normal aging, although to a lesser degree in most cases, and in Parkinson's disease and Down's syndrome. Dr Anderton told us about the chemical properties of the neurofibrillary tangles (NFT) and senile plaques (SP). Although the matter is not definitely settled it appears that the NFT and SP are products arising as a consequence of neuronal cell degeneration. If this is so, the relatively poor correlation between these phenomena and the occurrence of dementia may be due to different localization—at the cellular level—of NFT and SP in cases with and without dementia, respectively. It remains to be seen if the precise chemical definition of these changes will reveal any important clues to the aetiology or pathogenesis of AD/SDAT.

Different views were expressed, as to whether the NFT or SP were the primary lesions in AD/SDAT (see e.g. Dr Winblad's paper). A third possibility would be that both changes are secondary to biochemical alterations, which in turn may lead to cellular degeneration. Besides, AD/SDAT may not necessarily have one *single* cause. It may not even be entirely due to nerve cell degeneration. It should be recalled that even relatively severe neuronal cell losses can be compensated for by feedback mechanisms. Maybe failures of other kinds have to be added in order to induce overt functional deficiencies. For example, a combination of degeneration of nerve cells with an insufficient transport of nutrients across the brain capillaries may be considered. The regionally uniform reduction of 5-hydroxyindoleacetic acid levels in cases of AD/SDAT may be interpreted as evidence of a failure of amino acid transport into the brain, although other alternatives may also be considered.

The grafting technique has attracted a lot of attention in brain research during recent years, mostly among experimental workers, although a few therapeutic attempts have also been made in cases of Parkinson's disease. It seems questionable if this approach will lead to a major breakthrough in the treatment of degenerative brain disorders. However, experimental work in this area may provide important information about factors involved in regeneration, as illustrated by Dr Wyatt's paper.

These lectures have amply demonstrated the enormous complexity of the aging process and its functional consequences. The papers presented as well as the comments and discussions were very stimulating and thought provocative. We are all grateful to Sandoz for organizing meetings of this type, which I think are of tremendous importance for this research field.

Reference

Carlsson, M., Svensson, K., Eriksson, E. and Carlsson, A. (1985). Rat brain serotonin: biochemical and functional evidence for a sex difference. *J. Neural. Transm.* **63**, 297-313.

Conclusion to the 1986 Sandoz Lectures in Gerontology

M. Bergener

Rheinische Landesklinik, Cologne, FRG

Gerontologists are trying to develop interdisciplinary approaches to research. Starting with the concept of the aging process as a complicated and multiply levelled framework of conditions, we have set out from different positions and via various routes to discover the junctions of this structure. We are trying to understand the multidimensionality of this process. Biologists, physicians, psychologists and sociologists have endeavoured to make a contribution. Has this really been the case? Do we already have the methodological tools of interdisciplinary research? Is interdisciplinary thinking already a matter of course or is it still, despite assertions to the contrary, no more than lip service? It would seem appropriate and advisable to retain a degree of scepticism here. In particular, one should exercise restraint and display critical modesty without disencouraging others. Resignation would be the worst solution; even if no one has yet managed to put forward a masterpiece of interdisciplinary thinking. The different scientists have become too entangled and entrapped in their self-made mazes of specialist knowledge: mazes into which no outsider will ever venture until he himself has developed the ability to leap over the ever-rising boundaries of his own discipline. As long as this is the case, the scientists' ivory towers will prove to be solitary cells.

It is said that Christian ascetics living atop a pillar measure their success by the height of the pillar. They have to remain visible to their admirers, a circumstance that somewhat limits the height of the pillar—unless of course the followers are equipped with opera glasses.

Of one thing I am convinced: the development of interdisciplinary research methods will depend particularly on which scientific languages scientists have at their disposal, and what vocabulary they can master. Are they able to express themselves only in one language, or can they use others? We must not forget

Dimensions in Aging
ISBN 0 12 090162 5

Copyright © 1986 Academic Press, London
All rights of reproduction in any form reserved.

that there cannot be other languages without reference to the one, the first, the original language.

Interdisciplinarity requires that one is able to think and write in at least two scientific languages. The problems of a language's translatability into another show the limits, or at least the particular difficulties with which the claim of interdisciplinary thinking, of interdisciplinary scientific methodology has to come to terms with. Will there ever be a completely synonymous vocabulary? I rather doubt it! And this despite all the encouraging contributions to this symposium. A further difficulty is that the different sciences have developed their own separate and rich vocabularies, that the meaning of individual words changes from discipline to discipline, and that the respective landscape is dependent on many external and temporary preconditions. Another problem is the ever-narrowing gap between what is thought and written and what goes to print, and the ever-widening gap between what is printed and what is read. So many consumers in science are at pains to keep abreast of progress, and there is hardly a breathing space between the development of ideas and the discovery of relationships. The particular level of understanding that goes beyond merely absorbing explanations has long fallen by the wayside. Even when one tries to adapt, there is a danger of dropping out of the running: to confine oneself more and more to scientific explanation could be more detrimental to the understanding of the whole relationship than being in complete ignorance of these explanations. Let us use the remaining "Spielraum" for interdisciplinary research. Bearing in mind the attitude of some sceptics, who believe that this "Spielraum" has long been filled in, since life—as the people of ancient times thought—cannot examine itself without once again casting out the lifeline of reductionism.

"Things were easier in the inanimate world . . ." wrote Erwin Chargaff. ". . . the objectives appeared to be well and clearly defined, and the methods elaborated to attain them were so close to each other that the close-meshed network they formed allowed only few possibilities of not recording unknown information". But what is this compared with the living beings, mankind— his individual fate, his wishes and founderings, his succumbing, failures and subjection, of which the eternally present proof, death, is clear to everyone, day and night. Of what relevance is it to use and to the public, Roger Sperry asked, "if we locate a few new neuronal links in the brain, a few unknown transmitters or receptors of the likes (or even this or that biological, psychological, social, and medical aspect of aging processes), when the quality, or even the survival, of civilized society is in potential danger?" In a world "that has to struggle with population imbalances in the order of hundreds of millions." While the worldwide *per capita* development of almost all important products from elementary resources has already reached an apex and has begun a slow downward slide, the world population is still growing by 6 million a month.

Gerontology, as an interdisciplinary science of all aging processes, must also offer a solution to this development. In view of this development, it would most certainly be no solution to proceed with "good old-fashioned" science. What we need above all is a new paradigm!